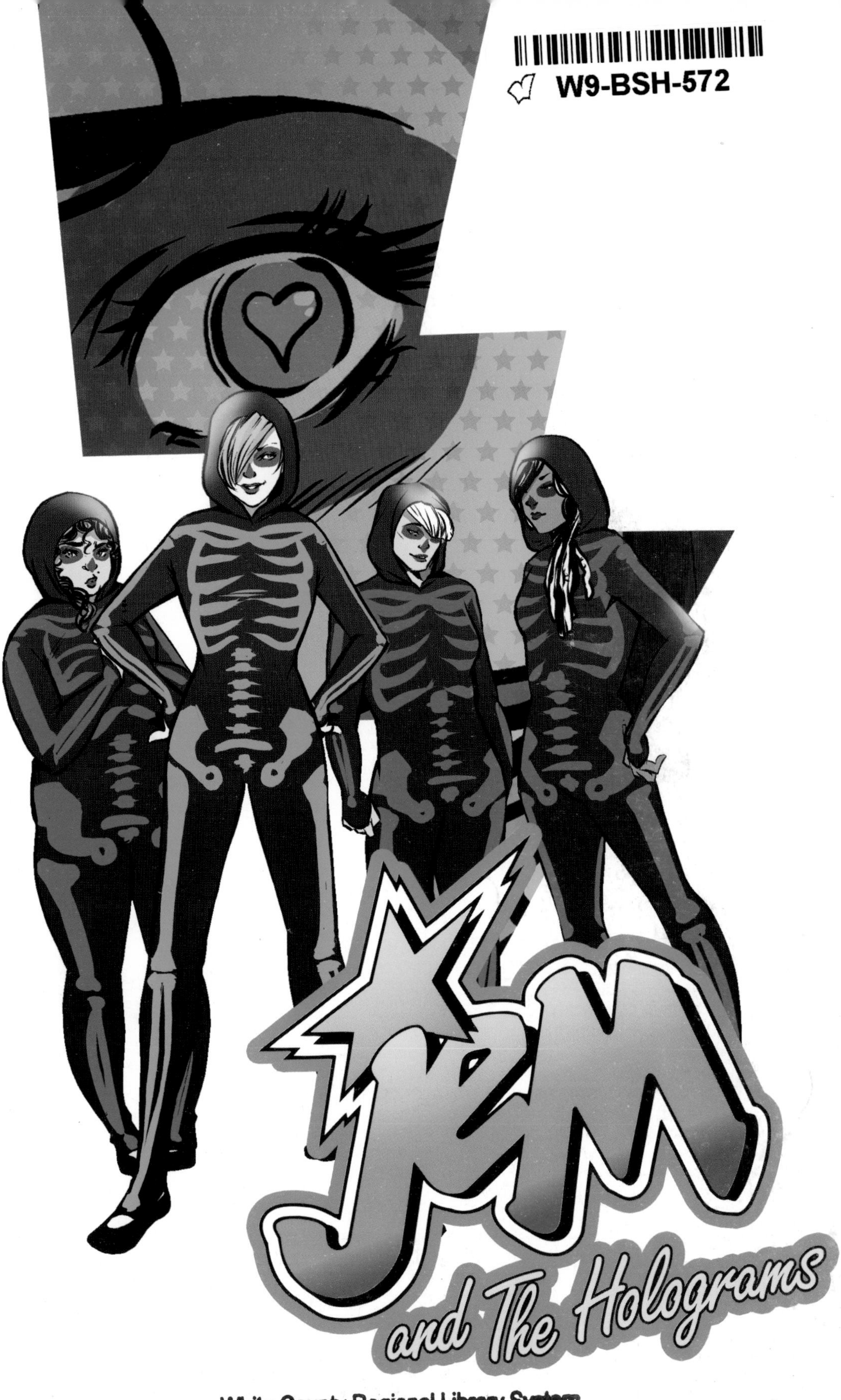
Jem
and The Holograms

WRITTEN BY **KELLY THOMPSON**

VIRAL
ART BY **EMMA VIECELI** · COLORS BY **M. VICTORIA ROBADO**

RIO PACHECO, BOY REPORTER
ART BY **CORIN HOWELL** · COLORS BY **M. VICTORIA ROBADO**

HOLIDAY SPECIAL
ART BY **AMY MEBBERSON** · COLORS BY **M. VICTORIA ROBADO**

ANNUAL 2015
WIRED
ART AND COLORS BY **AMY MEBBERSON**
JEM WOLF
ART BY **ARIELLE JOVELLANO** · COLORS BY **JOSH BURCHAM**
ANGRY AJA
ART BY **REBEKAH ISAACS** · COLORS BY **JOANA LAFUENTE**
SHANA WARS
ART AND COLORS BY **JEN BARTEL**
JEM BABIES
ART AND COLORS BY **AGNES GARBOWSKA** · COLOR ASSIST BY **LAUREN PERRY**

LETTERS BY **SHAWN LEE** AND **TOM B. LONG**
SERIES EDITS BY **JOHN BARBER**

COVER BY **JEN BARTEL**
COLLECTION EDITS BY **JUSTIN EISINGER** AND **ALONZO SIMON**
PUBLISHED BY **TED ADAMS**
COLLECTION DESIGN BY **SHAWN LEE**

Special thanks to Hasbro's Andrea Hopelain, Heather Hopkins, Ed Lane, Elizabeth Malkin, and Michael Kelly for their invaluable assistance.   For international rights, contact **licensing@idwpublishing.com**

ISBN: 978-1-63140-579-2   19 18 17 16   2 3 4 5

Licensed By: Hasbro

www.IDWPUBLISHING.com

Ted Adams, CEO & Publisher
Greg Goldstein, President & COO
Robbie Robbins, EVP/Sr. Graphic Artist
Chris Ryall, Chief Creative Officer/Editor-in-Chief
Matthew Ruzicka, CPA, Chief Financial Officer
Dirk Wood, VP of Marketing
Lorelei Bunjes, VP of Digital Services
Jeff Webber, VP of Licensing, Digital and Subsidiary Rights
Jerry Bennington, VP of New Product Development

Facebook: **facebook.com/idwpublishing**
Twitter: **@idwpublishing**
YouTube: **youtube.com/idwpublishing**
Tumblr: **tumblr.idwpublishing.com**
Instagram: **instagram.com/idwpublishing**

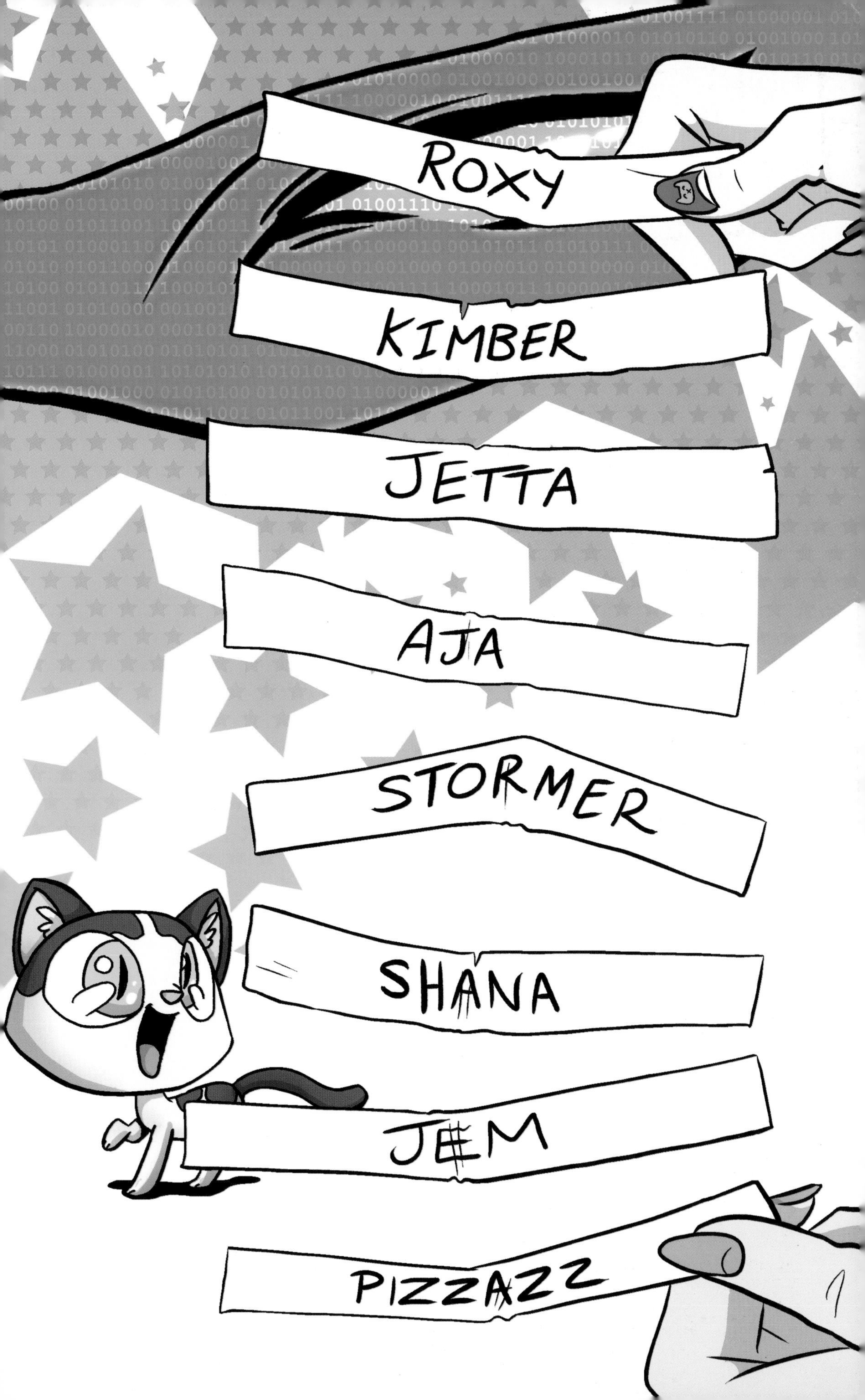
ROXY
KIMBER
JETTA
AJA
STORMER
SHANA
JEM
PIZZAZZ

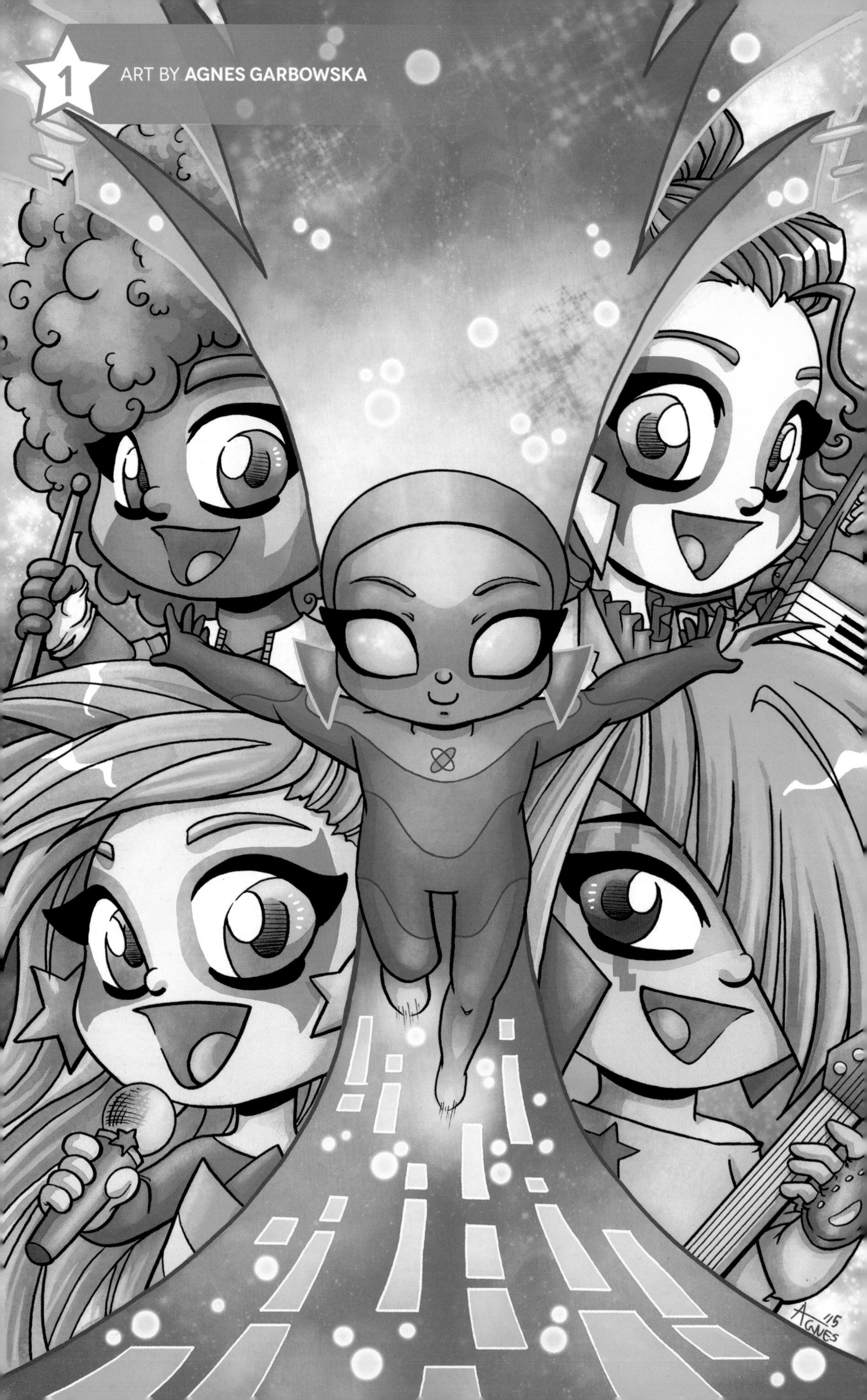
AGNES '15

1 ART BY AGNES GARBOWSKA

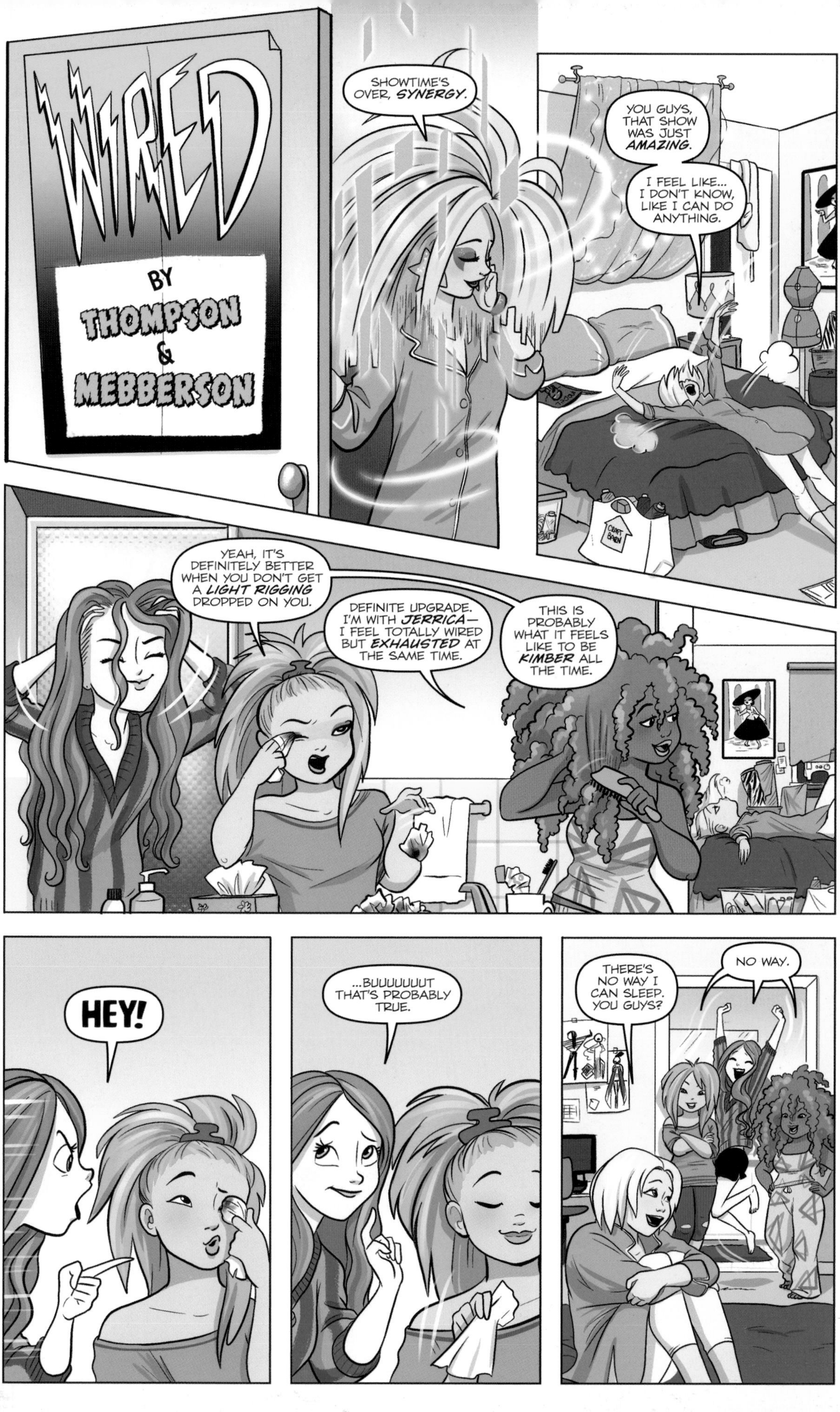
WIRED
BY THOMPSON & MEBBERSON
SHOWTIME'S OVER, SYNERGY.
YOU GUYS, THAT SHOW WAS JUST AMAZING.
I FEEL LIKE... I DON'T KNOW, LIKE I CAN DO ANYTHING.
CRAFT BARN
YEAH, IT'S DEFINITELY BETTER WHEN YOU DON'T GET A LIGHT RIGGING DROPPED ON YOU.
DEFINITE UPGRADE. I'M WITH JERRICA— I FEEL TOTALLY WIRED BUT EXHAUSTED AT THE SAME TIME.
THIS IS PROBABLY WHAT IT FEELS LIKE TO BE KIMBER ALL THE TIME.
HEY!
...BUUUUUUUT THAT'S PROBABLY TRUE.
THERE'S NO WAY I CAN SLEEP. YOU GUYS?
NO WAY.

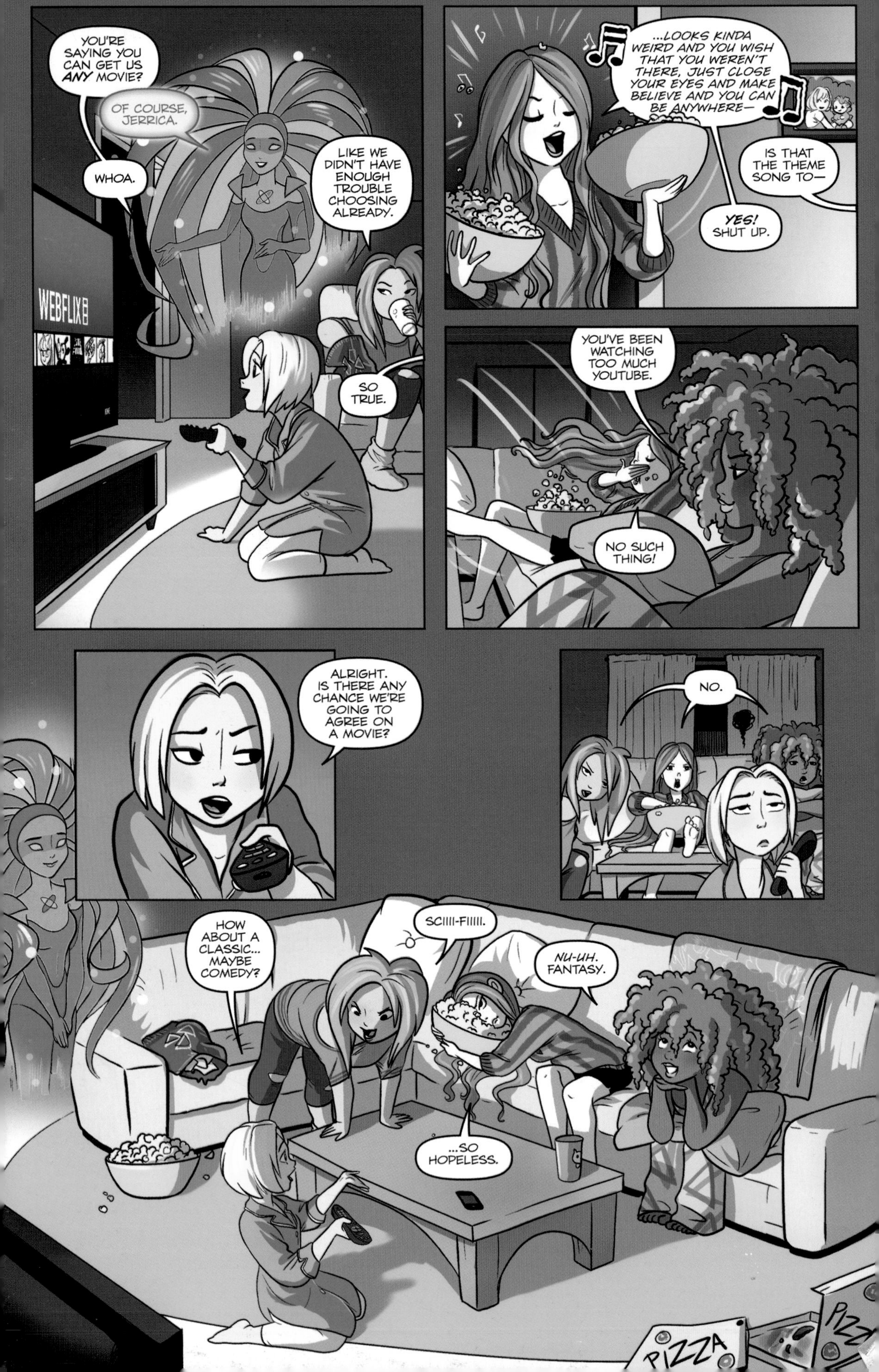
YOU'RE SAYING YOU CAN GET US ANY MOVIE?
OF COURSE, JERRICA.
WHOA.
LIKE WE DIDN'T HAVE ENOUGH TROUBLE CHOOSING ALREADY.
SO TRUE.
WEBFLIX
...LOOKS KINDA WEIRD AND YOU WISH THAT YOU WEREN'T THERE, JUST CLOSE YOUR EYES AND MAKE BELIEVE AND YOU CAN BE ANYWHERE—
IS THAT THE THEME SONG TO—
YES! SHUT UP.
YOU'VE BEEN WATCHING TOO MUCH YOUTUBE.
NO SUCH THING!
ALRIGHT. IS THERE ANY CHANCE WE'RE GOING TO AGREE ON A MOVIE?
NO.
HOW ABOUT A CLASSIC... MAYBE COMEDY?
SCIIIII-FIIIII.
NU-UH. FANTASY.
...SO HOPELESS.
PIZZA
PIZZ

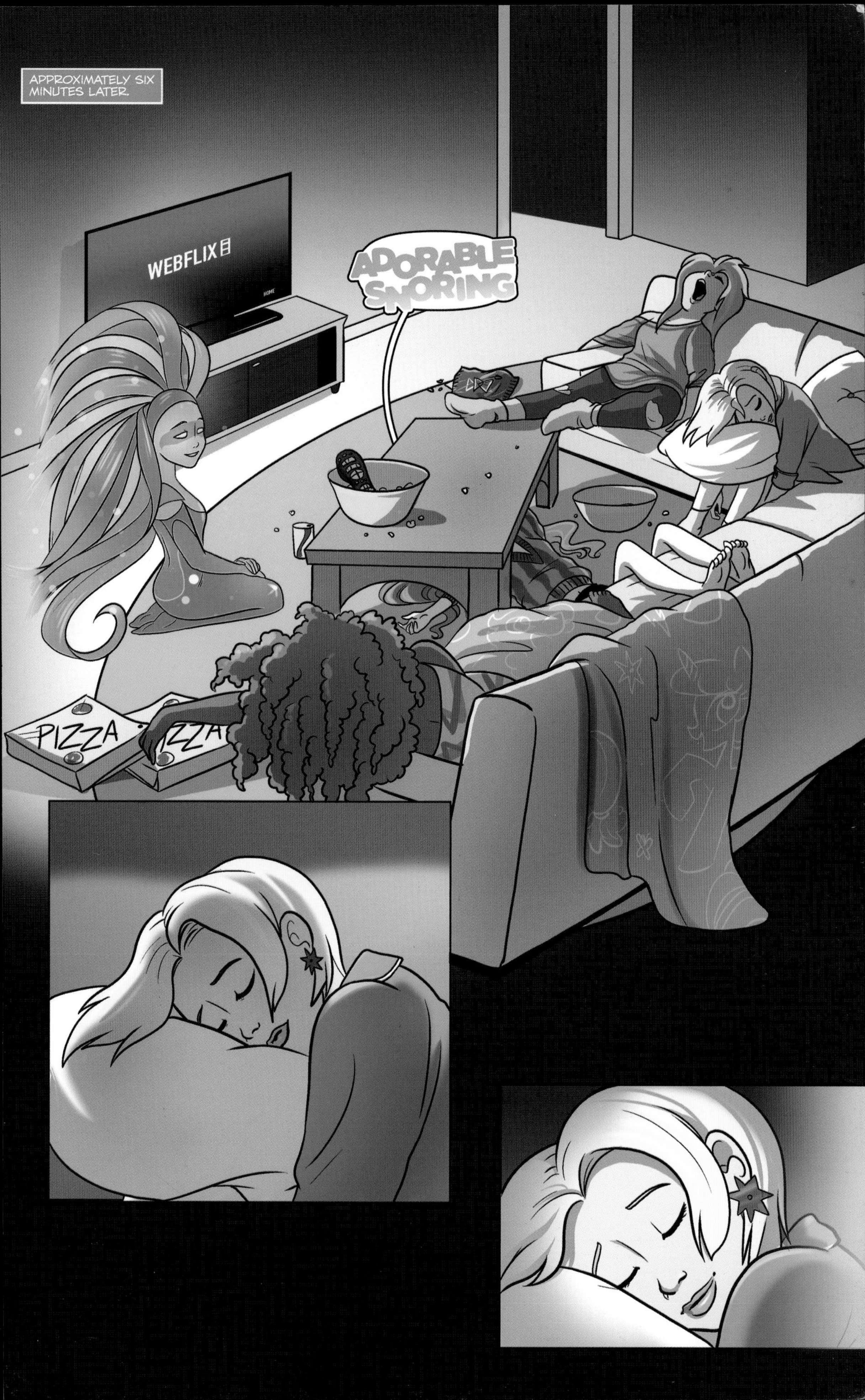
APPROXIMATELY SIX MINUTES LATER.
WEBFLIX
HOME
ADORABLE SNORING
PIZZA
PIZZA

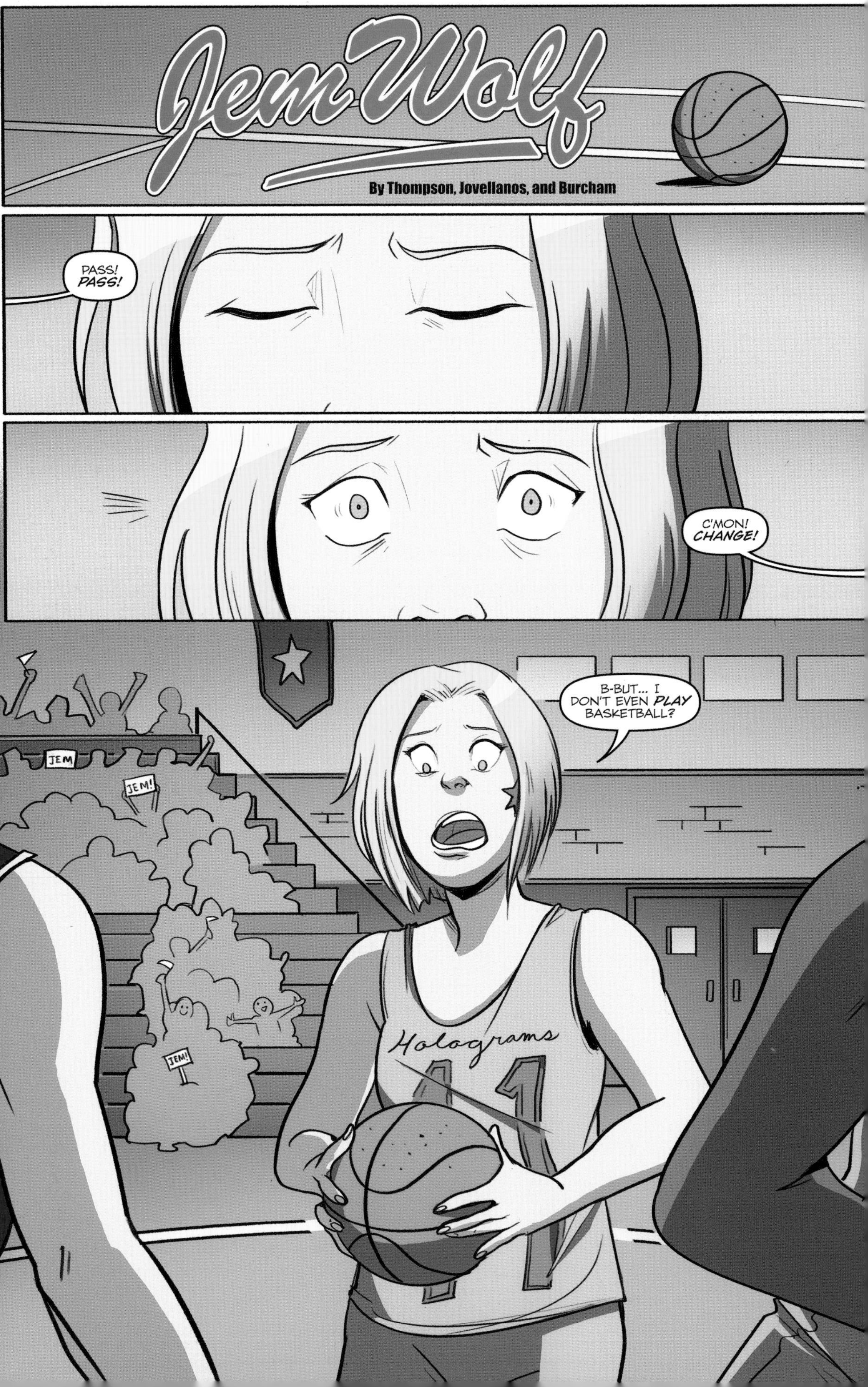
Jem Wolf
By Thompson, Jovellanos, and Burcham
PASS! PASS!
C'MON! CHANGE!
B-BUT... I DON'T EVEN PLAY BASKETBALL?
JEM
JEM!
Holograms
JEM!

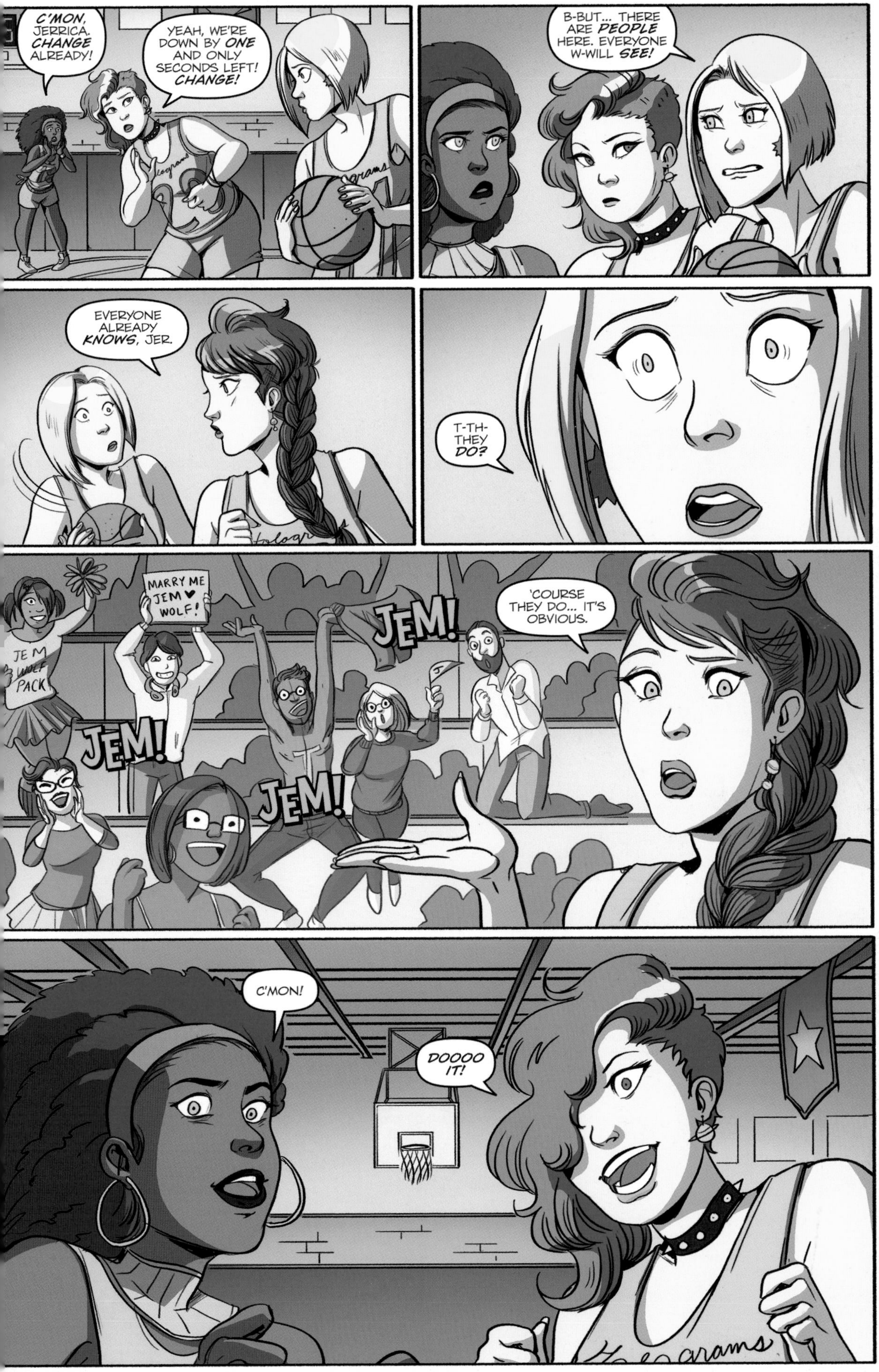
C'MON, JERRICA. CHANGE ALREADY!
YEAH, WE'RE DOWN BY ONE AND ONLY SECONDS LEFT! CHANGE!
B-BUT... THERE ARE PEOPLE HERE. EVERYONE W-WILL SEE!
EVERYONE ALREADY KNOWS, JER.
T-TH-THEY DO?
MARRY ME JEM ♥ WOLF!
JEM WOLF PACK
JEM!
'COURSE THEY DO... IT'S OBVIOUS.
JEM!
JEM!
C'MON!
DOOOO IT!

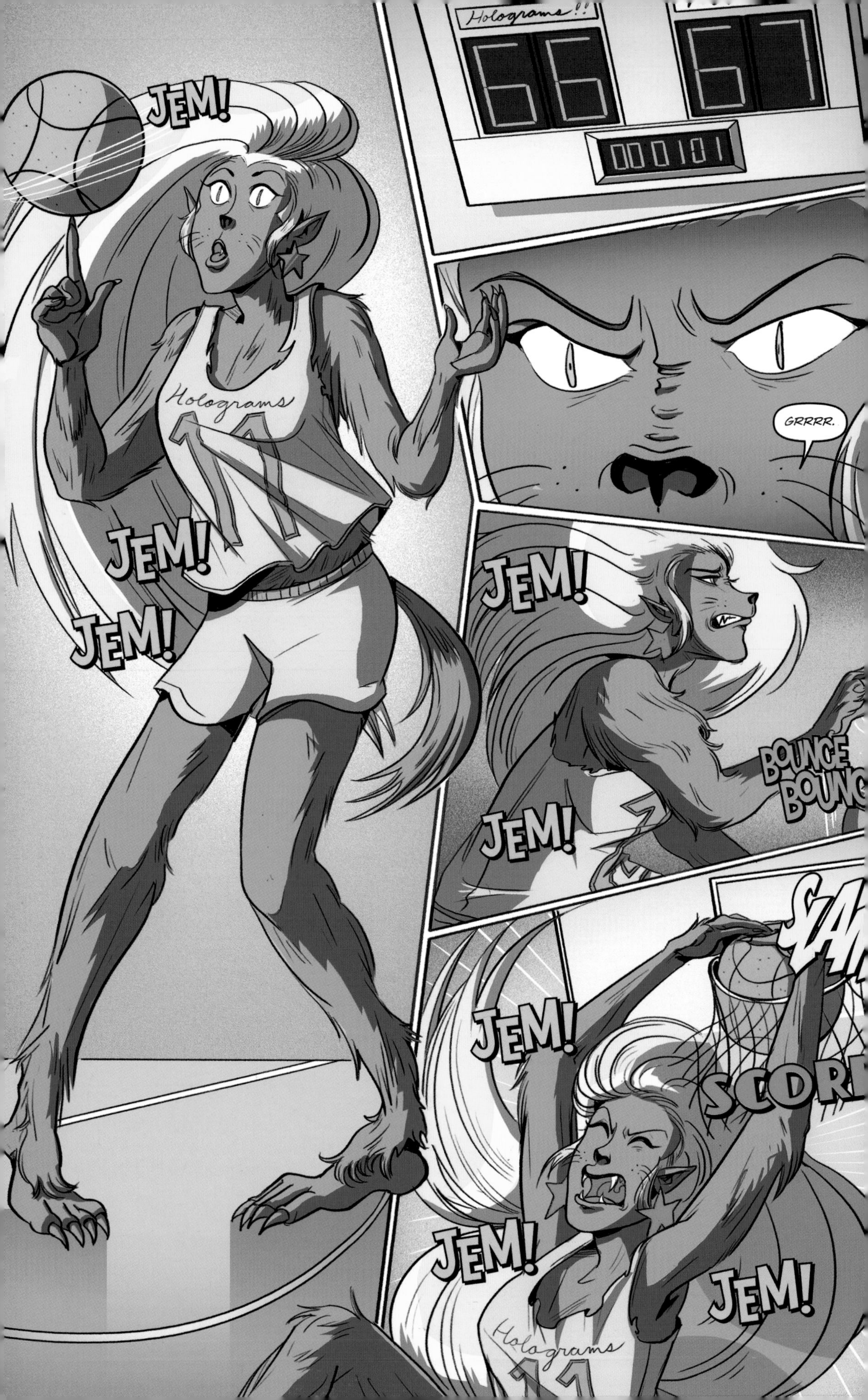
Holograms!!
66
67
JEM!
Holograms
JEM!
JEM!
GRRRR.
JEM!
BOUNCE
JEM!
JEM!
JEM!
JEM!
Holograms

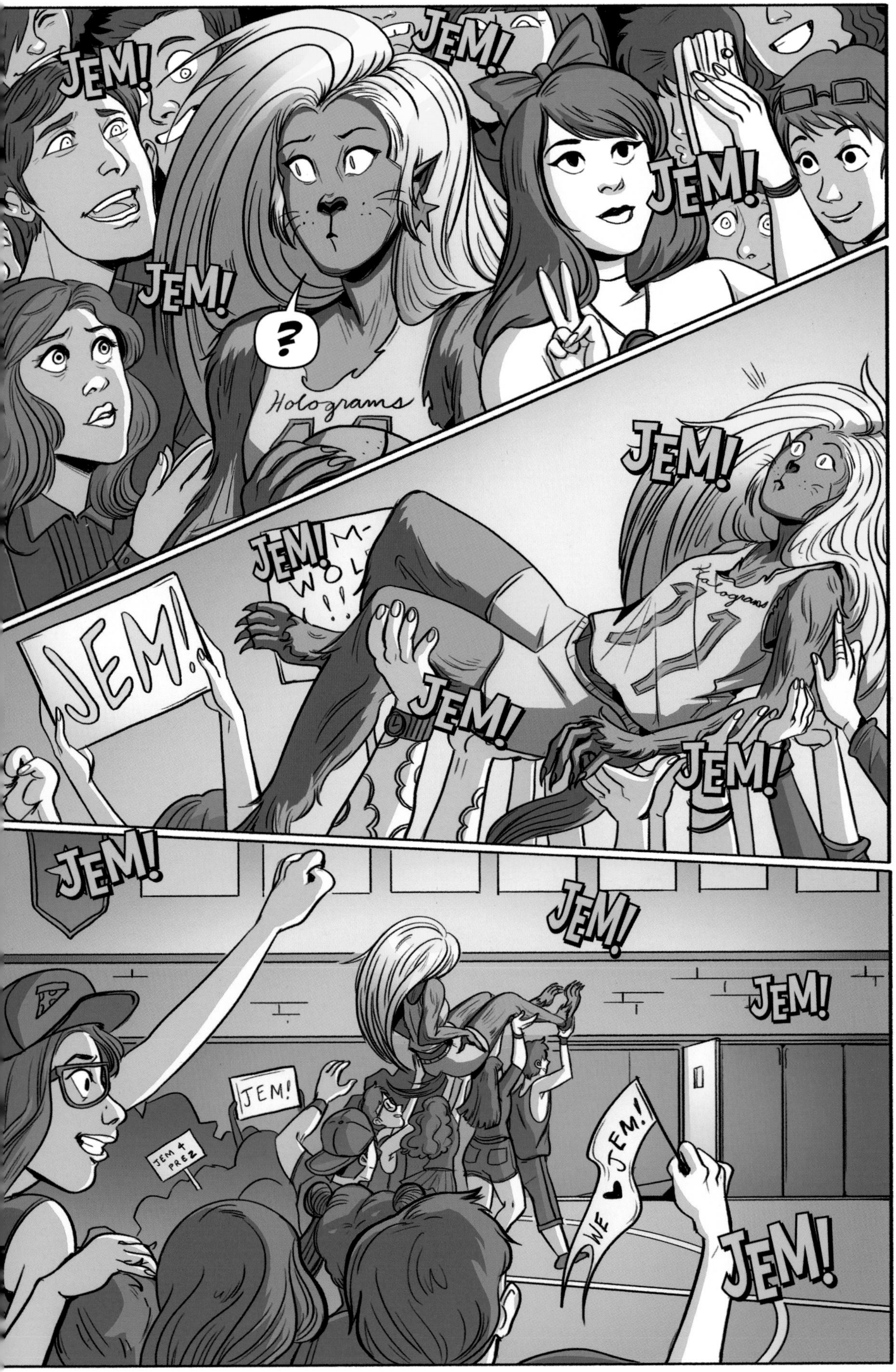
JEM!
JEM!
JEM!
JEM!
?
Holograms
JEM!
JEM!
JEM!
JEM!
JEM!
Holograms
JEM!
JEM!
JEM!
JEM!
JEM 4 PREZ
WE ♥ JEM!
JEM!

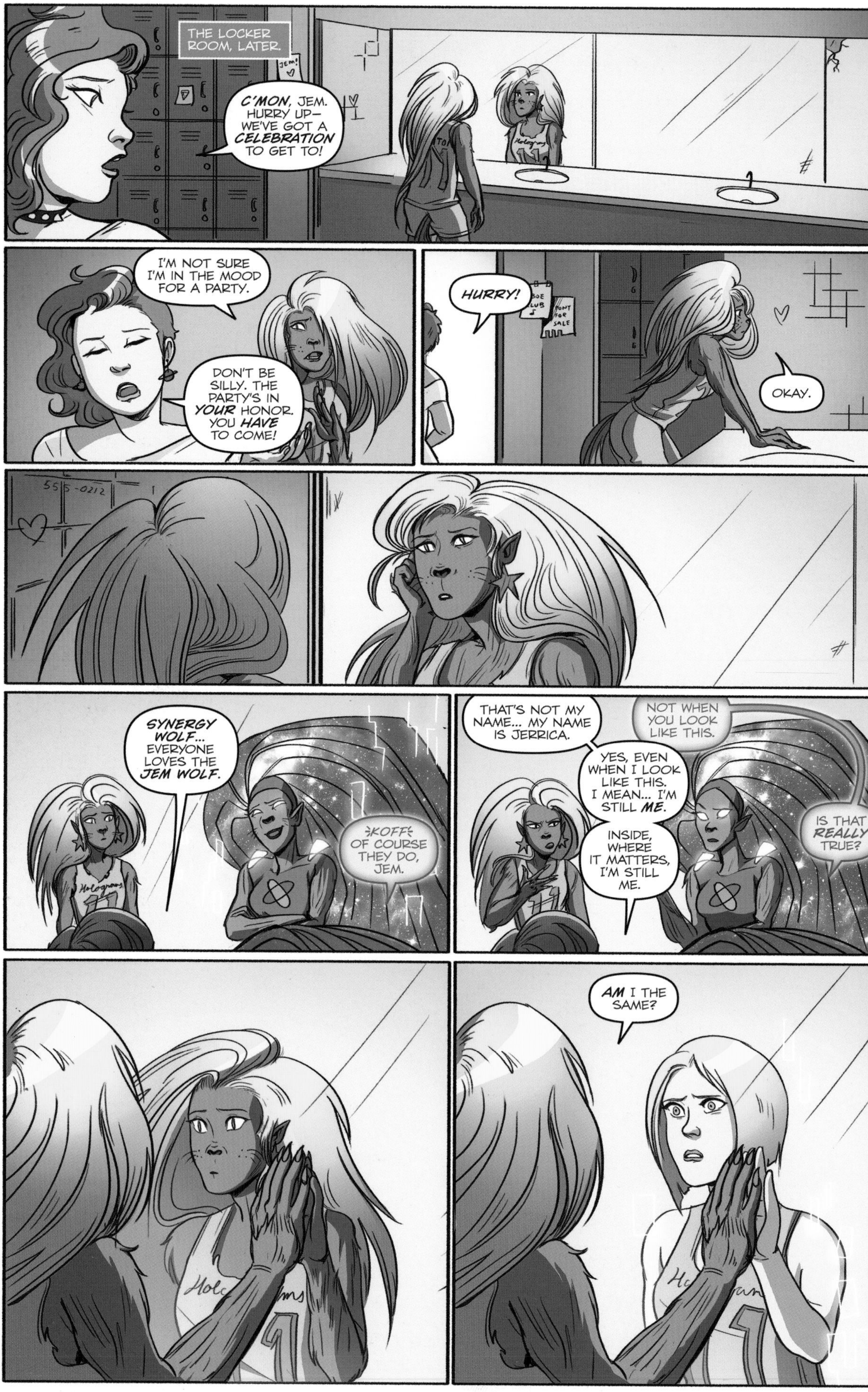
THE LOCKER ROOM, LATER.
JEM!
C'MON, JEM. HURRY UP— WE'VE GOT A CELEBRATION TO GET TO!
I'M NOT SURE I'M IN THE MOOD FOR A PARTY.
DON'T BE SILLY. THE PARTY'S IN YOUR HONOR. YOU HAVE TO COME!
HURRY!
PONY FOR SALE
OKAY.
555-0212
SYNERGY WOLF... EVERYONE LOVES THE JEM WOLF.
KOFF OF COURSE THEY DO, JEM.
THAT'S NOT MY NAME... MY NAME IS JERRICA.
NOT WHEN YOU LOOK LIKE THIS.
YES, EVEN WHEN I LOOK LIKE THIS. I MEAN... I'M STILL ME.
INSIDE, WHERE IT MATTERS, I'M STILL ME.
IS THAT REALLY TRUE?
AM I THE SAME?

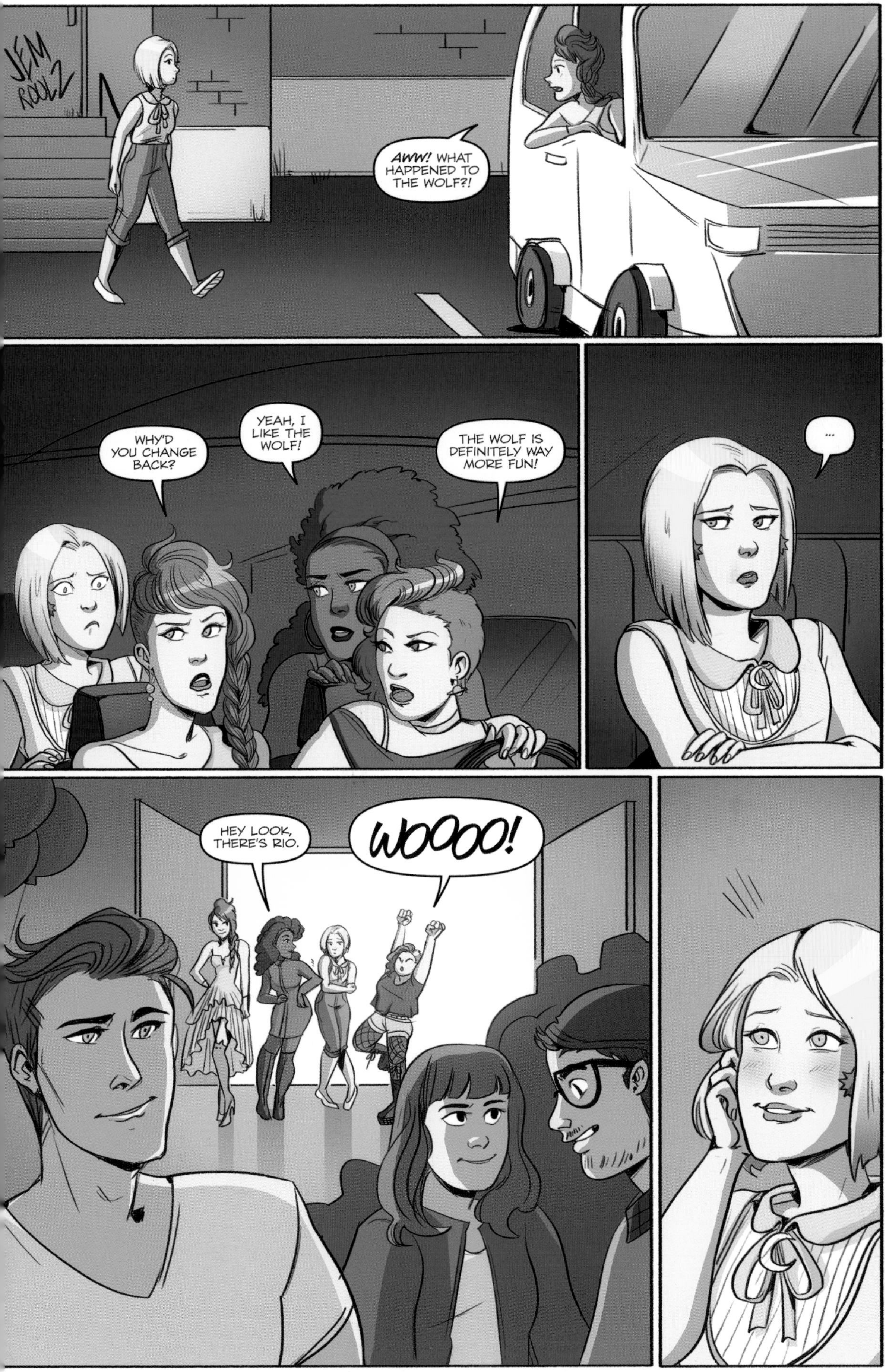
JEM ROOLZ
AWW! WHAT HAPPENED TO THE WOLF?!
WHY'D YOU CHANGE BACK?
YEAH, I LIKE THE WOLF!
THE WOLF IS DEFINITELY WAY MORE FUN!
...
HEY LOOK, THERE'S RIO.
WOOOO!

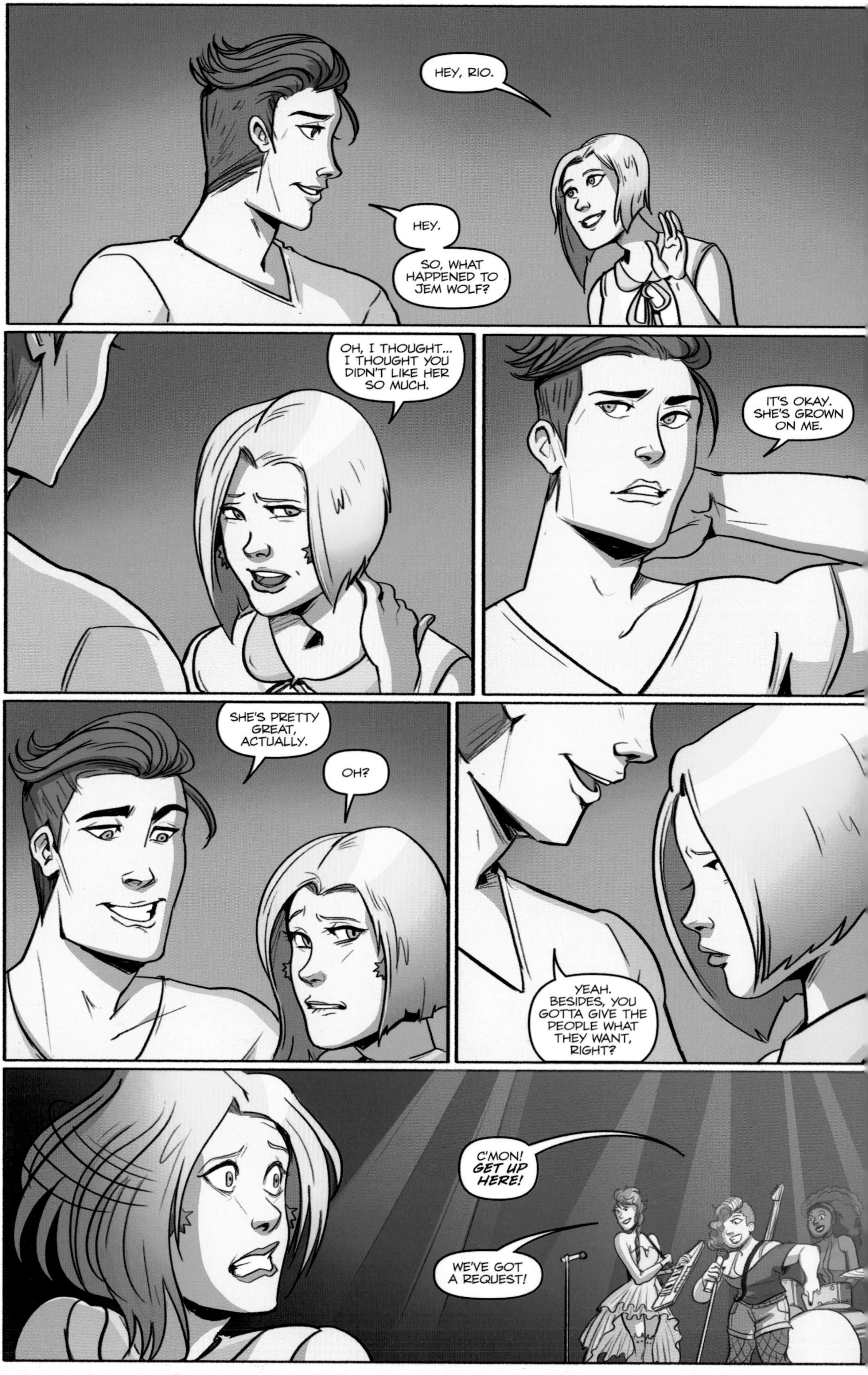
HEY, RIO.
HEY.
SO, WHAT HAPPENED TO JEM WOLF?
OH, I THOUGHT... I THOUGHT YOU DIDN'T LIKE HER SO MUCH.
IT'S OKAY. SHE'S GROWN ON ME.
SHE'S PRETTY GREAT, ACTUALLY.
OH?
YEAH. BESIDES, YOU GOTTA GIVE THE PEOPLE WHAT THEY WANT, RIGHT?
C'MON! GET UP HERE!
WE'VE GOT A REQUEST!

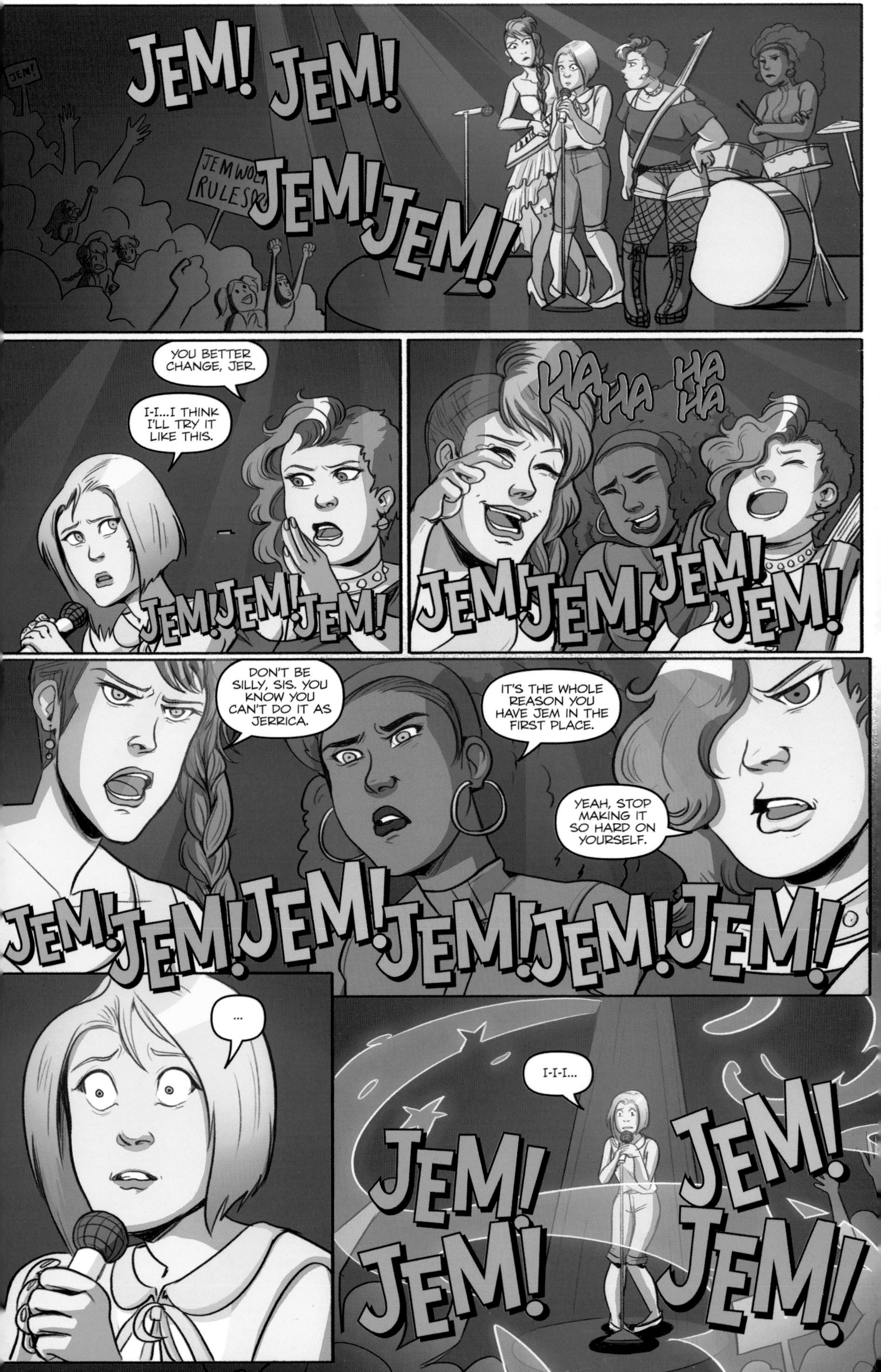
JEM
JEM! JEM!
JEMWOLF RULES!
JEM! JEM!
YOU BETTER CHANGE, JER.
I-I...I THINK I'LL TRY IT LIKE THIS.
JEM! JEM! JEM!
HA HA HA HA
JEM! JEM! JEM! JEM!
DON'T BE SILLY, SIS. YOU KNOW YOU CAN'T DO IT AS JERRICA.
IT'S THE WHOLE REASON YOU HAVE JEM IN THE FIRST PLACE.
YEAH, STOP MAKING IT SO HARD ON YOURSELF.
JEM! JEM! JEM! JEM! JEM! JEM!
...
I-I-I...
JEM! JEM! JEM! JEM!

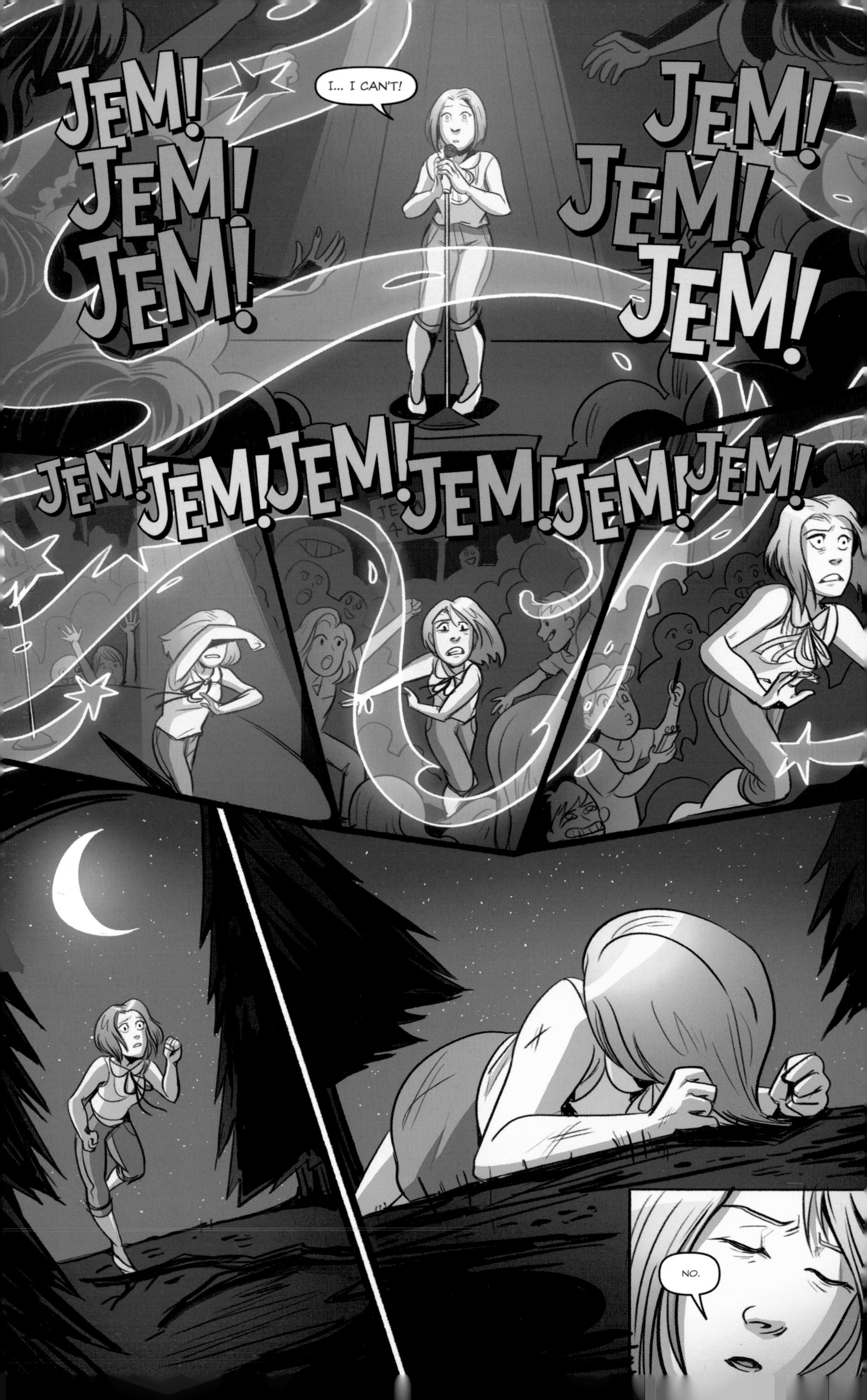

JEM! JEM! JEM!
I... I CAN'T!
JEM! JEM! JEM!
JEM! JEM! JEM! JEM! JEM! JEM!
NO.

ANGRY AJA
BEYOND THUNDER-ROTUNDA
BY THOMPSON, ISAACS, & LAFUENTE

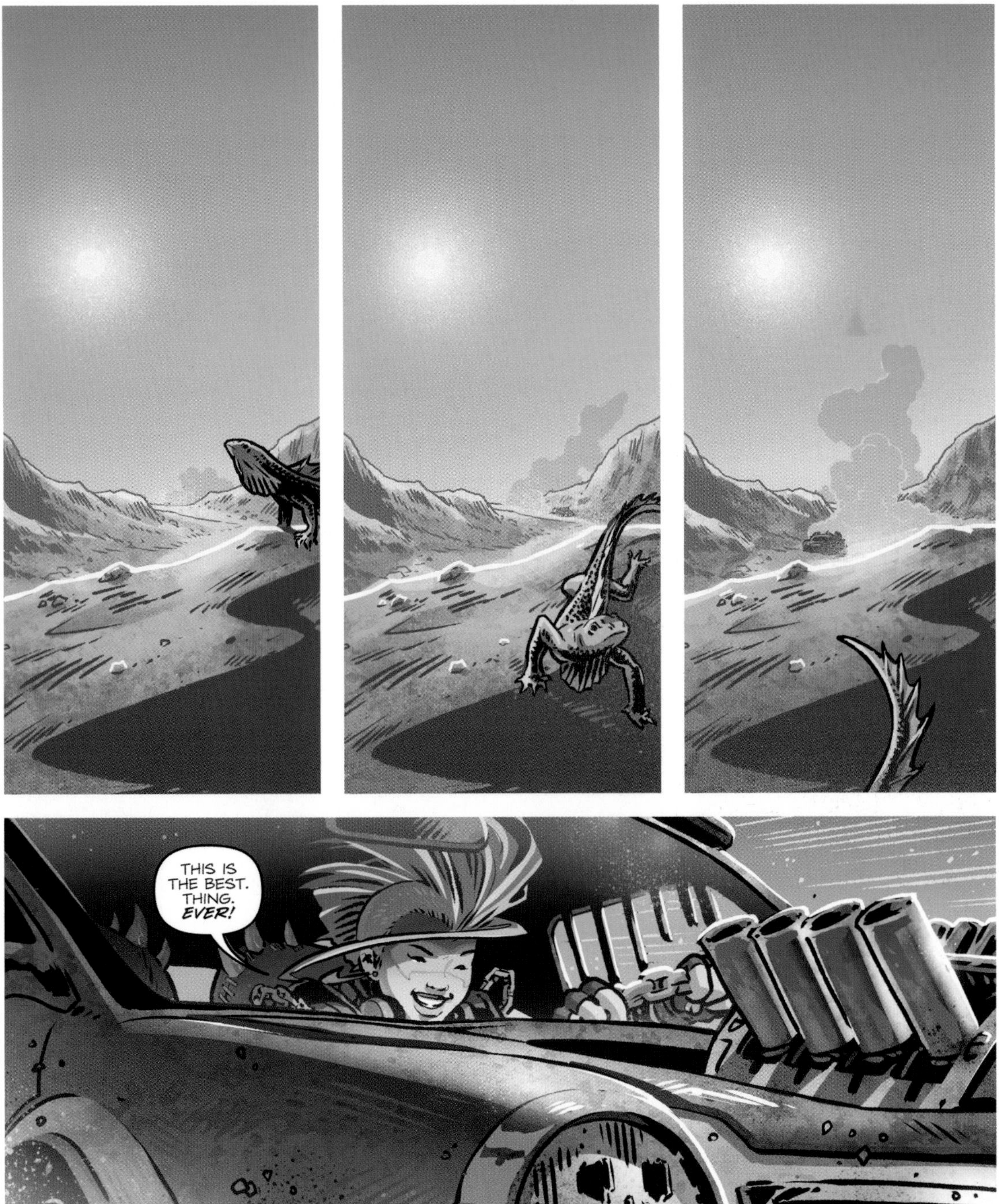
THIS IS THE BEST. THING. *EVER!*

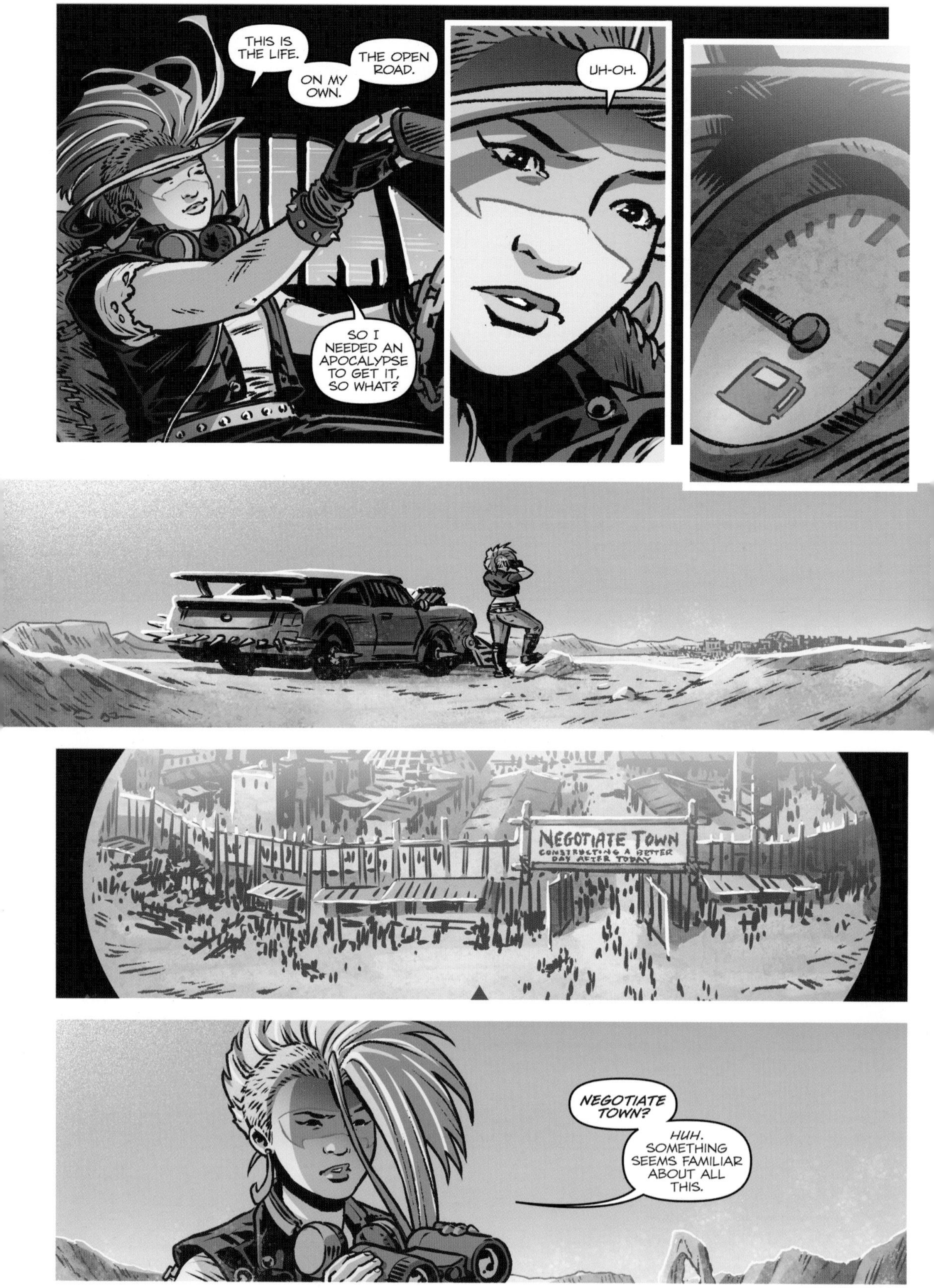
THIS IS THE LIFE.
ON MY OWN.
THE OPEN ROAD.
SO I NEEDED AN APOCALYPSE TO GET IT, SO WHAT?
UH-OH.
NEGOTIATE TOWN
CONSTRUCTING A BETTER DAY AFTER TODAY
NEGOTIATE TOWN?
HUH. SOMETHING SEEMS FAMILIAR ABOUT ALL THIS.

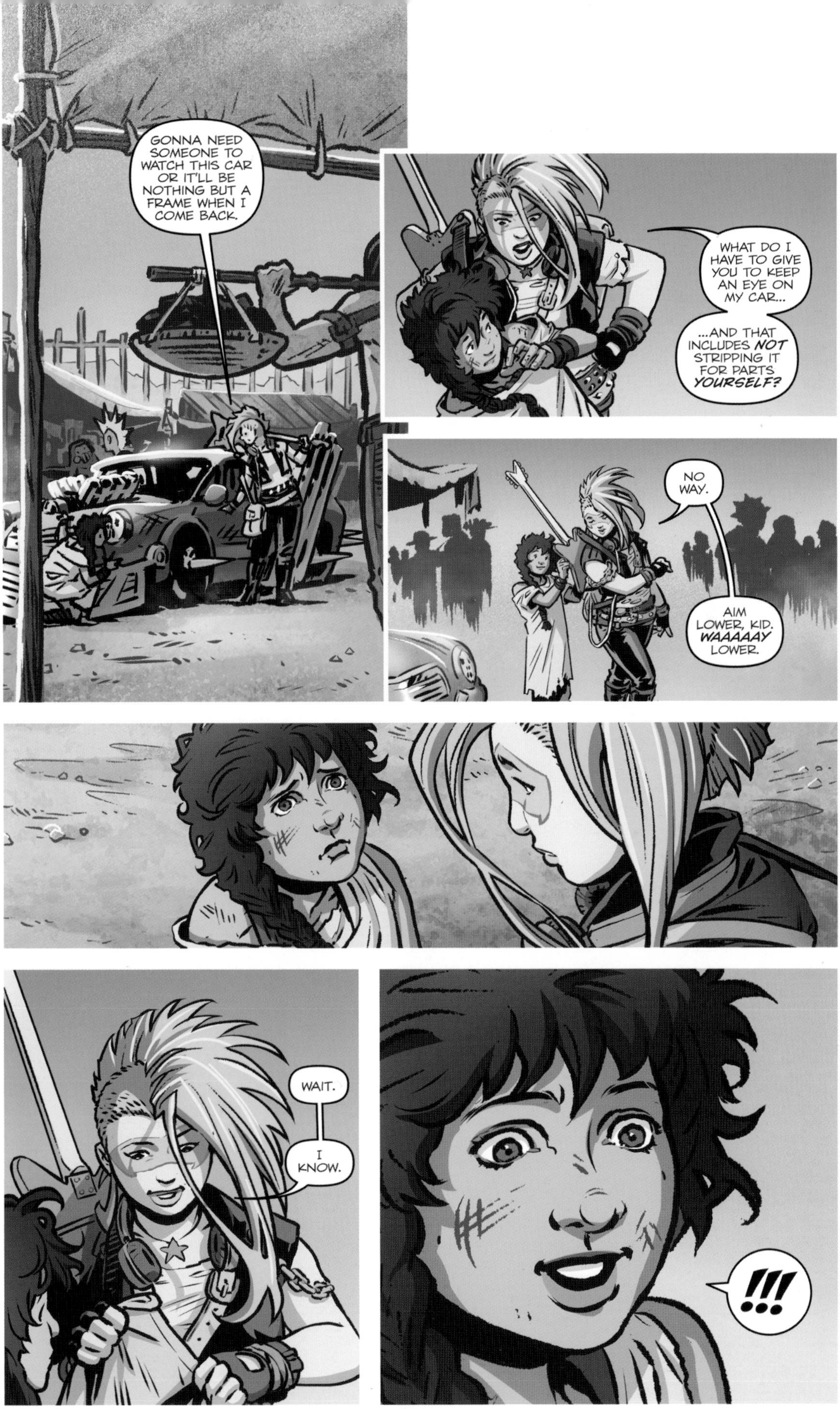
GONNA NEED SOMEONE TO WATCH THIS CAR OR IT'LL BE NOTHING BUT A FRAME WHEN I COME BACK.
WHAT DO I HAVE TO GIVE YOU TO KEEP AN EYE ON MY CAR...
...AND THAT INCLUDES NOT STRIPPING IT FOR PARTS YOURSELF?
NO WAY.
AIM LOWER, KID. WAAAAAY LOWER.
WAIT.
I KNOW.
!!!

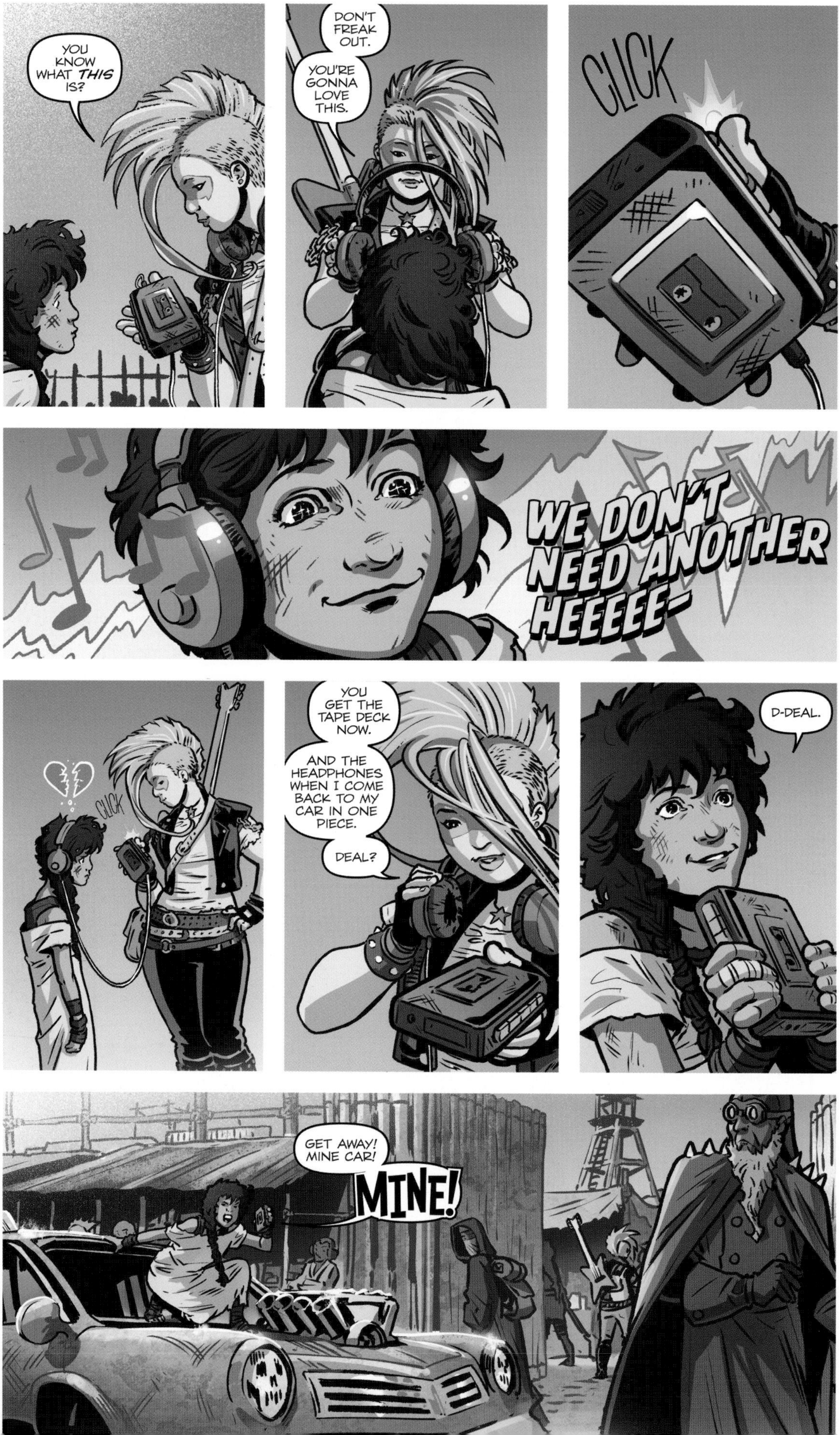
YOU KNOW WHAT THIS IS?
DON'T FREAK OUT.
YOU'RE GONNA LOVE THIS.
CLICK
WE DON'T NEED ANOTHER HEEEEE-
CLICK
YOU GET THE TAPE DECK NOW.
AND THE HEADPHONES WHEN I COME BACK TO MY CAR IN ONE PIECE.
DEAL?
D-DEAL.
GET AWAY! MINE CAR!
MINE!

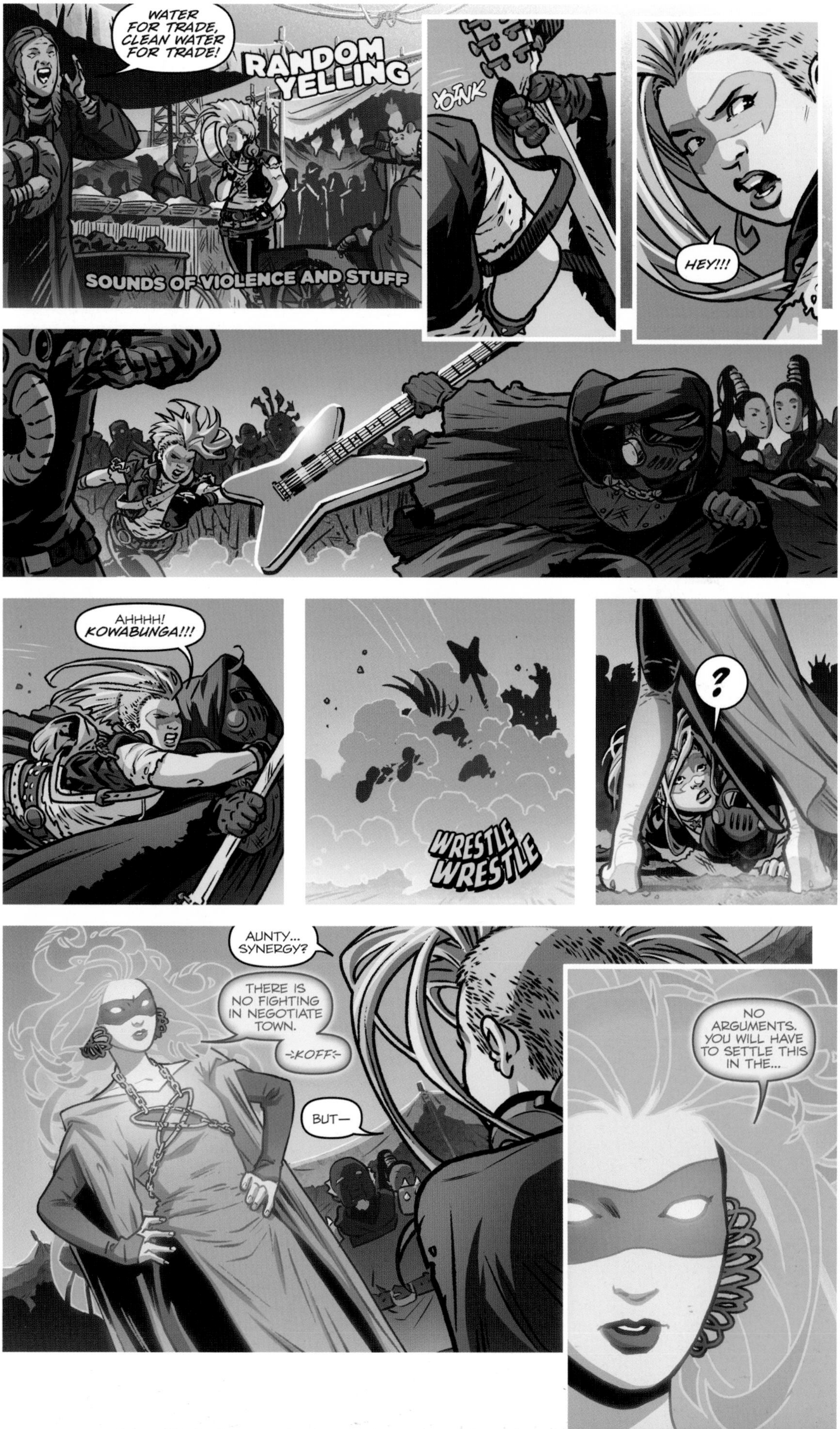
WATER FOR TRADE, CLEAN WATER FOR TRADE!
RANDOM YELLING
SOUNDS OF VIOLENCE AND STUFF
YOINK
HEY!!!
AHHHH! KOWABUNGA!!!
WRESTLE WRESTLE
?
AUNTY... SYNERGY?
THERE IS NO FIGHTING IN NEGOTIATE TOWN.
-KOFF-
BUT—
NO ARGUMENTS. YOU WILL HAVE TO SETTLE THIS IN THE...

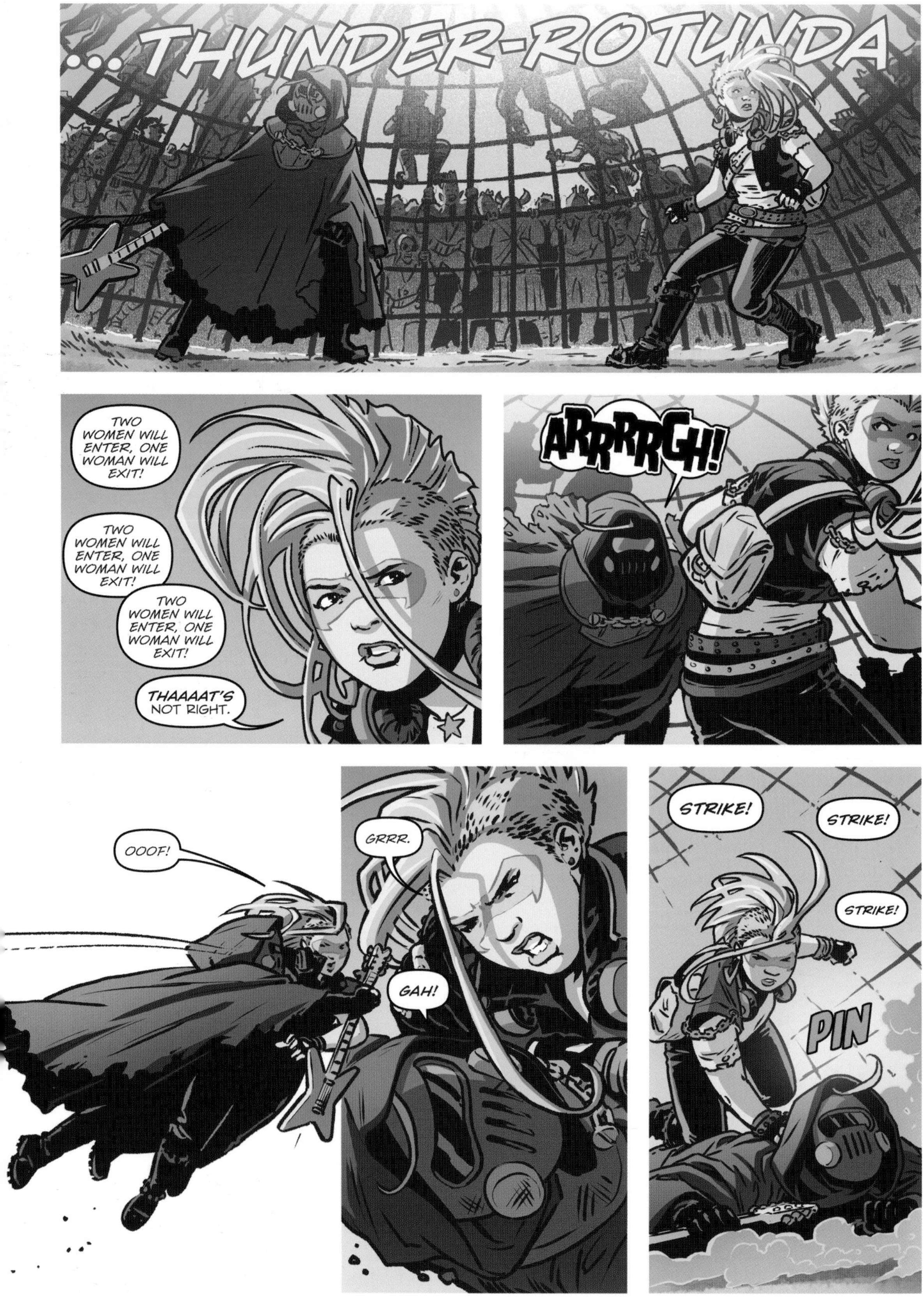
...THUNDER-ROTUNDA
TWO WOMEN WILL ENTER, ONE WOMAN WILL EXIT!
TWO WOMEN WILL ENTER, ONE WOMAN WILL EXIT!
TWO WOMEN WILL ENTER, ONE WOMAN WILL EXIT!
THAAAAT'S NOT RIGHT.
ARRRRGH!
OOOF!
GRRR.
GAH!
STRIKE!
STRIKE!
STRIKE!
PIN

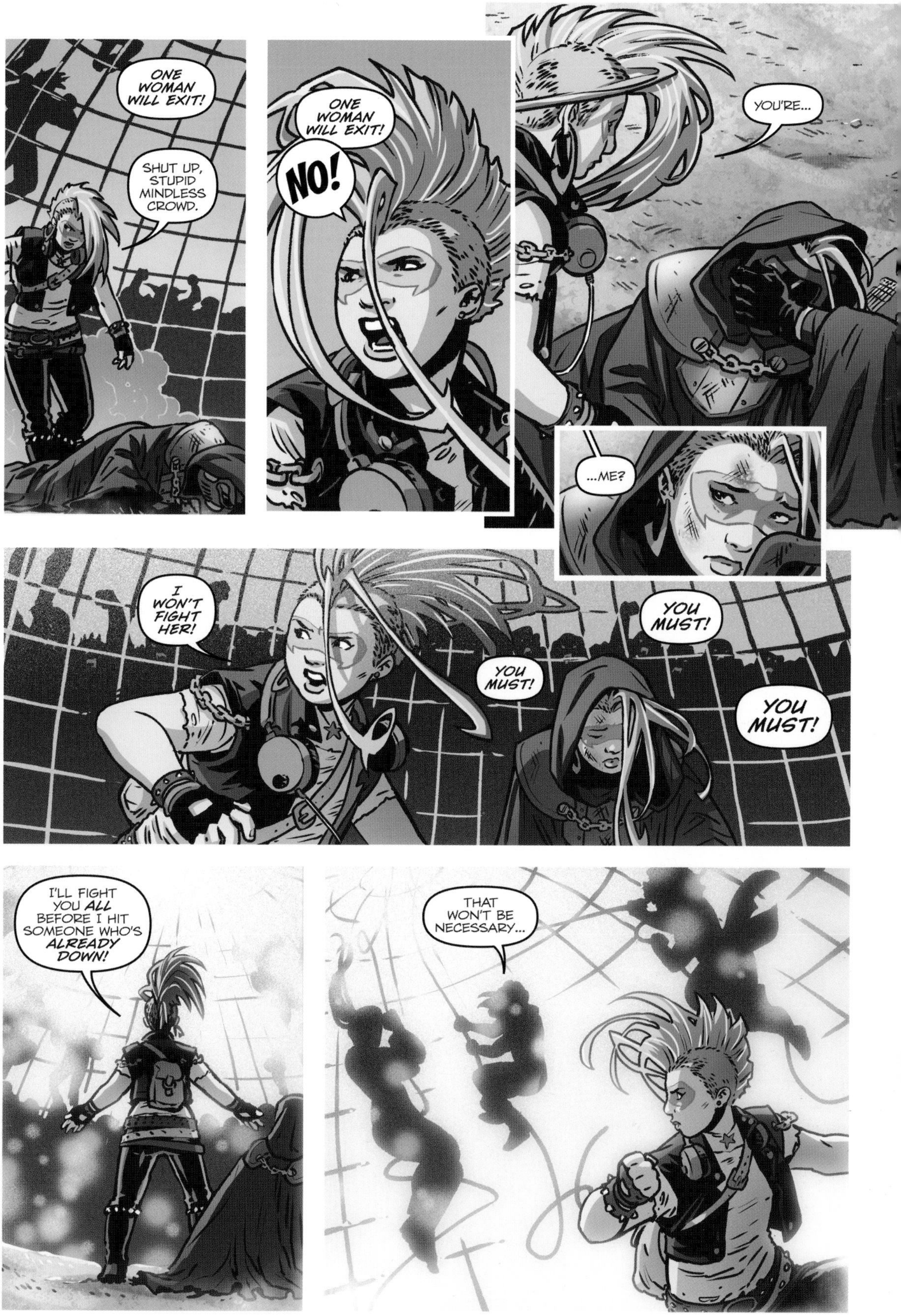
ONE WOMAN WILL EXIT!
SHUT UP, STUPID MINDLESS CROWD.
ONE WOMAN WILL EXIT!
NO!
YOU'RE...
...ME?
I WON'T FIGHT HER!
YOU MUST!
YOU MUST!
YOU MUST!
I'LL FIGHT YOU ALL BEFORE I HIT SOMEONE WHO'S ALREADY DOWN!
THAT WON'T BE NECESSARY...

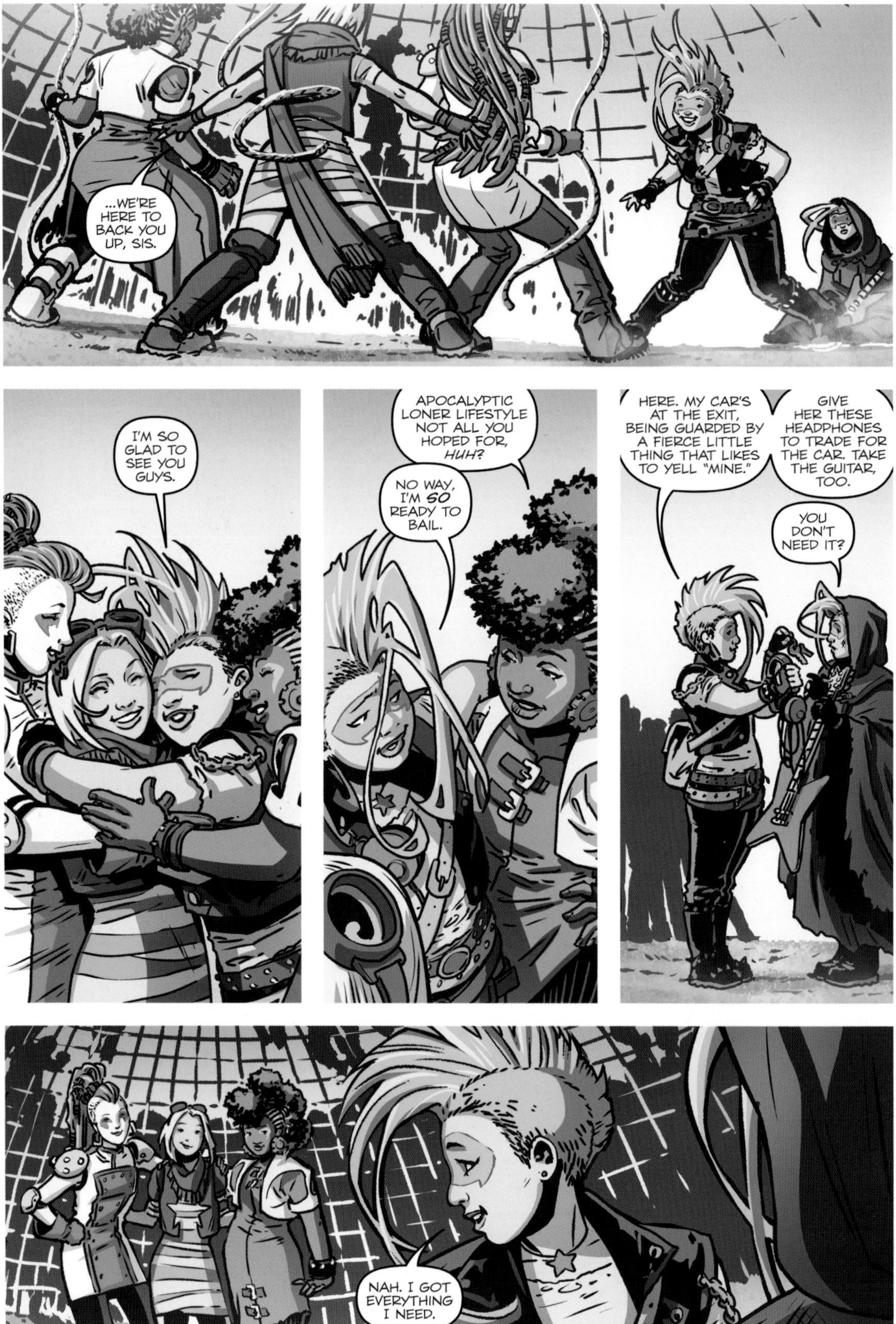
...WE'RE HERE TO BACK YOU UP, SIS.
I'M SO GLAD TO SEE YOU GUYS.
APOCALYPTIC LONER LIFESTYLE NOT ALL YOU HOPED FOR, *HUH*?
NO WAY, I'M *SO* READY TO BAIL.
HERE. MY CAR'S AT THE EXIT, BEING GUARDED BY A FIERCE LITTLE THING THAT LIKES TO YELL "MINE."
GIVE HER THESE HEADPHONES TO TRADE FOR THE CAR. TAKE THE GUITAR, TOO.
YOU DON'T NEED IT?
NAH. I GOT EVERYTHING I NEED.

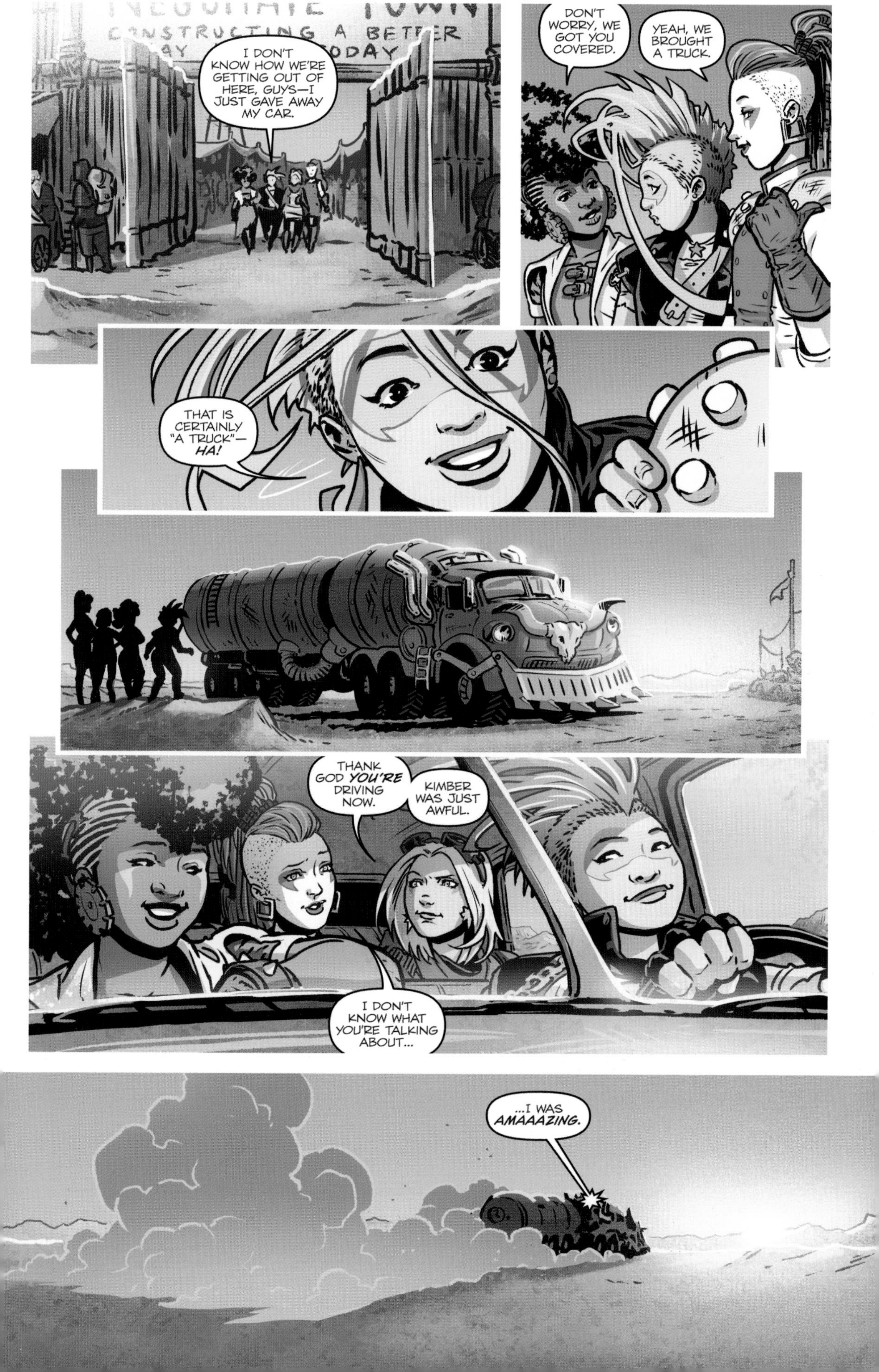

CONSTRUCTING A BETTER
I DON'T KNOW HOW WE'RE GETTING OUT OF HERE, GUYS—I JUST GAVE AWAY MY CAR.
DON'T WORRY, WE GOT YOU COVERED.
YEAH, WE BROUGHT A TRUCK.
THAT IS CERTAINLY "A TRUCK"— *HA!*
THANK GOD *YOU'RE* DRIVING NOW.
KIMBER WAS JUST AWFUL.
I DON'T KNOW WHAT YOU'RE TALKING ABOUT...
...I WAS *AMAAAZING.*

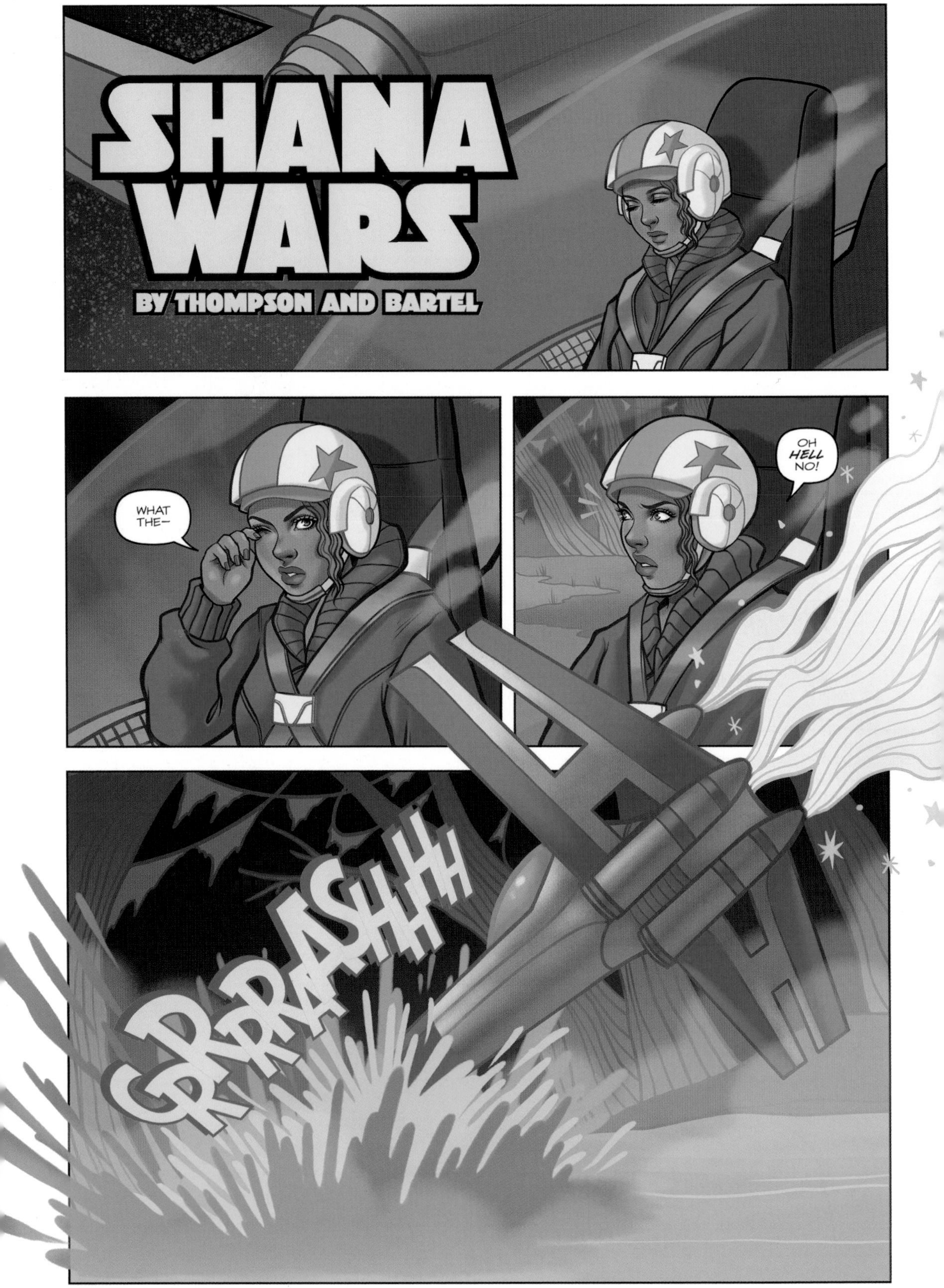
SHANA WARS
BY THOMPSON AND BARTEL
WHAT THE–
OH HELL NO!
GRRRASHHHH

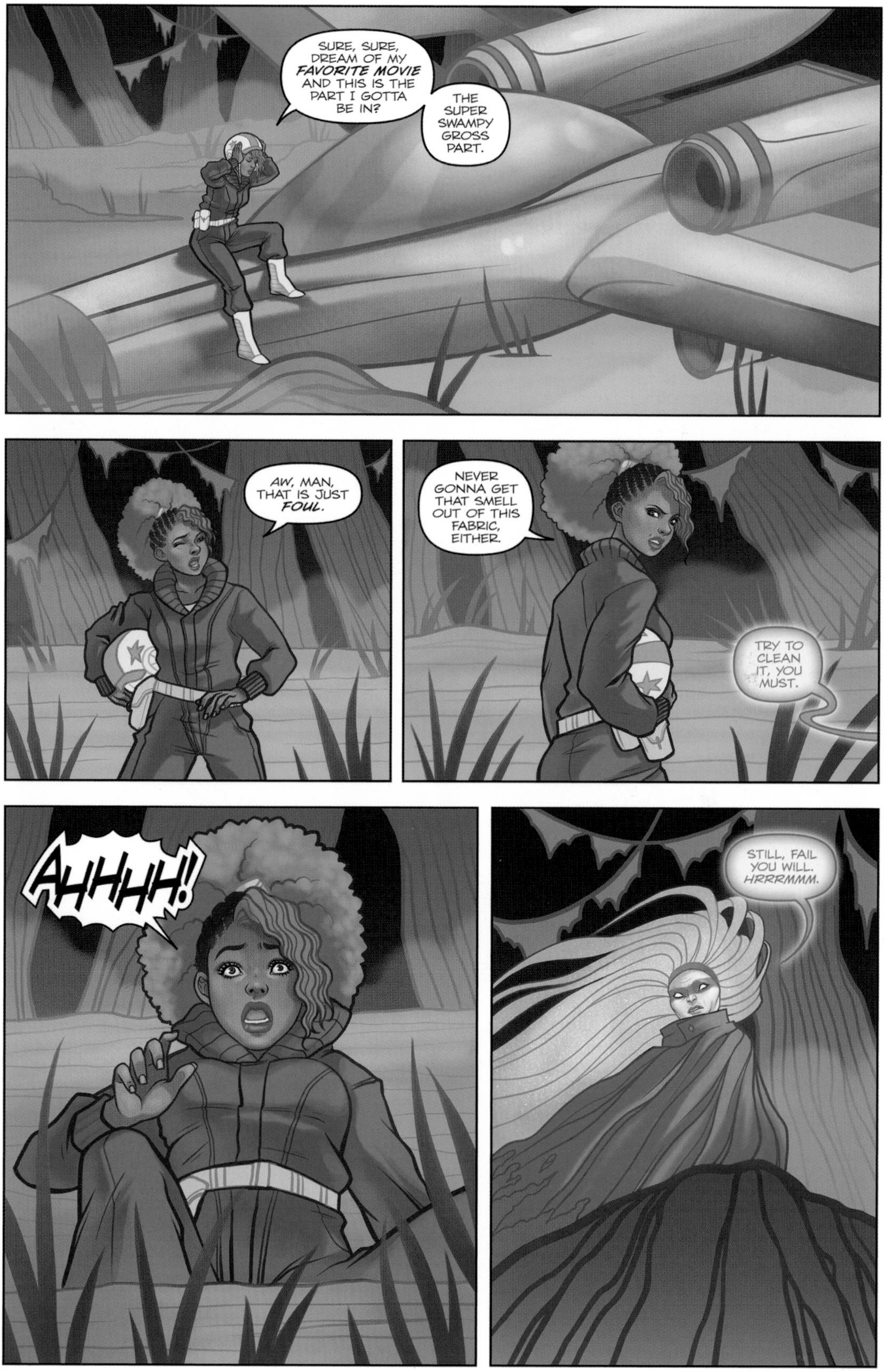
SURE, SURE, DREAM OF MY *FAVORITE MOVIE* AND THIS IS THE PART I GOTTA BE IN?
THE SUPER SWAMPY GROSS PART.
AW, MAN, THAT IS JUST *FOUL.*
NEVER GONNA GET THAT SMELL OUT OF THIS FABRIC, EITHER.
TRY TO CLEAN IT, YOU MUST.
AHHHH!
STILL, FAIL YOU WILL. *HRRRMMM.*

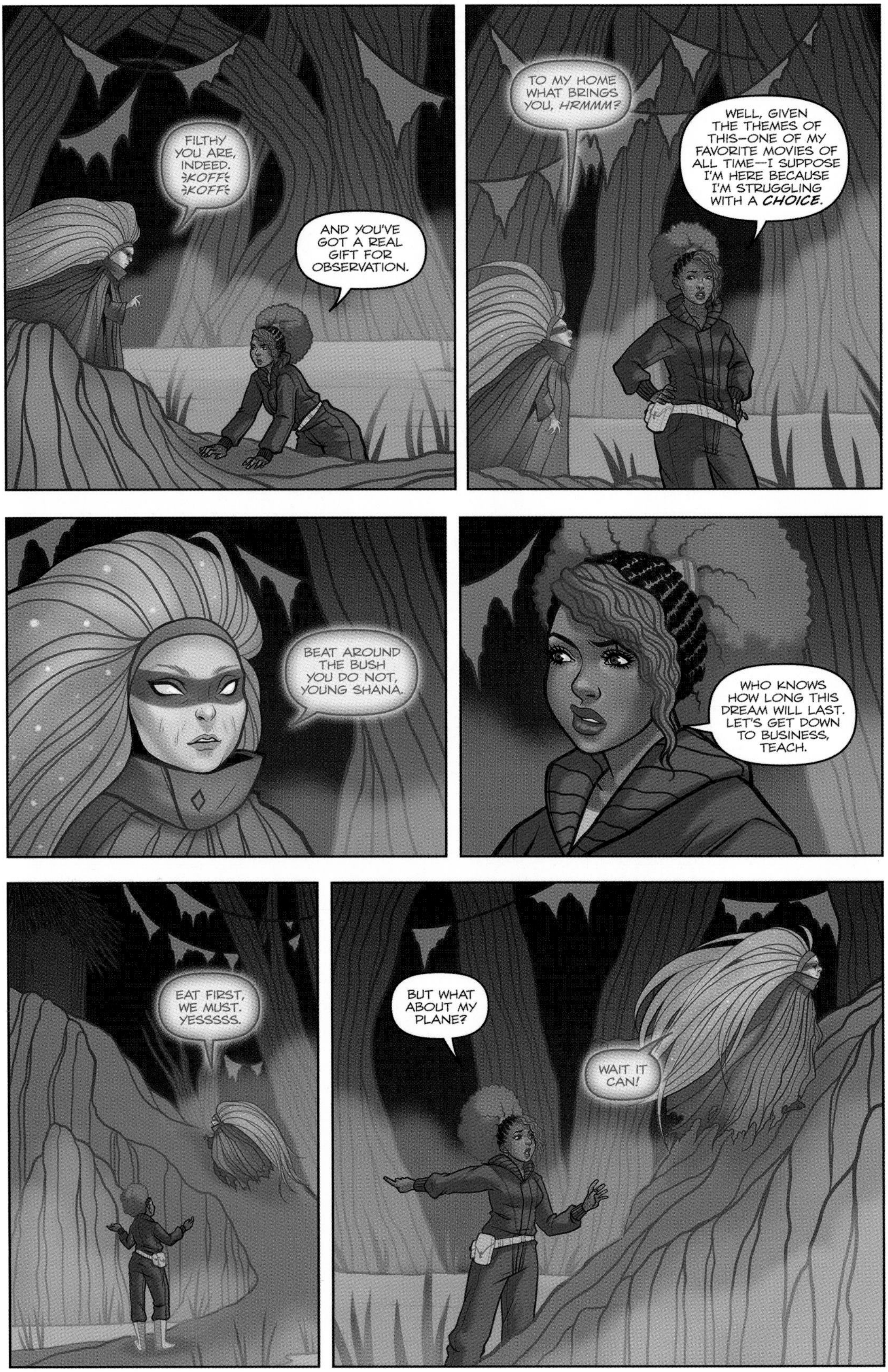
FILTHY YOU ARE, INDEED. *KOFF* *KOFF*
AND YOU'VE GOT A REAL GIFT FOR OBSERVATION.
TO MY HOME WHAT BRINGS YOU, *HRMMM?*
WELL, GIVEN THE THEMES OF THIS—ONE OF MY FAVORITE MOVIES OF ALL TIME—I SUPPOSE I'M HERE BECAUSE I'M STRUGGLING WITH A ***CHOICE***.
BEAT AROUND THE BUSH YOU DO NOT, YOUNG SHANA.
WHO KNOWS HOW LONG THIS DREAM WILL LAST. LET'S GET DOWN TO BUSINESS, TEACH.
EAT FIRST, WE MUST. YESSSSS.
BUT WHAT ABOUT MY PLANE?
WAIT IT CAN!

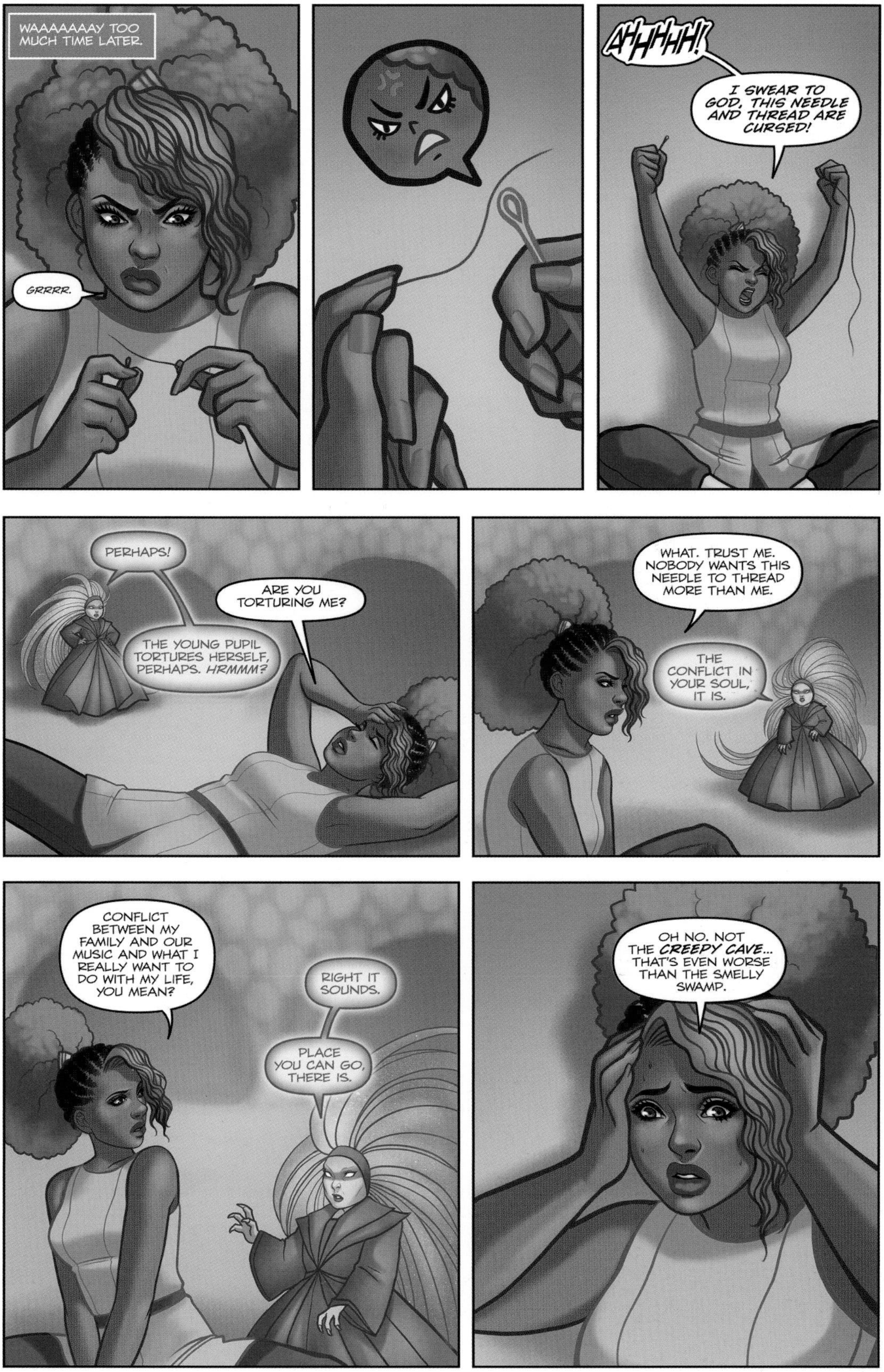
WAAAAAAAY TOO MUCH TIME LATER.
GRRRR.
AHHHHH!
I SWEAR TO GOD, THIS NEEDLE AND THREAD ARE CURSED!
PERHAPS!
ARE YOU TORTURING ME?
THE YOUNG PUPIL TORTURES HERSELF, PERHAPS. HRMMM?
WHAT. TRUST ME. NOBODY WANTS THIS NEEDLE TO THREAD MORE THAN ME.
THE CONFLICT IN YOUR SOUL, IT IS.
CONFLICT BETWEEN MY FAMILY AND OUR MUSIC AND WHAT I REALLY WANT TO DO WITH MY LIFE, YOU MEAN?
RIGHT IT SOUNDS.
PLACE YOU CAN GO, THERE IS.
OH NO. NOT THE CREEPY CAVE... THAT'S EVEN WORSE THAN THE SMELLY SWAMP.

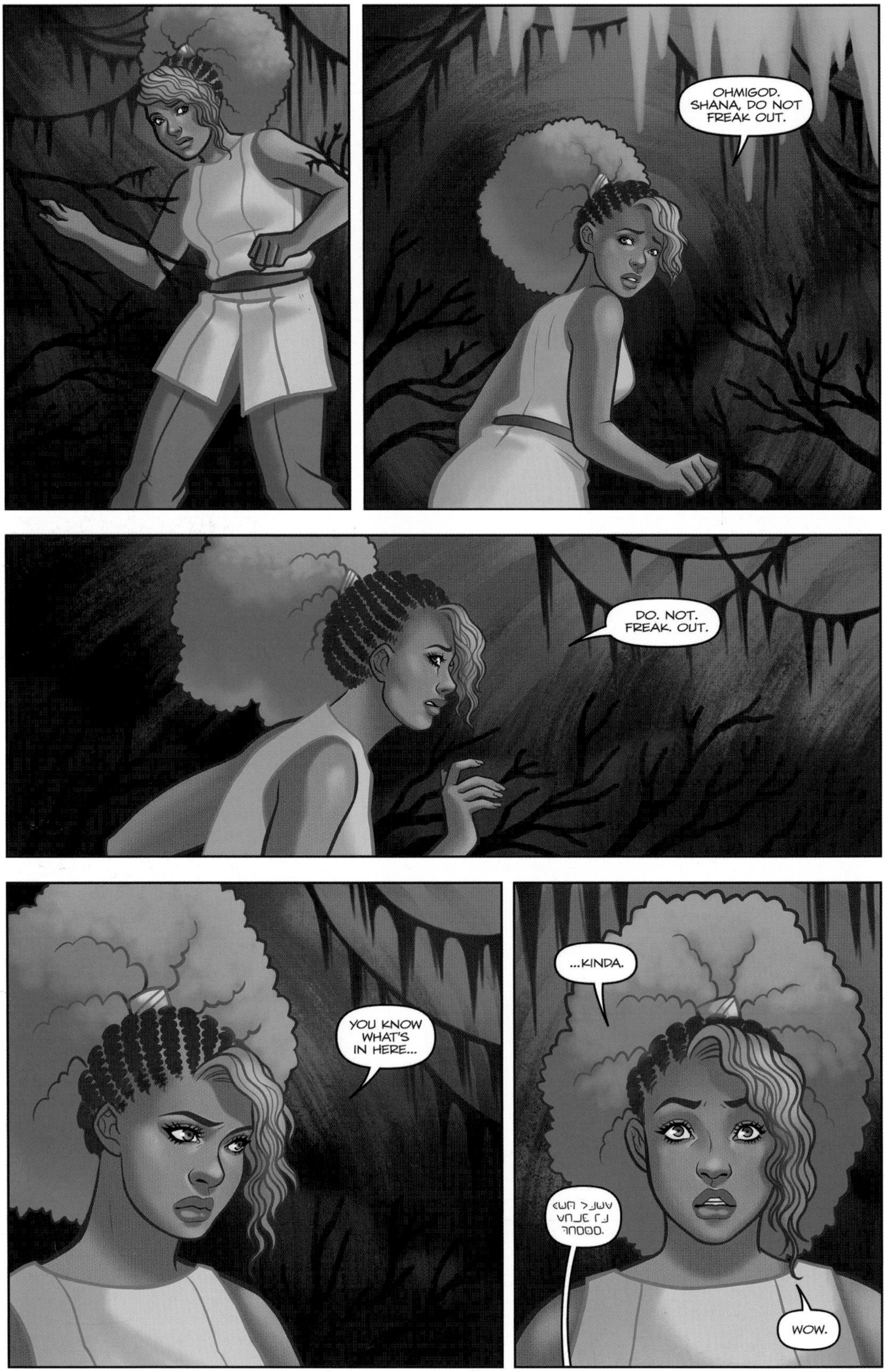
OHMIGOD. SHANA, DO NOT FREAK OUT.
DO. NOT. FREAK. OUT.
YOU KNOW WHAT'S IN HERE...
...KINDA.
WOW.

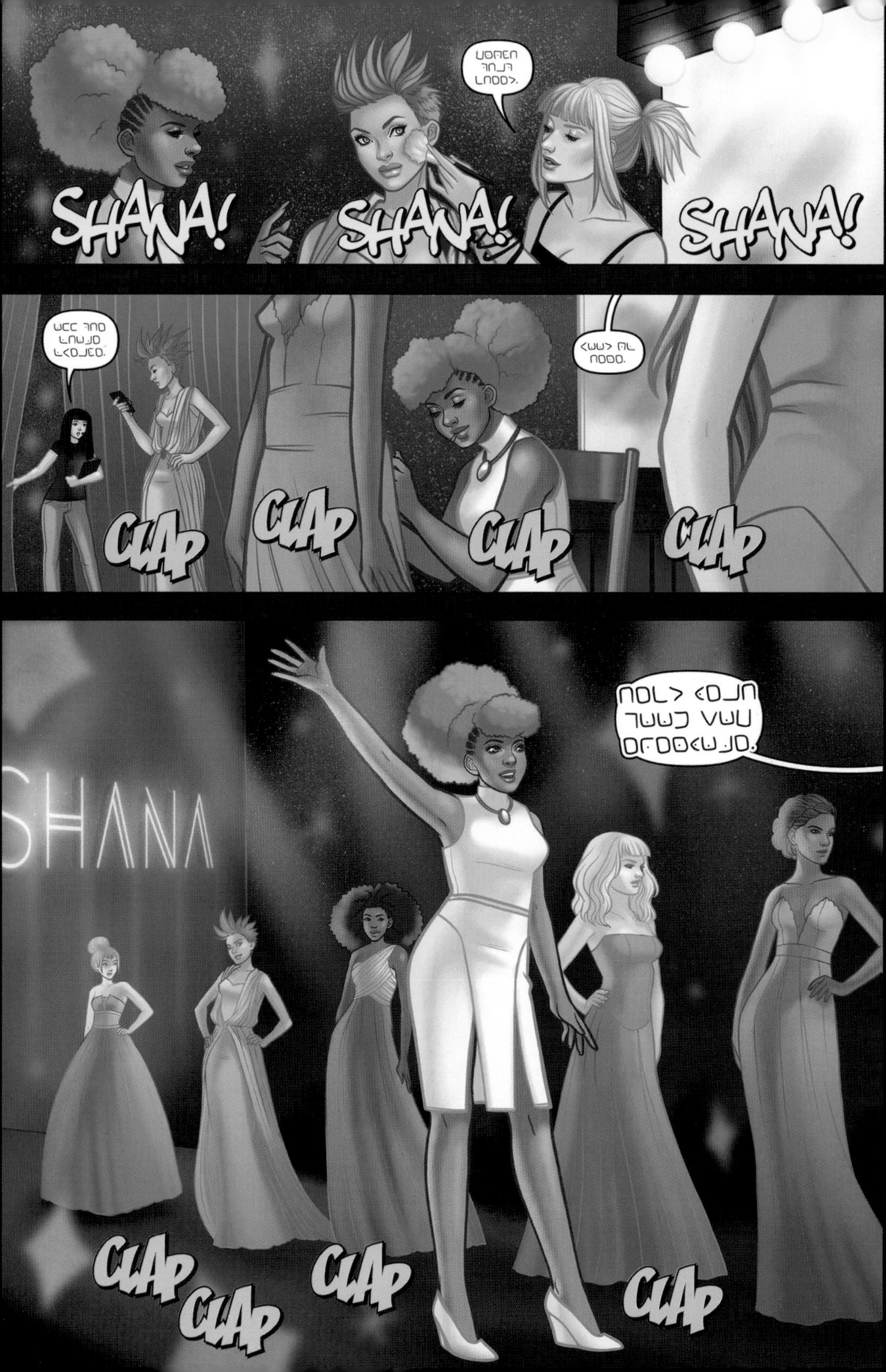
SHANA!
SHANA!
SHANA!
CLAP
CLAP
CLAP
CLAP
SHANA
CLAP
CLAP
CLAP
CLAP

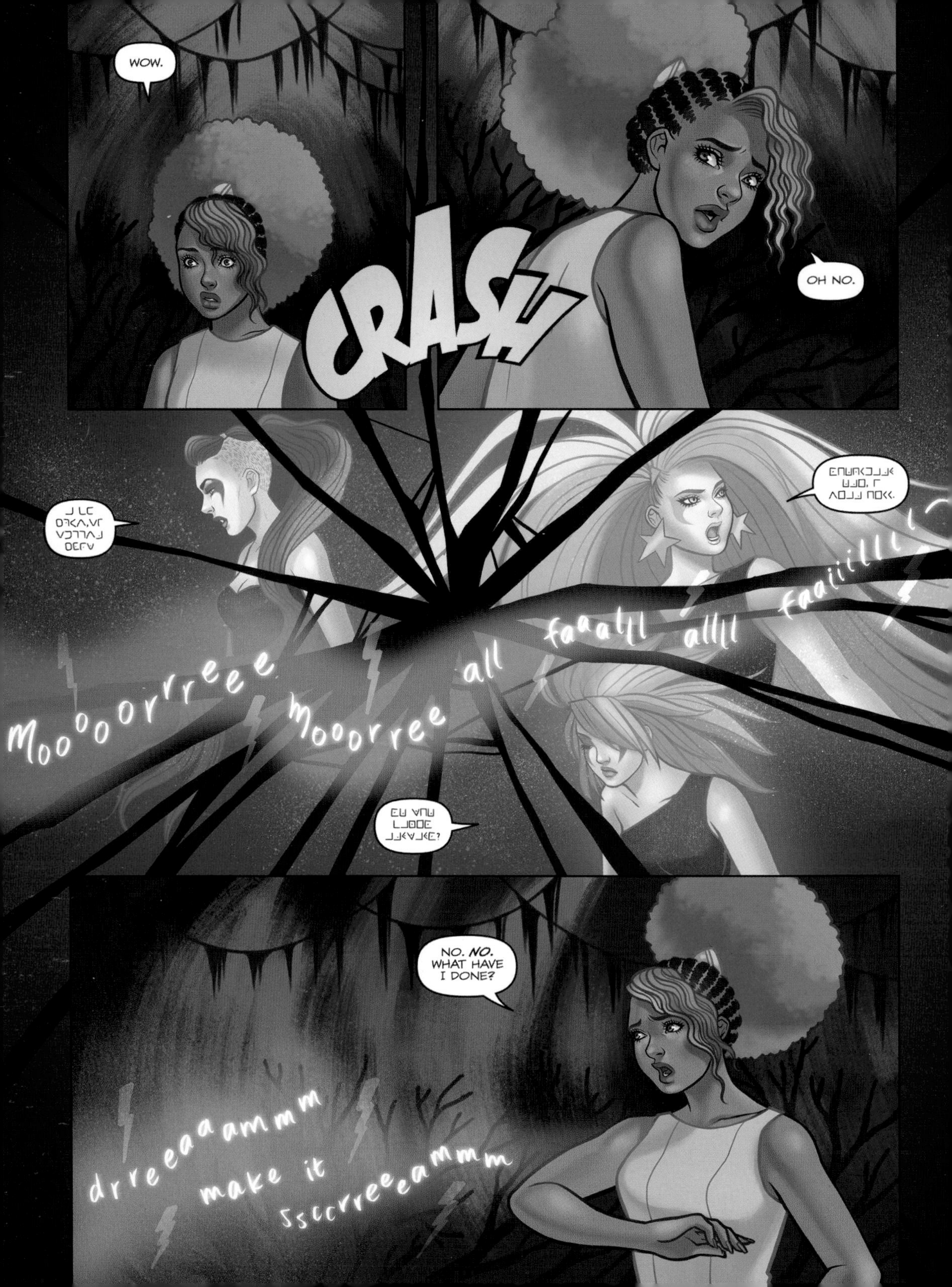
WOW.
CRASH
OH NO.
Mooooorrreee mooorree all faaalll allll faaiiilll
NO. *NO.* WHAT HAVE I DONE?
drreeaaammm make it sscrreeeammm

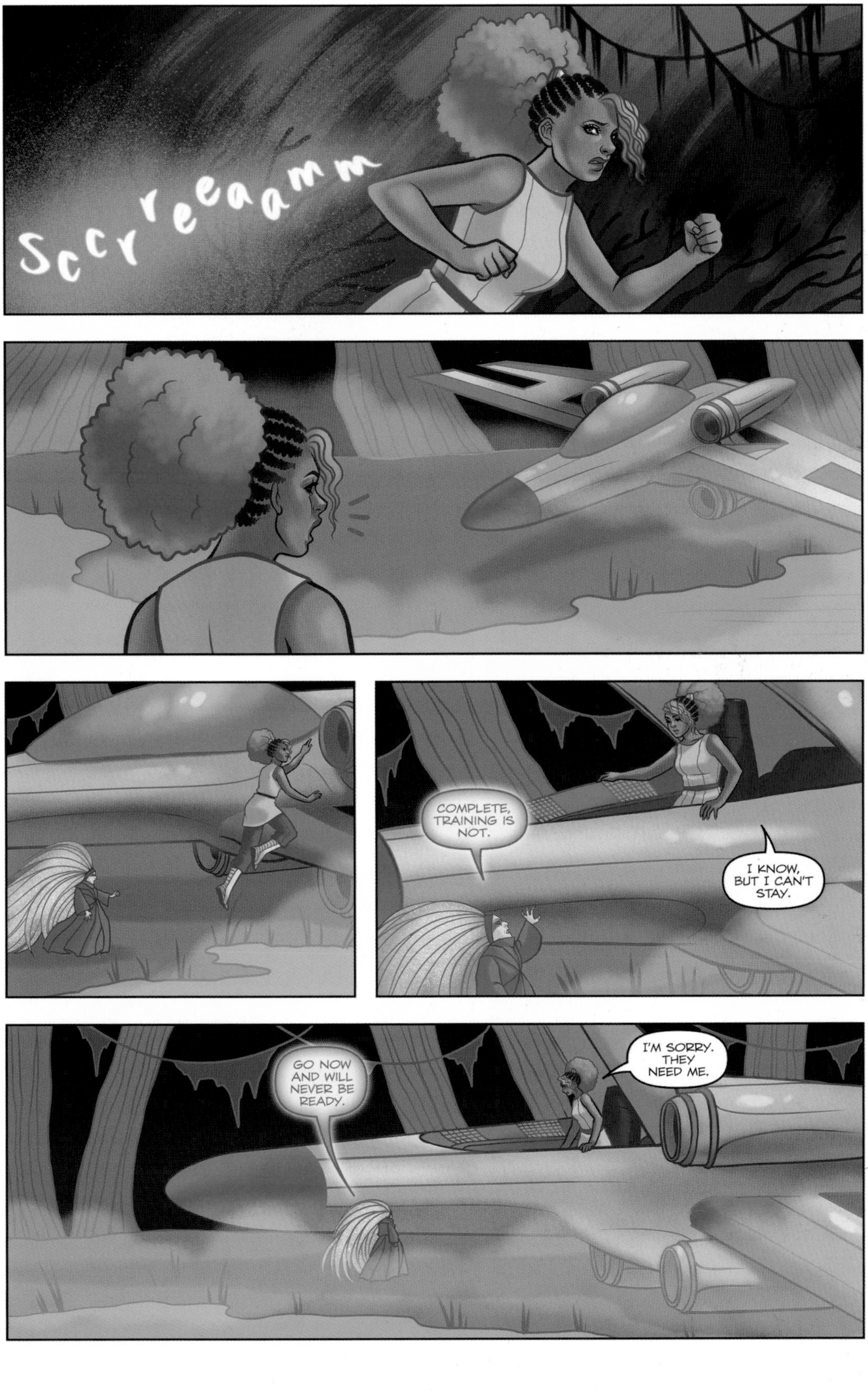
Sccreeaamm
COMPLETE, TRAINING IS NOT.
I KNOW, BUT I CAN'T STAY.
GO NOW AND WILL NEVER BE READY.
I'M SORRY. THEY NEED ME.

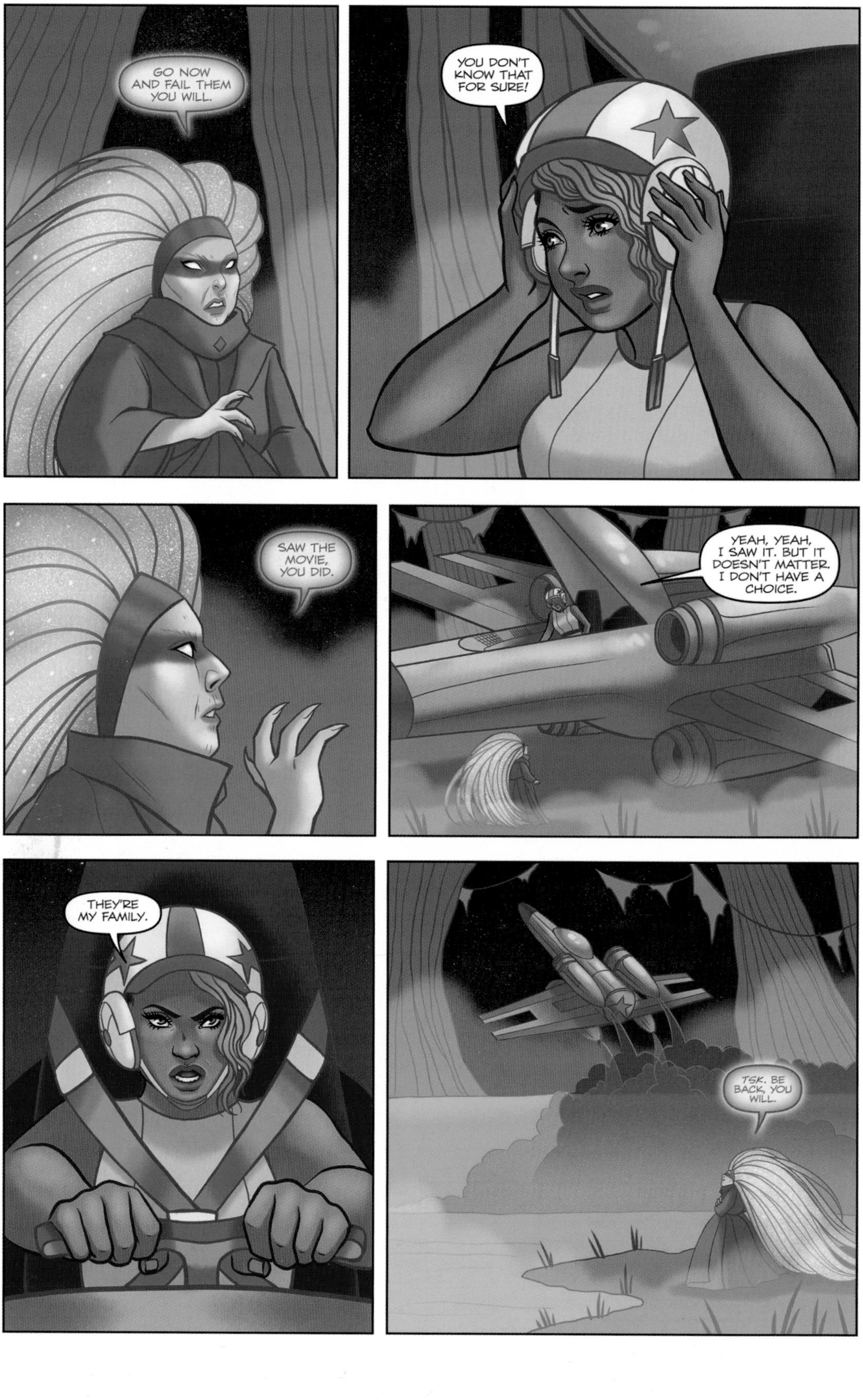
GO NOW AND FAIL THEM YOU WILL.
YOU DON'T KNOW THAT FOR SURE!
SAW THE MOVIE, YOU DID.
YEAH, YEAH, I SAW IT. BUT IT DOESN'T MATTER. I DON'T HAVE A CHOICE.
THEY'RE MY FAMILY.
TSK. BE BACK, YOU WILL.

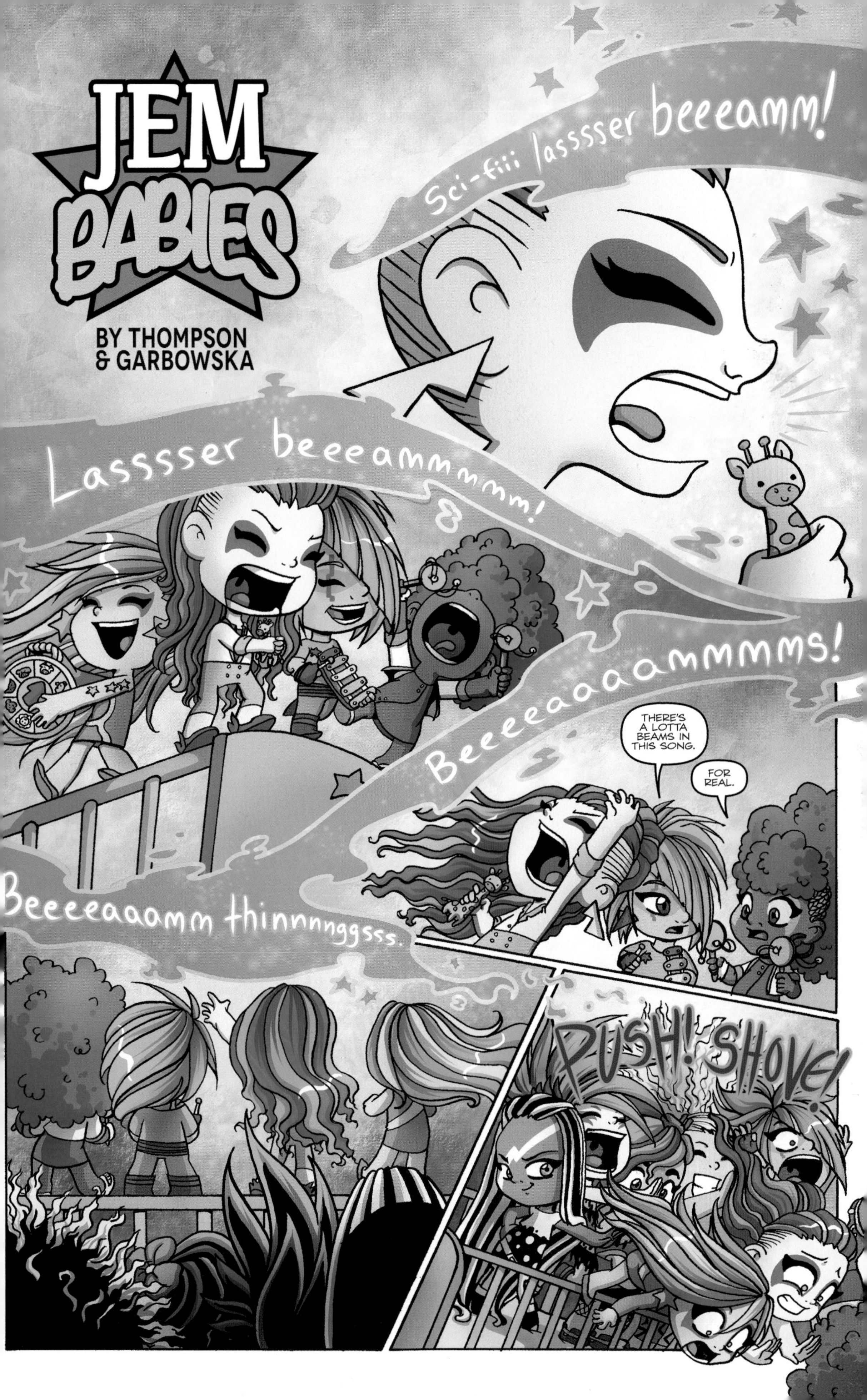
JEM BABIES
BY THOMPSON & GARBOWSKA
Sci-fiii lasssser beeeamm!
Lasssser beeeammmmm!
Beeeeaaaammmms!
THERE'S A LOTTA BEAMS IN THIS SONG.
FOR REAL.
Beeeeaaaamm thinnnnggsss.
PUSH! SHOVE!

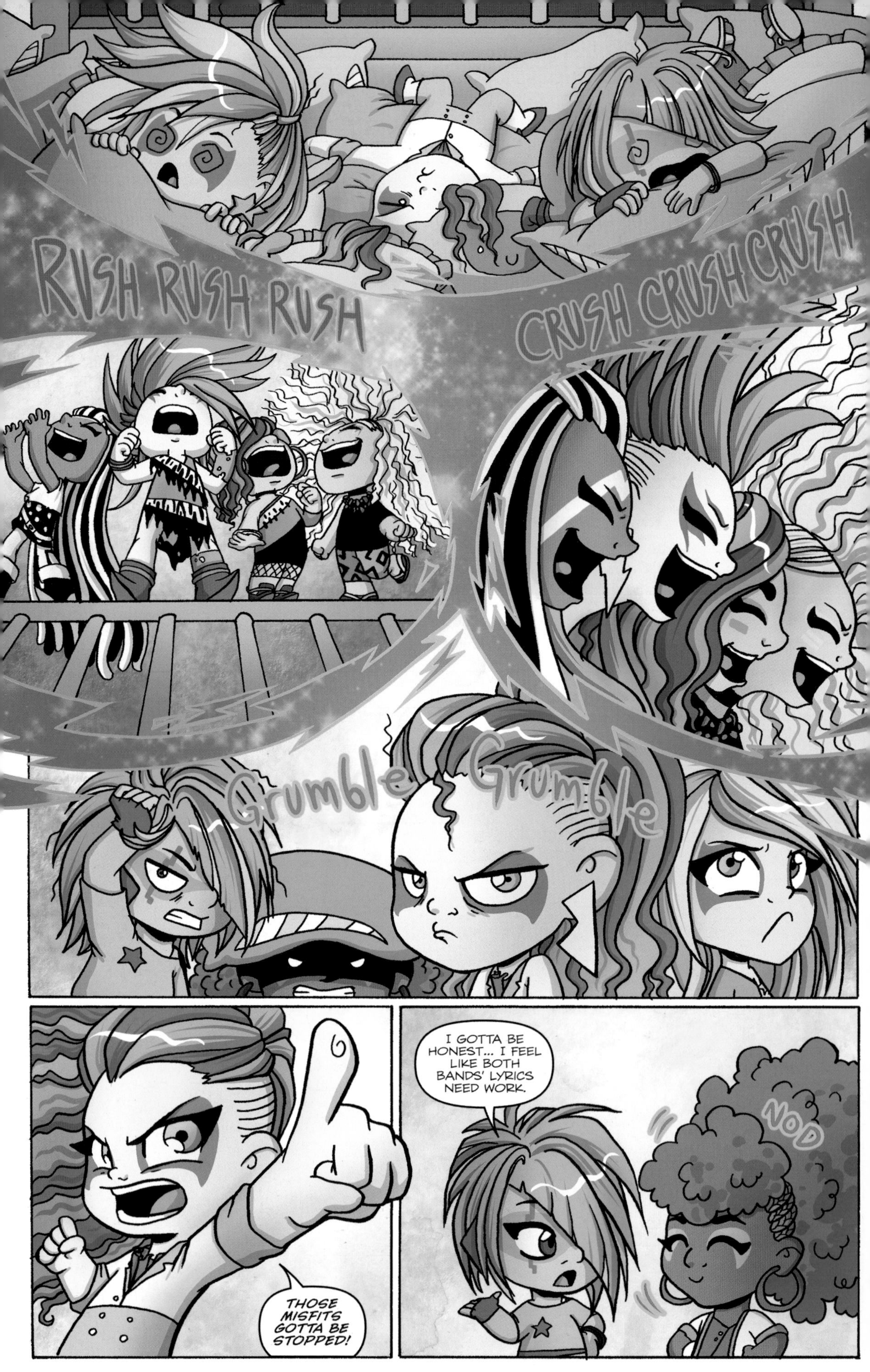

RUSH RUSH RUSH
CRUSH CRUSH CRUSH
Grumble Grumble
THOSE MISFITS GOTTA BE STOPPED!
I GOTTA BE HONEST... I FEEL LIKE BOTH BANDS' LYRICS NEED WORK.
NOD

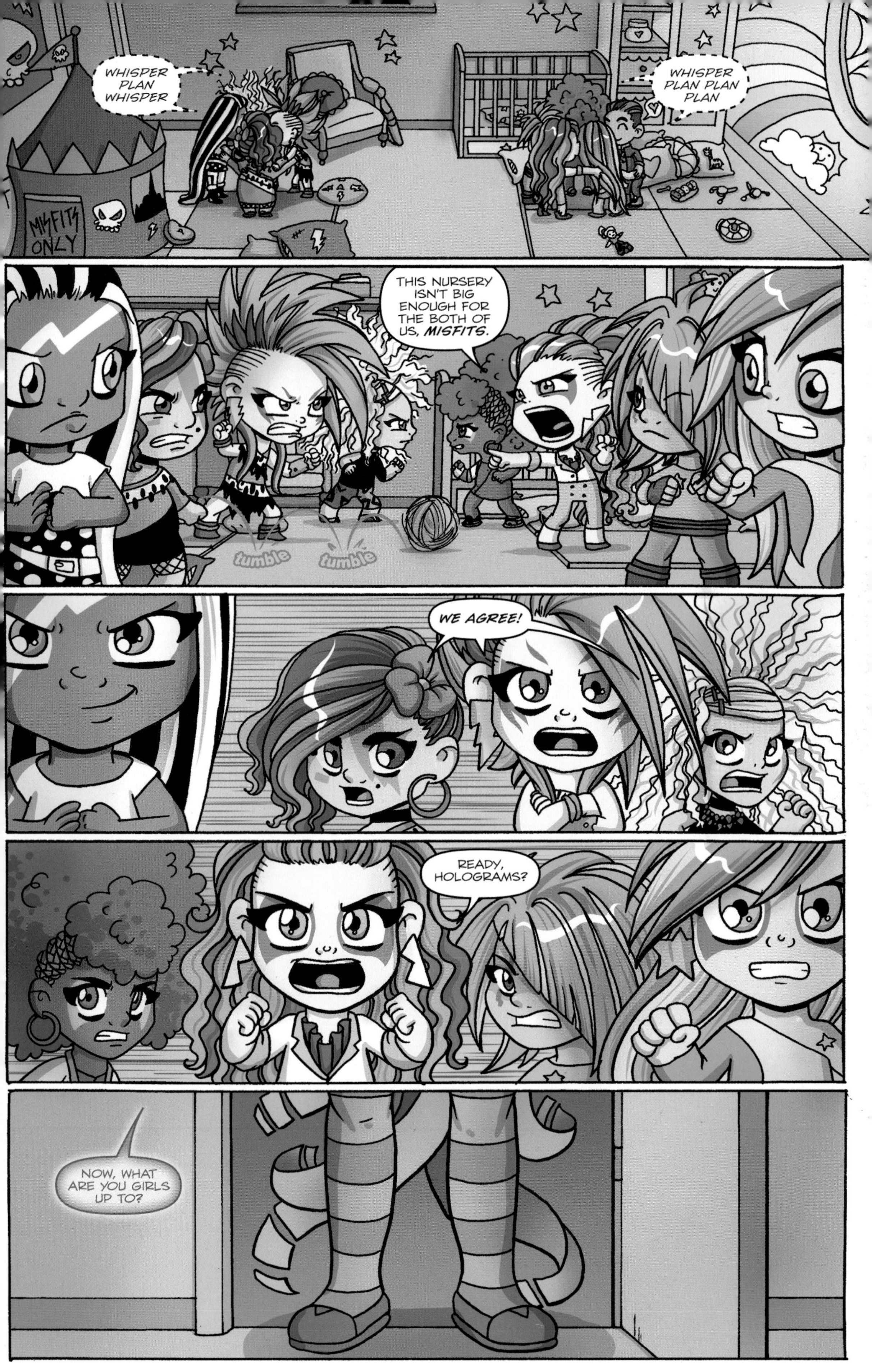
WHISPER PLAN WHISPER
WHISPER PLAN PLAN PLAN
MISFITS ONLY
THIS NURSERY ISN'T BIG ENOUGH FOR THE BOTH OF US, MISFITS.
tumble
tumble
WE AGREE!
READY, HOLOGRAMS?
NOW, WHAT ARE YOU GIRLS UP TO?

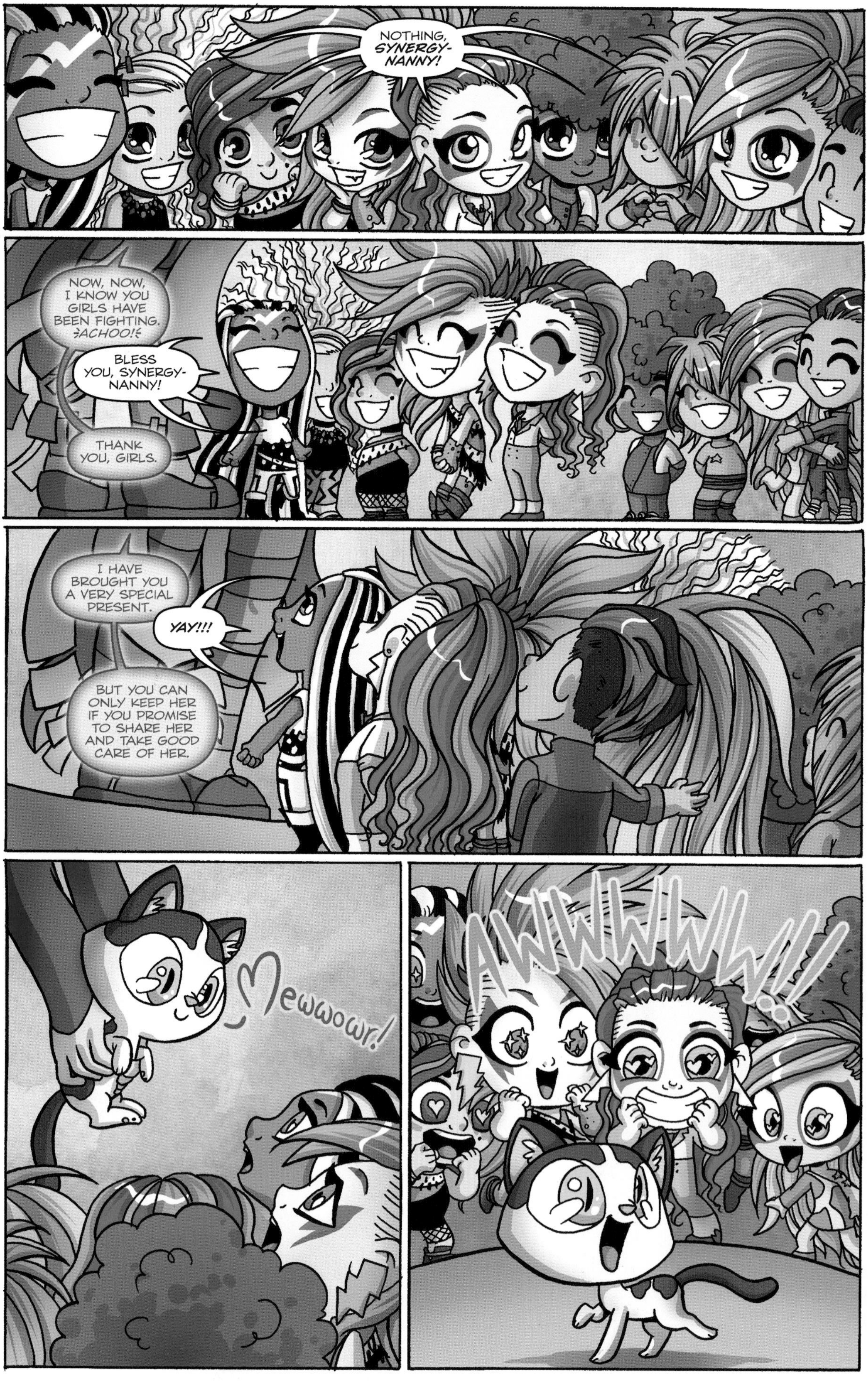
NOTHING, SYNERGY-NANNY!
NOW, NOW, I KNOW YOU GIRLS HAVE BEEN FIGHTING. ACHOO!
BLESS YOU, SYNERGY-NANNY!
THANK YOU, GIRLS.
I HAVE BROUGHT YOU A VERY SPECIAL PRESENT.
YAY!!!
BUT YOU CAN ONLY KEEP HER IF YOU PROMISE TO SHARE HER AND TAKE GOOD CARE OF HER.
Mewwowr!
AWWWWW!!

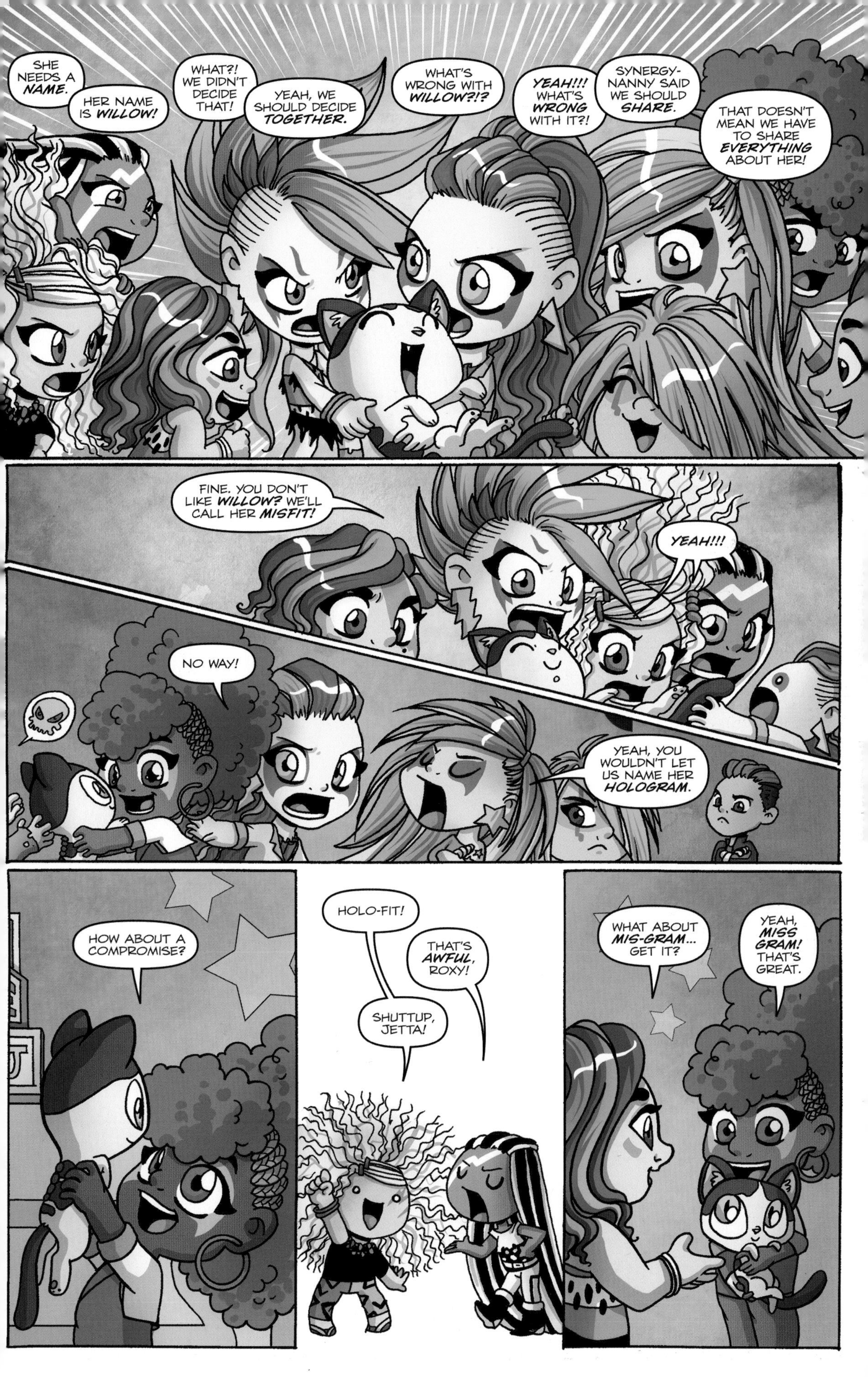
SHE NEEDS A NAME.
HER NAME IS WILLOW!
WHAT?! WE DIDN'T DECIDE THAT!
YEAH, WE SHOULD DECIDE TOGETHER.
WHAT'S WRONG WITH WILLOW?!?
YEAH!!! WHAT'S WRONG WITH IT?!
SYNERGY-NANNY SAID WE SHOULD SHARE.
THAT DOESN'T MEAN WE HAVE TO SHARE EVERYTHING ABOUT HER!
FINE. YOU DON'T LIKE WILLOW? WE'LL CALL HER MISFIT!
YEAH!!!
NO WAY!
YEAH, YOU WOULDN'T LET US NAME HER HOLOGRAM.
HOW ABOUT A COMPROMISE?
HOLO-FIT!
THAT'S AWFUL, ROXY!
SHUTTUP, JETTA!
WHAT ABOUT MIS-GRAM... GET IT?
YEAH, MISS GRAM! THAT'S GREAT.

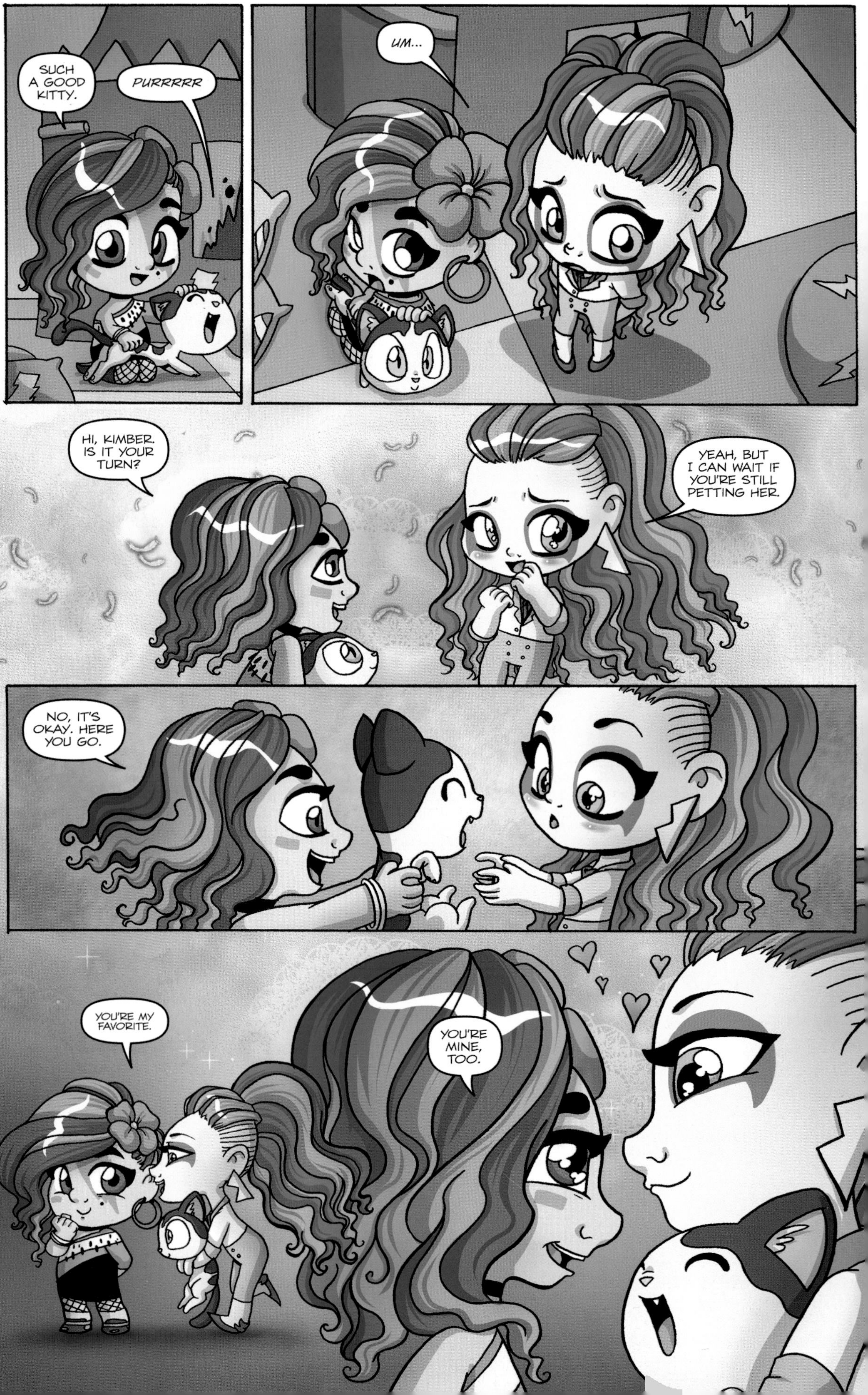
SUCH A GOOD KITTY.
PURRRRR
UM...
HI, KIMBER. IS IT YOUR TURN?
YEAH, BUT I CAN WAIT IF YOU'RE STILL PETTING HER.
NO, IT'S OKAY. HERE YOU GO.
YOU'RE MY FAVORITE.
YOU'RE MINE, TOO.

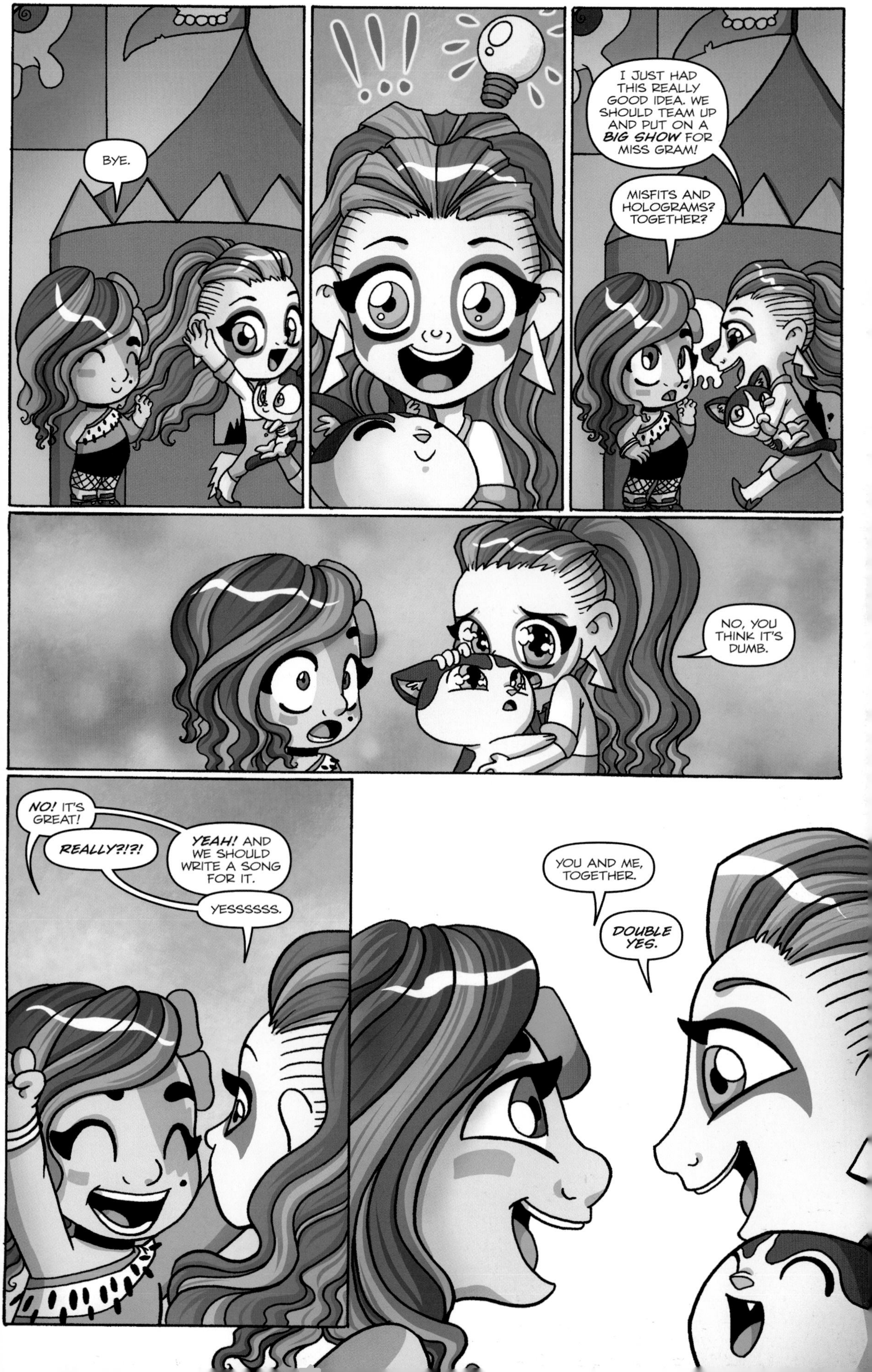

BYE.
I JUST HAD THIS REALLY GOOD IDEA. WE SHOULD TEAM UP AND PUT ON A BIG SHOW FOR MISS GRAM!
MISFITS AND HOLOGRAMS? TOGETHER?
NO, YOU THINK IT'S DUMB.
NO! IT'S GREAT!
REALLY?!?!
YEAH! AND WE SHOULD WRITE A SONG FOR IT.
YESSSSSS.
YOU AND ME, TOGETHER.
DOUBLE YES.

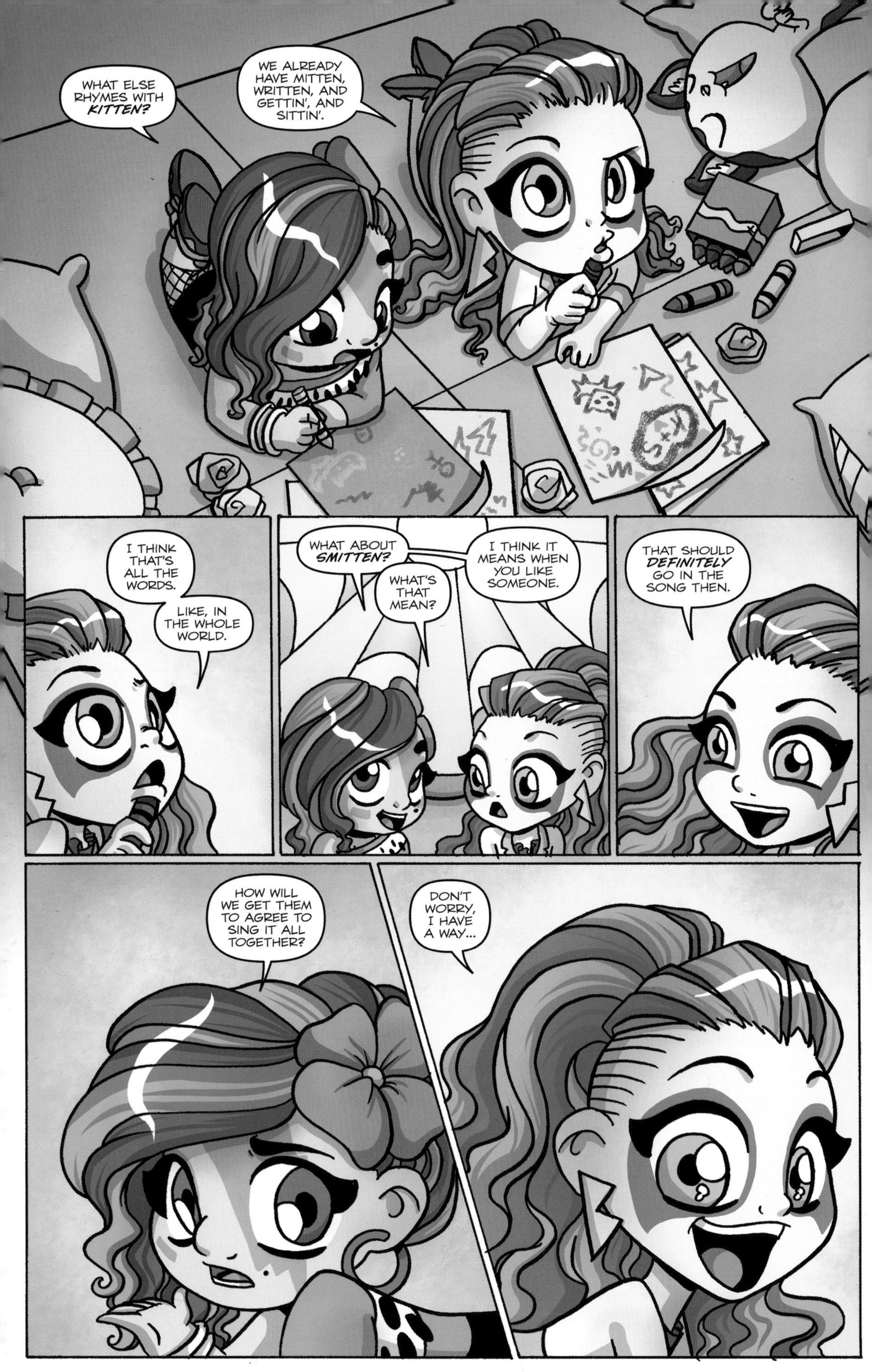
WHAT ELSE RHYMES WITH KITTEN?
WE ALREADY HAVE MITTEN, WRITTEN, AND GETTIN', AND SITTIN'.
I THINK THAT'S ALL THE WORDS.
LIKE, IN THE WHOLE WORLD.
WHAT ABOUT SMITTEN?
WHAT'S THAT MEAN?
I THINK IT MEANS WHEN YOU LIKE SOMEONE.
THAT SHOULD DEFINITELY GO IN THE SONG THEN.
HOW WILL WE GET THEM TO AGREE TO SING IT ALL TOGETHER?
DON'T WORRY, I HAVE A WAY...

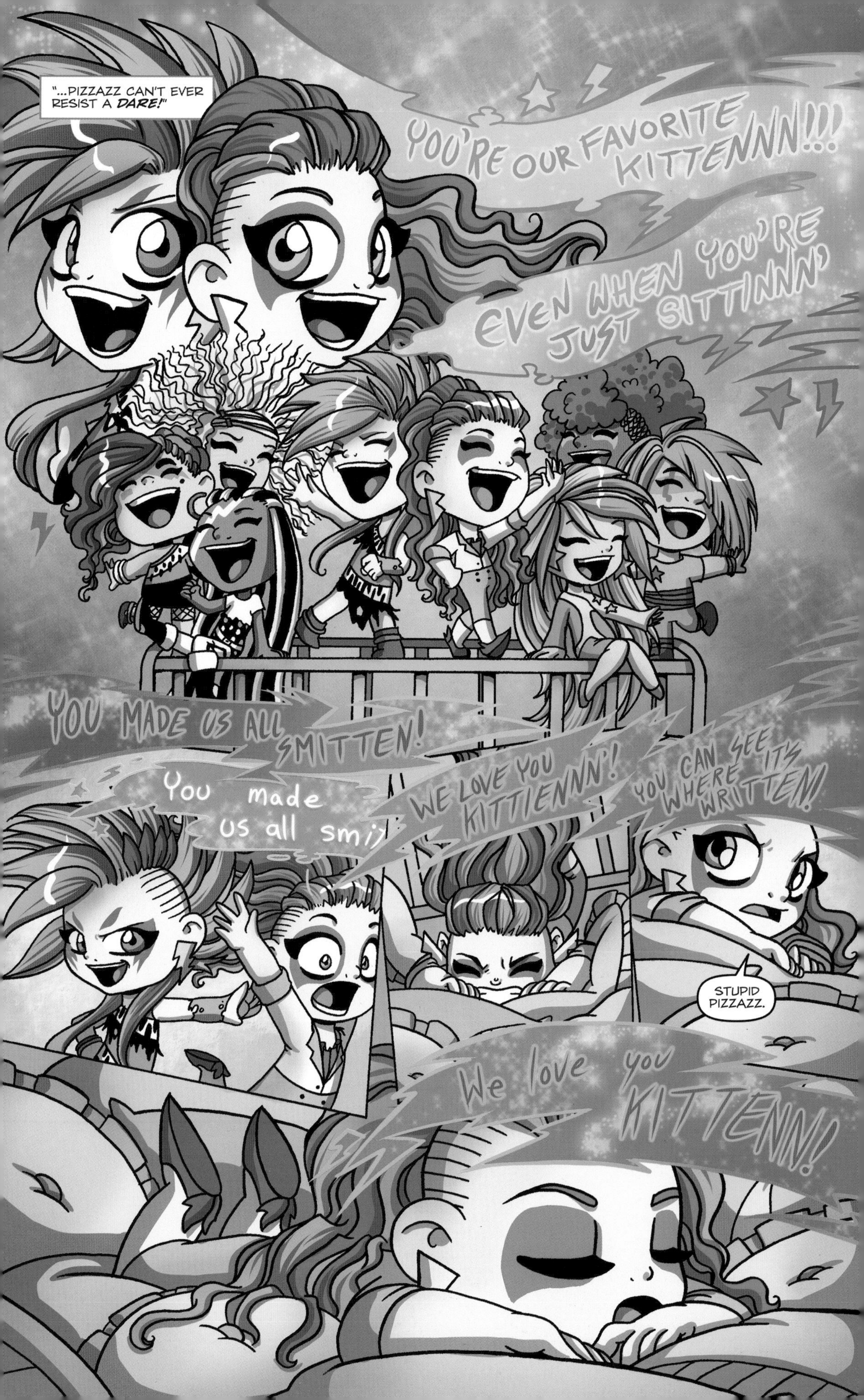
"...PIZZAZZ CAN'T EVER RESIST A *DARE!*"
YOU'RE OUR FAVORITE KITTENNN!!!
EVEN WHEN YOU'RE JUST SITTINNN'
YOU MADE US ALL SMITTEN!
You made us all smi
WE LOVE YOU KITTIENNN'!
YOU CAN SEE WHERE IT'S WRITTEN!
STUPID PIZZAZZ.
We love you KITTENN!

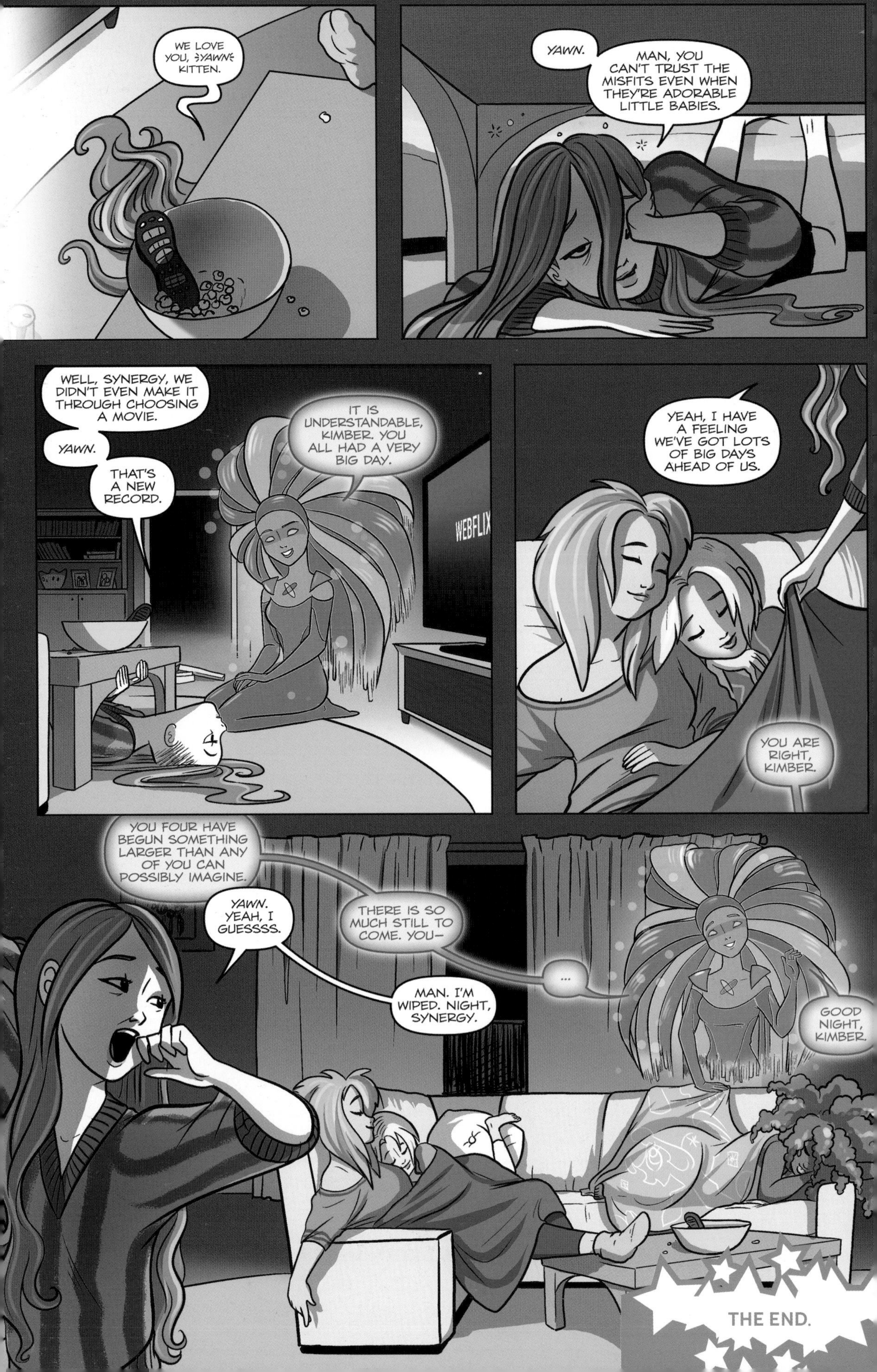
WE LOVE YOU, ⋟YAWN⋞ KITTEN.
YAWN.
MAN, YOU CAN'T TRUST THE MISFITS EVEN WHEN THEY'RE ADORABLE LITTLE BABIES.
WELL, SYNERGY, WE DIDN'T EVEN MAKE IT THROUGH CHOOSING A MOVIE.
YAWN.
THAT'S A NEW RECORD.
IT IS UNDERSTANDABLE, KIMBER. YOU ALL HAD A VERY BIG DAY.
WEBFLIX
YEAH, I HAVE A FEELING WE'VE GOT LOTS OF BIG DAYS AHEAD OF US.
YOU ARE RIGHT, KIMBER.
YOU FOUR HAVE BEGUN SOMETHING LARGER THAN ANY OF YOU CAN POSSIBLY IMAGINE.
YAWN. YEAH, I GUESSSS.
THERE IS SO MUCH STILL TO COME. YOU–
...
MAN. I'M WIPED. NIGHT, SYNERGY.
GOOD NIGHT, KIMBER.
THE END.

ART BY **AMY MEBBERSON**

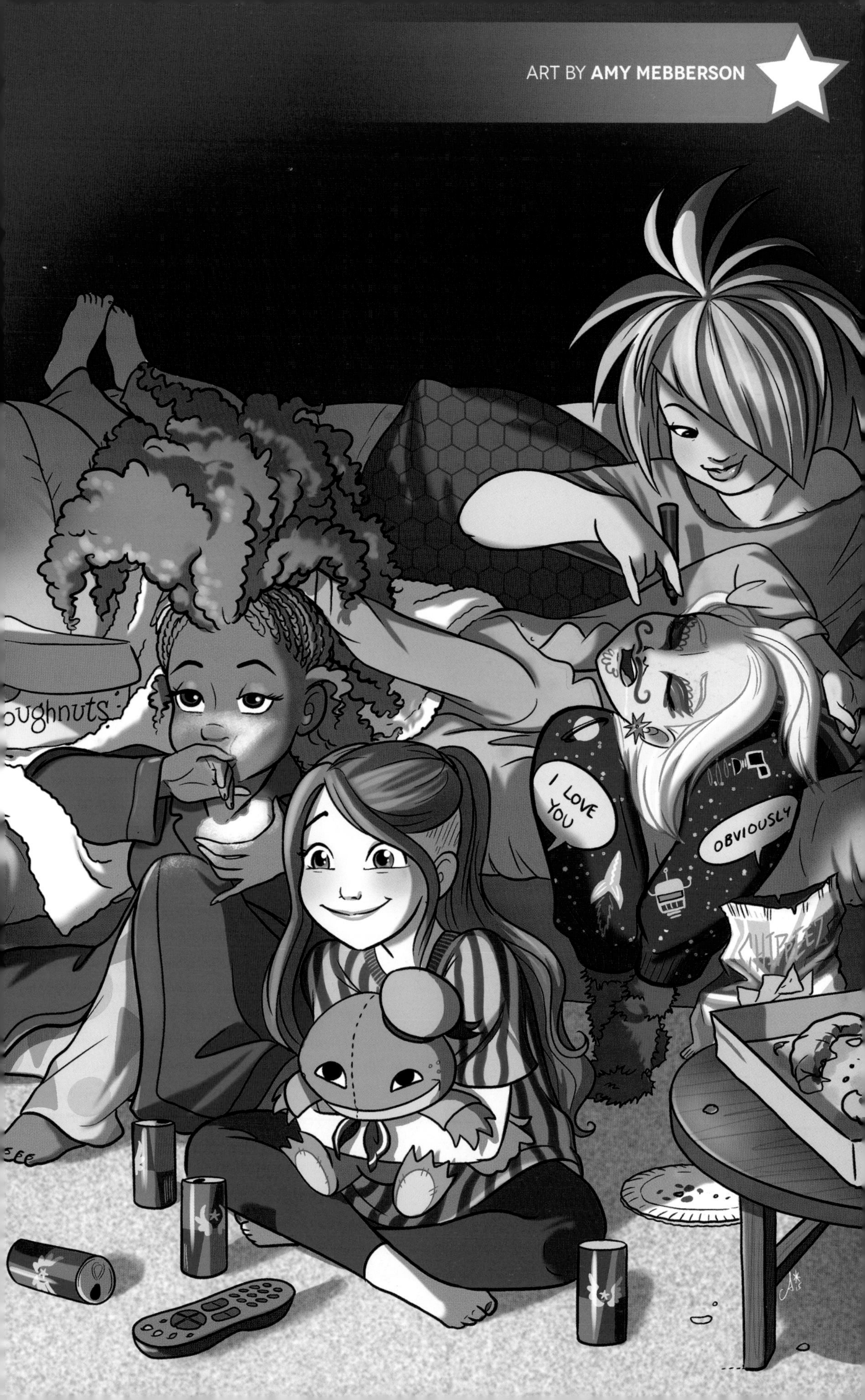
oughnuts
I LOVE YOU
OBVIOUSLY

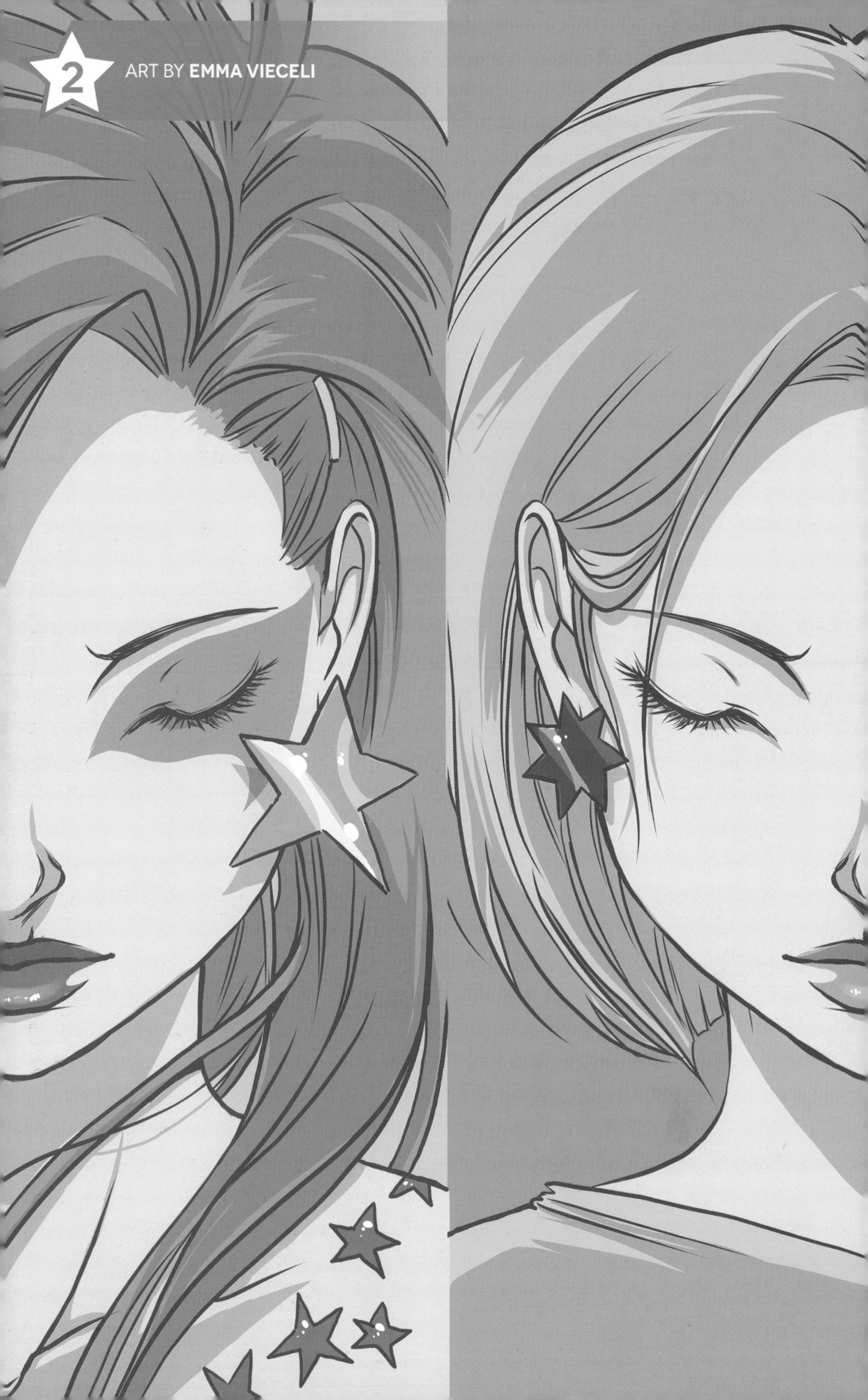
2
ART BY EMMA VIECELI

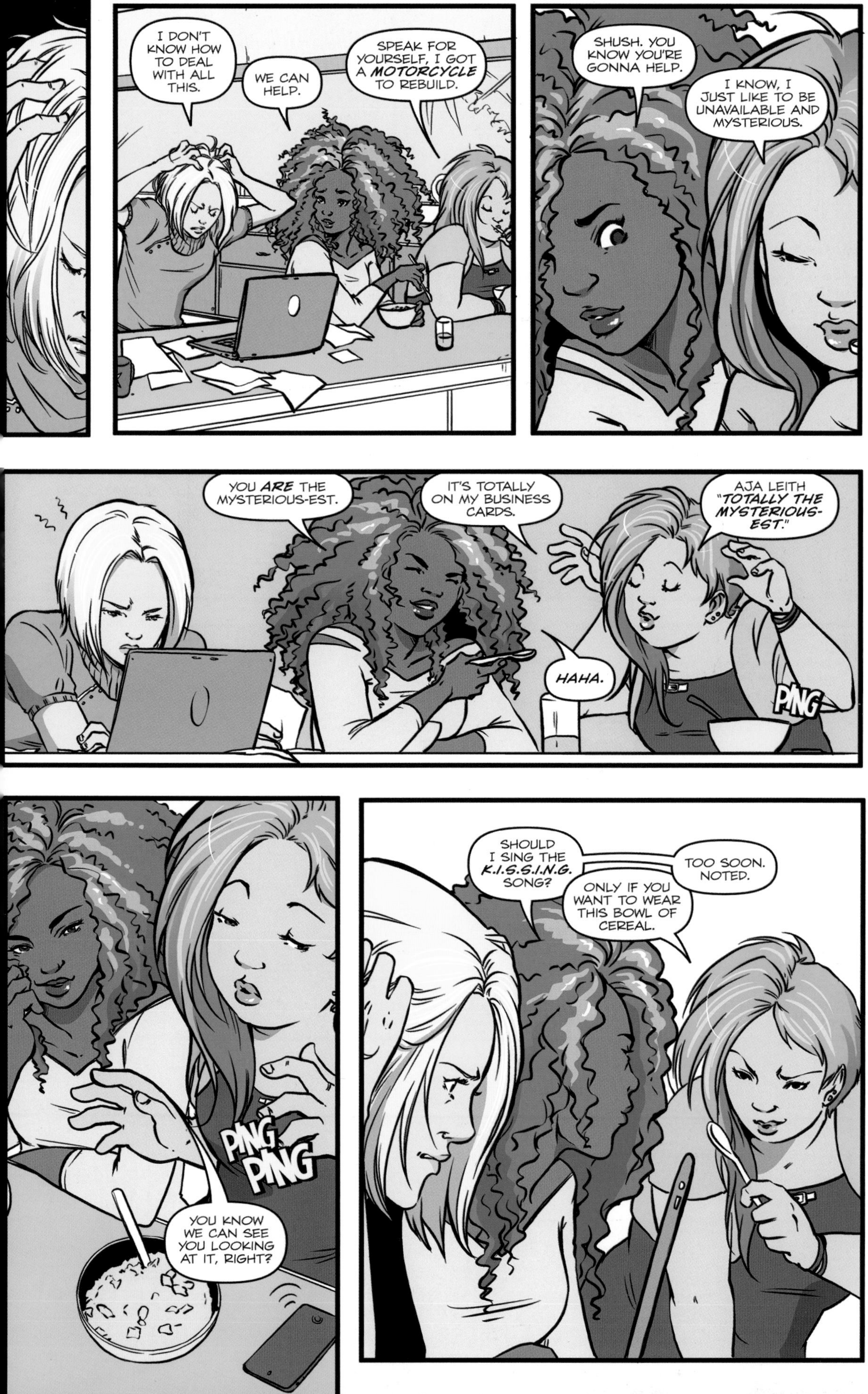
I DON'T KNOW HOW TO DEAL WITH ALL THIS.
WE CAN HELP.
SPEAK FOR YOURSELF, I GOT A *MOTORCYCLE* TO REBUILD.
SHUSH. YOU KNOW YOU'RE GONNA HELP.
I KNOW, I JUST LIKE TO BE UNAVAILABLE AND MYSTERIOUS.
YOU *ARE* THE MYSTERIOUS-EST.
IT'S TOTALLY ON MY BUSINESS CARDS.
AJA LEITH "*TOTALLY THE MYSTERIOUS-EST.*"
HAHA.
PING
PING PING
YOU KNOW WE CAN SEE YOU LOOKING AT IT, RIGHT?
SHOULD I SING THE *K.I.S.S.I.N.G.* SONG?
ONLY IF YOU WANT TO WEAR THIS BOWL OF CEREAL.
TOO SOON. NOTED.

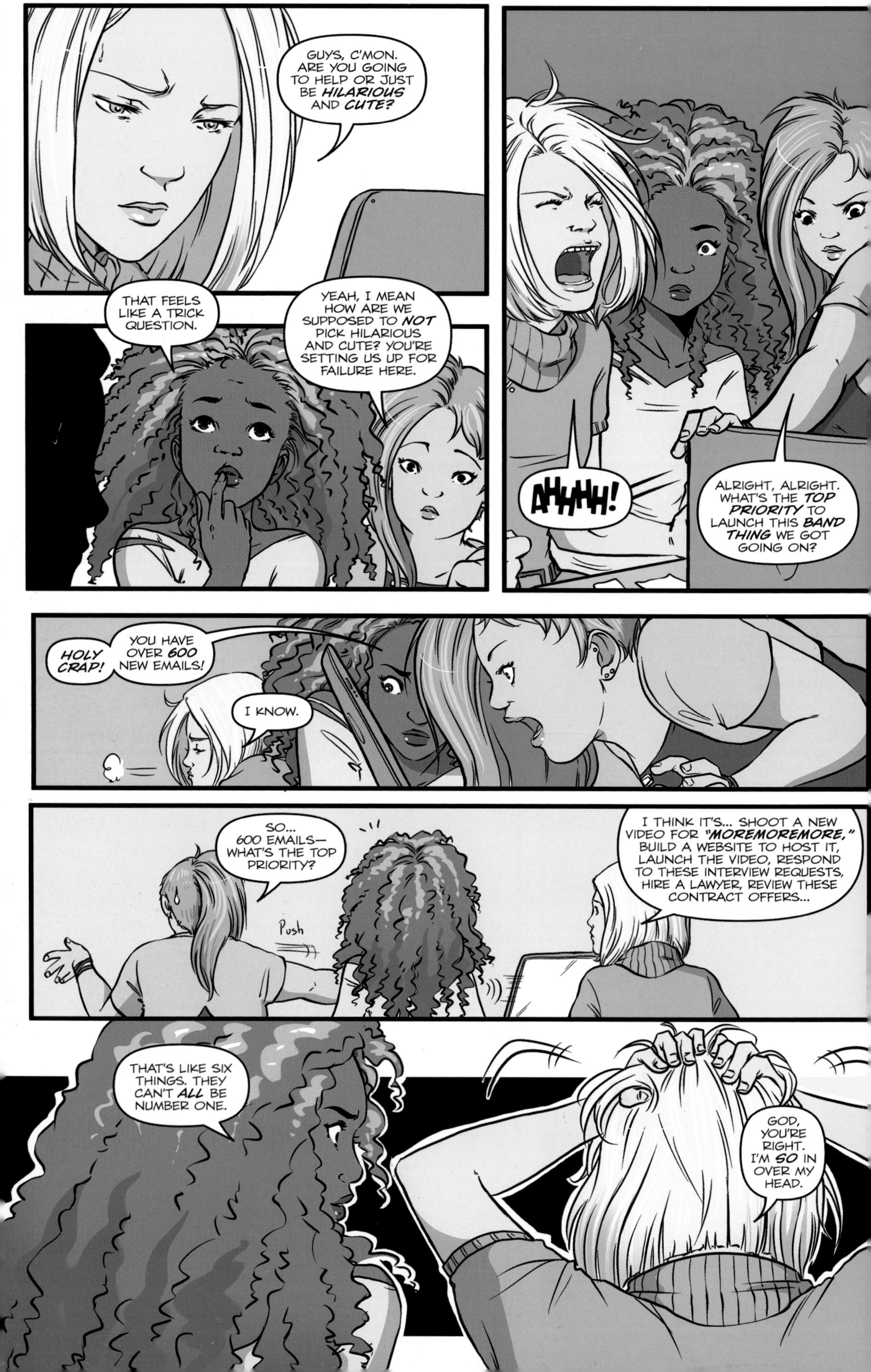
GUYS, C'MON. ARE YOU GOING TO HELP OR JUST BE *HILARIOUS* AND *CUTE?*
THAT FEELS LIKE A TRICK QUESTION.
YEAH, I MEAN HOW ARE WE SUPPOSED TO *NOT* PICK HILARIOUS AND CUTE? YOU'RE SETTING US UP FOR FAILURE HERE.
AHHHH!
ALRIGHT, ALRIGHT. WHAT'S THE *TOP PRIORITY* TO LAUNCH THIS *BAND THING* WE GOT GOING ON?
HOLY CRAP!
YOU HAVE OVER *600* NEW EMAILS!
I KNOW.
SO... 600 EMAILS— WHAT'S THE TOP PRIORITY?
Push
I THINK IT'S... SHOOT A NEW VIDEO FOR *"MOREMOREMORE,"* BUILD A WEBSITE TO HOST IT, LAUNCH THE VIDEO, RESPOND TO THESE INTERVIEW REQUESTS, HIRE A LAWYER, REVIEW THESE CONTRACT OFFERS...
THAT'S LIKE SIX THINGS. THEY CAN'T *ALL* BE NUMBER ONE.
GOD, YOU'RE RIGHT. I'M *SO* IN OVER MY HEAD.

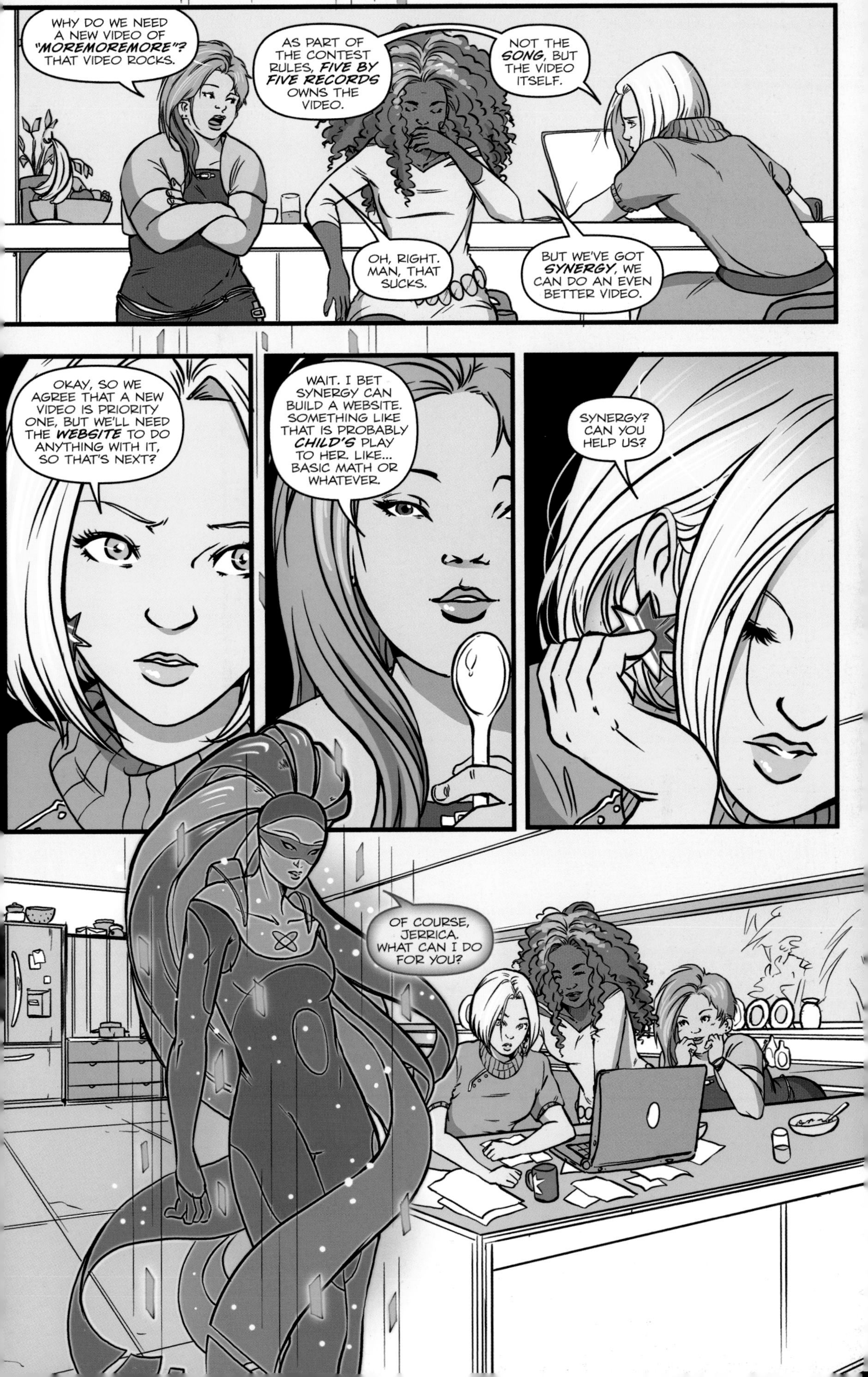
WHY DO WE NEED A NEW VIDEO OF "MOREMOREMORE"? THAT VIDEO ROCKS.
AS PART OF THE CONTEST RULES, FIVE BY FIVE RECORDS OWNS THE VIDEO.
NOT THE SONG, BUT THE VIDEO ITSELF.
OH, RIGHT. MAN, THAT SUCKS.
BUT WE'VE GOT SYNERGY, WE CAN DO AN EVEN BETTER VIDEO.
OKAY, SO WE AGREE THAT A NEW VIDEO IS PRIORITY ONE, BUT WE'LL NEED THE WEBSITE TO DO ANYTHING WITH IT, SO THAT'S NEXT?
WAIT. I BET SYNERGY CAN BUILD A WEBSITE. SOMETHING LIKE THAT IS PROBABLY CHILD'S PLAY TO HER. LIKE... BASIC MATH OR WHATEVER.
SYNERGY? CAN YOU HELP US?
OF COURSE, JERRICA. WHAT CAN I DO FOR YOU?

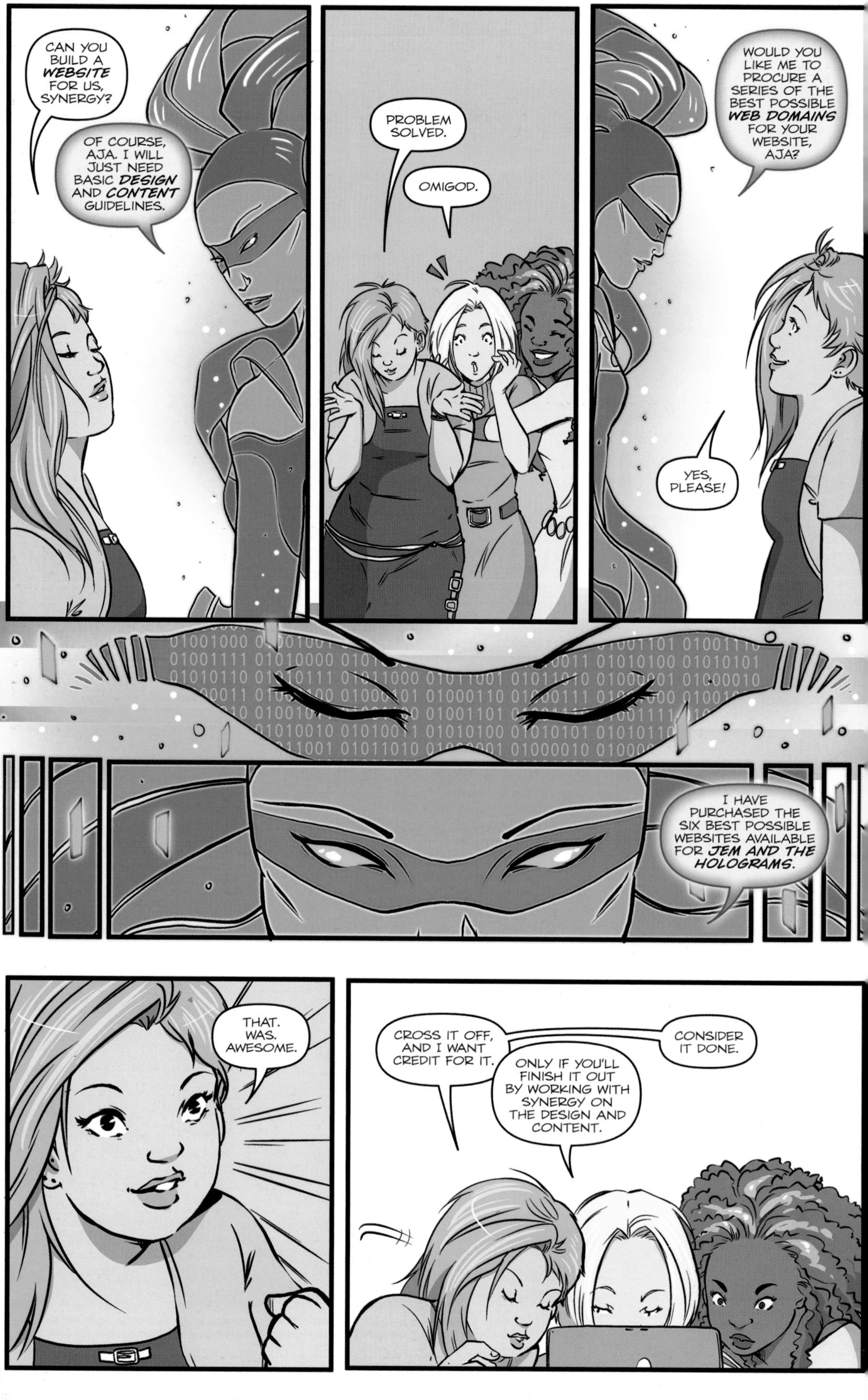
CAN YOU BUILD A **WEBSITE** FOR US, SYNERGY?
OF COURSE, AJA. I WILL JUST NEED BASIC **DESIGN** AND **CONTENT** GUIDELINES.
PROBLEM SOLVED.
OMIGOD.
WOULD YOU LIKE ME TO PROCURE A SERIES OF THE BEST POSSIBLE **WEB DOMAINS** FOR YOUR WEBSITE, AJA?
YES, PLEASE!
I HAVE PURCHASED THE SIX BEST POSSIBLE WEBSITES AVAILABLE FOR **JEM AND THE HOLOGRAMS**.
THAT. WAS. AWESOME.
CROSS IT OFF, AND I WANT CREDIT FOR IT.
CONSIDER IT DONE.
ONLY IF YOU'LL FINISH IT OUT BY WORKING WITH SYNERGY ON THE DESIGN AND CONTENT.

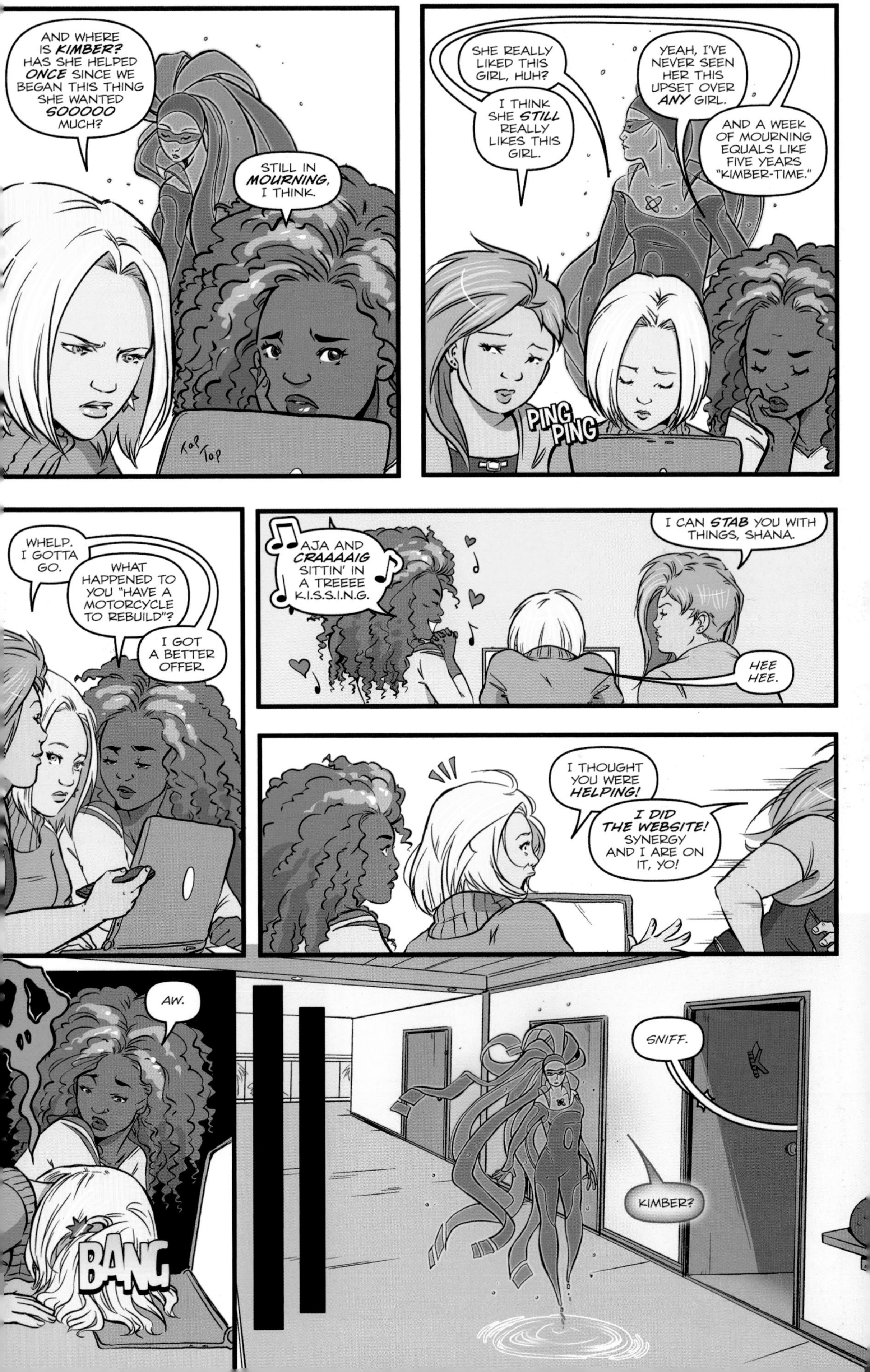
AND WHERE IS KIMBER? HAS SHE HELPED ONCE SINCE WE BEGAN THIS THING SHE WANTED SOOOOO MUCH?
STILL IN MOURNING, I THINK.
TAP TAP
SHE REALLY LIKED THIS GIRL, HUH?
I THINK SHE STILL REALLY LIKES THIS GIRL.
YEAH, I'VE NEVER SEEN HER THIS UPSET OVER ANY GIRL.
AND A WEEK OF MOURNING EQUALS LIKE FIVE YEARS "KIMBER-TIME."
PING PING
WHELP. I GOTTA GO.
WHAT HAPPENED TO YOU "HAVE A MOTORCYCLE TO REBUILD"?
I GOT A BETTER OFFER.
AJA AND CRAAAAIG SITTIN' IN A TREEEE K.I.S.S.I.N.G.
I CAN STAB YOU WITH THINGS, SHANA.
HEE HEE.
I THOUGHT YOU WERE HELPING!
I DID THE WEBSITE! SYNERGY AND I ARE ON IT, YO!
AW.
BANG
SNIFF.
KIMBER?

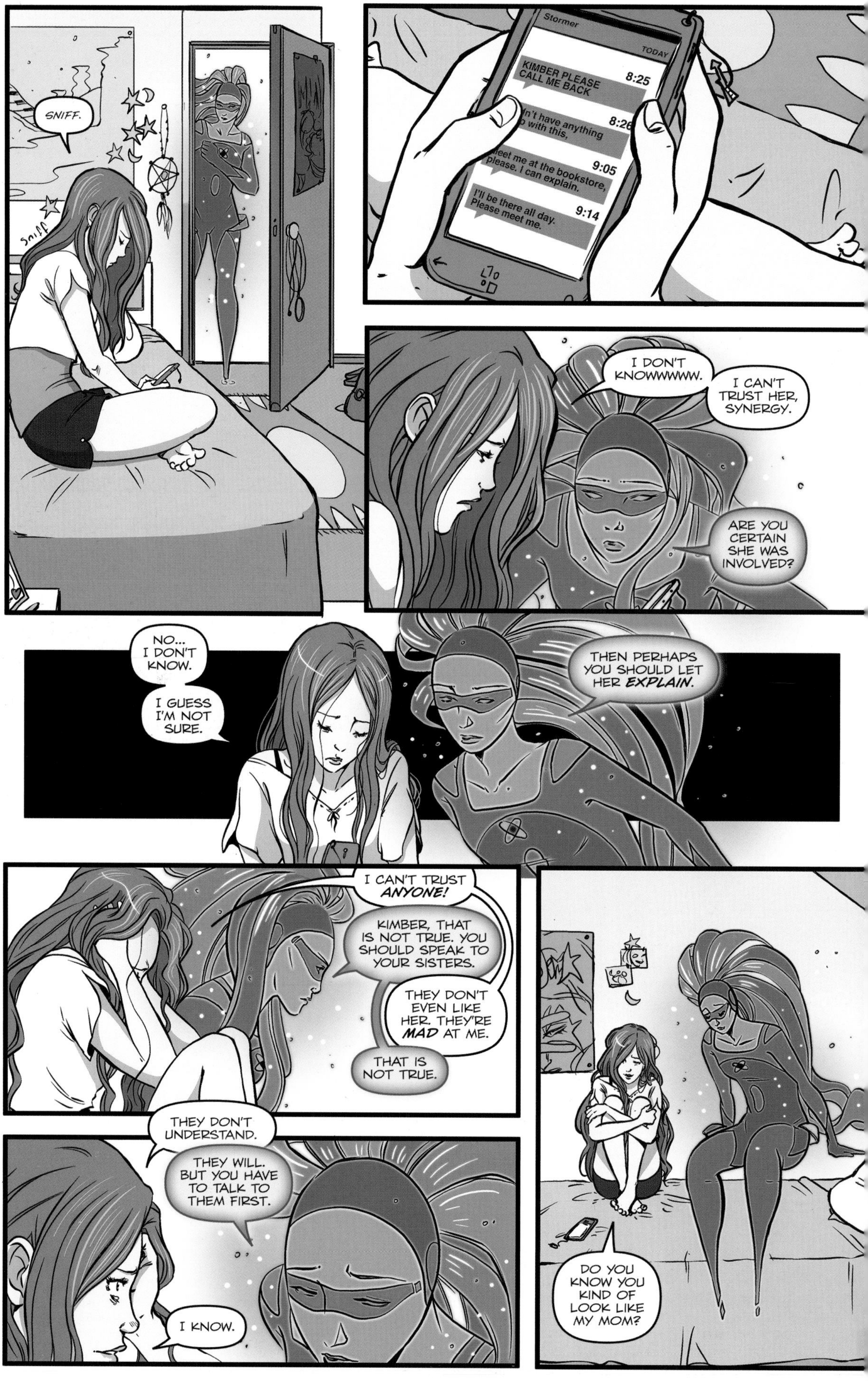
SNIFF.
Sniff
Stormer
TODAY
KIMBER PLEASE CALL ME BACK
8:25
have anything
with this,
8:26
at the bookstore,
please. I can explain.
9:05
I'll be there all day.
Please meet me.
9:14
I DON'T KNOWWWWW.
I CAN'T TRUST HER, SYNERGY.
ARE YOU CERTAIN SHE WAS INVOLVED?
NO... I DON'T KNOW.
I GUESS I'M NOT SURE.
THEN PERHAPS YOU SHOULD LET HER *EXPLAIN*.
I CAN'T TRUST *ANYONE!*
KIMBER, THAT IS NOT TRUE. YOU SHOULD SPEAK TO YOUR SISTERS.
THEY DON'T EVEN LIKE HER. THEY'RE *MAD* AT ME.
THAT IS NOT TRUE.
THEY DON'T UNDERSTAND.
THEY WILL. BUT YOU HAVE TO TALK TO THEM FIRST.
I KNOW.
DO YOU KNOW YOU KIND OF LOOK LIKE MY MOM?

I MEAN... A WEIRD FUTURE-Y SCI-FI VERSION OF MY MOM, BUT STILL.

I HOPE THIS DOES NOT BOTHER YOU.

NO. I LIKE IT.

SOMETIMES I CAN'T REMEMBER HER FACE.

SO I LIKE TO LOOK AT YOU. IT REMINDS ME.

...

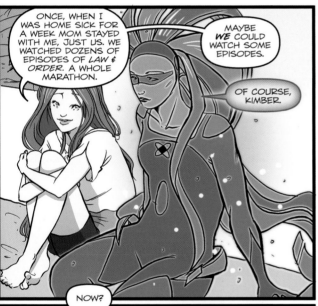

ONCE, WHEN I WAS HOME SICK FOR A WEEK MOM STAYED WITH ME, JUST US. WE WATCHED DOZENS OF EPISODES OF LAW & ORDER. A WHOLE MARATHON.

MAYBE WE COULD WATCH SOME EPISODES.

OF COURSE, KIMBER.

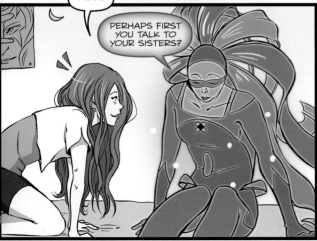

NOW?

PERHAPS FIRST YOU TALK TO YOUR SISTERS?

OH YEAH.

EVERYTHING IS A DISASTER.

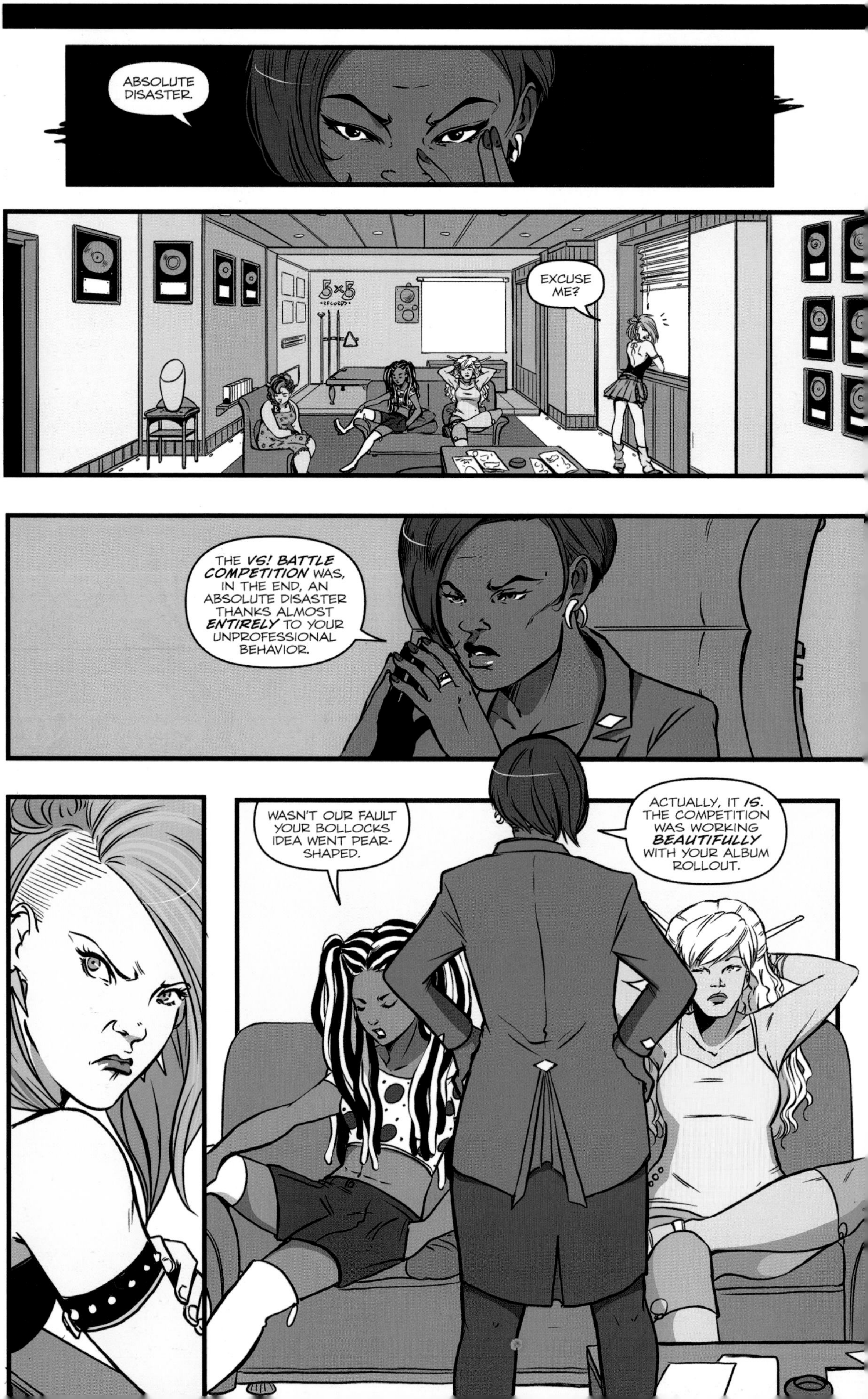
ABSOLUTE DISASTER.
EXCUSE ME?
THE VS! BATTLE COMPETITION WAS, IN THE END, AN ABSOLUTE DISASTER THANKS ALMOST ENTIRELY TO YOUR UNPROFESSIONAL BEHAVIOR.
WASN'T OUR FAULT YOUR BOLLOCKS IDEA WENT PEAR-SHAPED.
ACTUALLY, IT IS. THE COMPETITION WAS WORKING BEAUTIFULLY WITH YOUR ALBUM ROLLOUT.

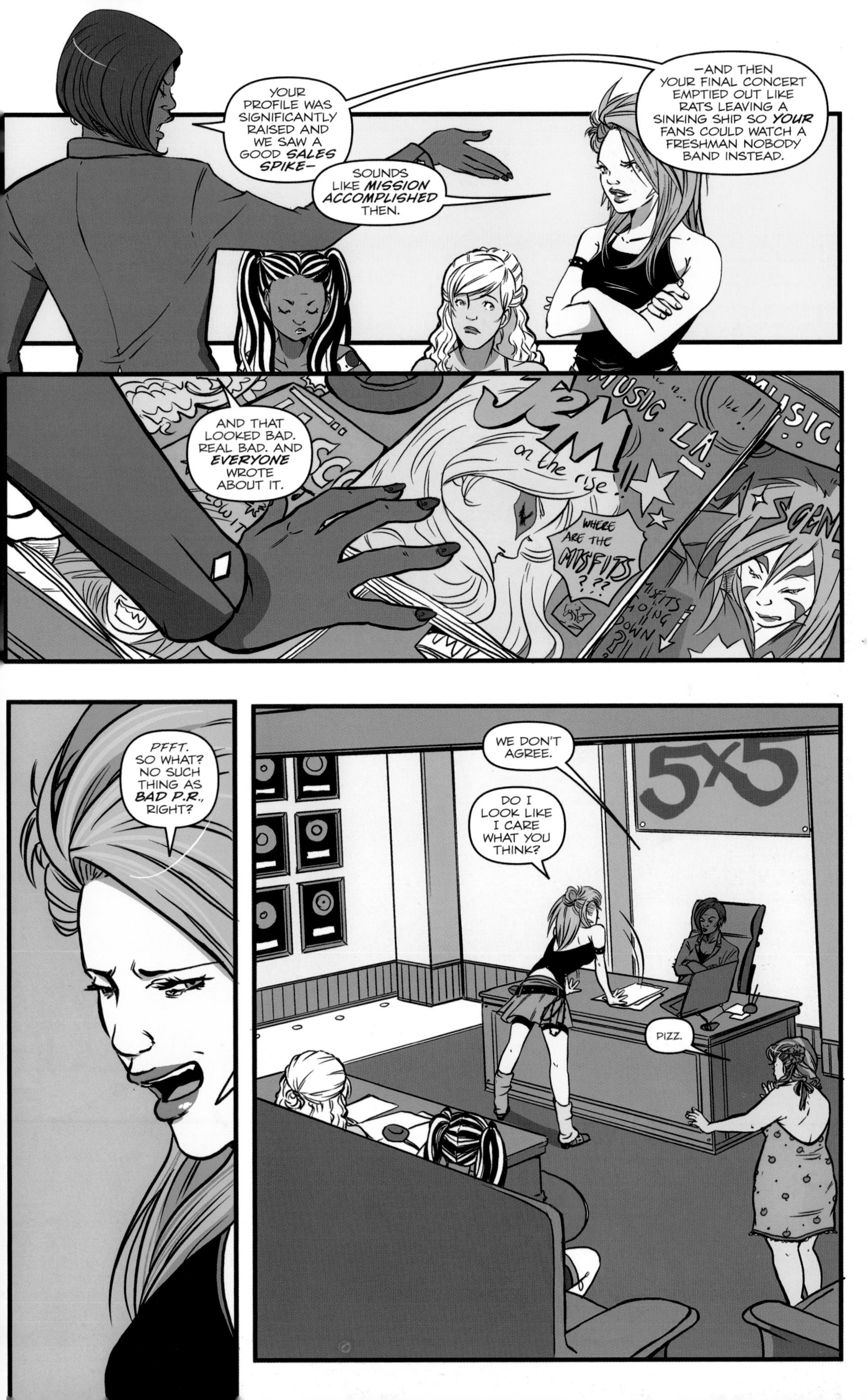
YOUR PROFILE WAS SIGNIFICANTLY RAISED AND WE SAW A GOOD SALES SPIKE—
—AND THEN YOUR FINAL CONCERT EMPTIED OUT LIKE RATS LEAVING A SINKING SHIP SO YOUR FANS COULD WATCH A FRESHMAN NOBODY BAND INSTEAD.
SOUNDS LIKE MISSION ACCOMPLISHED THEN.
AND THAT LOOKED BAD. REAL BAD. AND EVERYONE WROTE ABOUT IT.
JEM on the rise!!
MUSIC . L.A.
WHERE ARE THE MISFITS ???
MISFITS GOING DOWN ?!
PFFT. SO WHAT? NO SUCH THING AS BAD P.R., RIGHT?
WE DON'T AGREE.
DO I LOOK LIKE I CARE WHAT YOU THINK?
5x5
PIZZ.

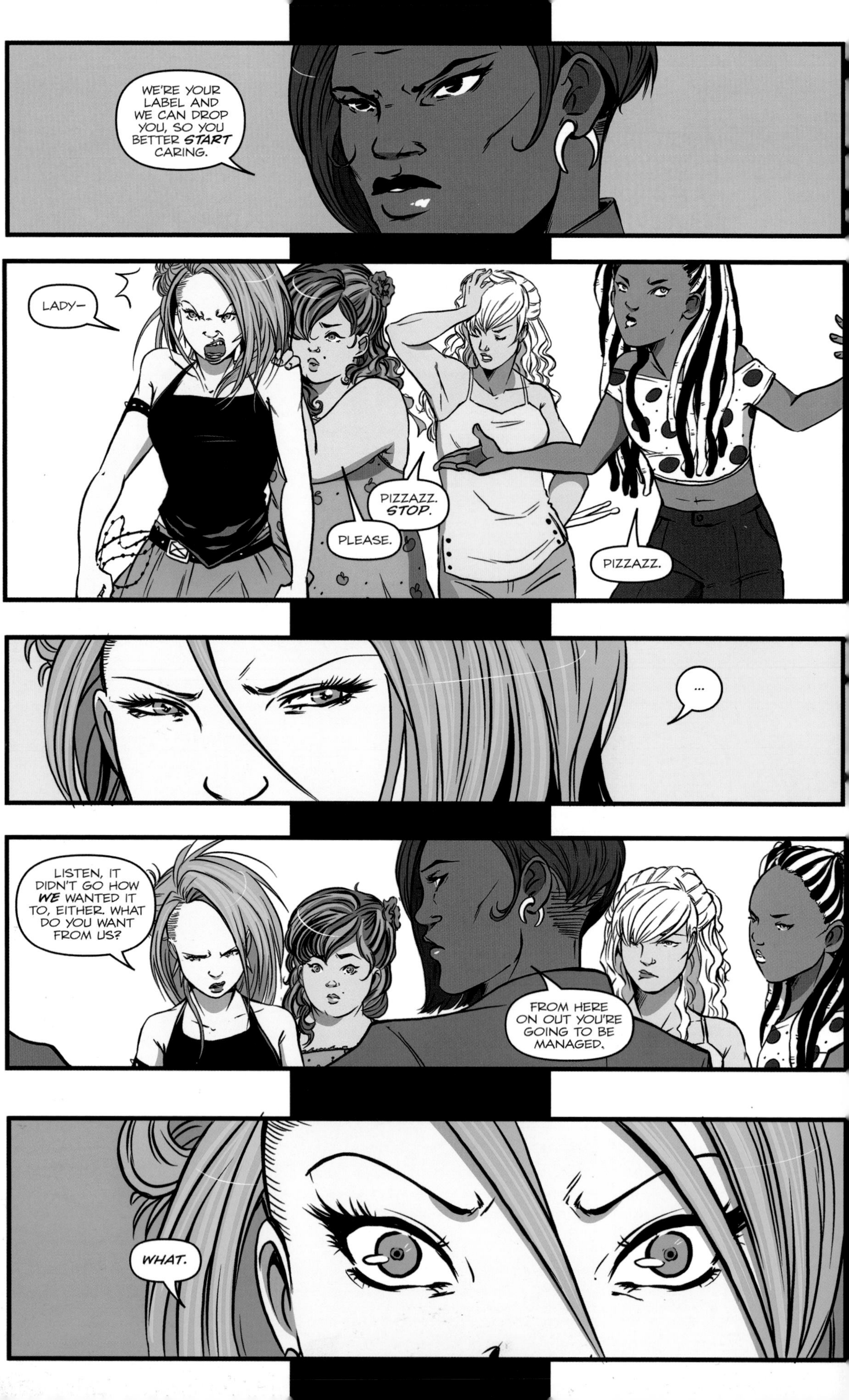
WE'RE YOUR LABEL AND WE CAN DROP YOU, SO YOU BETTER *START* CARING.
LADY—
PIZZAZZ. *STOP.*
PLEASE.
PIZZAZZ.
...
LISTEN, IT DIDN'T GO HOW *WE* WANTED IT TO, EITHER. WHAT DO YOU WANT FROM US?
FROM HERE ON OUT YOU'RE GOING TO BE MANAGED.
WHAT.

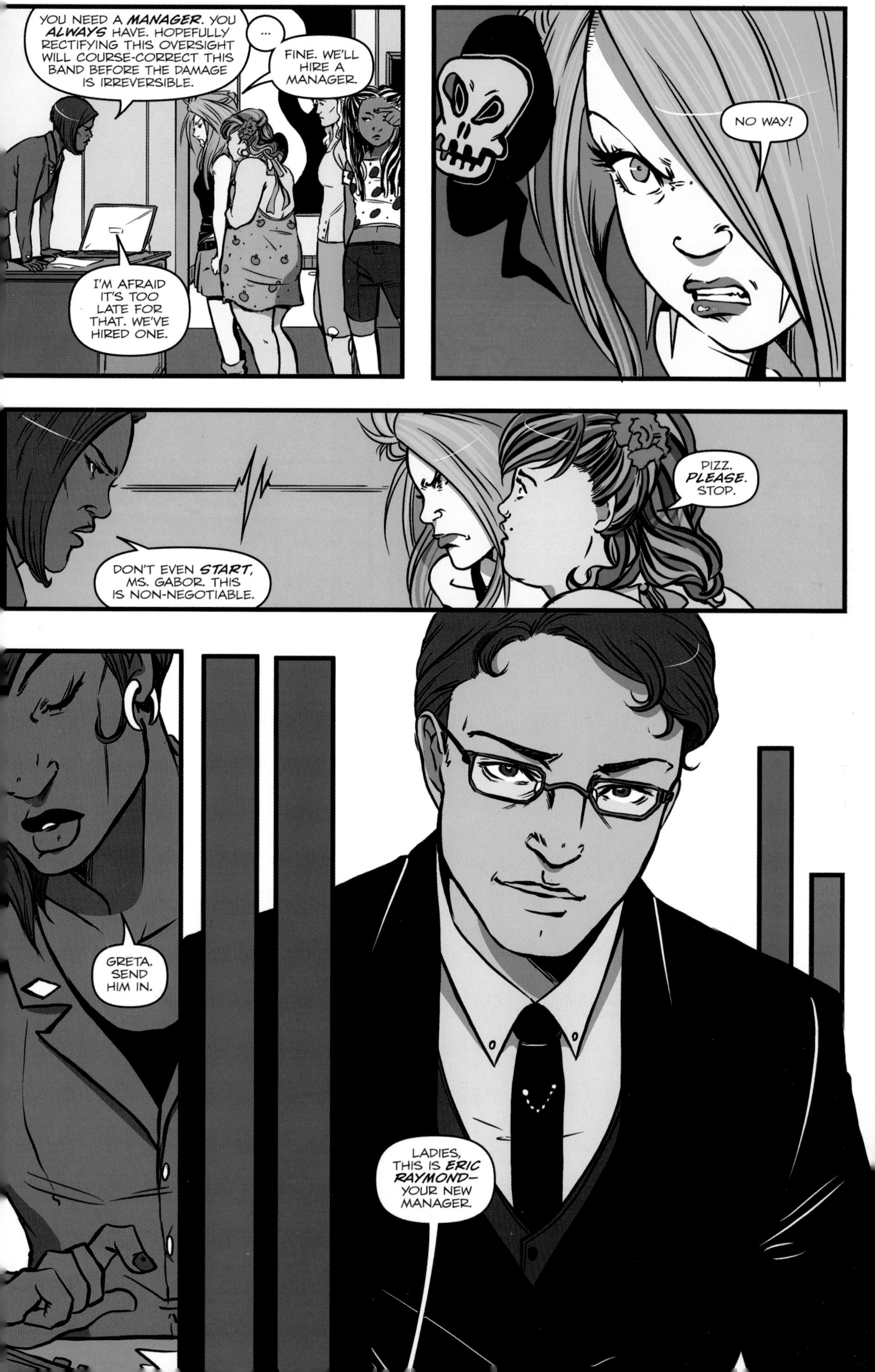
YOU NEED A MANAGER. YOU ALWAYS HAVE. HOPEFULLY RECTIFYING THIS OVERSIGHT WILL COURSE-CORRECT THIS BAND BEFORE THE DAMAGE IS IRREVERSIBLE.
...
FINE. WE'LL HIRE A MANAGER.
I'M AFRAID IT'S TOO LATE FOR THAT. WE'VE HIRED ONE.
NO WAY!
PIZZ. PLEASE. STOP.
DON'T EVEN START, MS. GABOR. THIS IS NON-NEGOTIABLE.
GRETA. SEND HIM IN.
LADIES, THIS IS ERIC RAYMOND— YOUR NEW MANAGER.

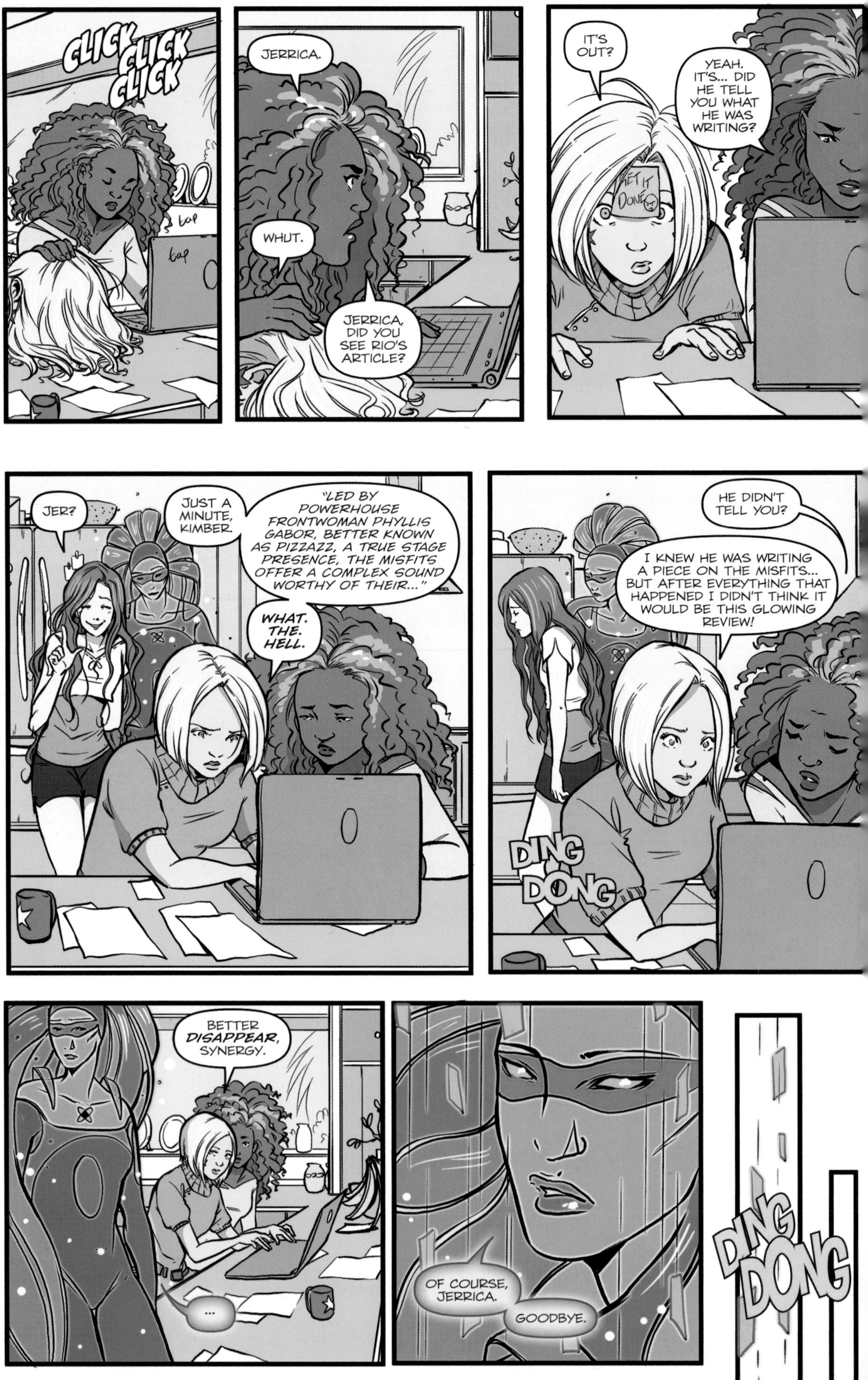

CLICK CLICK CLICK
tap
tap
JERRICA.
WHUT.
JERRICA, DID YOU SEE RIO'S ARTICLE?
IT'S OUT?
YEAH. IT'S... DID HE TELL YOU WHAT HE WAS WRITING?
GET IT DONE
JER?
JUST A MINUTE, KIMBER.
"LED BY POWERHOUSE FRONTWOMAN PHYLLIS GABOR, BETTER KNOWN AS PIZZAZZ, A TRUE STAGE PRESENCE, THE MISFITS OFFER A COMPLEX SOUND WORTHY OF THEIR..."
WHAT. THE. HELL.
HE DIDN'T TELL YOU?
I KNEW HE WAS WRITING A PIECE ON THE MISFITS... BUT AFTER EVERYTHING THAT HAPPENED I DIDN'T THINK IT WOULD BE THIS GLOWING REVIEW!
DING DONG
BETTER DISAPPEAR, SYNERGY.
...
OF COURSE, JERRICA.
GOODBYE.
DING DONG

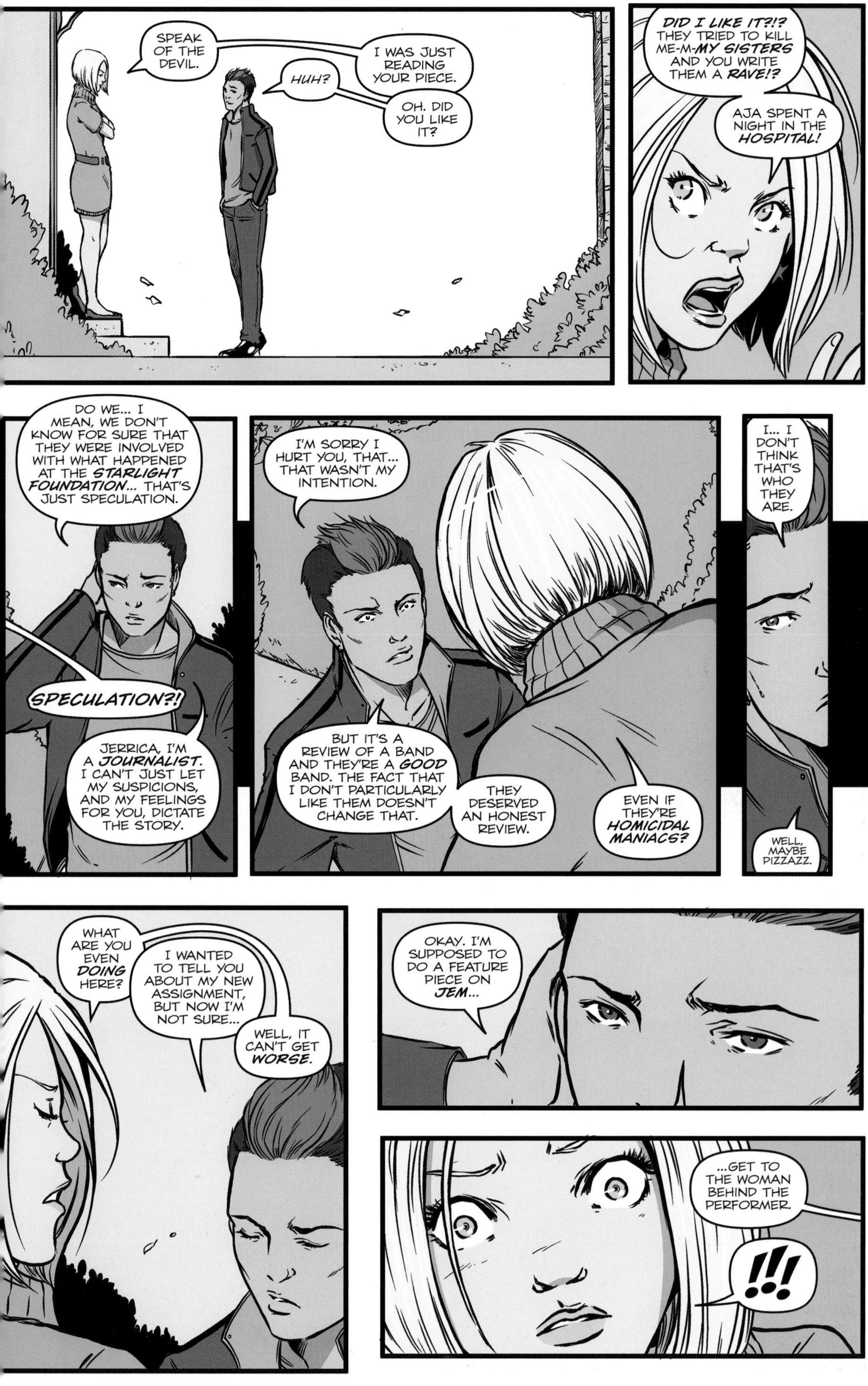
SPEAK OF THE DEVIL.
I WAS JUST READING YOUR PIECE.
HUH?
OH. DID YOU LIKE IT?
DID I LIKE IT?!? THEY TRIED TO KILL ME-M-MY SISTERS AND YOU WRITE THEM A RAVE!?
AJA SPENT A NIGHT IN THE HOSPITAL!
DO WE... I MEAN, WE DON'T KNOW FOR SURE THAT THEY WERE INVOLVED WITH WHAT HAPPENED AT THE STARLIGHT FOUNDATION... THAT'S JUST SPECULATION.
SPECULATION?!
JERRICA, I'M A JOURNALIST. I CAN'T JUST LET MY SUSPICIONS, AND MY FEELINGS FOR YOU, DICTATE THE STORY.
I'M SORRY I HURT YOU, THAT... THAT WASN'T MY INTENTION.
BUT IT'S A REVIEW OF A BAND AND THEY'RE A GOOD BAND. THE FACT THAT I DON'T PARTICULARLY LIKE THEM DOESN'T CHANGE THAT.
THEY DESERVED AN HONEST REVIEW.
EVEN IF THEY'RE HOMICIDAL MANIACS?
I... I DON'T THINK THAT'S WHO THEY ARE.
WELL, MAYBE PIZZAZZ.
WHAT ARE YOU EVEN DOING HERE?
I WANTED TO TELL YOU ABOUT MY NEW ASSIGNMENT, BUT NOW I'M NOT SURE...
WELL, IT CAN'T GET WORSE.
OKAY. I'M SUPPOSED TO DO A FEATURE PIECE ON JEM...
...GET TO THE WOMAN BEHIND THE PERFORMER.
!!!

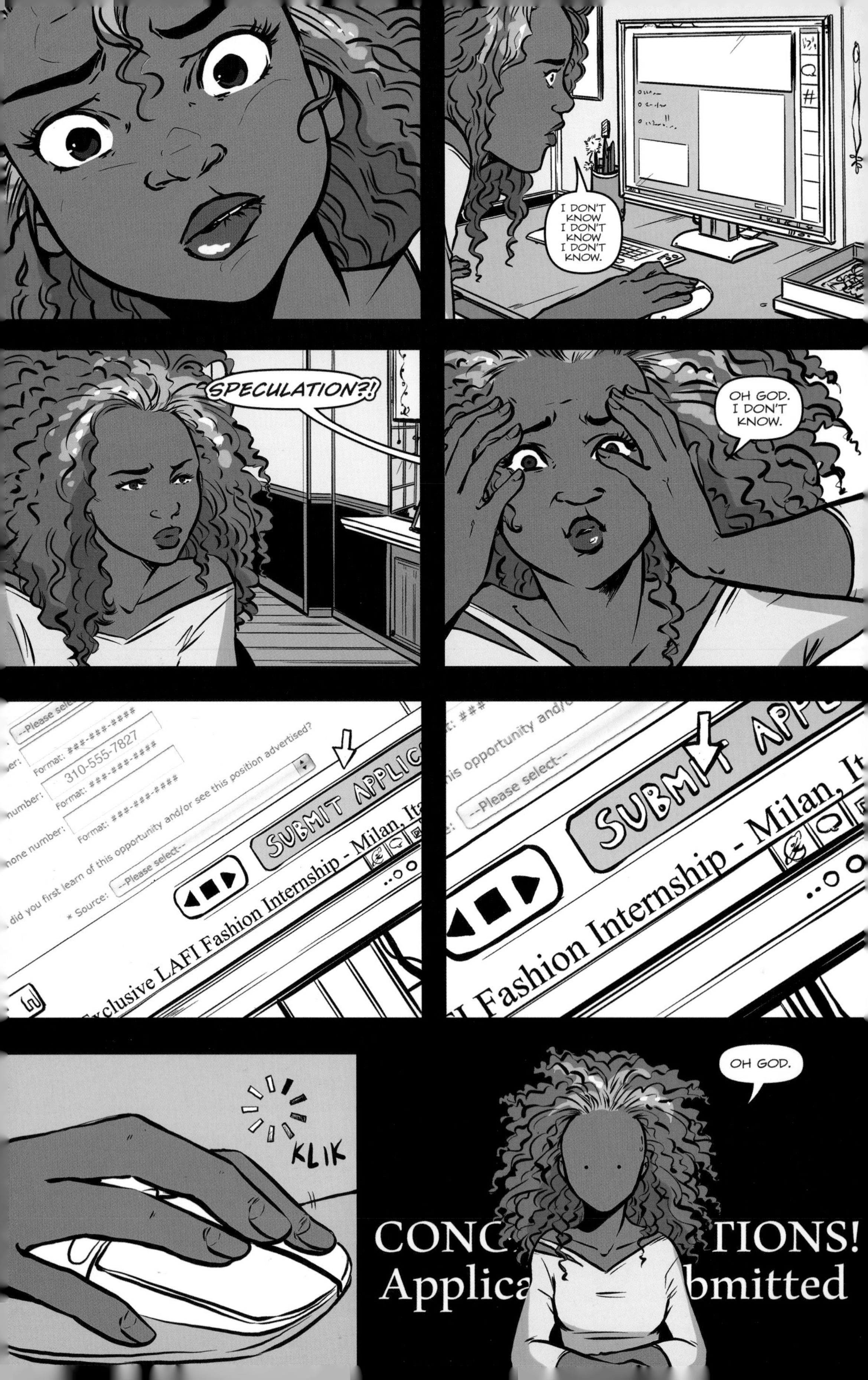

I DON'T KNOW I DON'T KNOW I DON'T KNOW.
SPECULATION?!
OH GOD. I DON'T KNOW.
SUBMIT APPLIC
Exclusive LAFI Fashion Internship - Milan, It
SUBMIT APPL
I Fashion Internship - Milan, It
KLIK
OH GOD.
CONG TIONS!
Applica bmitted

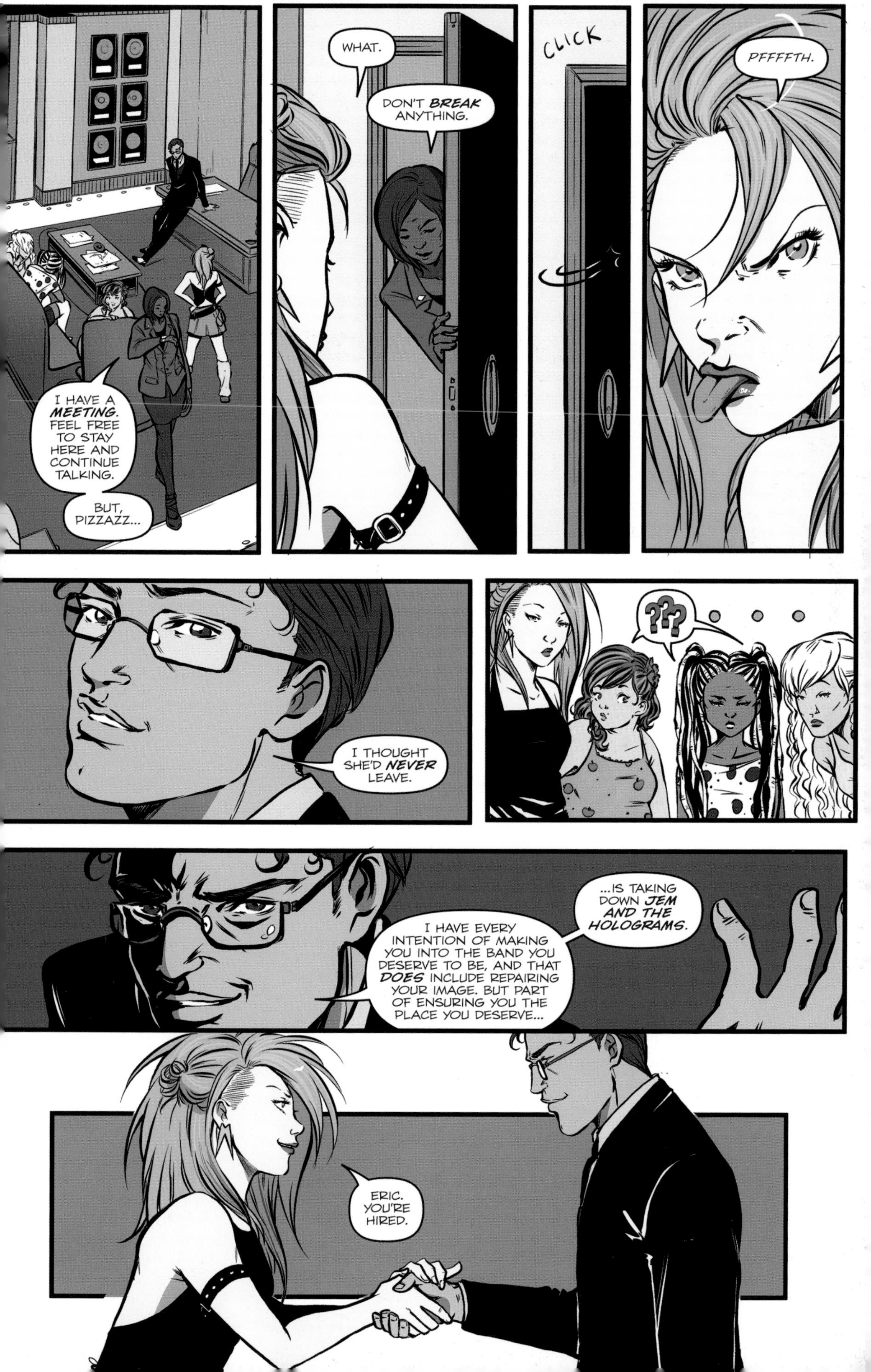
I HAVE A MEETING. FEEL FREE TO STAY HERE AND CONTINUE TALKING.
BUT, PIZZAZZ...
WHAT.
DON'T BREAK ANYTHING.
CLICK
PFFFFTH.
I THOUGHT SHE'D NEVER LEAVE.
???
I HAVE EVERY INTENTION OF MAKING YOU INTO THE BAND YOU DESERVE TO BE, AND THAT DOES INCLUDE REPAIRING YOUR IMAGE. BUT PART OF ENSURING YOU THE PLACE YOU DESERVE...
...IS TAKING DOWN JEM AND THE HOLOGRAMS.
ERIC. YOU'RE HIRED.

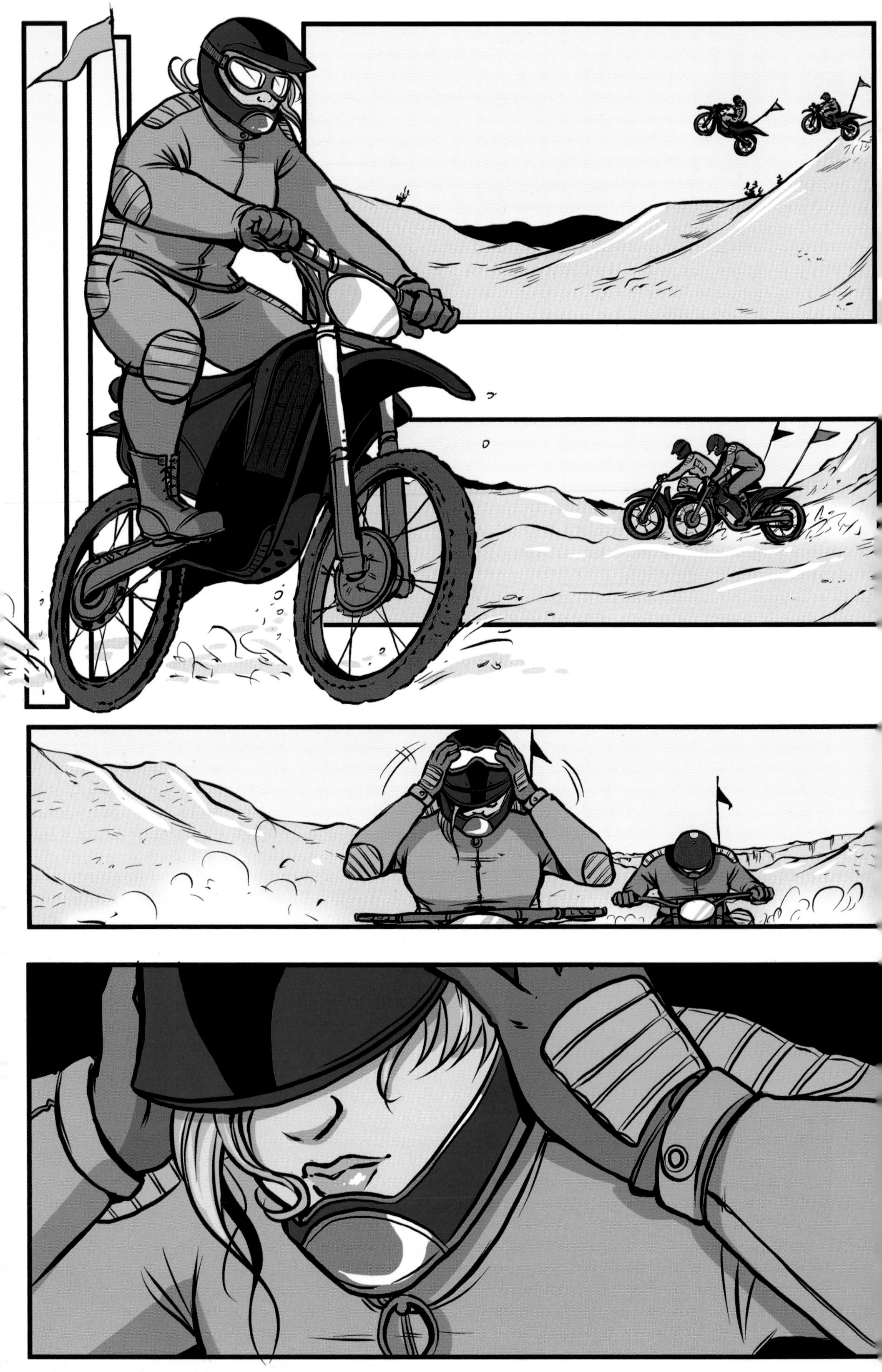

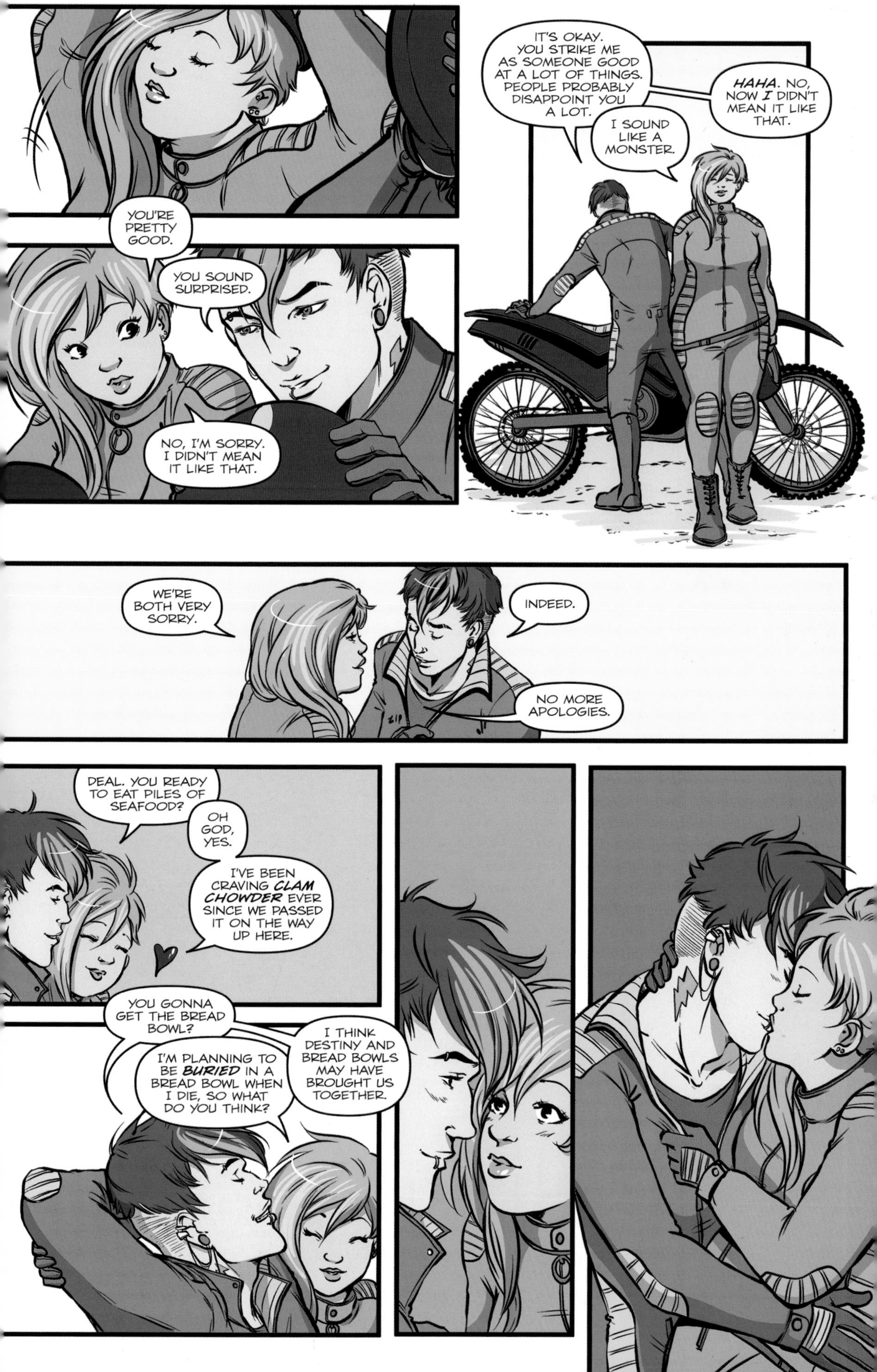

YOU'RE PRETTY GOOD.
YOU SOUND SURPRISED.
NO, I'M SORRY. I DIDN'T MEAN IT LIKE THAT.
IT'S OKAY. YOU STRIKE ME AS SOMEONE GOOD AT A LOT OF THINGS. PEOPLE PROBABLY DISAPPOINT YOU A LOT.
I SOUND LIKE A MONSTER.
HAHA. NO, NOW I DIDN'T MEAN IT LIKE THAT.
WE'RE BOTH VERY SORRY.
INDEED.
NO MORE APOLOGIES.
ZIP
DEAL. YOU READY TO EAT PILES OF SEAFOOD?
OH GOD, YES.
I'VE BEEN CRAVING CLAM CHOWDER EVER SINCE WE PASSED IT ON THE WAY UP HERE.
YOU GONNA GET THE BREAD BOWL?
I'M PLANNING TO BE BURIED IN A BREAD BOWL WHEN I DIE, SO WHAT DO YOU THINK?
I THINK DESTINY AND BREAD BOWLS MAY HAVE BROUGHT US TOGETHER.

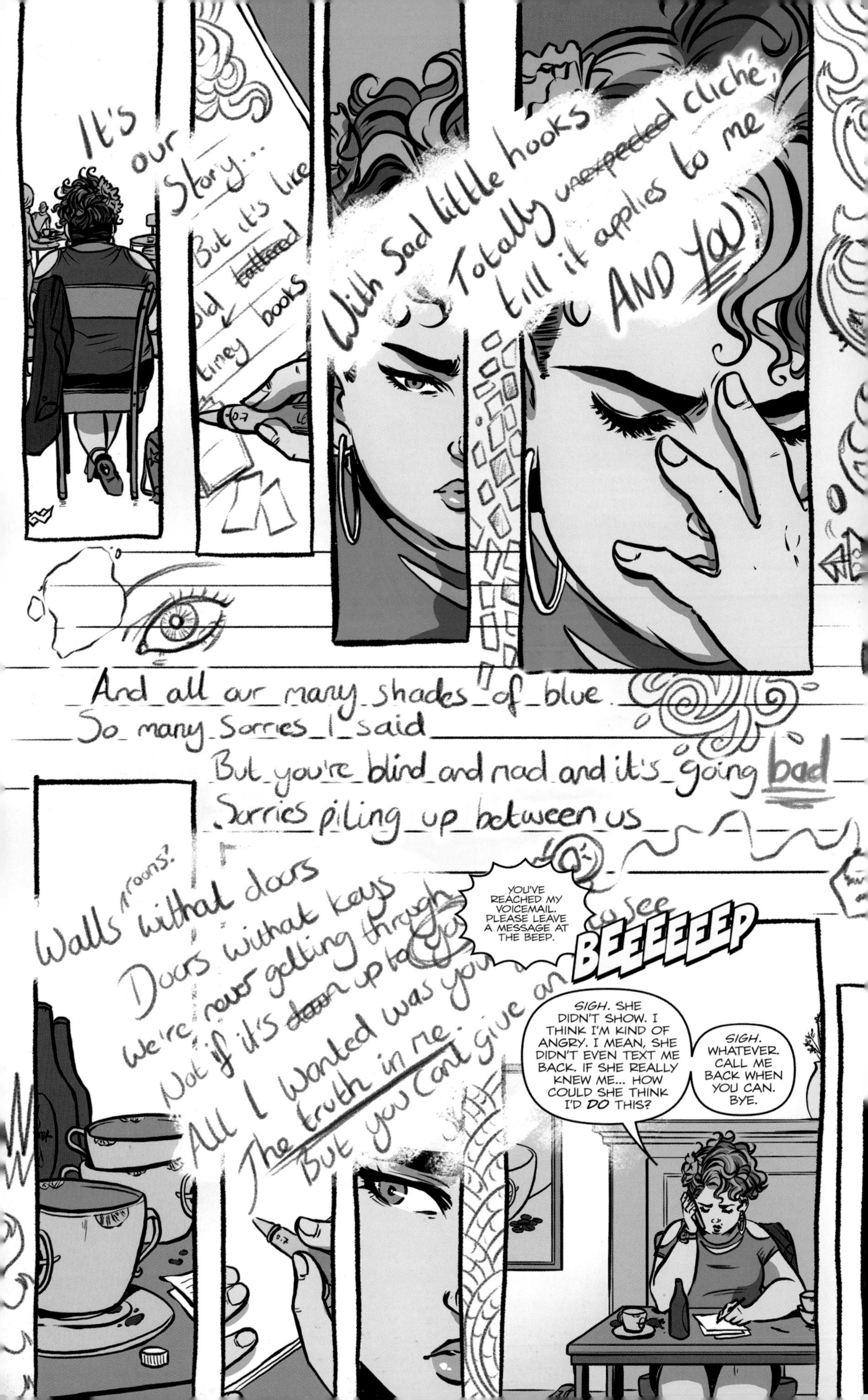

It's our Story...
But it's like old tattered timey books
With sad little hooks
Totally unexpected cliché,
till it applies to me
AND YOU
And all our many shades of blue
So many sorries I said
But you're blind and mad and it's going bad
Sorries piling up between us
Walls without doors
rooms?
Doors without keys
We're never getting through
Not if it's down up to you
All I wanted was you
to see
The truth in me
But you can't give an
YOU'VE REACHED MY VOICEMAIL. PLEASE LEAVE A MESSAGE AT THE BEEP.
BEEEEEEP
SIGH. SHE DIDN'T SHOW. I THINK I'M KIND OF ANGRY. I MEAN, SHE DIDN'T EVEN TEXT ME BACK. IF SHE REALLY KNEW ME... HOW COULD SHE THINK I'D DO THIS?
SIGH. WHATEVER. CALL ME BACK WHEN YOU CAN. BYE.

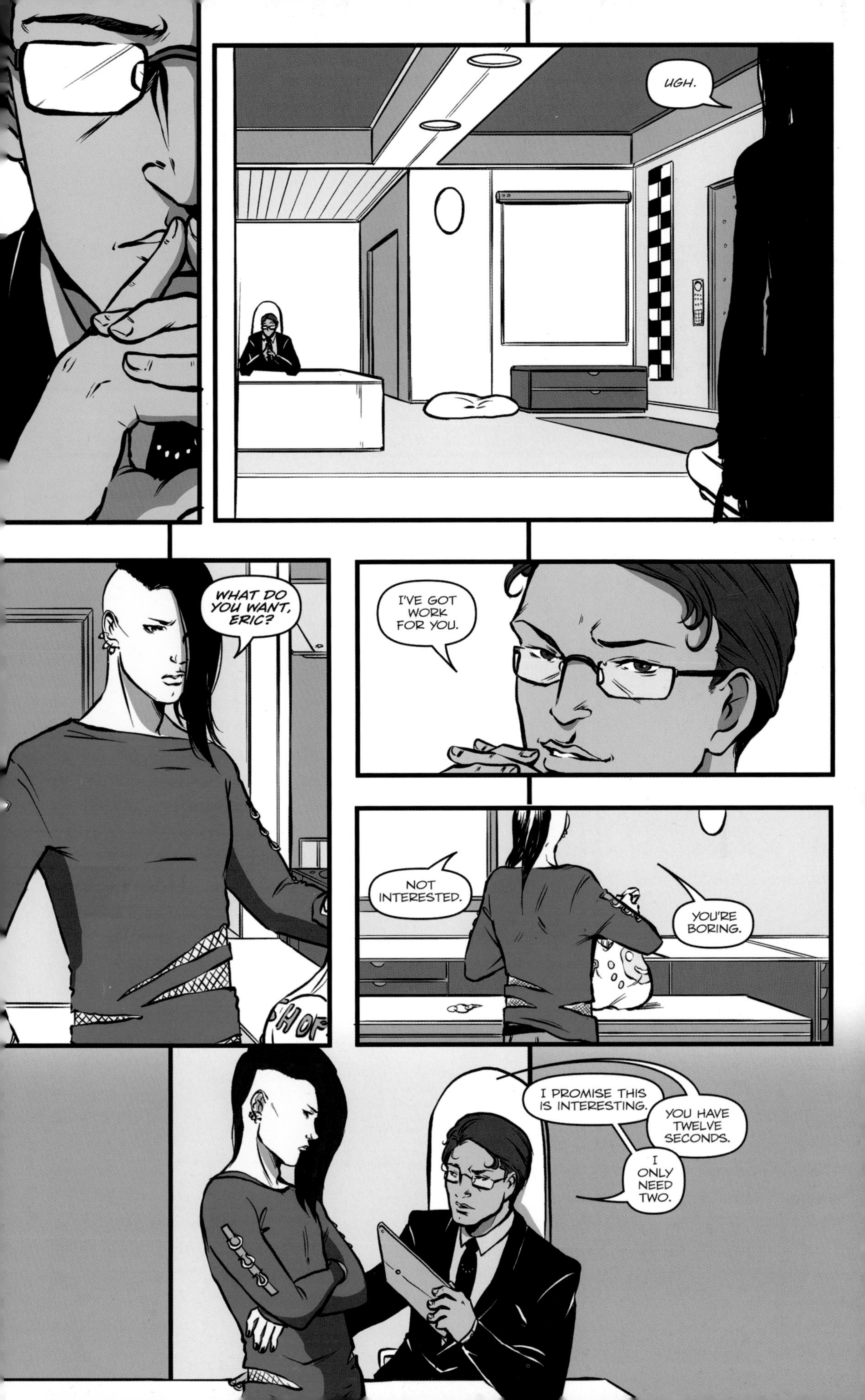
UGH.
WHAT DO YOU WANT, ERIC?
I'VE GOT WORK FOR YOU.
NOT INTERESTED.
YOU'RE BORING.
I PROMISE THIS IS INTERESTING.
YOU HAVE TWELVE SECONDS.
I ONLY NEED TWO.

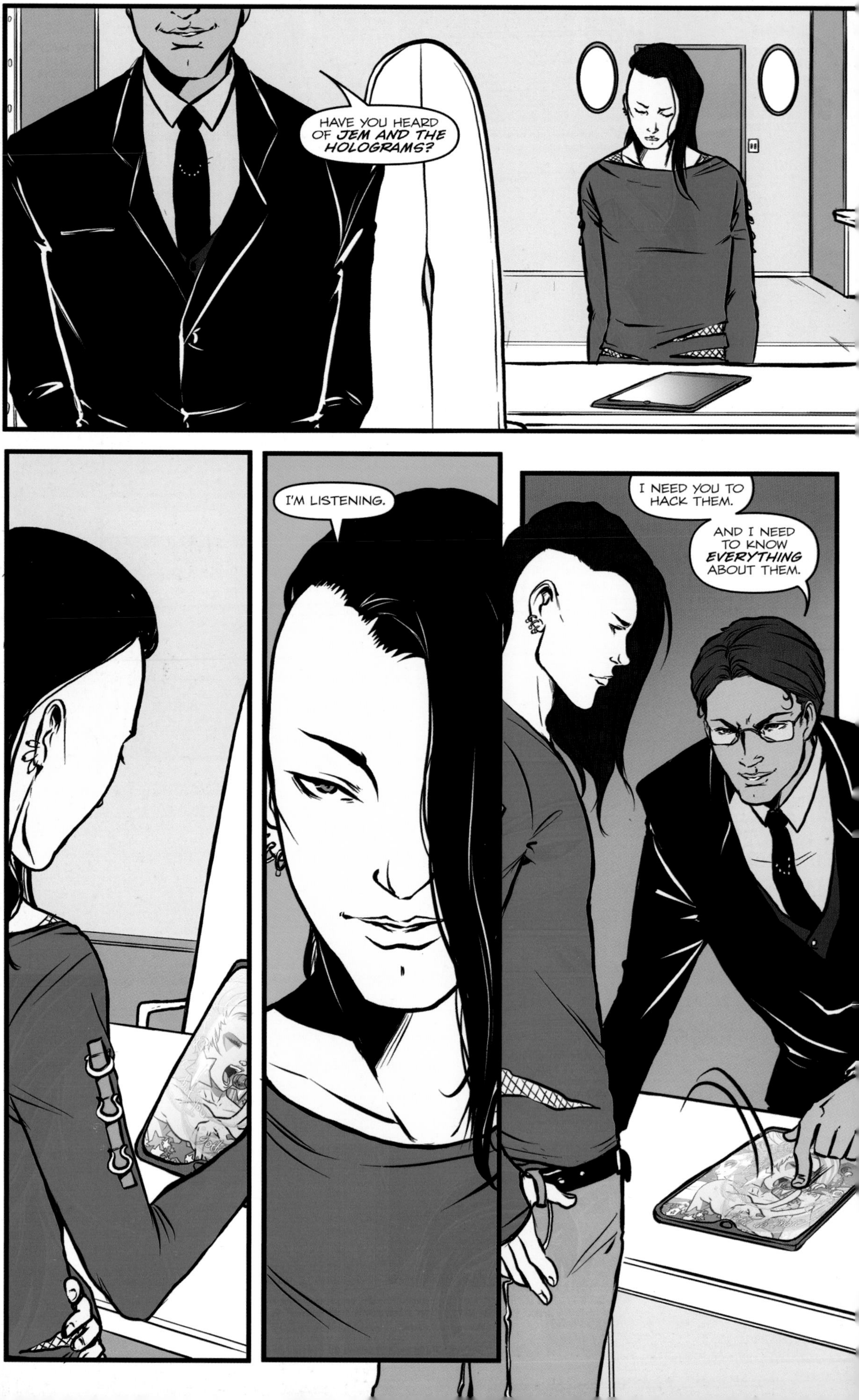
HAVE YOU HEARD OF ***JEM AND THE HOLOGRAMS?***
I'M LISTENING.
I NEED YOU TO HACK THEM.
AND I NEED TO KNOW ***EVERYTHING*** ABOUT THEM.

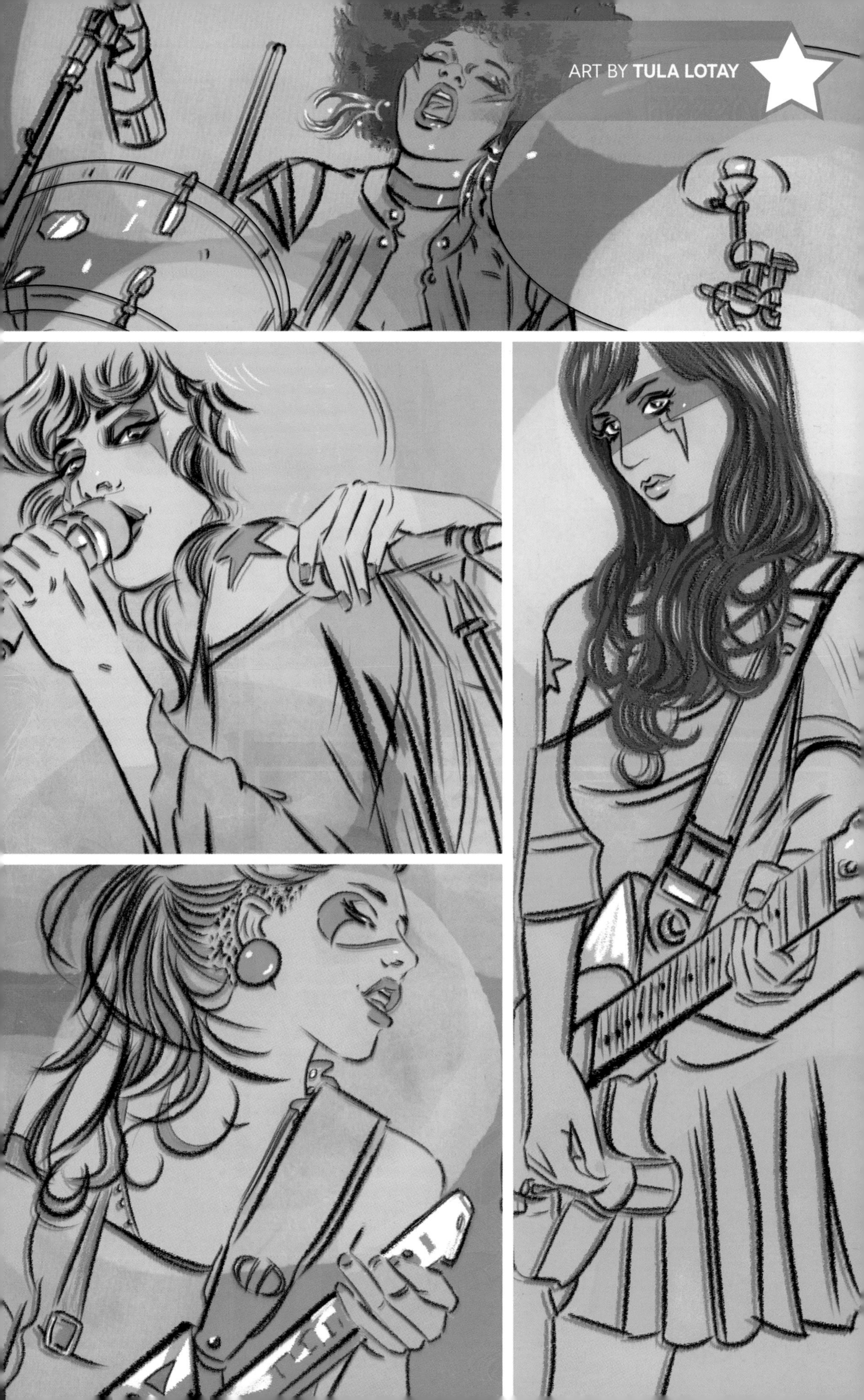
ART BY TULA LOTAY

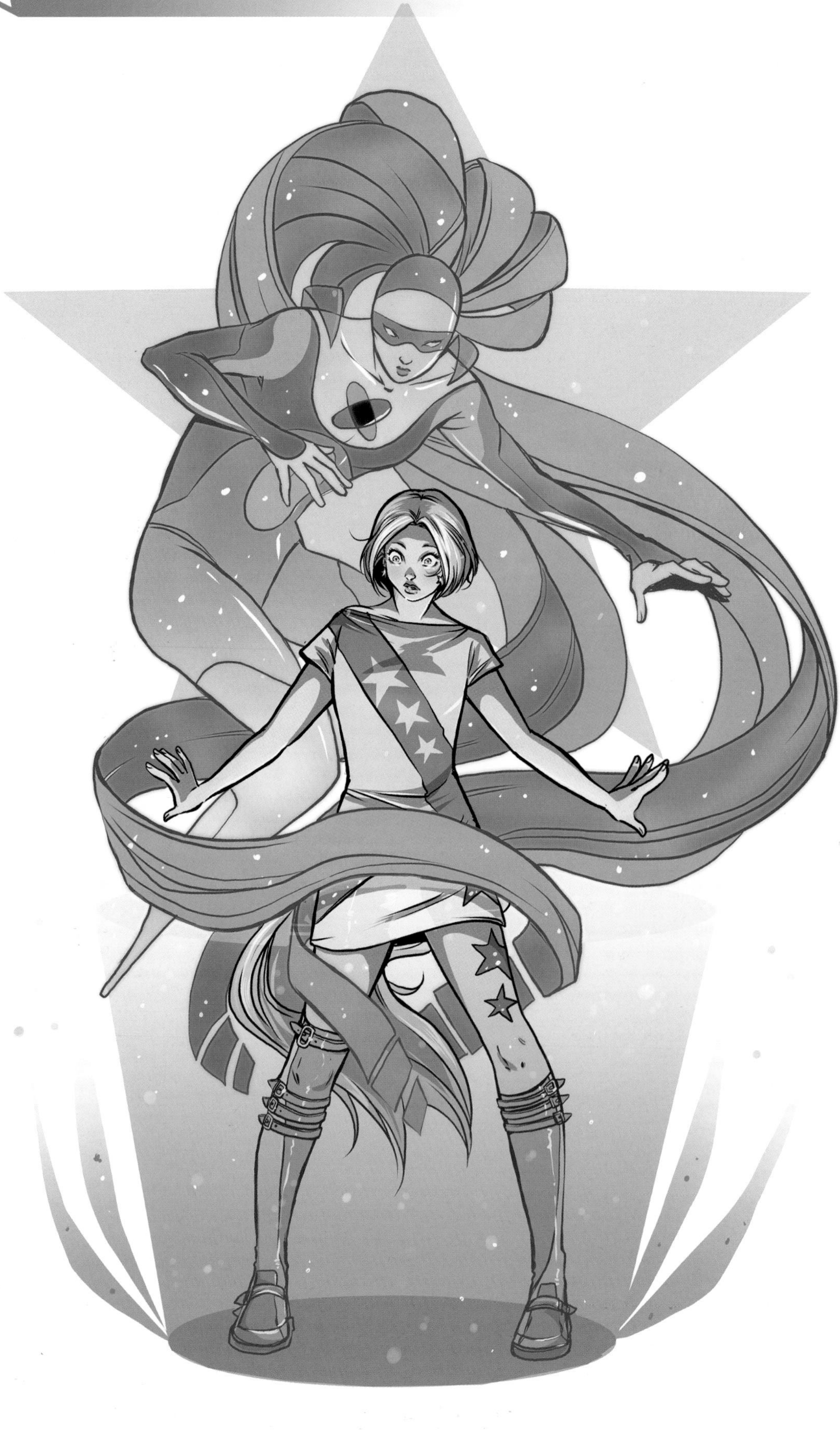

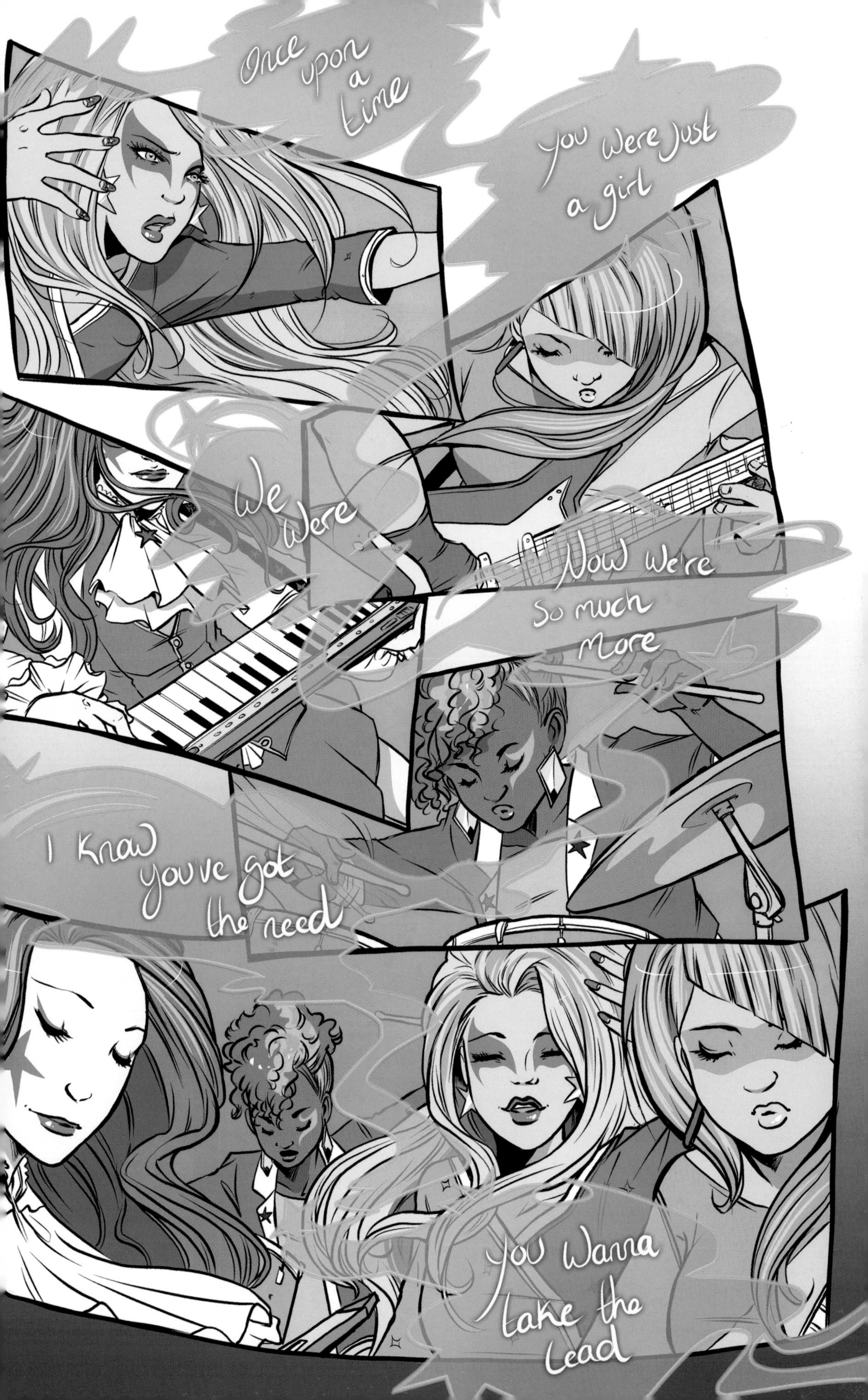
Once upon a time
You were just a girl
We were
Now we're so much more
I know you've got the need
You wanna take the lead

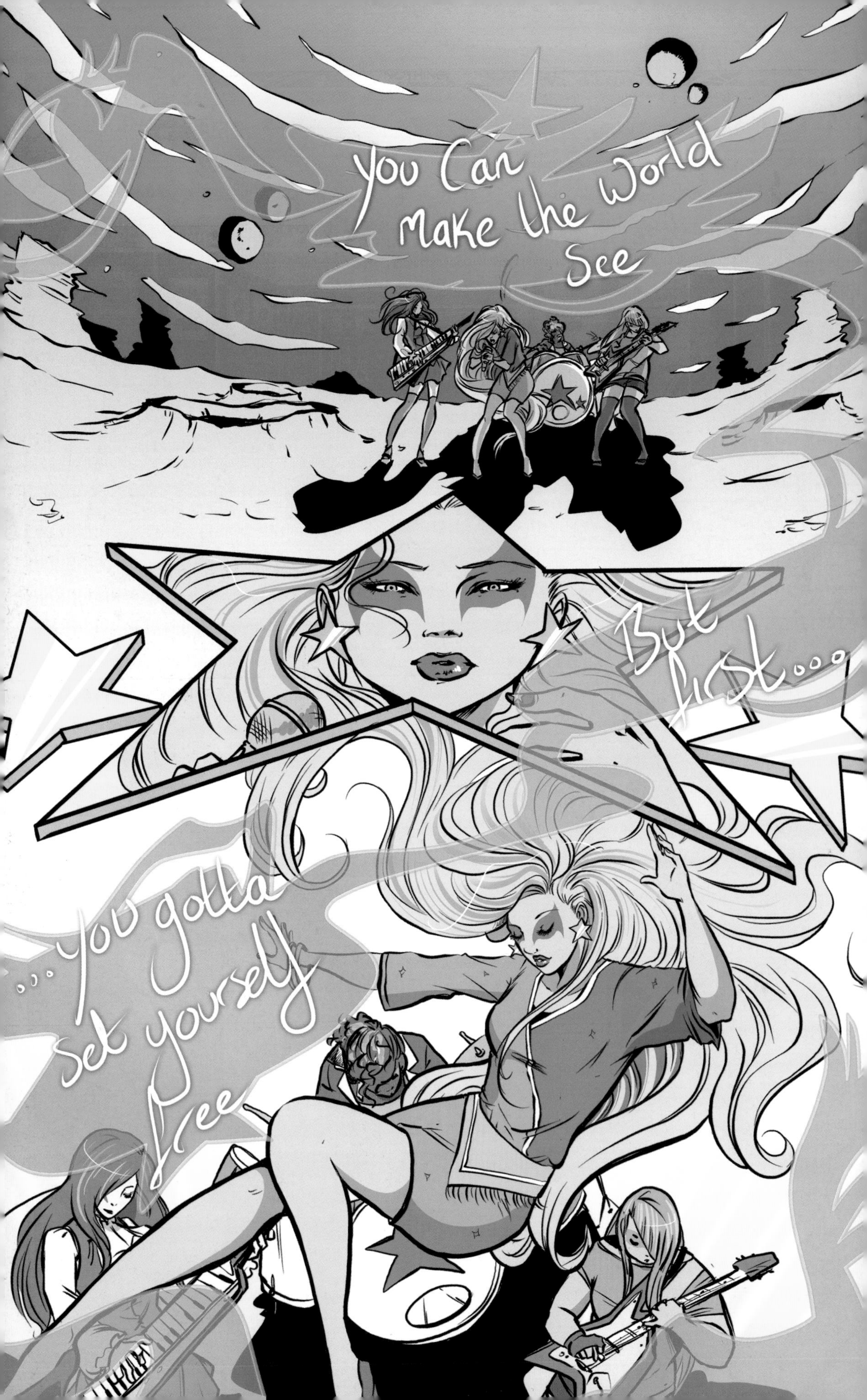
you Can Make the World See
But first...
...you gotta set yourself free

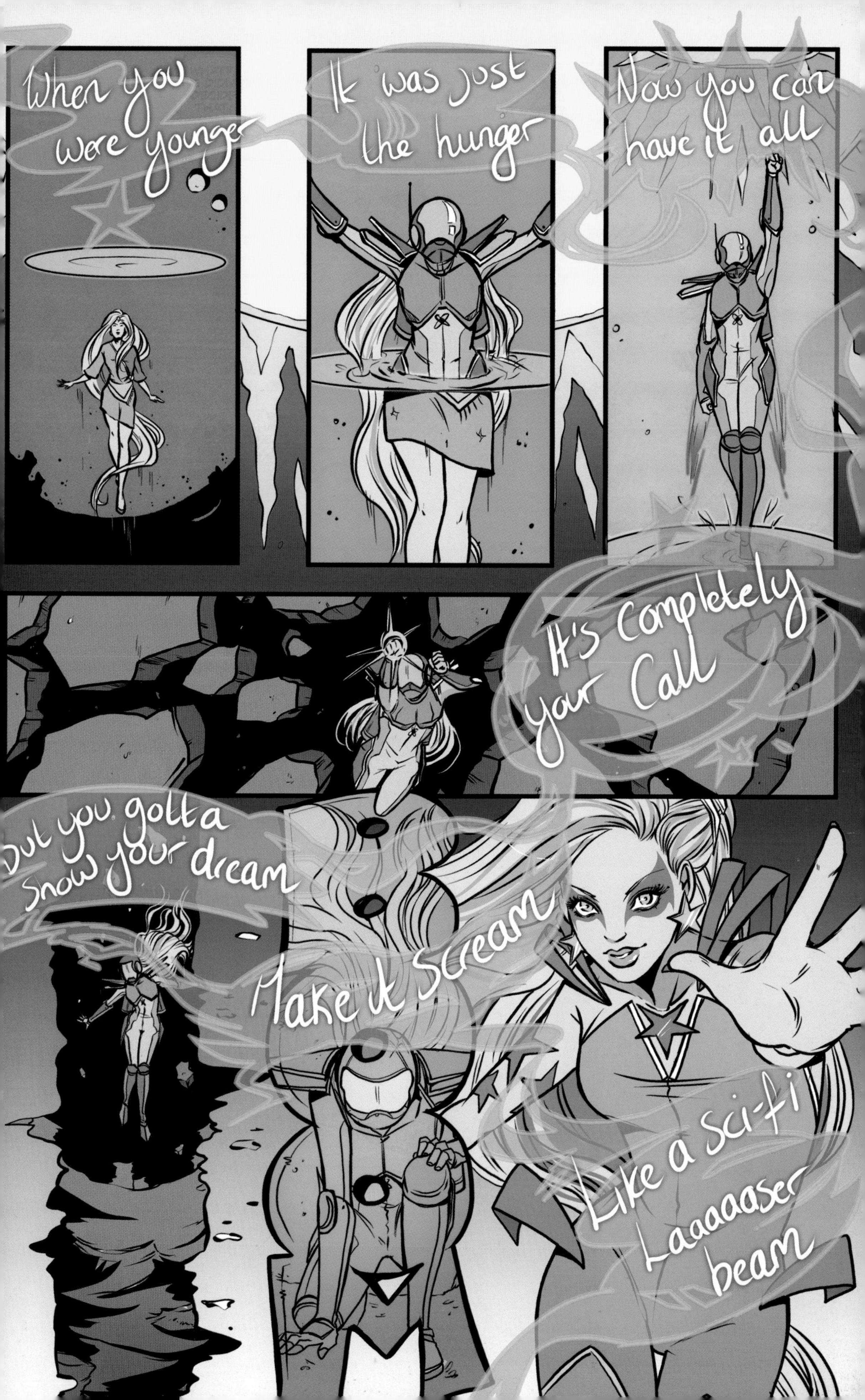
When you were younger
It was just the hunger
Now you can have it all
It's completely your Call
But you gotta show your dream
Make it Scream
Like a Sci-fi Laaaaaser beam

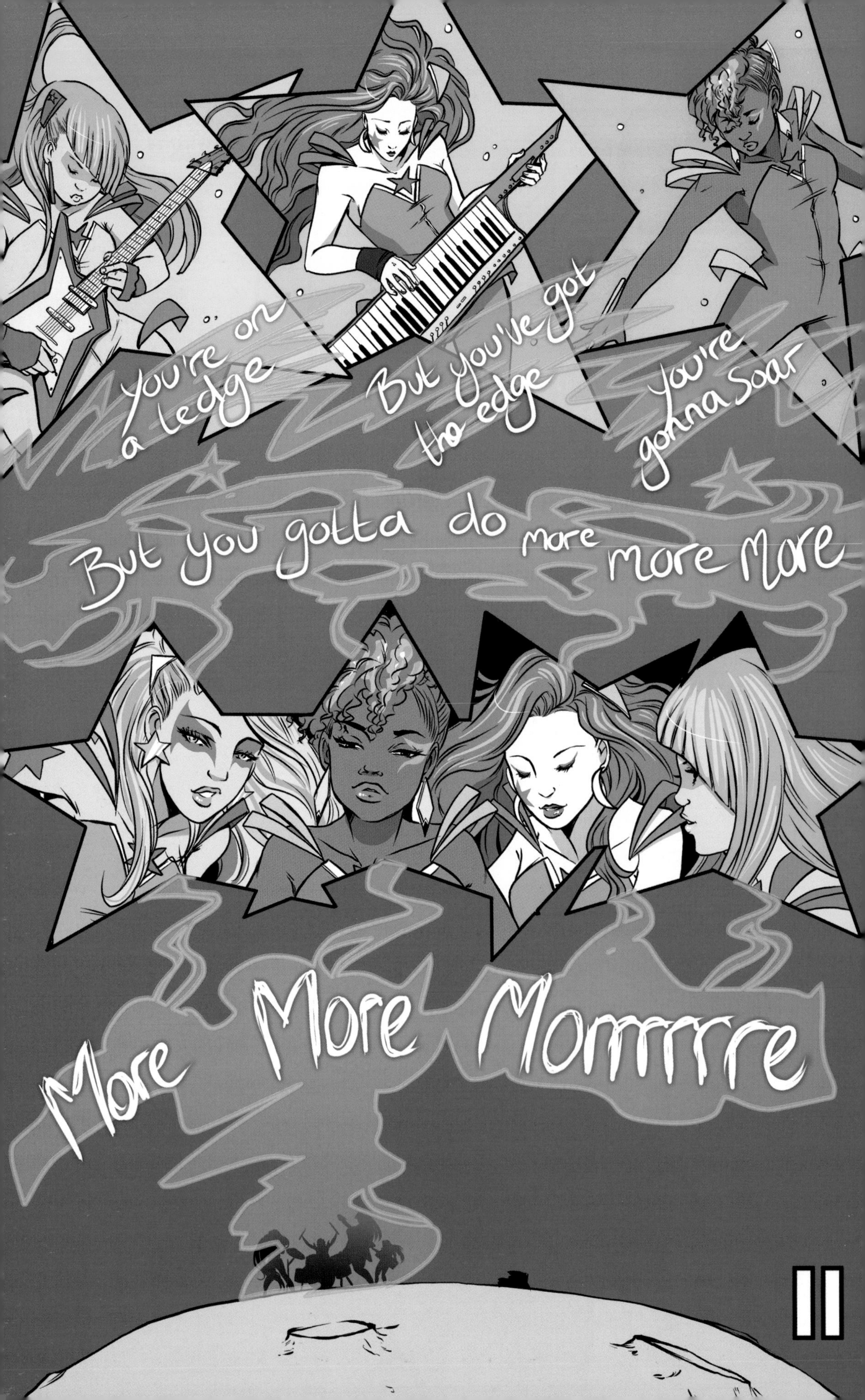
You're on a ledge
But you've got the edge
You're gonna Soar
But you gotta do more more More
More More Morrrrre

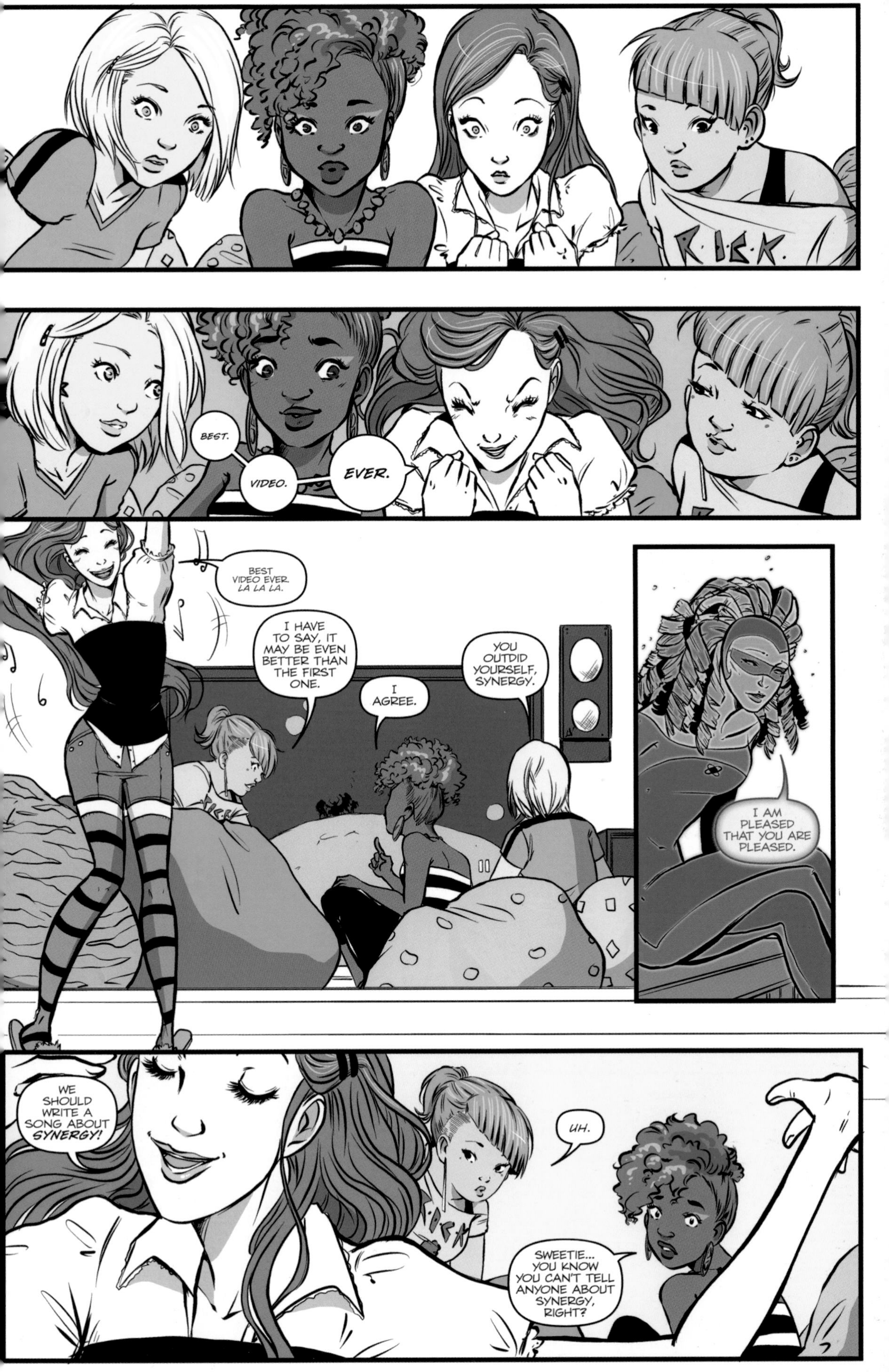
BEST.
VIDEO.
EVER.
BEST VIDEO EVER. LA LA LA.
I HAVE TO SAY, IT MAY BE EVEN BETTER THAN THE FIRST ONE.
I AGREE.
YOU OUTDID YOURSELF, SYNERGY.
I AM PLEASED THAT YOU ARE PLEASED.
WE SHOULD WRITE A SONG ABOUT SYNERGY!
UH.
SWEETIE... YOU KNOW YOU CAN'T TELL ANYONE ABOUT SYNERGY, RIGHT?

KIMBER, THIS IS *SO* IMPORTANT.

SYNERGY COULD BE *REALLY DANGEROUS* IN THE WRONG HANDS.

LIKE *THE MISFITS?*

YEAH... OF COURSE...

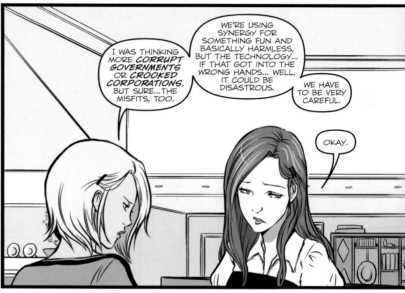

I WAS THINKING MORE *CORRUPT GOVERNMENTS* OR *CROOKED CORPORATIONS*, BUT SURE... THE MISFITS, TOO.

WE'RE USING SYNERGY FOR SOMETHING FUN AND BASICALLY HARMLESS, BUT THE TECHNOLOGY... IF THAT GOT INTO THE WRONG HANDS... WELL, IT COULD BE DISASTROUS.

WE HAVE TO BE VERY CAREFUL.

OKAY.

YOU HAVEN'T TOLD ANYONE ABOUT SYNERGY, HAVE YOU?

NO WAY!

WE'RE SORRY SWEETIE... WE JUST, YOU PANICKED US A LITTLE. THIS IS A *BIG DEAL.*

I KNOW. I REMEMBER *SYNER-KITTY.*

I'LL ALWAYS MISS *SYNER-KITTY.*

ARE YOU SURE? EVEN *STORMER?*

I SAID *NO, AJA! JEEZ!*

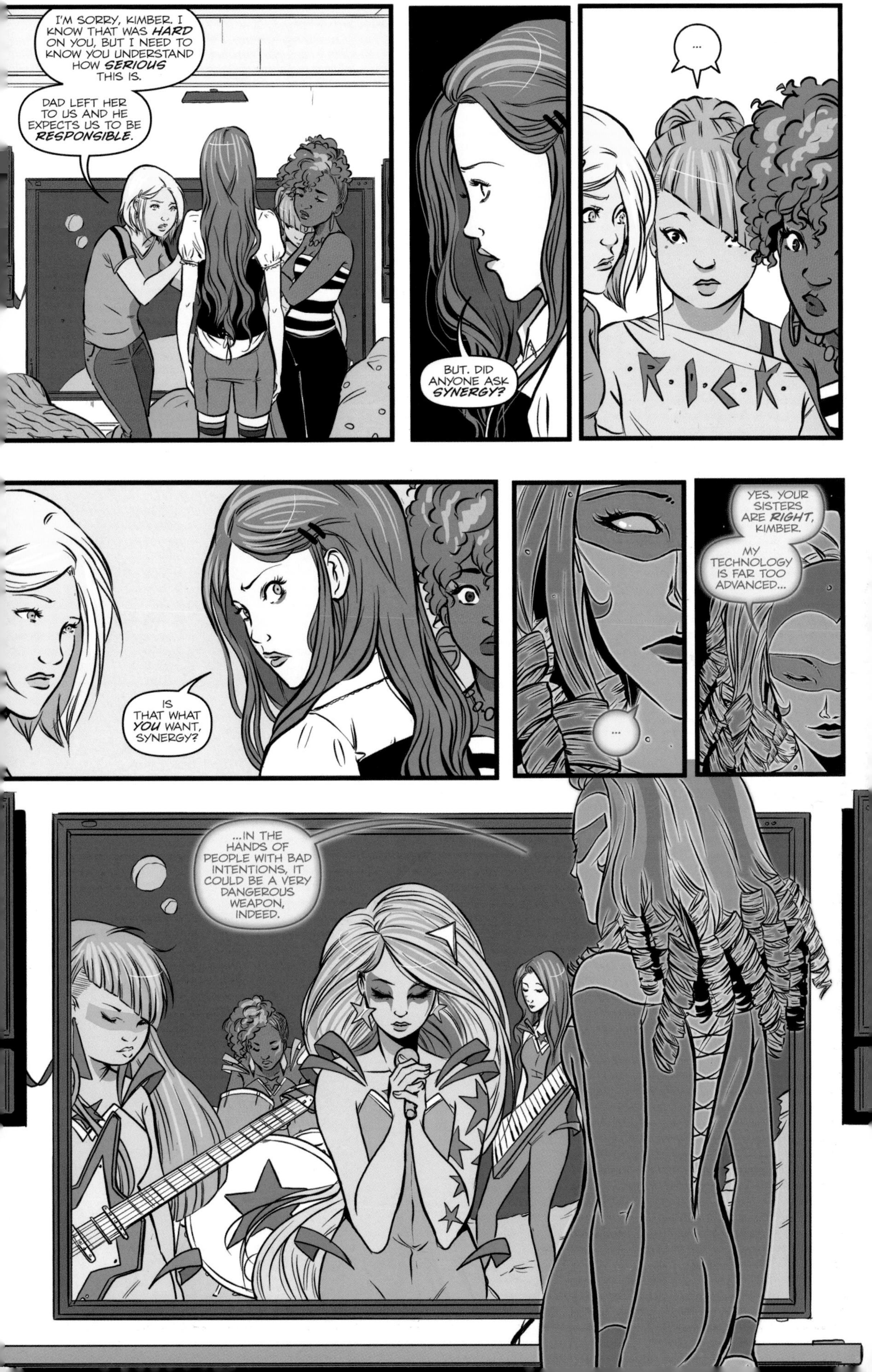
I'M SORRY, KIMBER. I KNOW THAT WAS HARD ON YOU, BUT I NEED TO KNOW YOU UNDERSTAND HOW SERIOUS THIS IS.
DAD LEFT HER TO US AND HE EXPECTS US TO BE RESPONSIBLE.
BUT. DID ANYONE ASK SYNERGY?
...
IS THAT WHAT YOU WANT, SYNERGY?
...
YES. YOUR SISTERS ARE RIGHT, KIMBER.
MY TECHNOLOGY IS FAR TOO ADVANCED...
...IN THE HANDS OF PEOPLE WITH BAD INTENTIONS, IT COULD BE A VERY DANGEROUS WEAPON, INDEED.

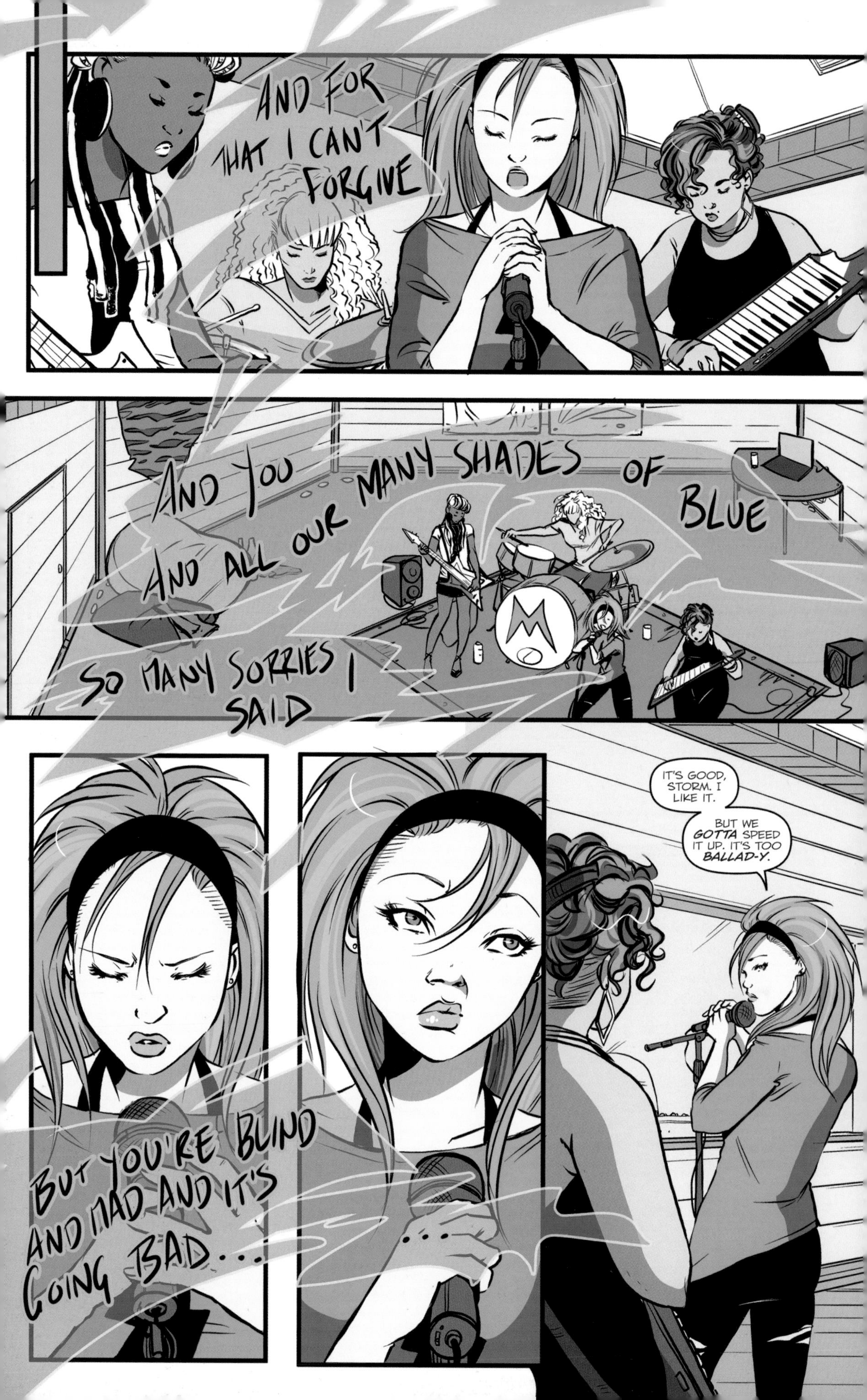
AND FOR THAT I CAN'T FORGIVE
AND YOU AND ALL OUR MANY SHADES OF BLUE
SO MANY SORRIES I SAID
BUT YOU'RE BLIND AND MAD AND IT'S GOING BAD...
...
IT'S GOOD, STORM. I LIKE IT.
BUT WE GOTTA SPEED IT UP. IT'S TOO BALLAD-Y.

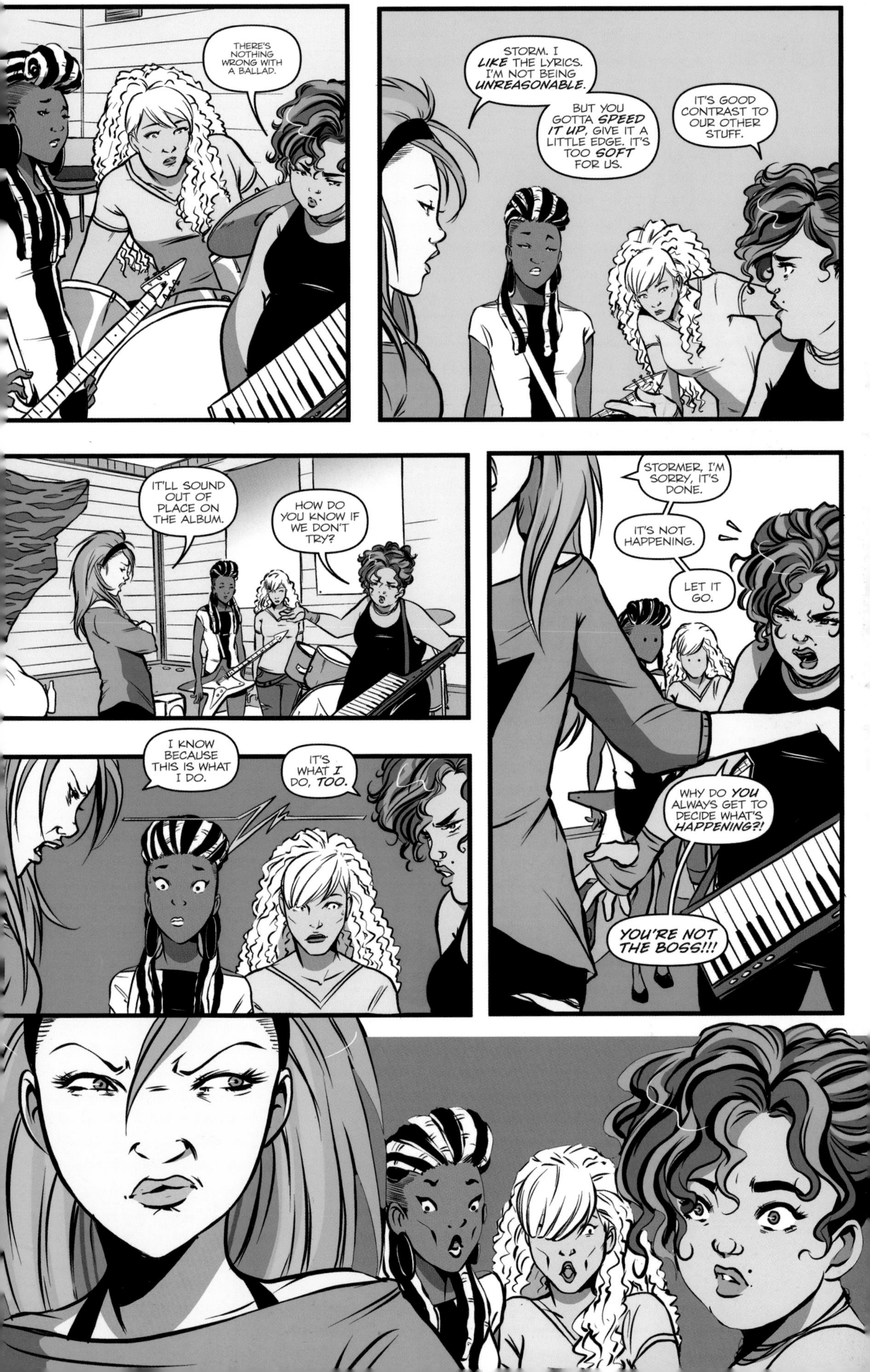

THERE'S NOTHING WRONG WITH A BALLAD.
STORM. I LIKE THE LYRICS. I'M NOT BEING UNREASONABLE.
BUT YOU GOTTA SPEED IT UP, GIVE IT A LITTLE EDGE. IT'S TOO SOFT FOR US.
IT'S GOOD CONTRAST TO OUR OTHER STUFF.
IT'LL SOUND OUT OF PLACE ON THE ALBUM.
HOW DO YOU KNOW IF WE DON'T TRY?
I KNOW BECAUSE THIS IS WHAT I DO.
IT'S WHAT I DO, TOO.
STORMER, I'M SORRY, IT'S DONE.
IT'S NOT HAPPENING.
LET IT GO.
WHY DO YOU ALWAYS GET TO DECIDE WHAT'S HAPPENING?!
YOU'RE NOT THE BOSS!!!

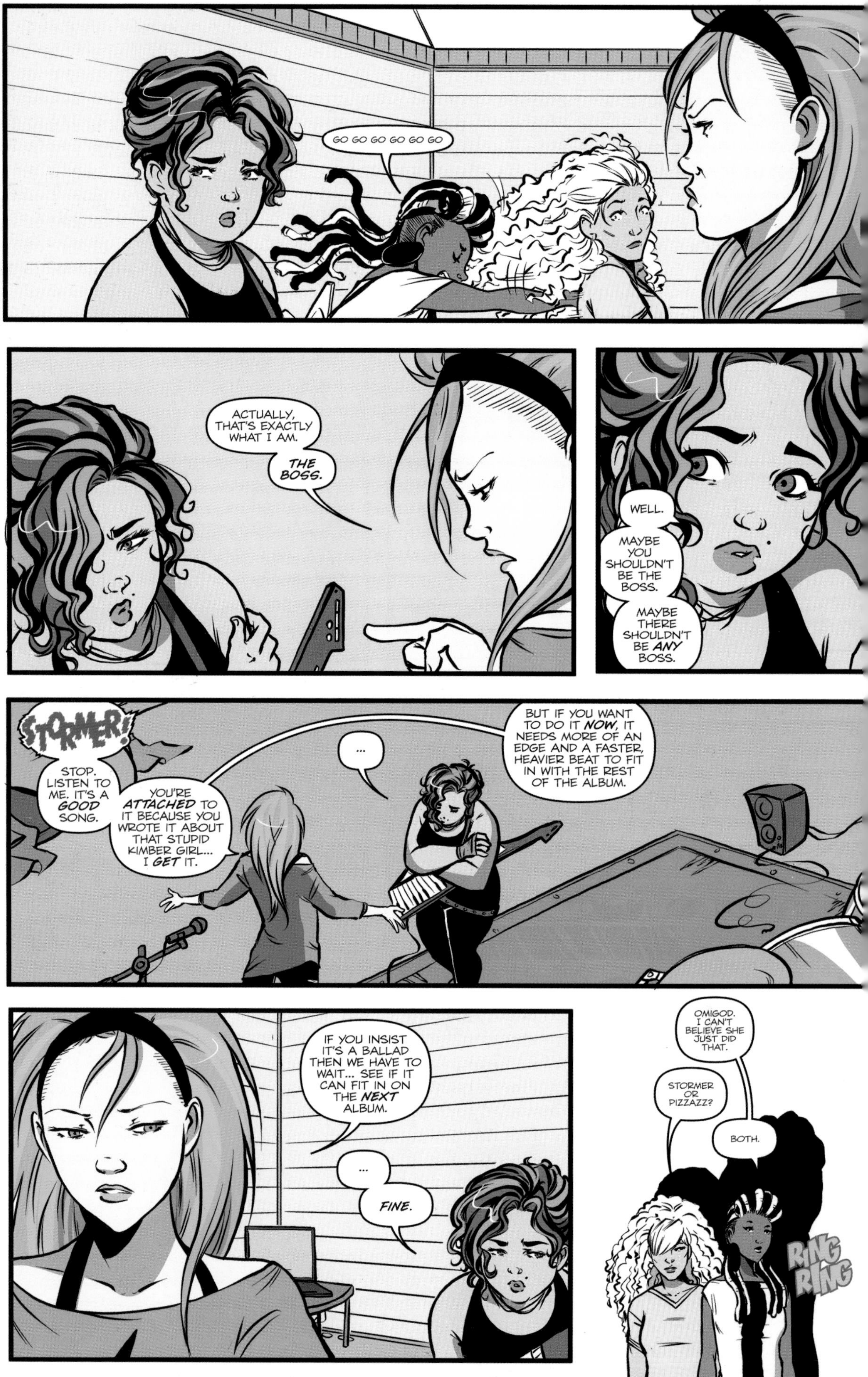
GO GO GO GO GO GO
ACTUALLY, THAT'S EXACTLY WHAT I AM.
THE BOSS.
WELL.
MAYBE YOU SHOULDN'T BE THE BOSS.
MAYBE THERE SHOULDN'T BE ANY BOSS.
STORMER!
STOP. LISTEN TO ME. IT'S A GOOD SONG.
YOU'RE ATTACHED TO IT BECAUSE YOU WROTE IT ABOUT THAT STUPID KIMBER GIRL... I GET IT.
...
BUT IF YOU WANT TO DO IT NOW, IT NEEDS MORE OF AN EDGE AND A FASTER, HEAVIER BEAT TO FIT IN WITH THE REST OF THE ALBUM.
IF YOU INSIST IT'S A BALLAD THEN WE HAVE TO WAIT... SEE IF IT CAN FIT IN ON THE NEXT ALBUM.
...
FINE.
OMIGOD. I CAN'T BELIEVE SHE JUST DID THAT.
STORMER OR PIZZAZZ?
BOTH.
RING RING

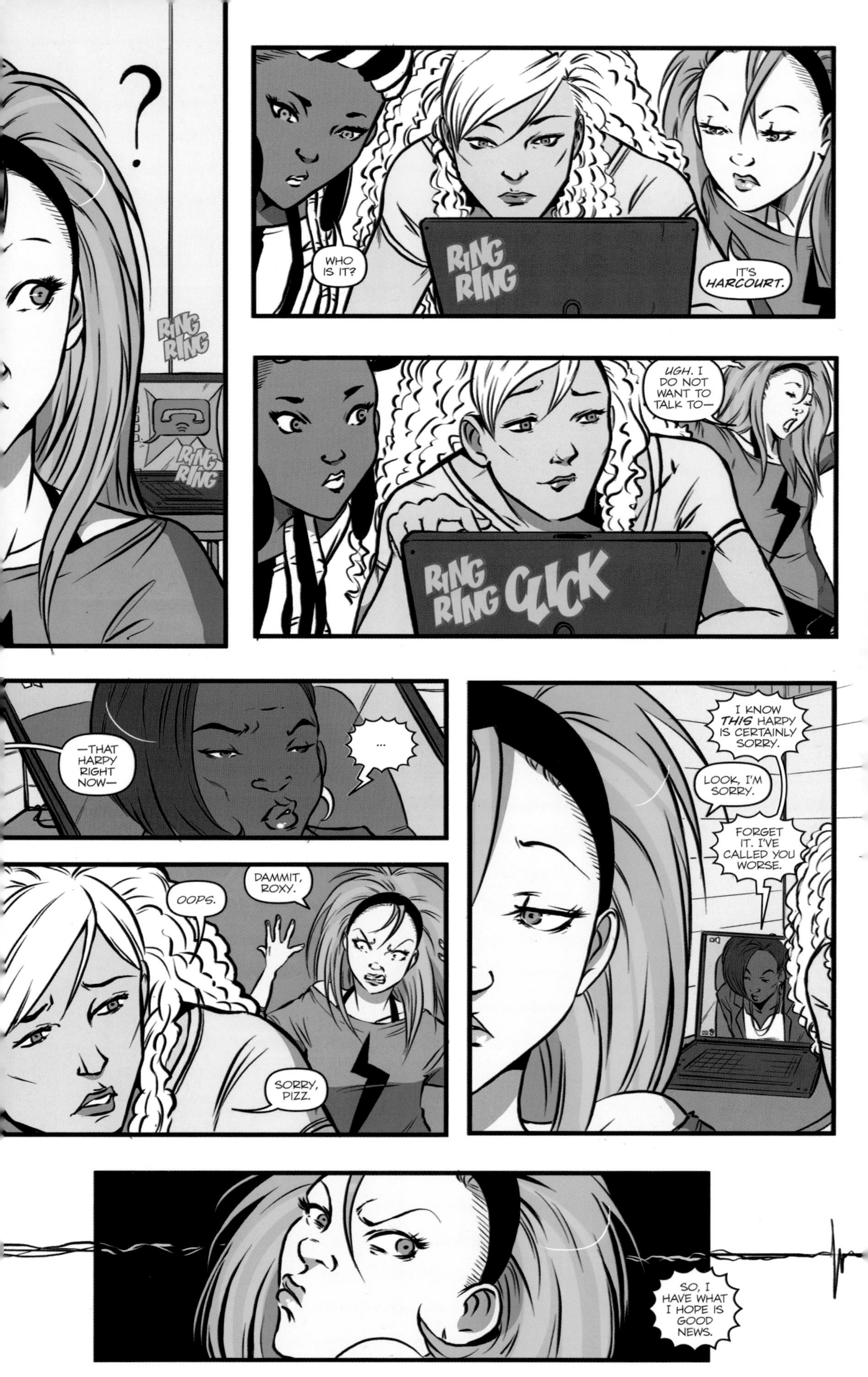
?
RING RING
RING RING
WHO IS IT?
RING RING
IT'S HARCOURT.
UGH. I DO NOT WANT TO TALK TO—
RING RING CLICK
—THAT HARPY RIGHT NOW—
...
OOPS.
DAMMIT, ROXY.
SORRY, PIZZ.
I KNOW THIS HARPY IS CERTAINLY SORRY.
LOOK, I'M SORRY.
FORGET IT. I'VE CALLED YOU WORSE.
SO, I HAVE WHAT I HOPE IS GOOD NEWS.

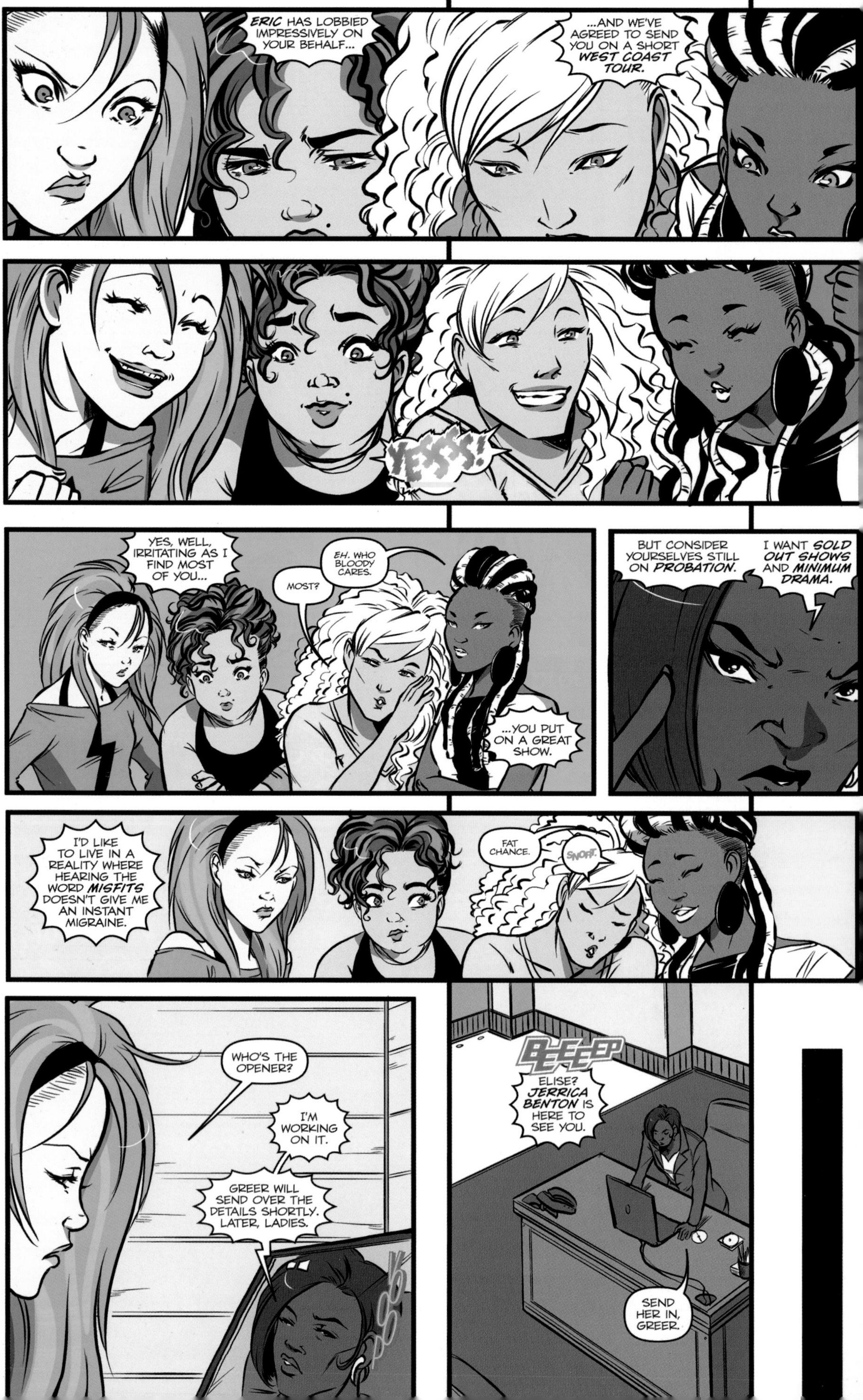
ERIC HAS LOBBIED IMPRESSIVELY ON YOUR BEHALF...
...AND WE'VE AGREED TO SEND YOU ON A SHORT WEST COAST TOUR.
YESSSS!
YES, WELL, IRRITATING AS I FIND MOST OF YOU...
MOST?
EH. WHO BLOODY CARES.
...YOU PUT ON A GREAT SHOW.
BUT CONSIDER YOURSELVES STILL ON PROBATION.
I WANT SOLD OUT SHOWS AND MINIMUM DRAMA.
I'D LIKE TO LIVE IN A REALITY WHERE HEARING THE WORD MISFITS DOESN'T GIVE ME AN INSTANT MIGRAINE.
FAT CHANCE.
SNORT.
WHO'S THE OPENER?
I'M WORKING ON IT.
GREER WILL SEND OVER THE DETAILS SHORTLY. LATER, LADIES.
BEEEEP
ELISE? JERICA BENTON IS HERE TO SEE YOU.
SEND HER IN, GREER.

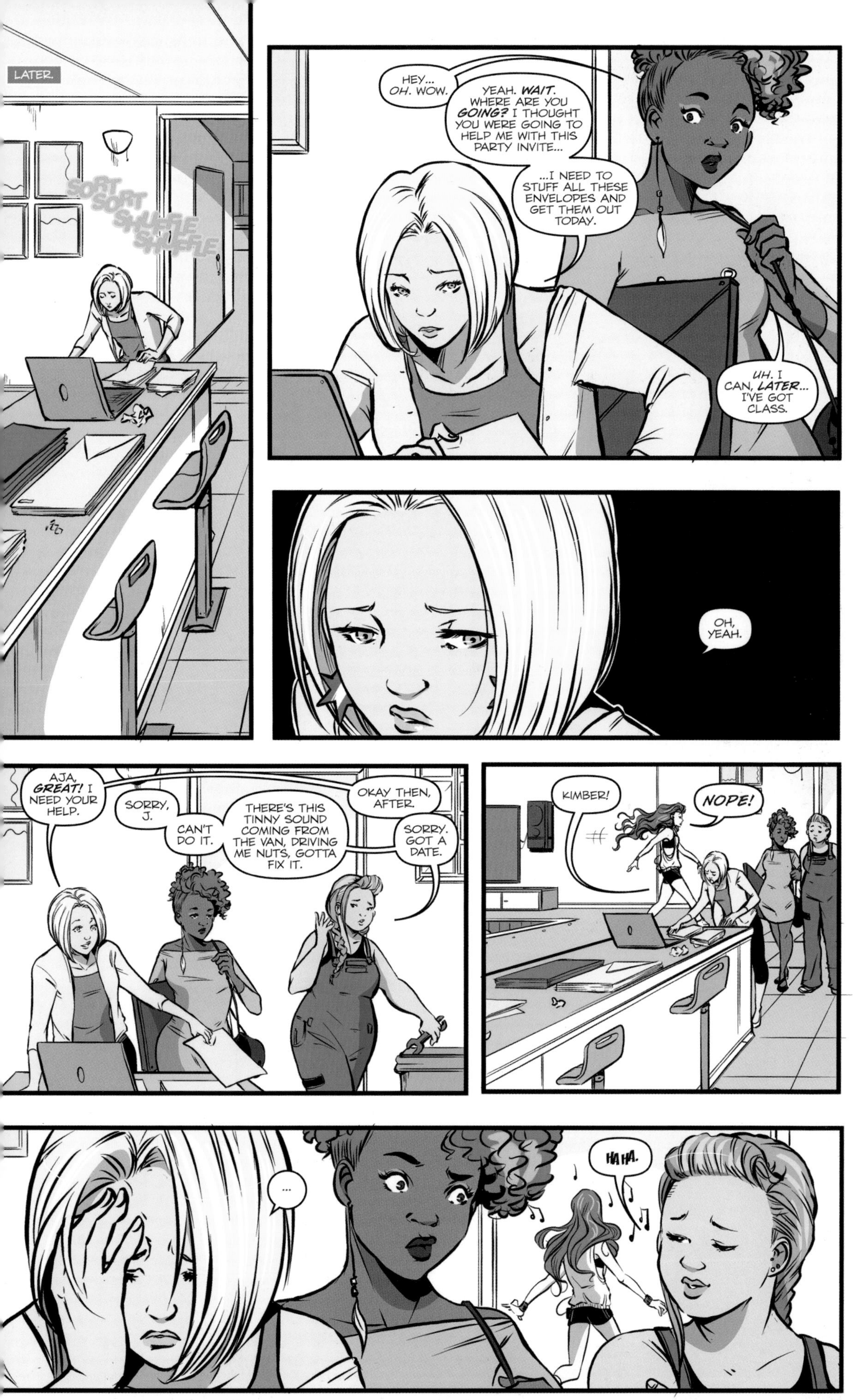

LATER.
SORT SORT
SHUFFLE SHUFFLE
HEY... OH. WOW.
YEAH. WAIT. WHERE ARE YOU GOING? I THOUGHT YOU WERE GOING TO HELP ME WITH THIS PARTY INVITE...
...I NEED TO STUFF ALL THESE ENVELOPES AND GET THEM OUT TODAY.
UH. I CAN, LATER... I'VE GOT CLASS.
OH, YEAH.
AJA, GREAT! I NEED YOUR HELP.
SORRY, J.
CAN'T DO IT.
THERE'S THIS TINNY SOUND COMING FROM THE VAN, DRIVING ME NUTS, GOTTA FIX IT.
OKAY THEN, AFTER.
SORRY. GOT A DATE.
KIMBER!
NOPE!
...
HA HA.

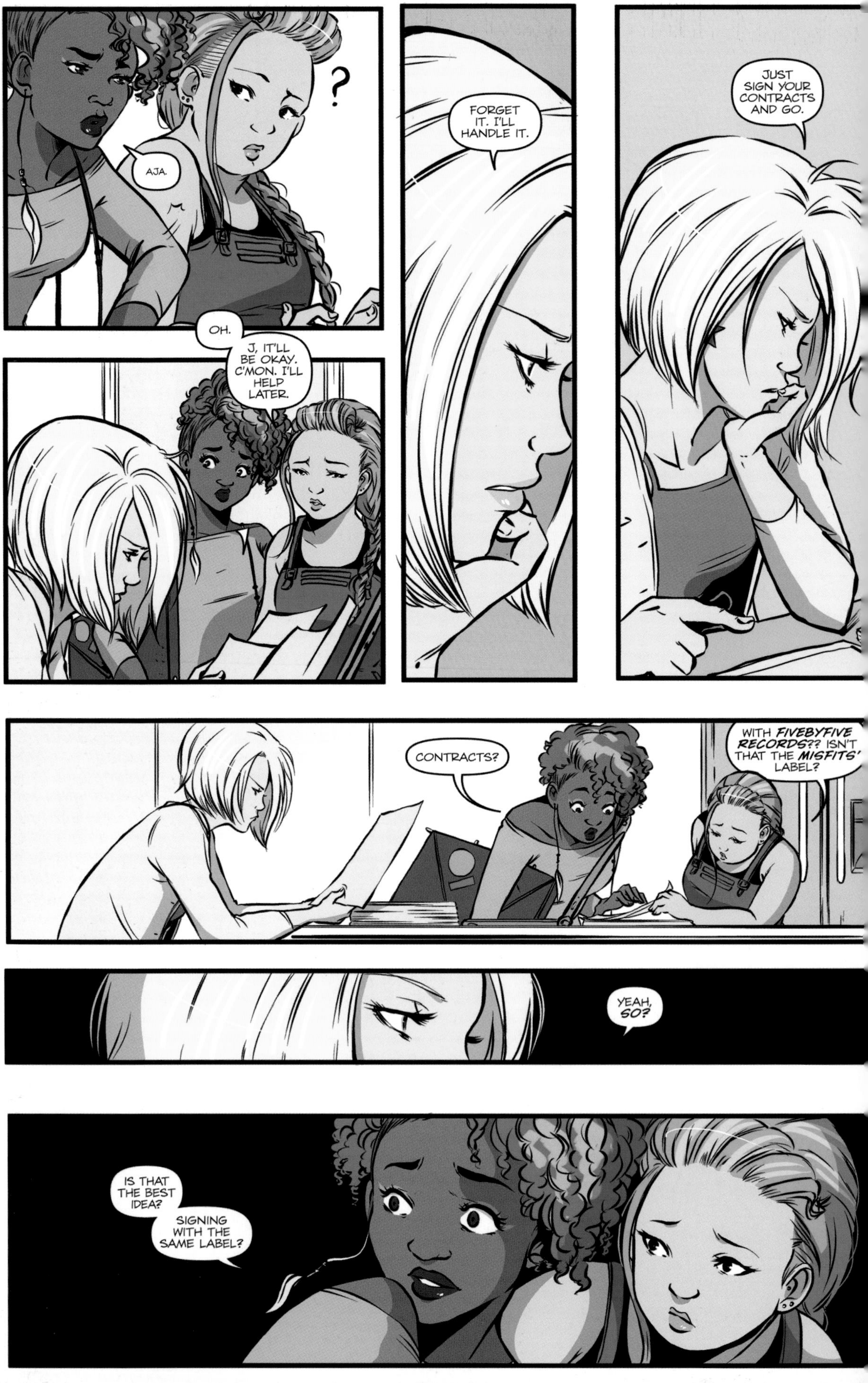
?
AJA.
FORGET IT. I'LL HANDLE IT.
JUST SIGN YOUR CONTRACTS AND GO.
OH.
J, IT'LL BE OKAY. C'MON. I'LL HELP LATER.
CONTRACTS?
WITH FIVEBYFIVE RECORDS?? ISN'T THAT THE MISFITS' LABEL?
YEAH, SO?
IS THAT THE BEST IDEA?
SIGNING WITH THE SAME LABEL?

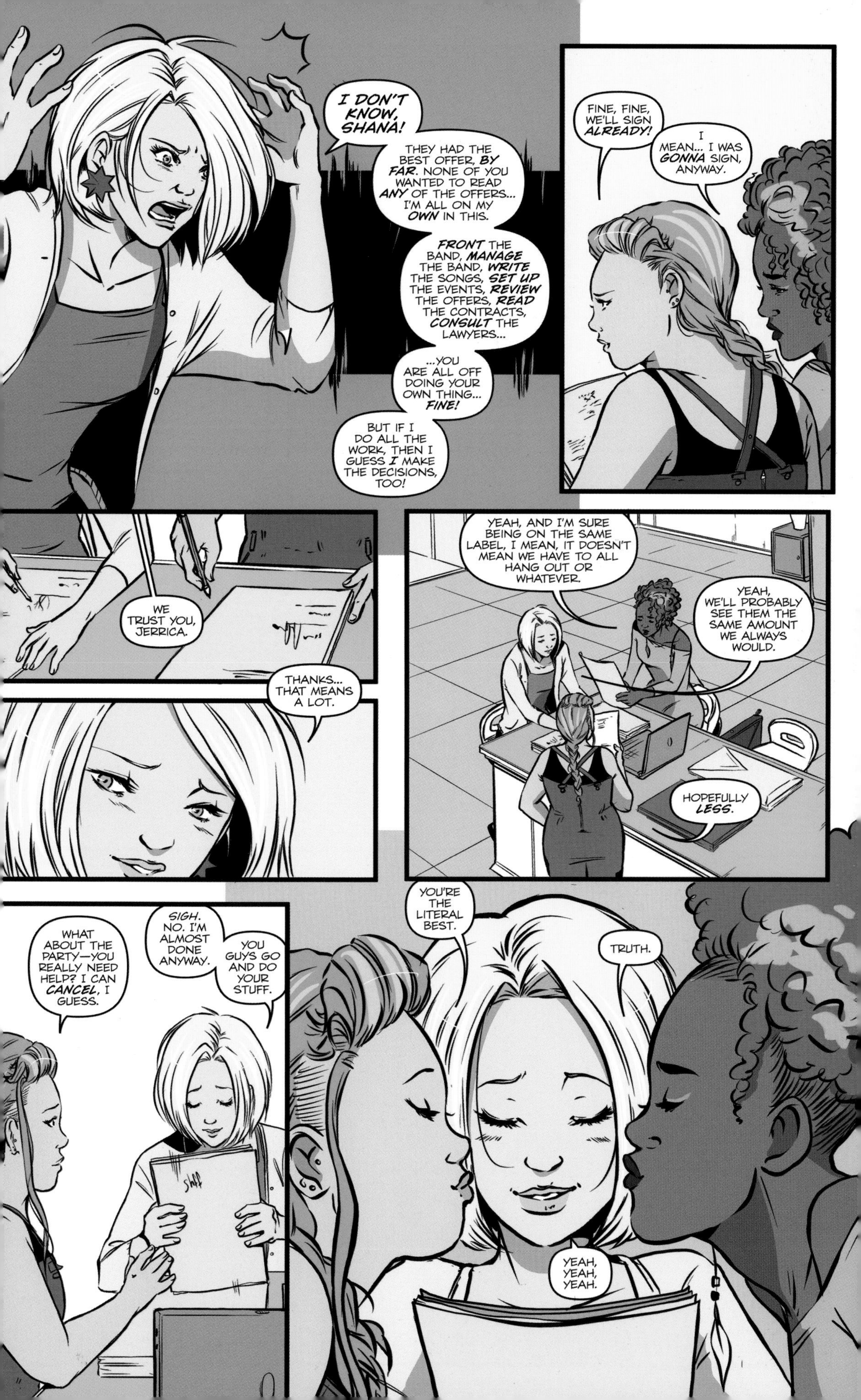
I DON'T KNOW, SHANA!
THEY HAD THE BEST OFFER, BY FAR. NONE OF YOU WANTED TO READ ANY OF THE OFFERS... I'M ALL ON MY OWN IN THIS.
FRONT THE BAND, MANAGE THE BAND, WRITE THE SONGS, SET UP THE EVENTS, REVIEW THE OFFERS, READ THE CONTRACTS, CONSULT THE LAWYERS...
...YOU ARE ALL OFF DOING YOUR OWN THING... FINE!
BUT IF I DO ALL THE WORK, THEN I GUESS I MAKE THE DECISIONS, TOO!
FINE, FINE, WE'LL SIGN ALREADY!
I MEAN... I WAS GONNA SIGN, ANYWAY.
WE TRUST YOU, JERRICA.
THANKS... THAT MEANS A LOT.
YEAH, AND I'M SURE BEING ON THE SAME LABEL, I MEAN, IT DOESN'T MEAN WE HAVE TO ALL HANG OUT OR WHATEVER.
YEAH, WE'LL PROBABLY SEE THEM THE SAME AMOUNT WE ALWAYS WOULD.
HOPEFULLY LESS.
WHAT ABOUT THE PARTY—YOU REALLY NEED HELP? I CAN CANCEL, I GUESS.
SIGH. NO. I'M ALMOST DONE ANYWAY.
YOU GUYS GO AND DO YOUR STUFF.
YOU'RE THE LITERAL BEST.
TRUTH.
YEAH, YEAH, YEAH.

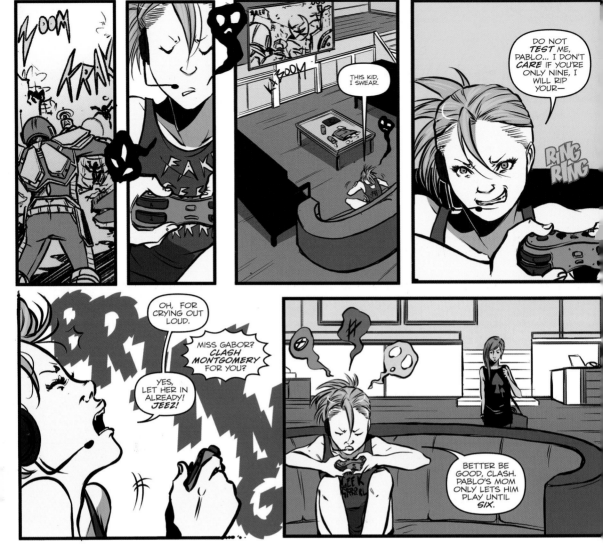

ZOOM

KRAK

THIS KID, I SWEAR.

DO NOT *TEST* ME, PABLO... I DON'T *CARE* IF YOU'RE ONLY NINE, I WILL RIP YOUR—

RING RING

BRRING

OH, FOR CRYING OUT LOUD.

MISS GABOR? *CLASH MONTGOMERY* FOR YOU?

YES, LET HER IN ALREADY! *JEEZ!*

BETTER BE GOOD, CLASH. PABLO'S MOM ONLY LETS HIM PLAY UNTIL *SIX*.

WHAT DID YOU...?!

YOU LITTLE—

—*YOUR* MOMMA, PABLO. *YOUR* MOMMA.

...

GOTTA GO, PABLO. CATCH YOU TOMORROW.

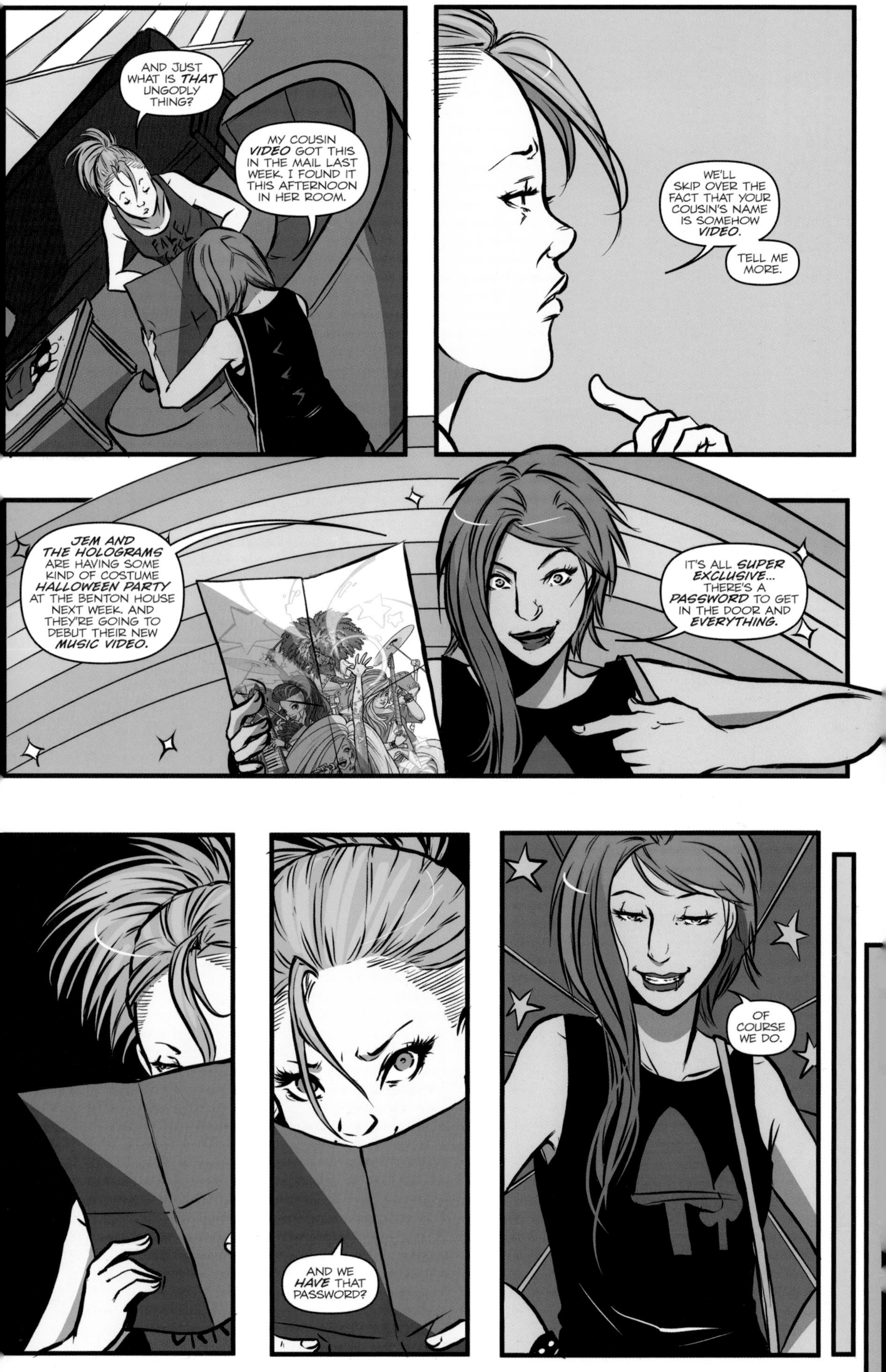
AND JUST WHAT IS THAT UNGODLY THING?
MY COUSIN VIDEO GOT THIS IN THE MAIL LAST WEEK. I FOUND IT THIS AFTERNOON IN HER ROOM.
WE'LL SKIP OVER THE FACT THAT YOUR COUSIN'S NAME IS SOMEHOW VIDEO.
TELL ME MORE.
JEM AND THE HOLOGRAMS ARE HAVING SOME KIND OF COSTUME HALLOWEEN PARTY AT THE BENTON HOUSE NEXT WEEK. AND THEY'RE GOING TO DEBUT THEIR NEW MUSIC VIDEO.
IT'S ALL SUPER EXCLUSIVE... THERE'S A PASSWORD TO GET IN THE DOOR AND EVERYTHING.
AND WE HAVE THAT PASSWORD?
OF COURSE WE DO.

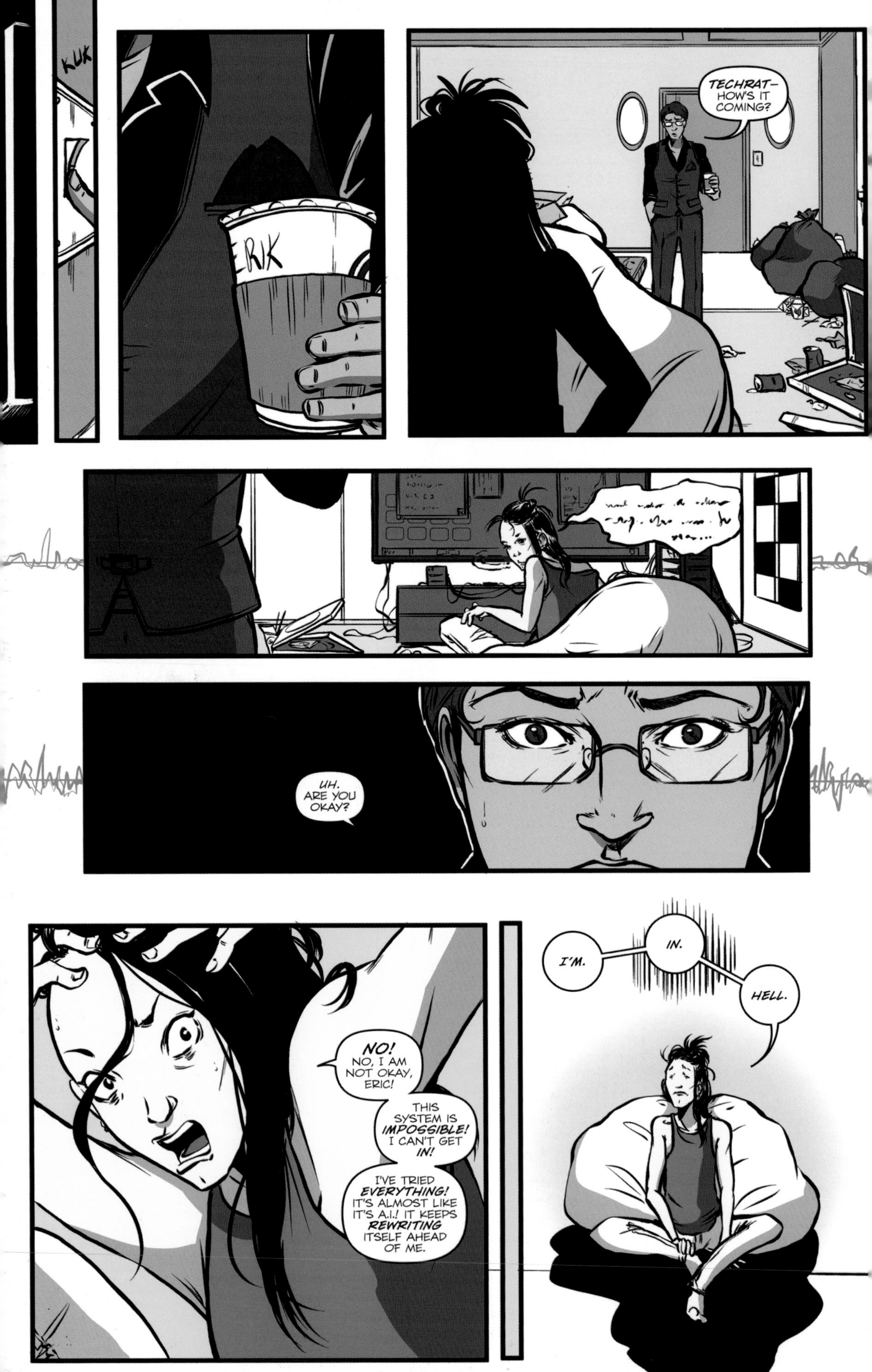
KLIK
ERIK
TECHRAT— HOW'S IT COMING?
UH. ARE YOU OKAY?
NO! NO, I AM NOT OKAY, ERIC!
THIS SYSTEM IS IMPOSSIBLE! I CAN'T GET IN!
I'VE TRIED EVERYTHING! IT'S ALMOST LIKE IT'S A.I.! IT KEEPS REWRITING ITSELF AHEAD OF ME.
I'M.
IN.
HELL.

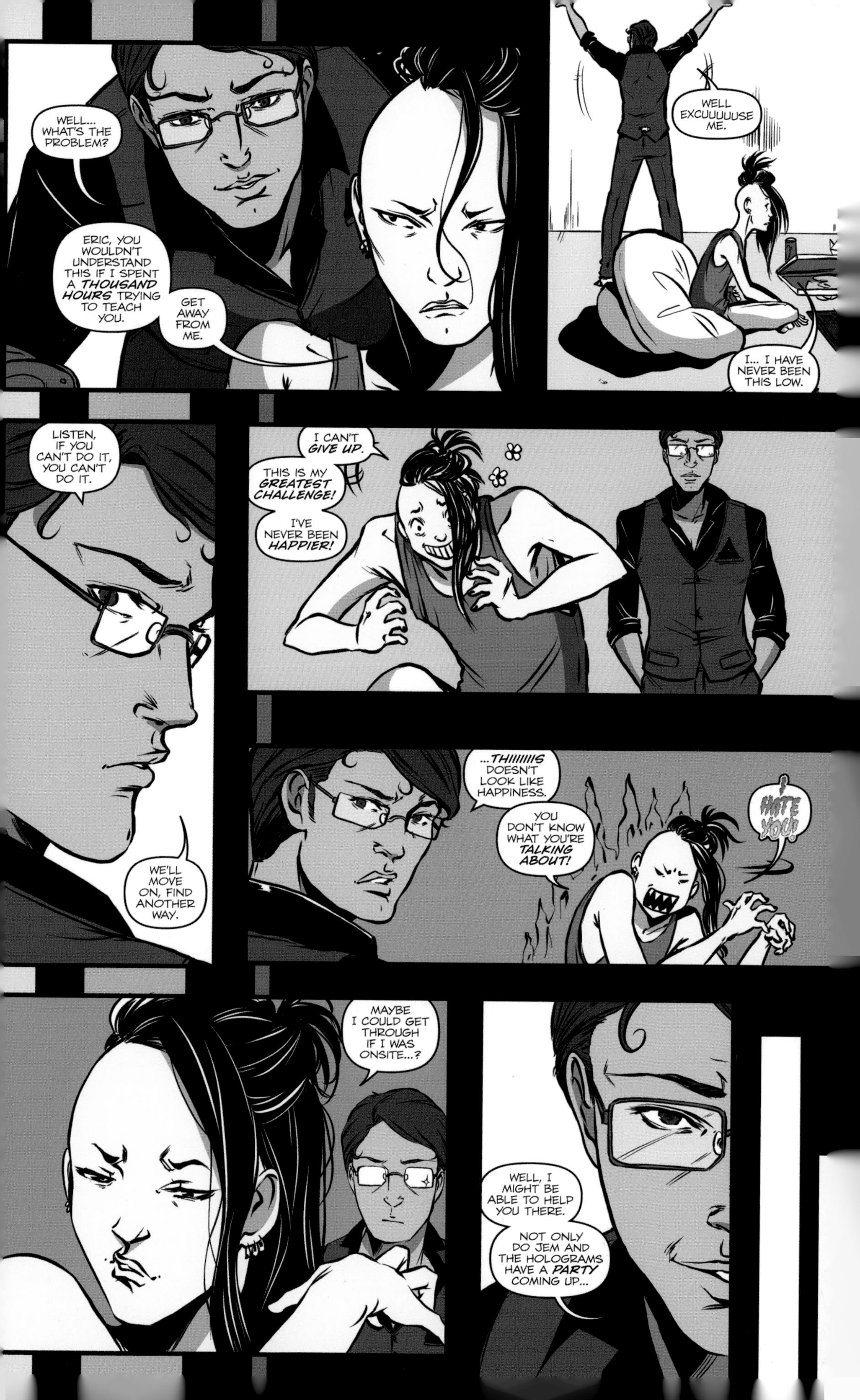
WELL... WHAT'S THE PROBLEM?
ERIC, YOU WOULDN'T UNDERSTAND THIS IF I SPENT A **THOUSAND HOURS** TRYING TO TEACH YOU.
GET AWAY FROM ME.
WELL EXCUUUUUSE ME.
I... I HAVE NEVER BEEN THIS LOW.
LISTEN, IF YOU CAN'T DO IT, YOU CAN'T DO IT.
WE'LL MOVE ON, FIND ANOTHER WAY.
I CAN'T ***GIVE UP.***
THIS IS MY ***GREATEST CHALLENGE!***
I'VE NEVER BEEN ***HAPPIER!***
...***THIIIIIIS*** DOESN'T LOOK LIKE HAPPINESS.
YOU DON'T KNOW WHAT YOU'RE ***TALKING ABOUT!***
I HATE YOU!
MAYBE I COULD GET THROUGH IF I WAS ONSITE...?
WELL, I MIGHT BE ABLE TO HELP YOU THERE.
NOT ONLY DO JEM AND THE HOLOGRAMS HAVE A ***PARTY*** COMING UP...

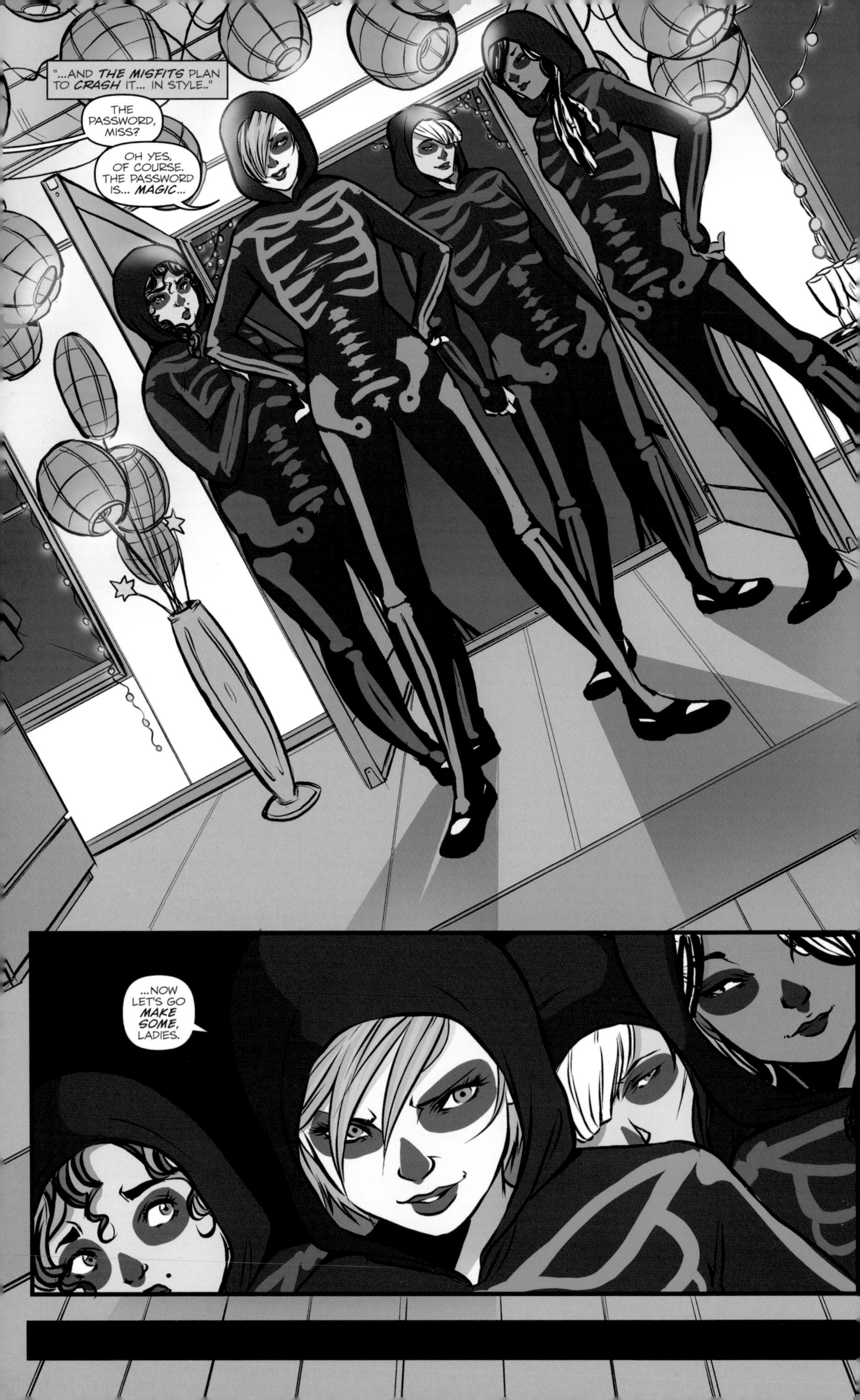
"...AND THE MISFITS PLAN TO CRASH IT... IN STYLE.."
THE PASSWORD, MISS?
OH YES, OF COURSE. THE PASSWORD IS... MAGIC...
...NOW LET'S GO MAKE SOME, LADIES.

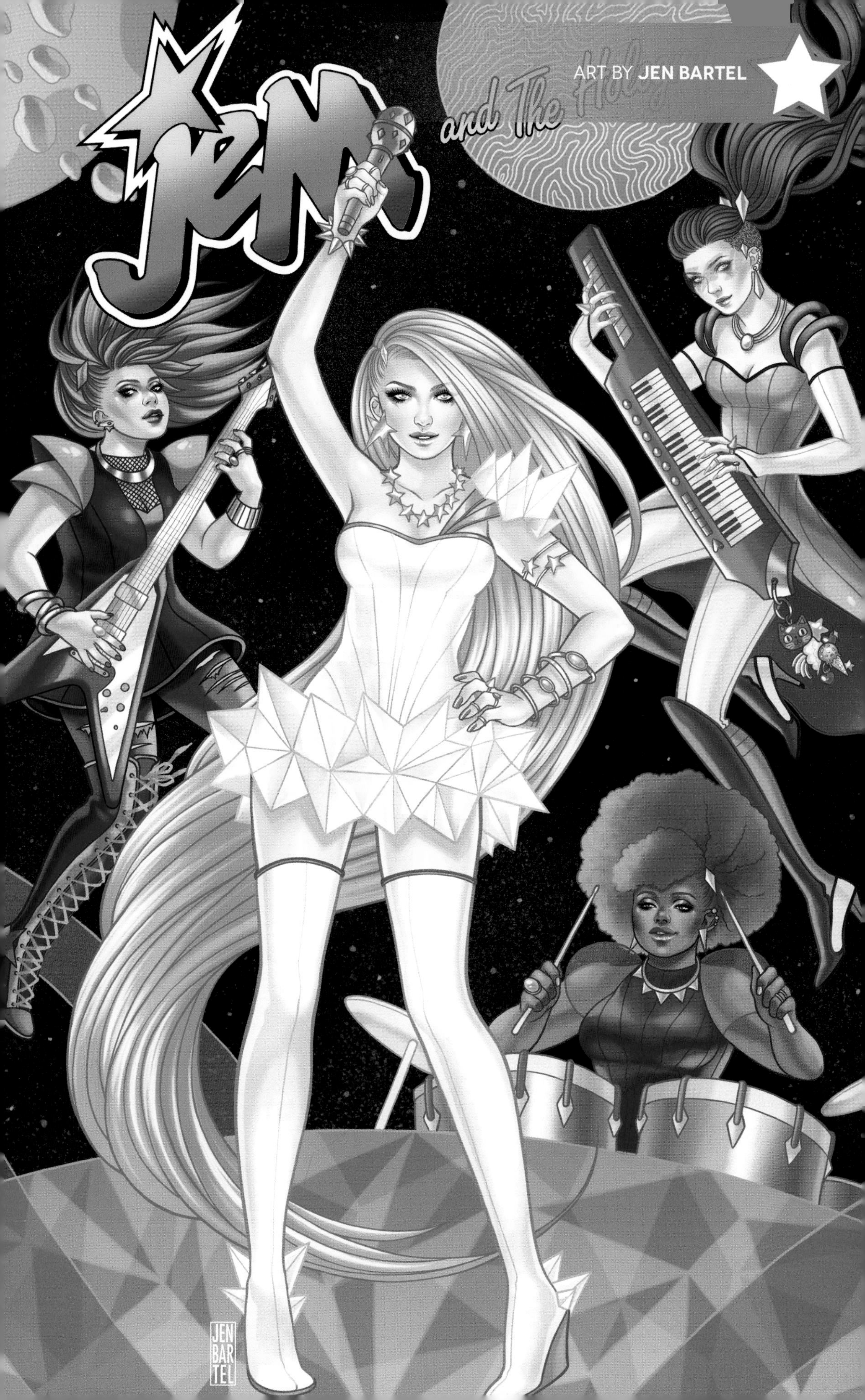
ART BY JEN BARTEL
Jem
and The Holograms
JEN BARTEL

4

ART BY **EMMA VIECELI**

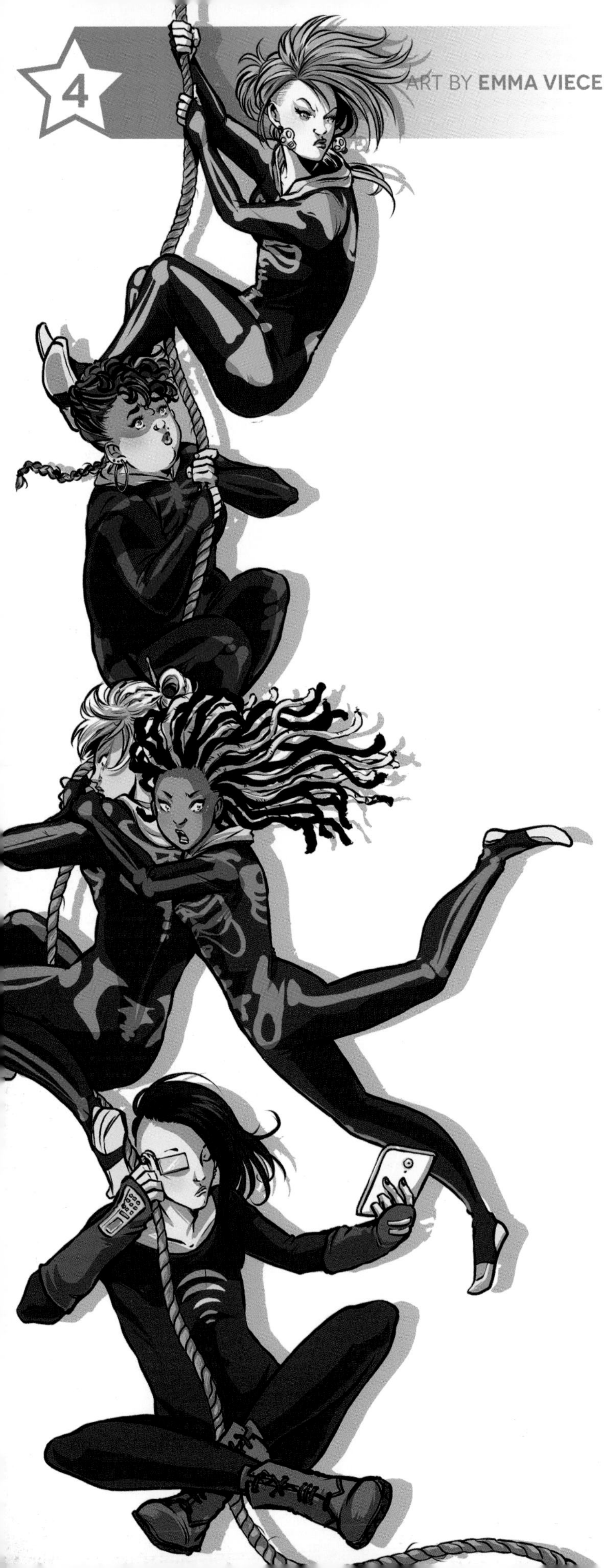

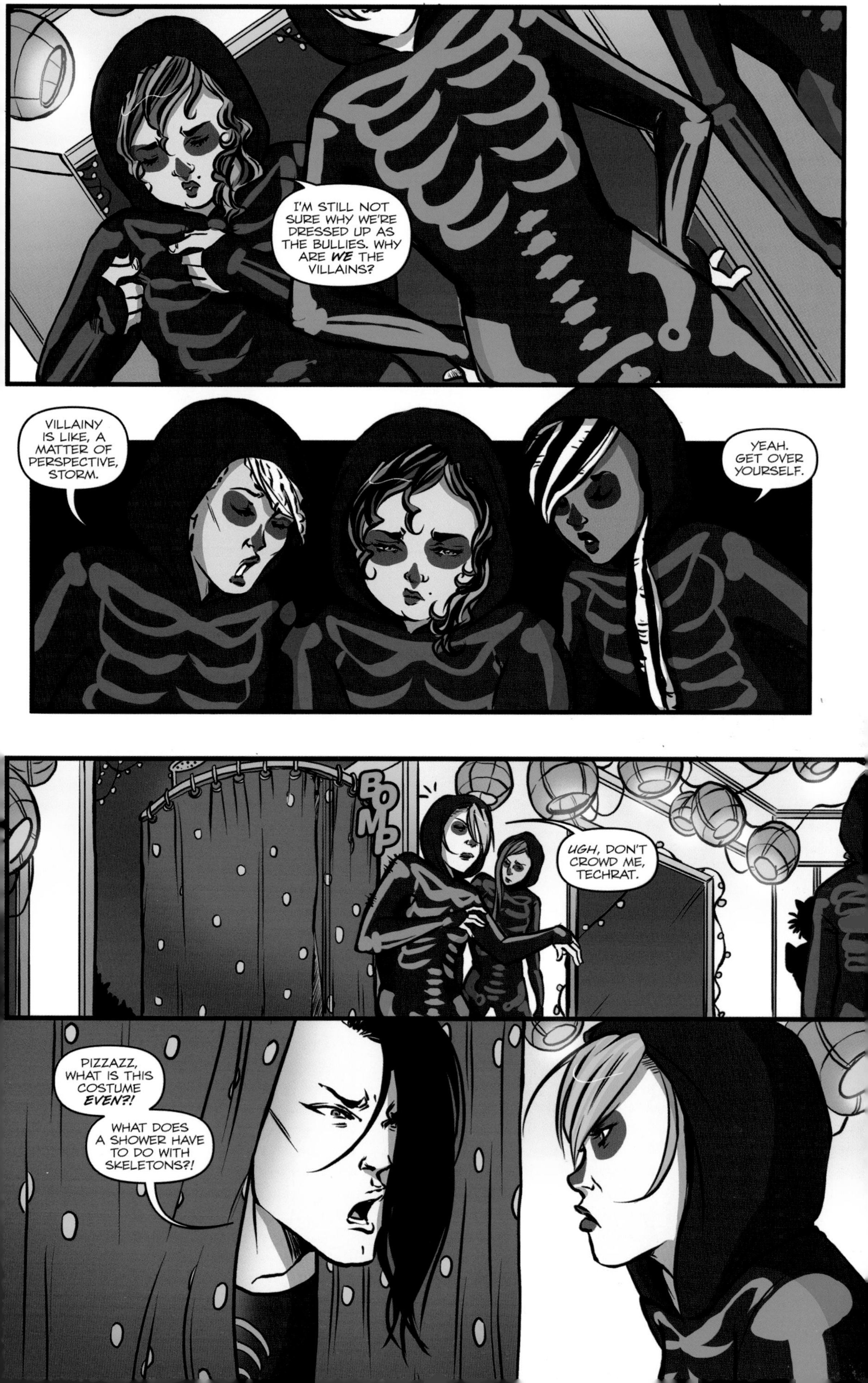

I'M STILL NOT SURE WHY WE'RE DRESSED UP AS THE BULLIES. WHY ARE *WE* THE VILLAINS?
VILLAINY IS LIKE, A MATTER OF PERSPECTIVE, STORM.
YEAH. GET OVER YOURSELF.
BOMP
UGH, DON'T CROWD ME, TECHRAT.
PIZZAZZ, WHAT IS THIS COSTUME *EVEN?!*
WHAT DOES A SHOWER HAVE TO DO WITH SKELETONS?!

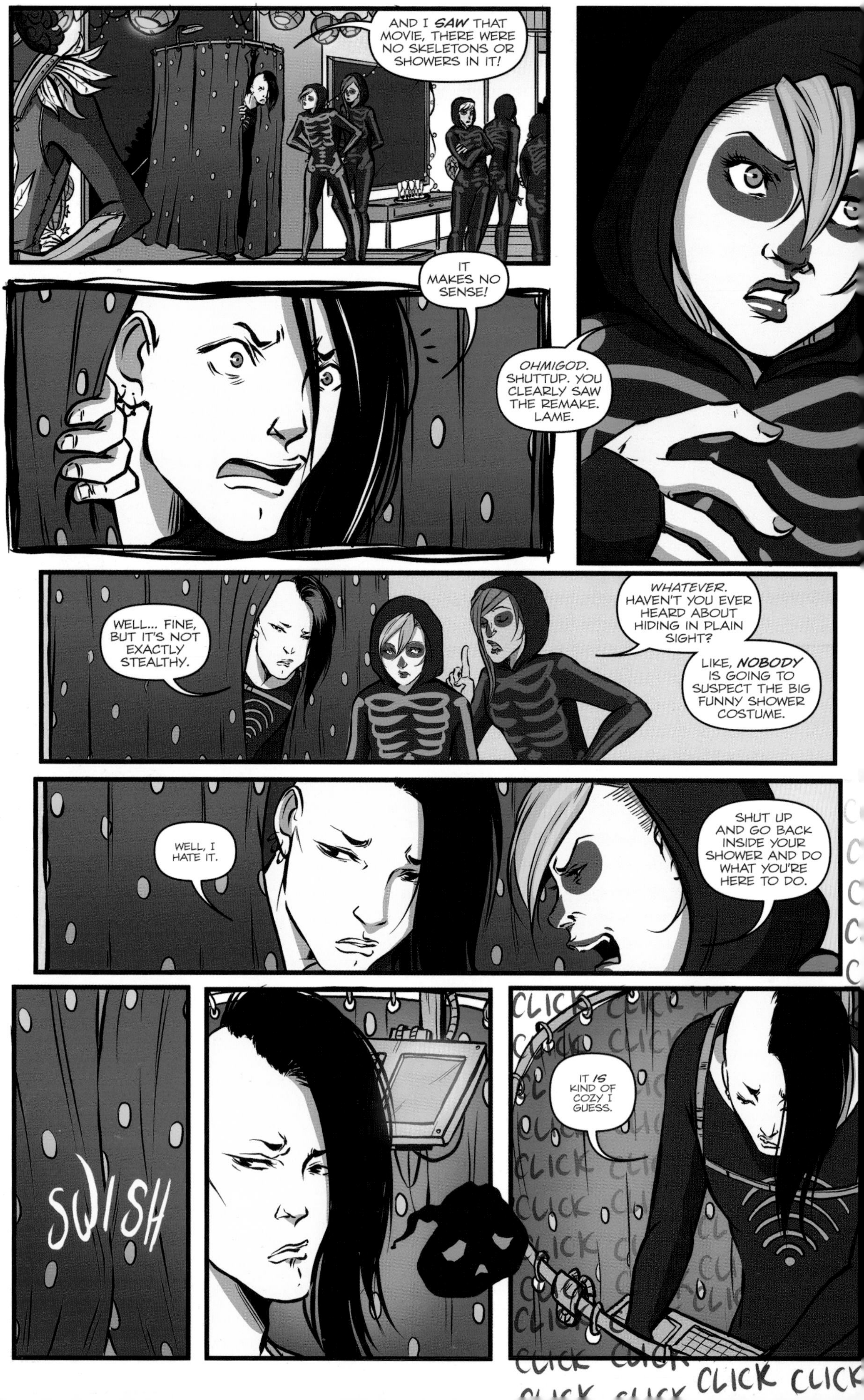

AND I SAW THAT MOVIE, THERE WERE NO SKELETONS OR SHOWERS IN IT!
IT MAKES NO SENSE!
OHMIGOD. SHUTTUP. YOU CLEARLY SAW THE REMAKE. LAME.
WELL... FINE, BUT IT'S NOT EXACTLY STEALTHY.
WHATEVER. HAVEN'T YOU EVER HEARD ABOUT HIDING IN PLAIN SIGHT?
LIKE, NOBODY IS GOING TO SUSPECT THE BIG FUNNY SHOWER COSTUME.
WELL, I HATE IT.
SHUT UP AND GO BACK INSIDE YOUR SHOWER AND DO WHAT YOU'RE HERE TO DO.
SWISH
IT IS KIND OF COZY I GUESS.
CLICK CLICK CLICK CLICK

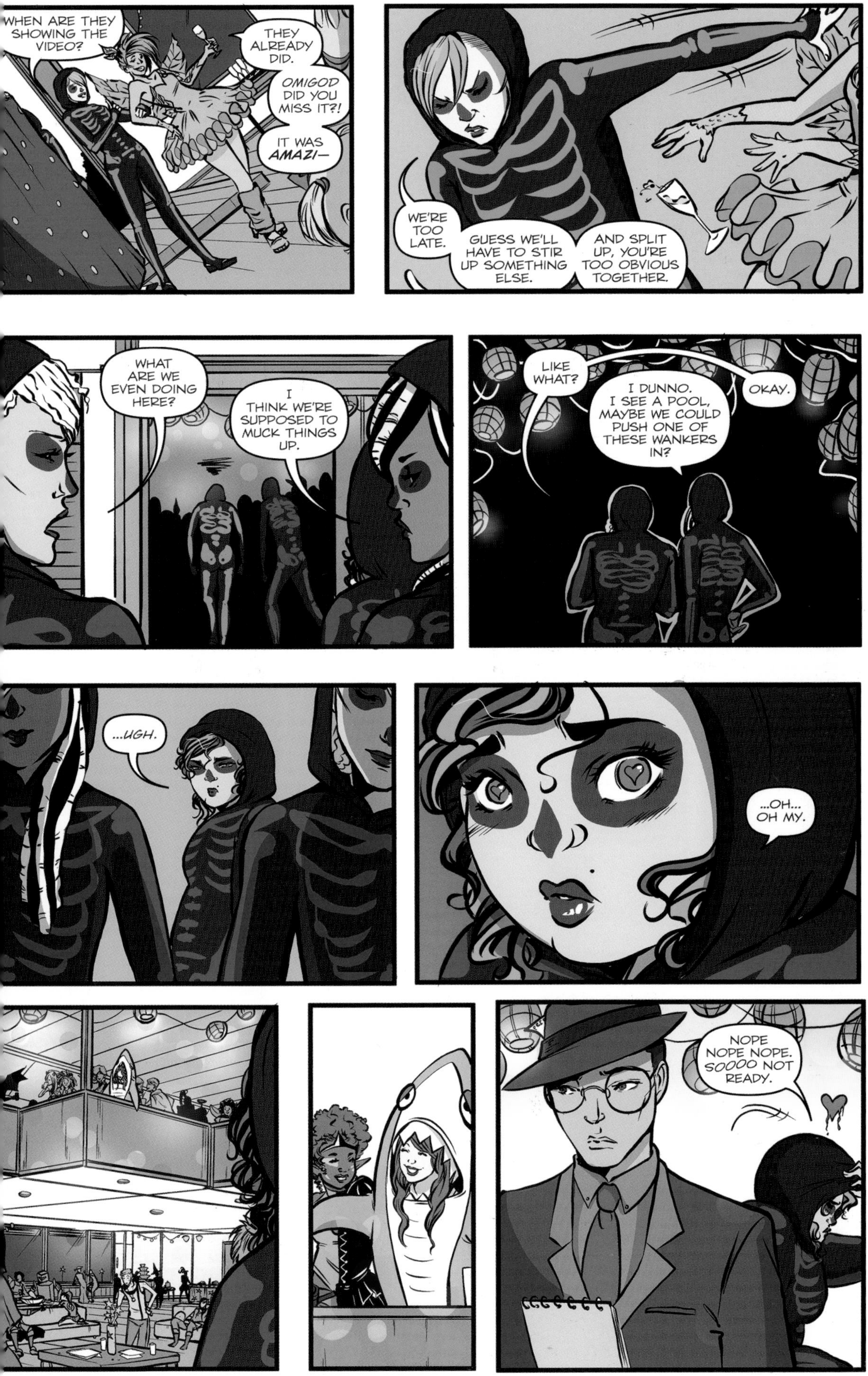
WHEN ARE THEY SHOWING THE VIDEO?
THEY ALREADY DID.
OMIGOD DID YOU MISS IT?!
IT WAS AMAZI—
WE'RE TOO LATE.
GUESS WE'LL HAVE TO STIR UP SOMETHING ELSE.
AND SPLIT UP, YOU'RE TOO OBVIOUS TOGETHER.
WHAT ARE WE EVEN DOING HERE?
I THINK WE'RE SUPPOSED TO MUCK THINGS UP.
LIKE WHAT?
I DUNNO. I SEE A POOL, MAYBE WE COULD PUSH ONE OF THESE WANKERS IN?
OKAY.
...UGH.
...OH... OH MY.
NOPE NOPE NOPE. SOOOO NOT READY.

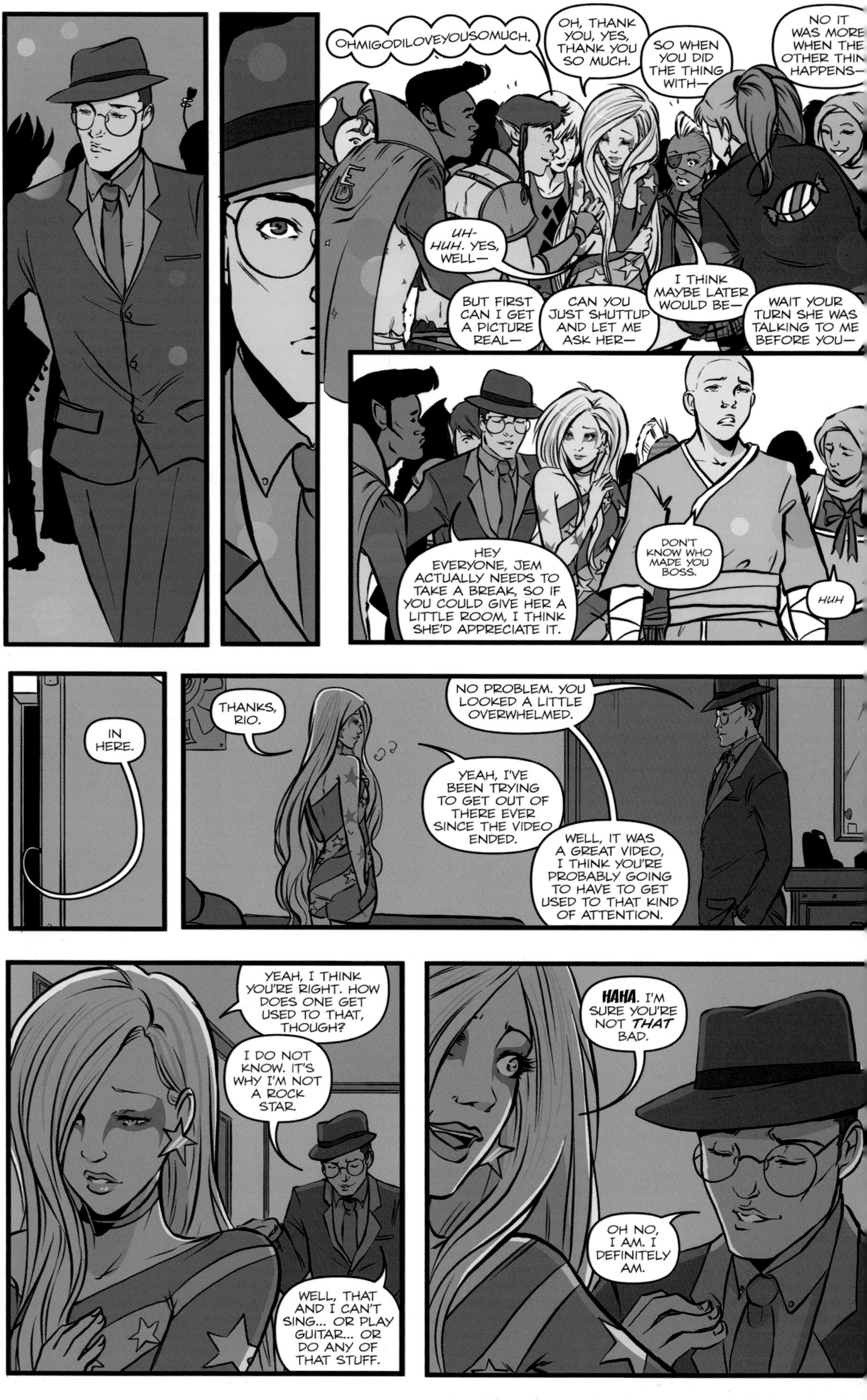

OHMIGODILOVEYOUSOMUCH.
OH, THANK YOU, YES, THANK YOU SO MUCH.
SO WHEN YOU DID THE THING WITH—
NO IT WAS MORE WHEN THE OTHER THIN HAPPENS—
UH-HUH. YES, WELL—
BUT FIRST CAN I GET A PICTURE REAL—
CAN YOU JUST SHUTTUP AND LET ME ASK HER—
I THINK MAYBE LATER WOULD BE—
WAIT YOUR TURN SHE WAS TALKING TO ME BEFORE YOU—
HEY EVERYONE, JEM ACTUALLY NEEDS TO TAKE A BREAK, SO IF YOU COULD GIVE HER A LITTLE ROOM, I THINK SHE'D APPRECIATE IT.
DON'T KNOW WHO MADE YOU BOSS.
HUH
IN HERE.
THANKS, RIO.
NO PROBLEM. YOU LOOKED A LITTLE OVERWHELMED.
YEAH, I'VE BEEN TRYING TO GET OUT OF THERE EVER SINCE THE VIDEO ENDED.
WELL, IT WAS A GREAT VIDEO, I THINK YOU'RE PROBABLY GOING TO HAVE TO GET USED TO THAT KIND OF ATTENTION.
YEAH, I THINK YOU'RE RIGHT. HOW DOES ONE GET USED TO THAT, THOUGH?
I DO NOT KNOW. IT'S WHY I'M NOT A ROCK STAR.
WELL, THAT AND I CAN'T SING... OR PLAY GUITAR... OR DO ANY OF THAT STUFF.
HAHA. I'M SURE YOU'RE NOT THAT BAD.
OH NO, I AM. I DEFINITELY AM.

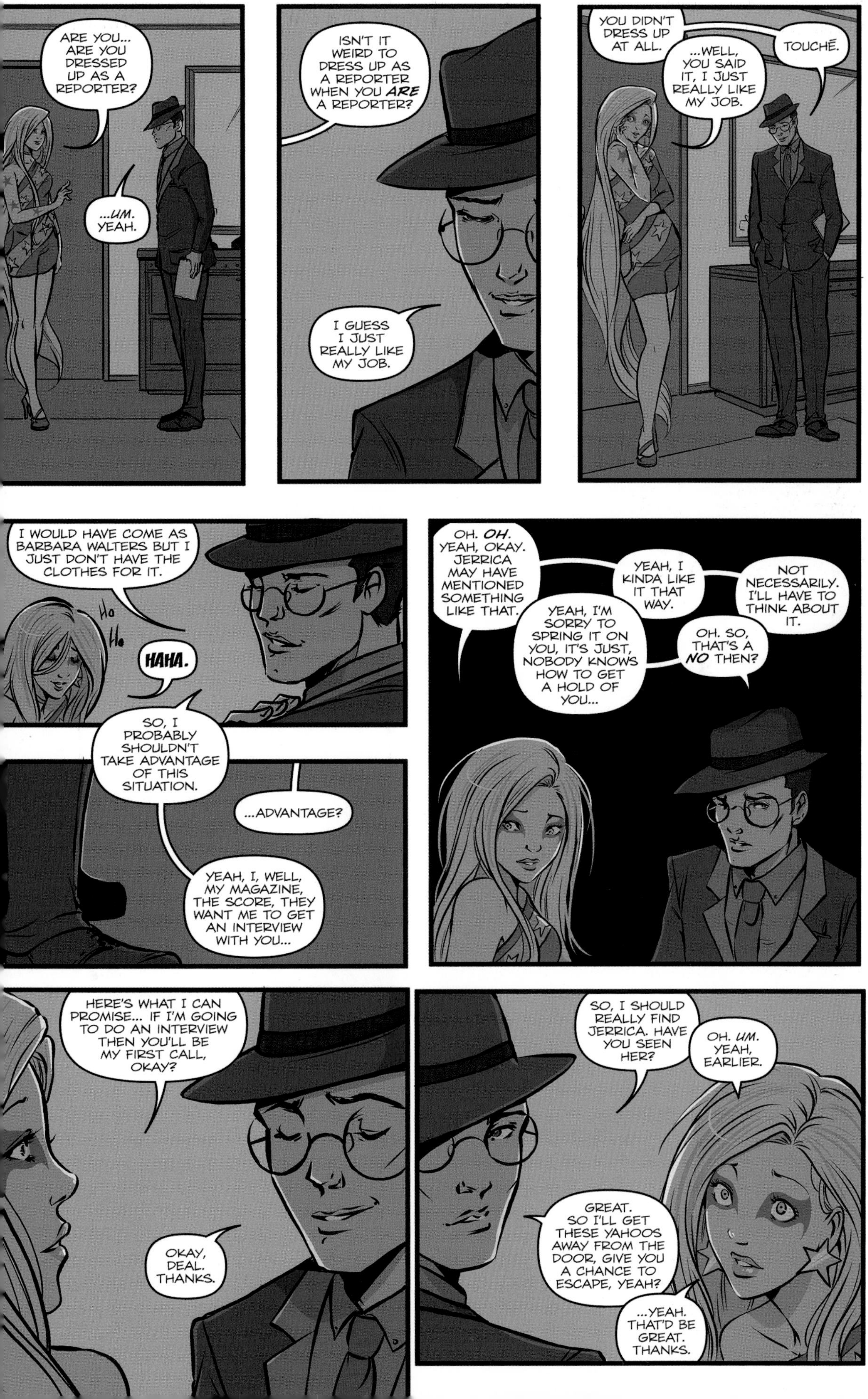
ARE YOU... ARE YOU DRESSED UP AS A REPORTER?
...UM. YEAH.
ISN'T IT WEIRD TO DRESS UP AS A REPORTER WHEN YOU ARE A REPORTER?
I GUESS I JUST REALLY LIKE MY JOB.
YOU DIDN'T DRESS UP AT ALL.
TOUCHÉ.
...WELL, YOU SAID IT, I JUST REALLY LIKE MY JOB.
I WOULD HAVE COME AS BARBARA WALTERS BUT I JUST DON'T HAVE THE CLOTHES FOR IT.
Ho Ho
HAHA.
SO, I PROBABLY SHOULDN'T TAKE ADVANTAGE OF THIS SITUATION.
...ADVANTAGE?
YEAH, I, WELL, MY MAGAZINE, THE SCORE, THEY WANT ME TO GET AN INTERVIEW WITH YOU...
OH. OH. YEAH, OKAY. JERRICA MAY HAVE MENTIONED SOMETHING LIKE THAT.
YEAH, I'M SORRY TO SPRING IT ON YOU, IT'S JUST, NOBODY KNOWS HOW TO GET A HOLD OF YOU...
YEAH, I KINDA LIKE IT THAT WAY.
OH. SO, THAT'S A NO THEN?
NOT NECESSARILY. I'LL HAVE TO THINK ABOUT IT.
HERE'S WHAT I CAN PROMISE... IF I'M GOING TO DO AN INTERVIEW THEN YOU'LL BE MY FIRST CALL, OKAY?
OKAY, DEAL. THANKS.
SO, I SHOULD REALLY FIND JERRICA. HAVE YOU SEEN HER?
OH. UM. YEAH, EARLIER.
GREAT. SO I'LL GET THESE YAHOOS AWAY FROM THE DOOR, GIVE YOU A CHANCE TO ESCAPE, YEAH?
...YEAH. THAT'D BE GREAT. THANKS.

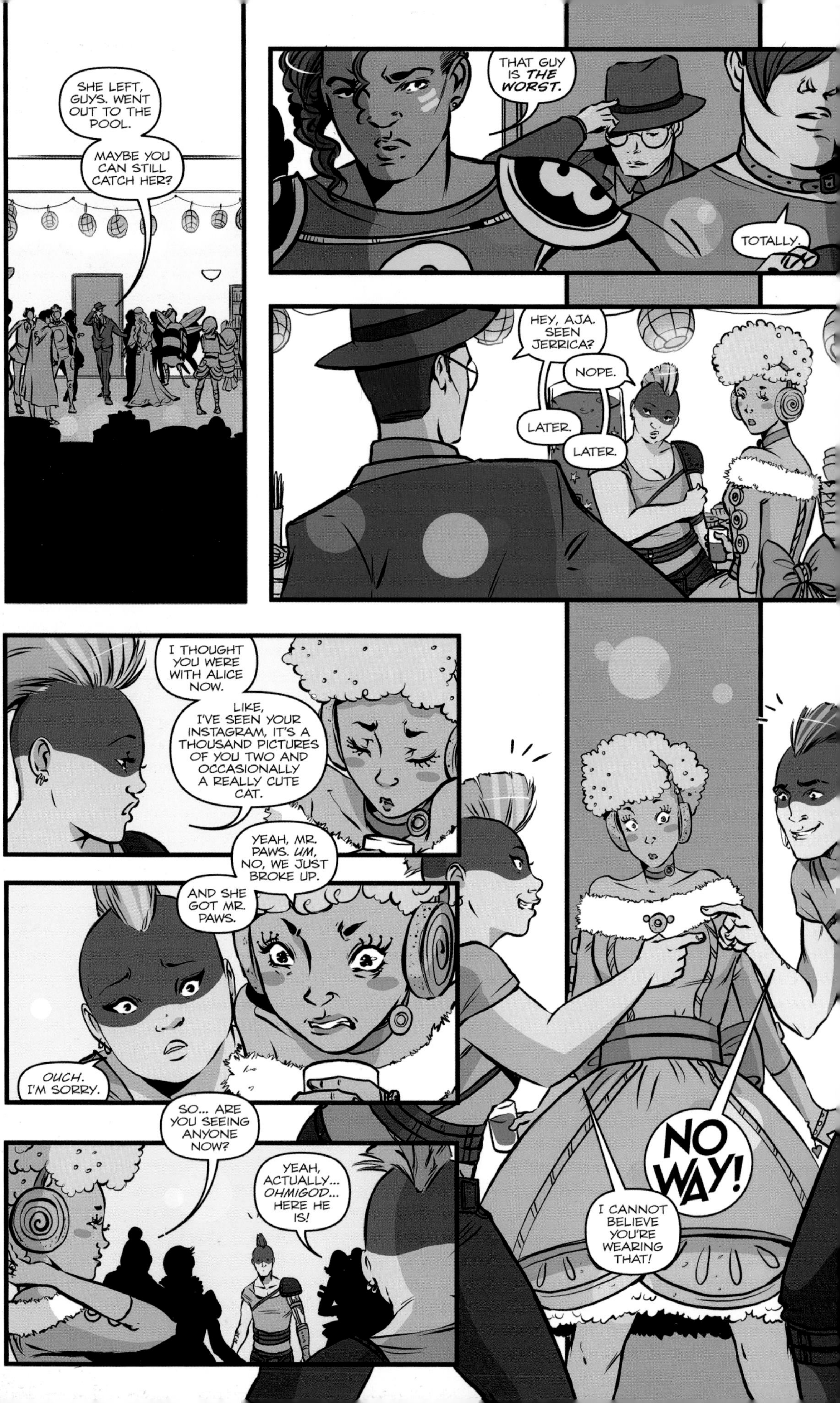
SHE LEFT, GUYS. WENT OUT TO THE POOL.
MAYBE YOU CAN STILL CATCH HER?
THAT GUY IS *THE WORST.*
TOTALLY.
HEY, AJA. SEEN JERRICA?
NOPE.
LATER.
LATER.
I THOUGHT YOU WERE WITH ALICE NOW.
LIKE, I'VE SEEN YOUR INSTAGRAM, IT'S A THOUSAND PICTURES OF YOU TWO AND OCCASIONALLY A REALLY CUTE CAT.
YEAH, MR. PAWS. *UM,* NO, WE JUST BROKE UP.
AND SHE GOT MR. PAWS.
OUCH. I'M SORRY.
SO... ARE YOU SEEING ANYONE NOW?
YEAH, ACTUALLY... *OHMIGOD*... HERE HE IS!
NO WAY!
I CANNOT BELIEVE YOU'RE WEARING THAT!

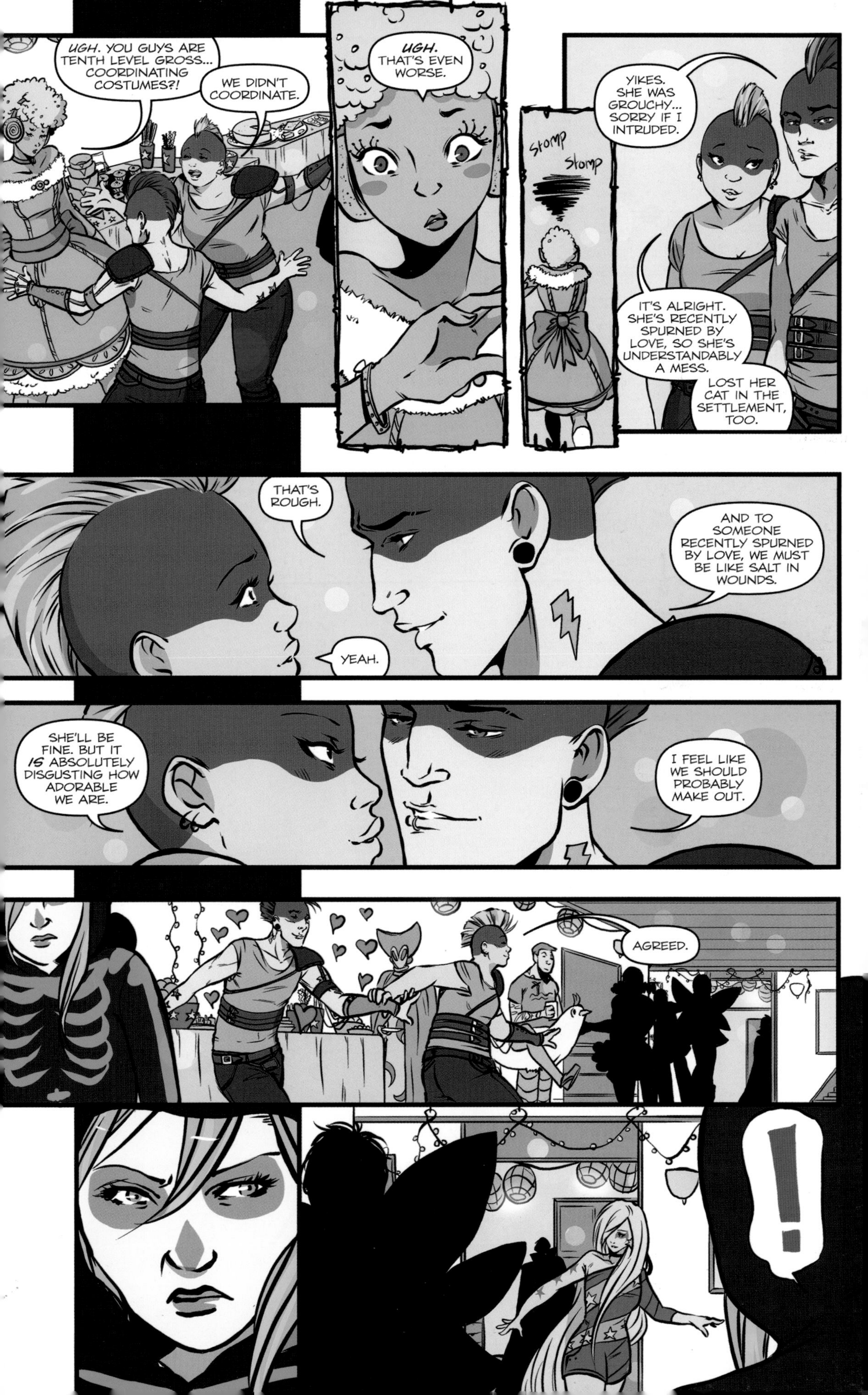
UGH. YOU GUYS ARE TENTH LEVEL GROSS... COORDINATING COSTUMES?!
WE DIDN'T COORDINATE.
UGH. THAT'S EVEN WORSE.
STOMP
STOMP
YIKES. SHE WAS GROUCHY... SORRY IF I INTRUDED.
IT'S ALRIGHT. SHE'S RECENTLY SPURNED BY LOVE, SO SHE'S UNDERSTANDABLY A MESS.
LOST HER CAT IN THE SETTLEMENT, TOO.
THAT'S ROUGH.
YEAH.
AND TO SOMEONE RECENTLY SPURNED BY LOVE, WE MUST BE LIKE SALT IN WOUNDS.
SHE'LL BE FINE. BUT IT IS ABSOLUTELY DISGUSTING HOW ADORABLE WE ARE.
I FEEL LIKE WE SHOULD PROBABLY MAKE OUT.
AGREED.
!

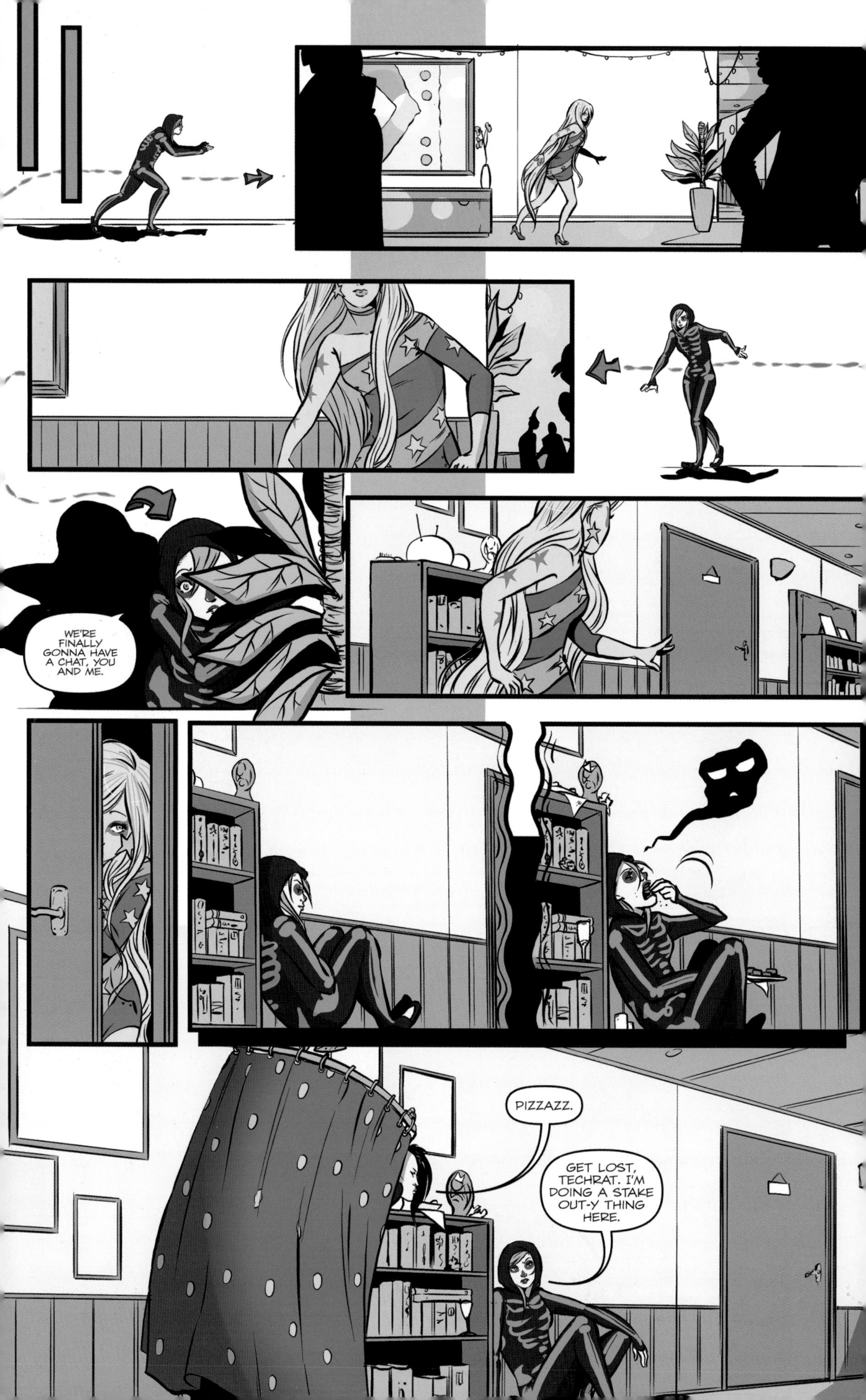
WE'RE FINALLY GONNA HAVE A CHAT, YOU AND ME.
PIZZAZZ.
GET LOST, TECHRAT. I'M DOING A STAKE OUT-Y THING HERE.

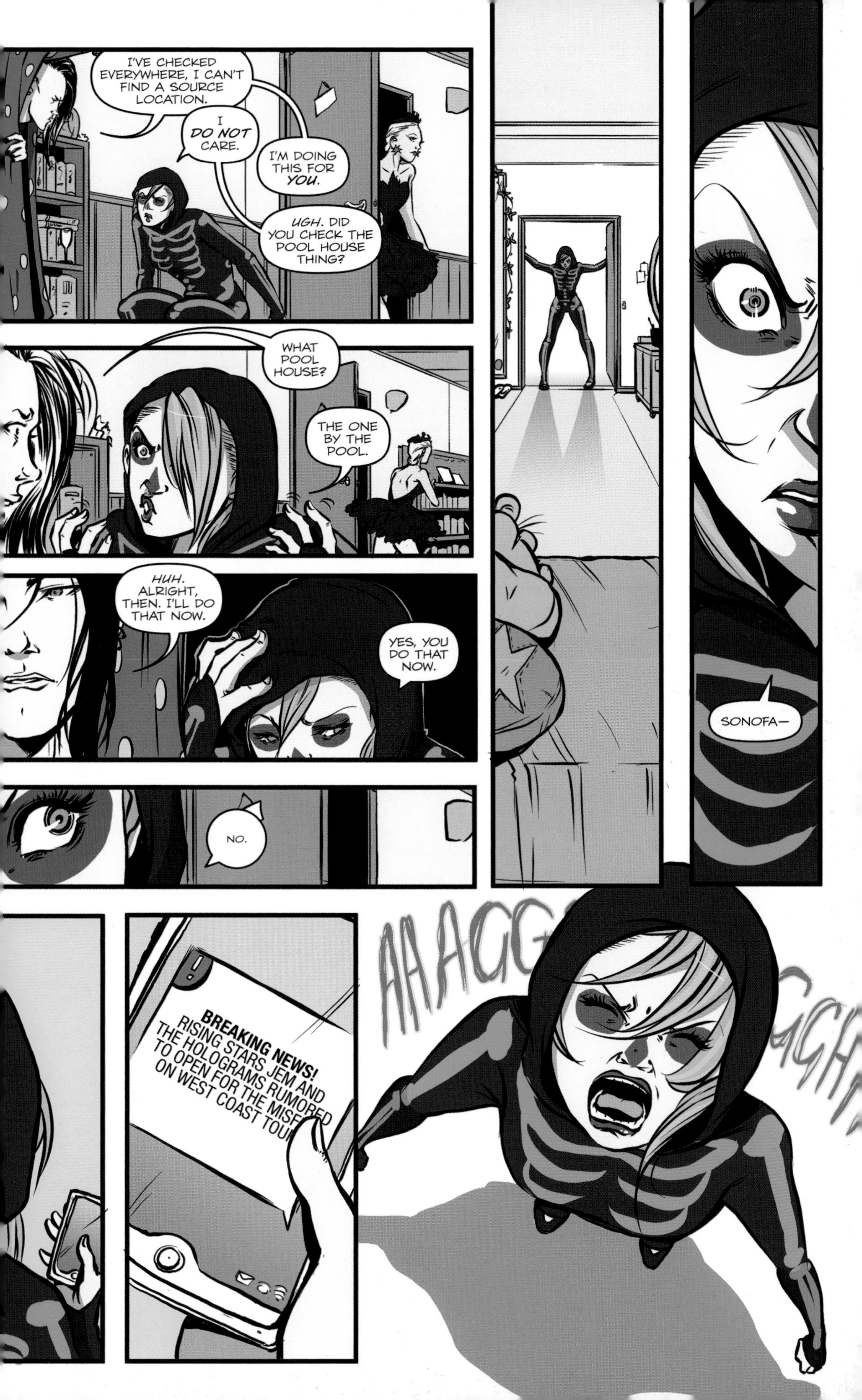
I'VE CHECKED EVERYWHERE, I CAN'T FIND A SOURCE LOCATION.
I DO NOT CARE.
I'M DOING THIS FOR YOU.
UGH. DID YOU CHECK THE POOL HOUSE THING?
WHAT POOL HOUSE?
THE ONE BY THE POOL.
HUH. ALRIGHT, THEN. I'LL DO THAT NOW.
YES, YOU DO THAT NOW.
NO.
SONOFA—
BREAKING NEWS!
RISING STARS JEM AND THE HOLOGRAMS RUMORED TO OPEN FOR THE MISF
ON WEST COAST TOU
AAAGG
GGH

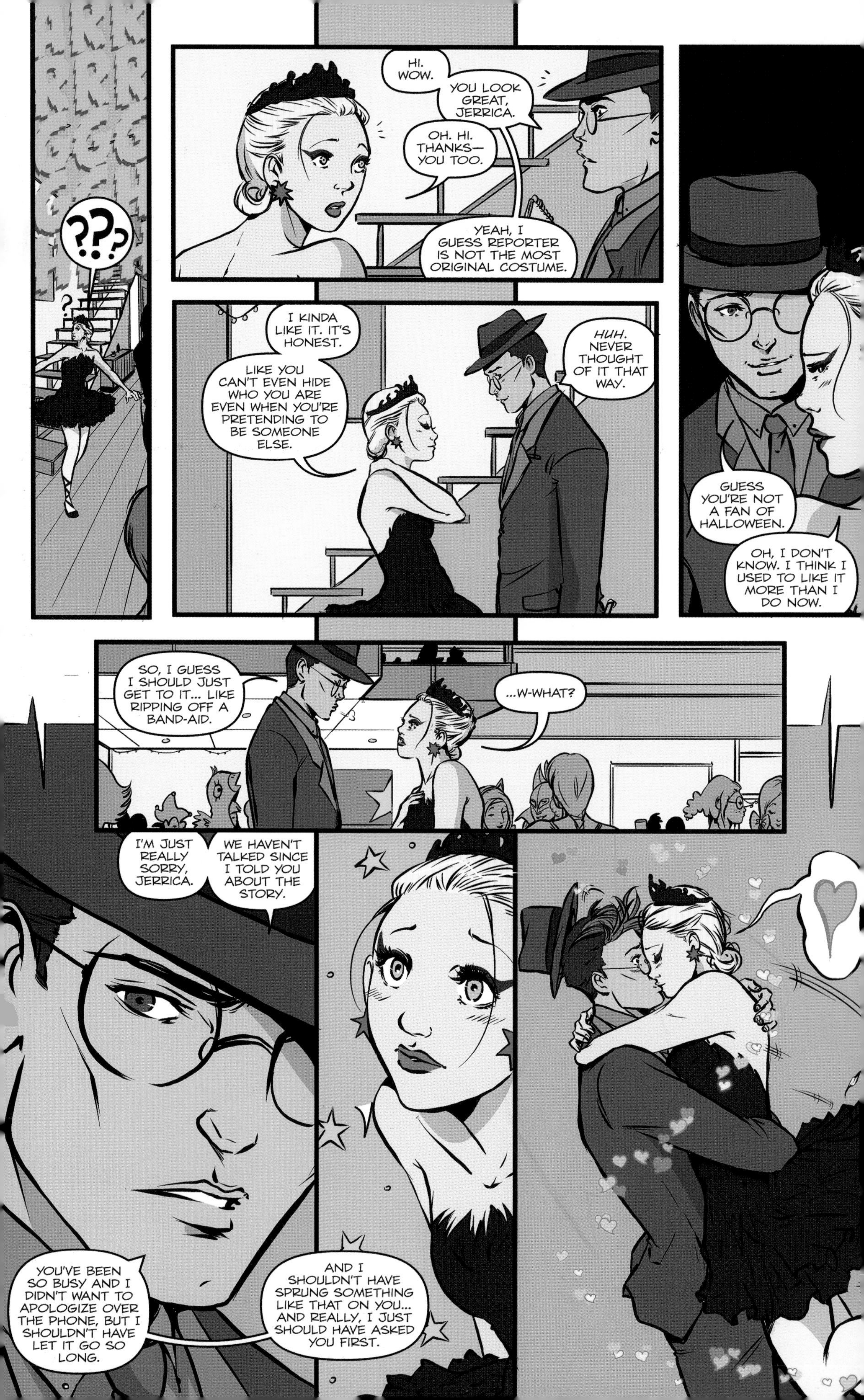
ARRRGGGGH
??
?
HI. WOW.
YOU LOOK GREAT, JERRICA.
OH. HI. THANKS— YOU TOO.
YEAH, I GUESS REPORTER IS NOT THE MOST ORIGINAL COSTUME.
I KINDA LIKE IT. IT'S HONEST.
LIKE YOU CAN'T EVEN HIDE WHO YOU ARE EVEN WHEN YOU'RE PRETENDING TO BE SOMEONE ELSE.
HUH. NEVER THOUGHT OF IT THAT WAY.
GUESS YOU'RE NOT A FAN OF HALLOWEEN.
OH, I DON'T KNOW. I THINK I USED TO LIKE IT MORE THAN I DO NOW.
SO, I GUESS I SHOULD JUST GET TO IT... LIKE RIPPING OFF A BAND-AID.
...W-WHAT?
I'M JUST REALLY SORRY, JERRICA.
WE HAVEN'T TALKED SINCE I TOLD YOU ABOUT THE STORY.
YOU'VE BEEN SO BUSY AND I DIDN'T WANT TO APOLOGIZE OVER THE PHONE, BUT I SHOULDN'T HAVE LET IT GO SO LONG.
AND I SHOULDN'T HAVE SPRUNG SOMETHING LIKE THAT ON YOU... AND REALLY, I JUST SHOULD HAVE ASKED YOU FIRST.

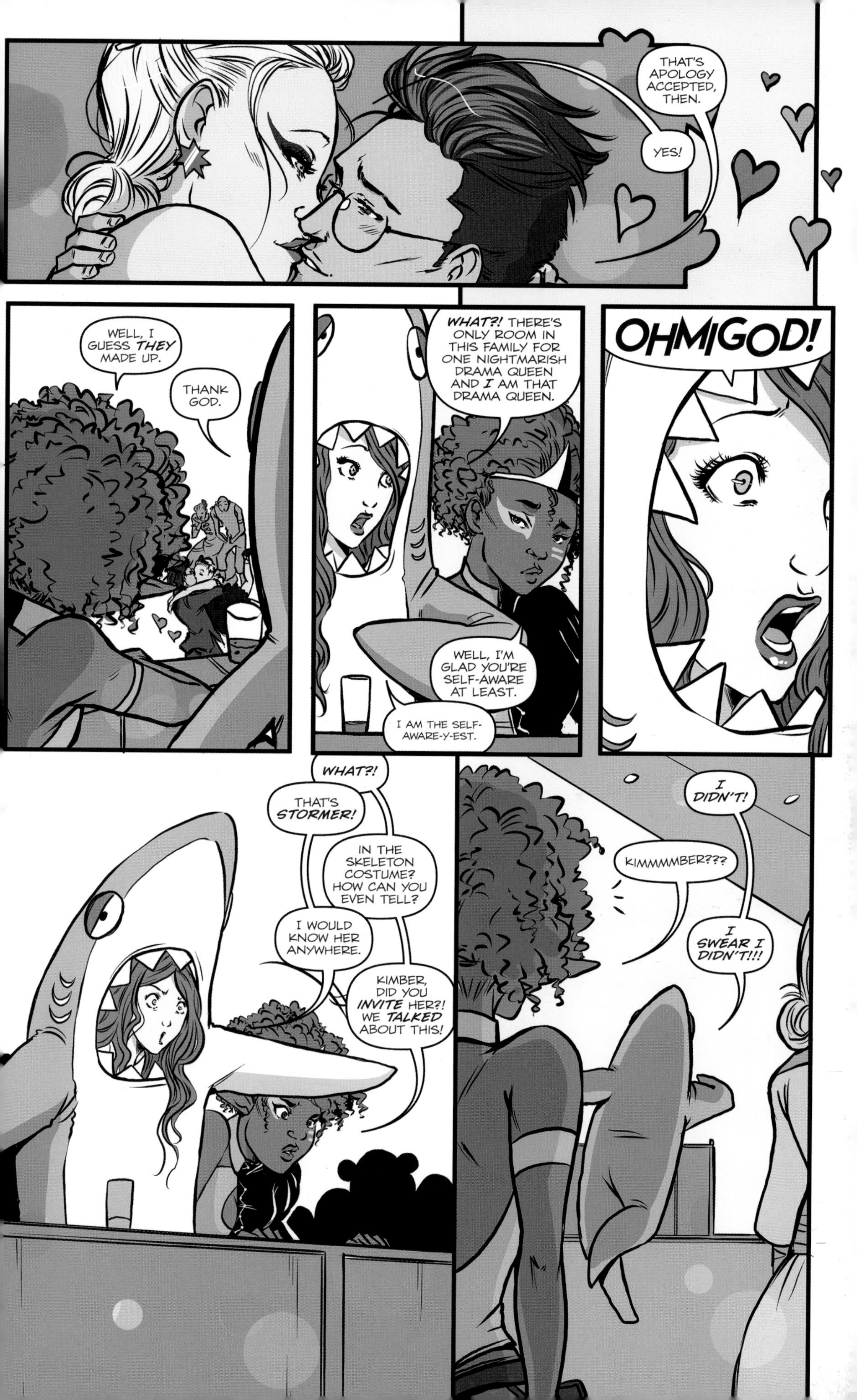
THAT'S APOLOGY ACCEPTED, THEN.
YES!
WELL, I GUESS THEY MADE UP.
THANK GOD.
WHAT?! THERE'S ONLY ROOM IN THIS FAMILY FOR ONE NIGHTMARISH DRAMA QUEEN AND I AM THAT DRAMA QUEEN.
WELL, I'M GLAD YOU'RE SELF-AWARE AT LEAST.
I AM THE SELF-AWARE-Y-EST.
OHMIGOD!
WHAT?!
THAT'S STORMER!
IN THE SKELETON COSTUME? HOW CAN YOU EVEN TELL?
I WOULD KNOW HER ANYWHERE.
KIMBER, DID YOU INVITE HER?! WE TALKED ABOUT THIS!
I DIDN'T!
KIMMMMBER???
I SWEAR I DIDN'T!!!

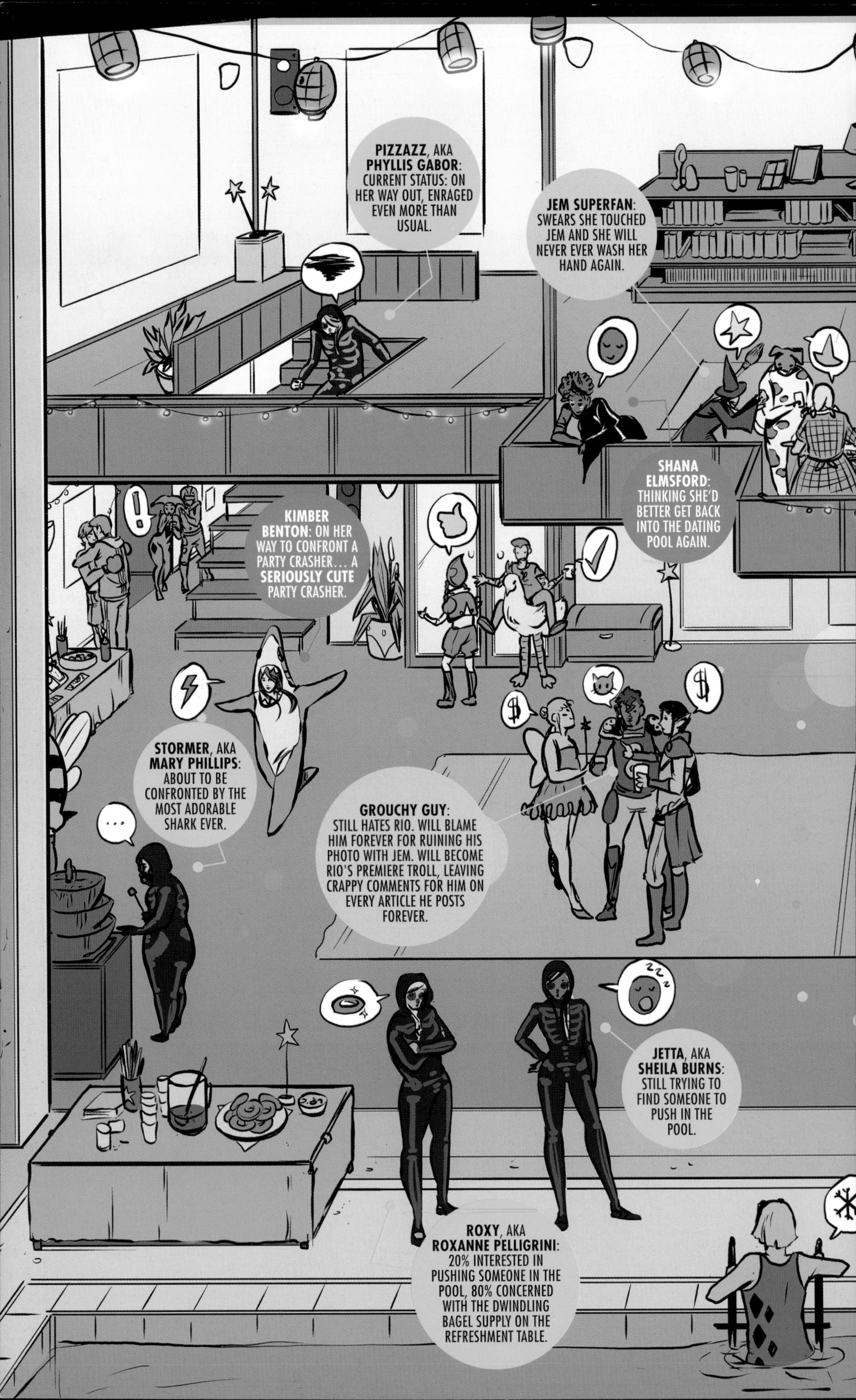
PIZZAZZ, AKA PHYLLIS GABOR: CURRENT STATUS: ON HER WAY OUT, ENRAGED EVEN MORE THAN USUAL.
JEM SUPERFAN: SWEARS SHE TOUCHED JEM AND SHE WILL NEVER EVER WASH HER HAND AGAIN.
SHANA ELMSFORD: THINKING SHE'D BETTER GET BACK INTO THE DATING POOL AGAIN.
KIMBER BENTON: ON HER WAY TO CONFRONT A PARTY CRASHER… A SERIOUSLY CUTE PARTY CRASHER.
STORMER, AKA MARY PHILLIPS: ABOUT TO BE CONFRONTED BY THE MOST ADORABLE SHARK EVER.
...
GROUCHY GUY: STILL HATES RIO. WILL BLAME HIM FOREVER FOR RUINING HIS PHOTO WITH JEM. WILL BECOME RIO'S PREMIERE TROLL, LEAVING CRAPPY COMMENTS FOR HIM ON EVERY ARTICLE HE POSTS FOREVER.
JETTA, AKA SHEILA BURNS: STILL TRYING TO FIND SOMEONE TO PUSH IN THE POOL.
ROXY, AKA ROXANNE PELLIGRINI: 20% INTERESTED IN PUSHING SOMEONE IN THE POOL, 80% CONCERNED WITH THE DWINDLING BAGEL SUPPLY ON THE REFRESHMENT TABLE.

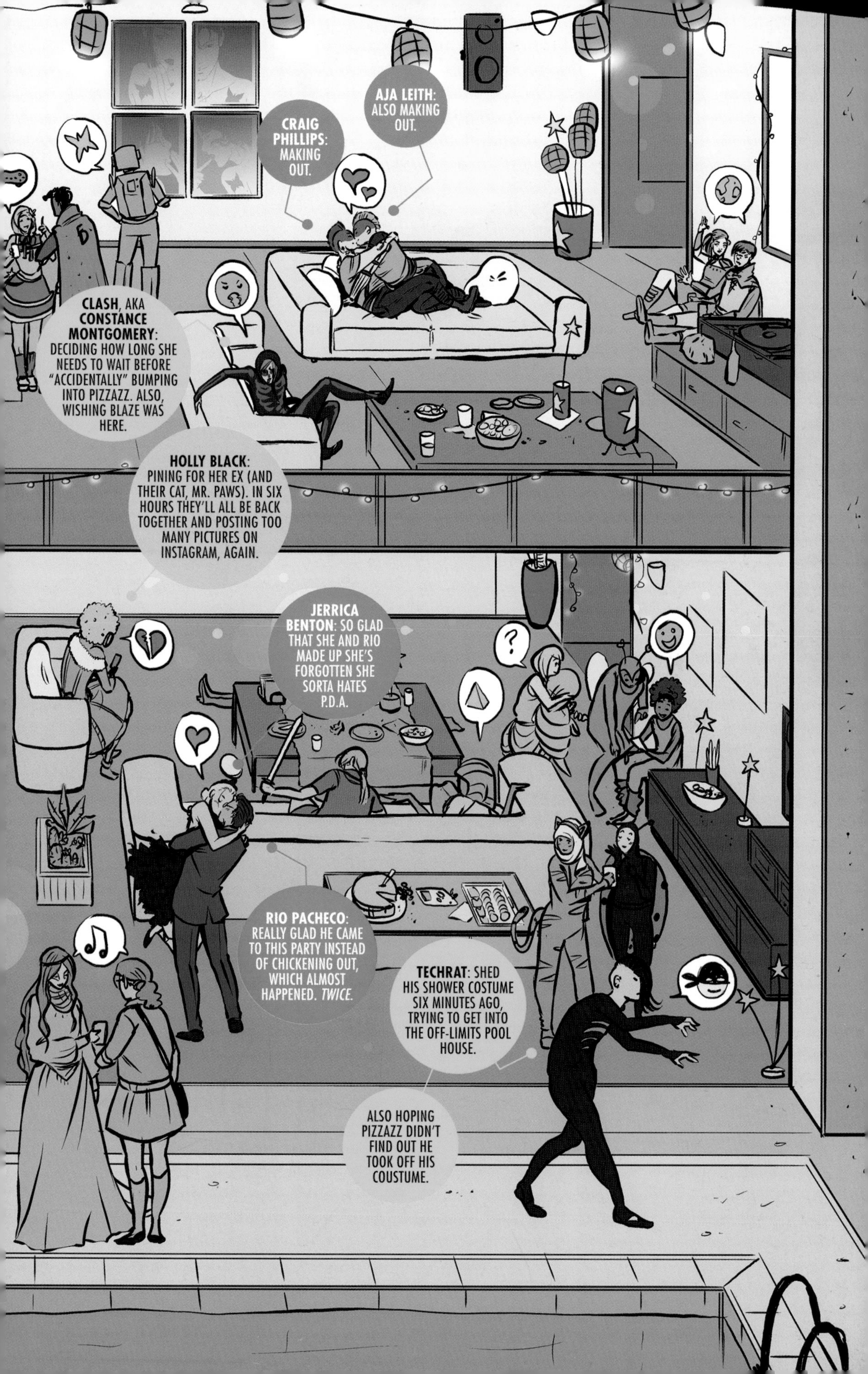
CRAIG PHILLIPS: MAKING OUT.
AJA LEITH: ALSO MAKING OUT.
CLASH, AKA CONSTANCE MONTGOMERY: DECIDING HOW LONG SHE NEEDS TO WAIT BEFORE "ACCIDENTALLY" BUMPING INTO PIZZAZZ. ALSO, WISHING BLAZE WAS HERE.
HOLLY BLACK: PINING FOR HER EX (AND THEIR CAT, MR. PAWS). IN SIX HOURS THEY'LL ALL BE BACK TOGETHER AND POSTING TOO MANY PICTURES ON INSTAGRAM, AGAIN.
JERRICA BENTON: SO GLAD THAT SHE AND RIO MADE UP SHE'S FORGOTTEN SHE SORTA HATES P.D.A.
RIO PACHECO: REALLY GLAD HE CAME TO THIS PARTY INSTEAD OF CHICKENING OUT, WHICH ALMOST HAPPENED. TWICE.
TECHRAT: SHED HIS SHOWER COSTUME SIX MINUTES AGO, TRYING TO GET INTO THE OFF-LIMITS POOL HOUSE.
ALSO HOPING PIZZAZZ DIDN'T FIND OUT HE TOOK OFF HIS COUSTUME.

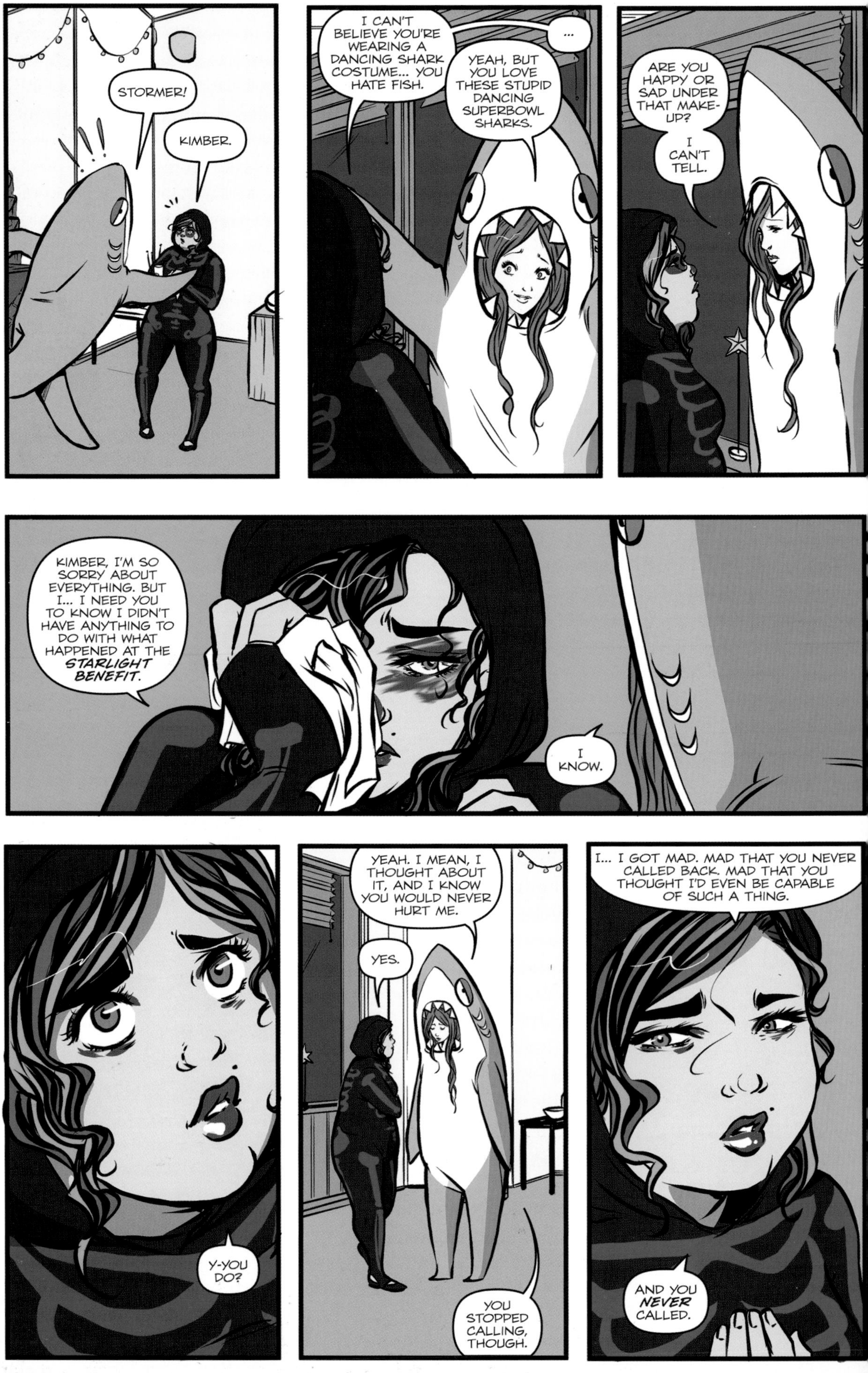
STORMER!
KIMBER.
I CAN'T BELIEVE YOU'RE WEARING A DANCING SHARK COSTUME... YOU HATE FISH.
...
YEAH, BUT YOU LOVE THESE STUPID DANCING SUPERBOWL SHARKS.
ARE YOU HAPPY OR SAD UNDER THAT MAKE-UP?
I CAN'T TELL.
KIMBER, I'M SO SORRY ABOUT EVERYTHING. BUT I... I NEED YOU TO KNOW I DIDN'T HAVE ANYTHING TO DO WITH WHAT HAPPENED AT THE STARLIGHT BENEFIT.
I KNOW.
Y-YOU DO?
YEAH. I MEAN, I THOUGHT ABOUT IT, AND I KNOW YOU WOULD NEVER HURT ME.
YES.
YOU STOPPED CALLING, THOUGH.
I... I GOT MAD. MAD THAT YOU NEVER CALLED BACK. MAD THAT YOU THOUGHT I'D EVEN BE CAPABLE OF SUCH A THING.
AND YOU NEVER CALLED.

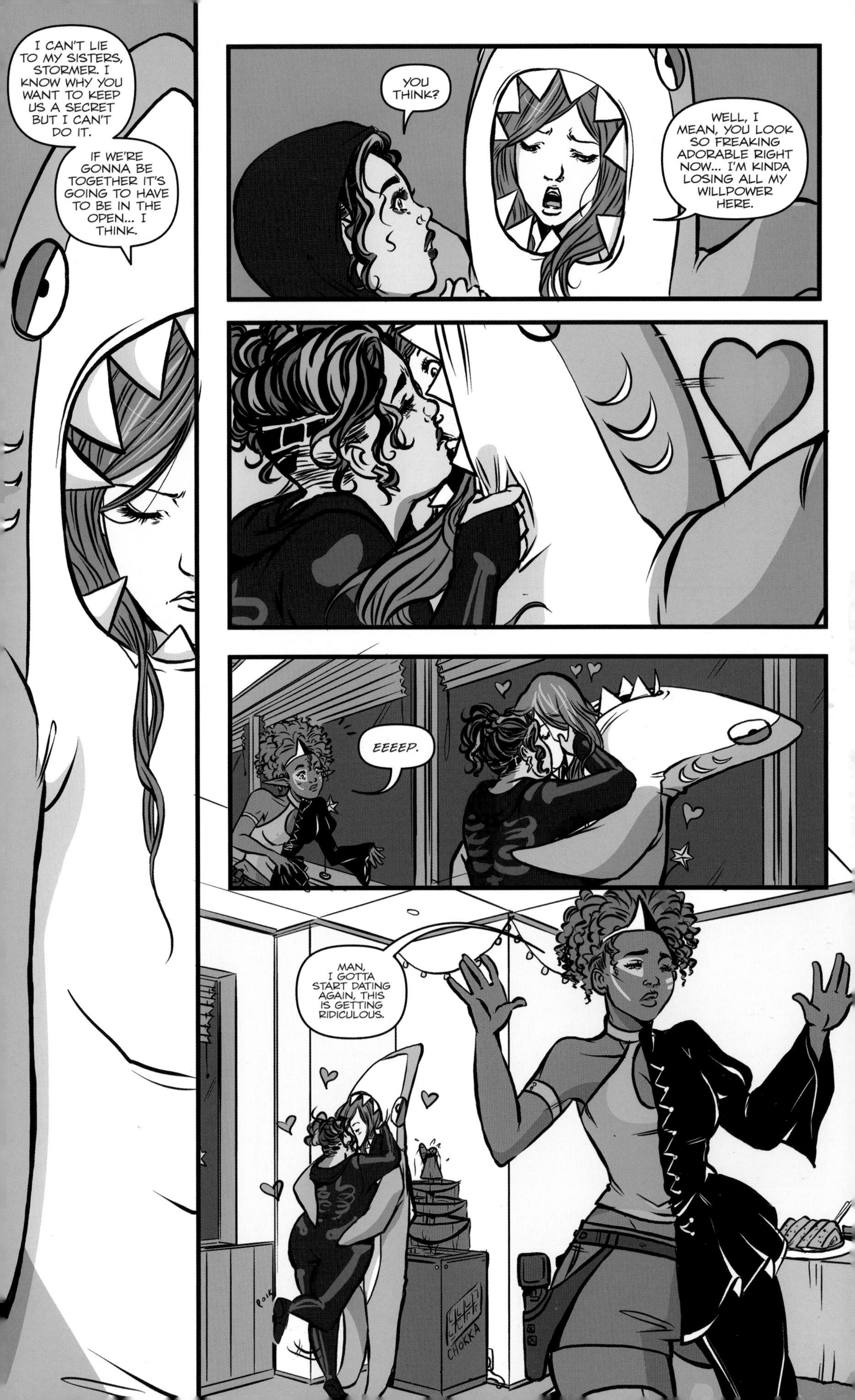
I CAN'T LIE TO MY SISTERS, STORMER. I KNOW WHY YOU WANT TO KEEP US A SECRET BUT I CAN'T DO IT.
IF WE'RE GONNA BE TOGETHER IT'S GOING TO HAVE TO BE IN THE OPEN... I THINK.
YOU THINK?
WELL, I MEAN, YOU LOOK SO FREAKING ADORABLE RIGHT NOW... I'M KINDA LOSING ALL MY WILLPOWER HERE.
EEEEP.
MAN, I GOTTA START DATING AGAIN, THIS IS GETTING RIDICULOUS.
CHOKKA

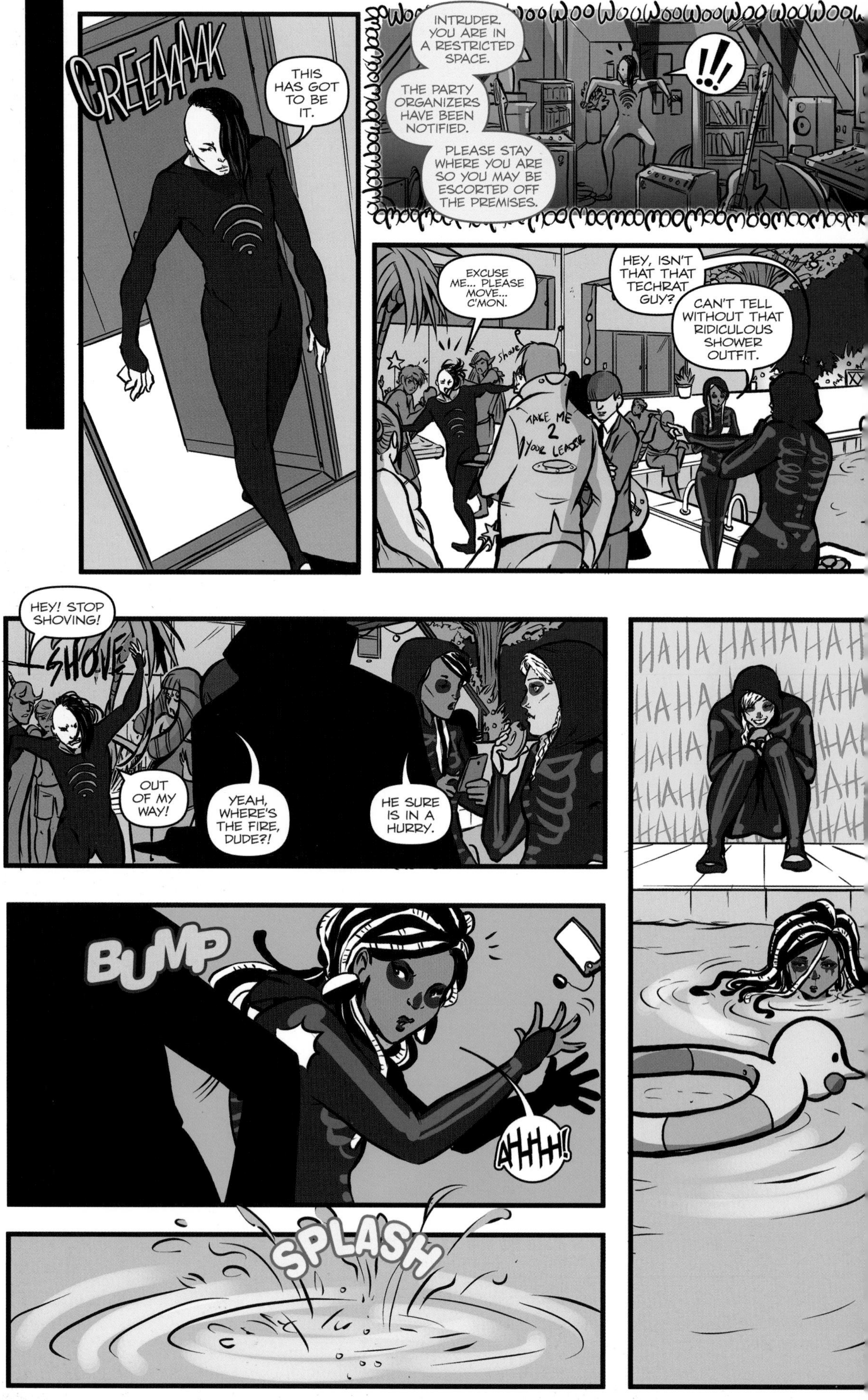
CREEAAAAK
THIS HAS GOT TO BE IT.
WOOWOOWOOWOOWOOWOOWOOWOOWOO
INTRUDER. YOU ARE IN A RESTRICTED SPACE.
THE PARTY ORGANIZERS HAVE BEEN NOTIFIED.
PLEASE STAY WHERE YOU ARE SO YOU MAY BE ESCORTED OFF THE PREMISES.
!!!
EXCUSE ME... PLEASE MOVE... C'MON.
shove
HEY, ISN'T THAT THAT TECHRAT GUY?
CAN'T TELL WITHOUT THAT RIDICULOUS SHOWER OUTFIT.
TAKE ME 2 YOUR LEADER
HEY! STOP SHOVING!
SHOVE
OUT OF MY WAY!
YEAH, WHERE'S THE FIRE, DUDE?!
HE SURE IS IN A HURRY.
HAHA HAHA HAHA
BUMP
AHHHH!
SPLASH

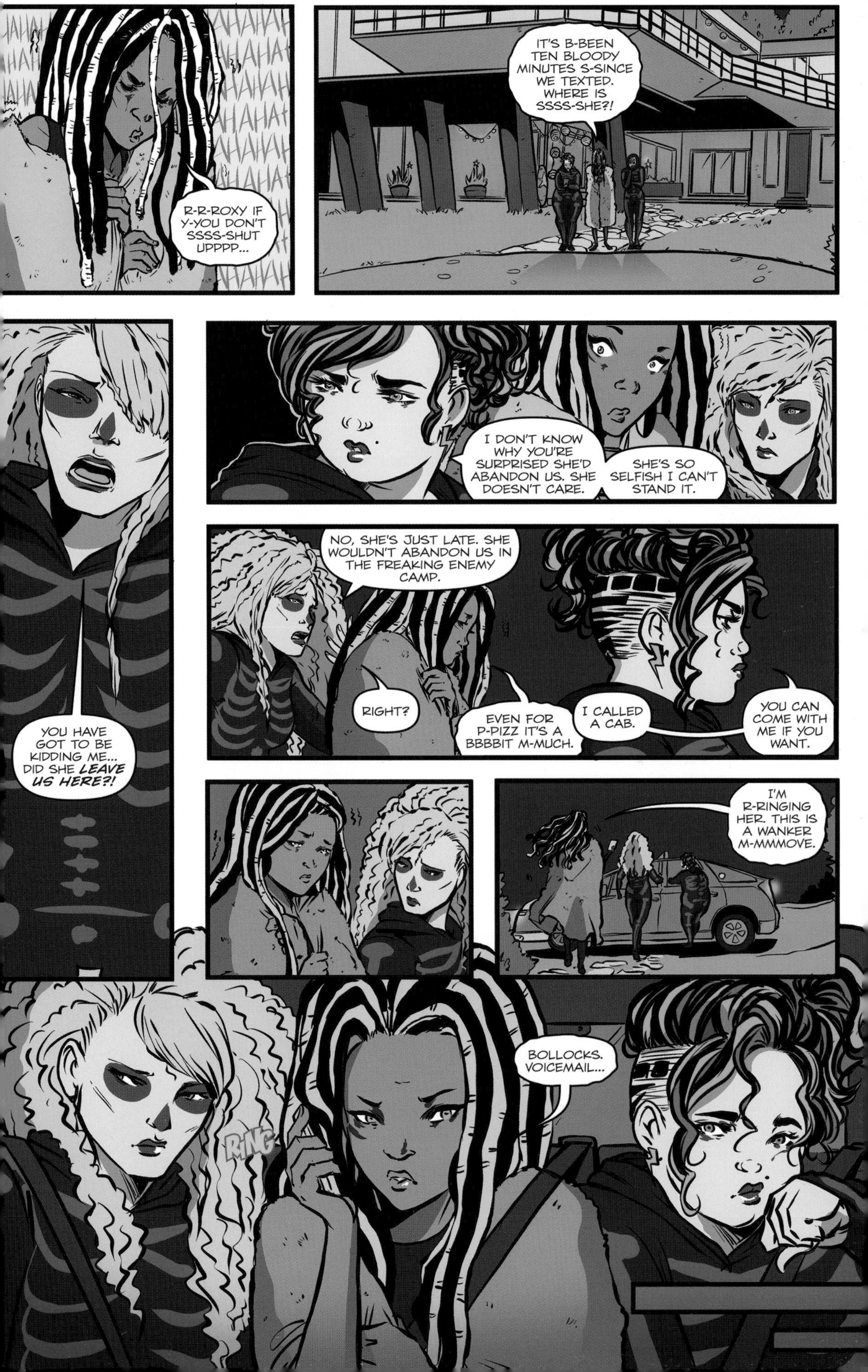
HAHAHA
R-R-ROXY IF Y-YOU DON'T SSSS-SHUT UPPPP...
IT'S B-BEEN TEN BLOODY MINUTES S-SINCE WE TEXTED. WHERE IS SSSS-SHE?!
YOU HAVE GOT TO BE KIDDING ME... DID SHE *LEAVE US HERE?!*
I DON'T KNOW WHY YOU'RE SURPRISED SHE'D ABANDON US. SHE DOESN'T CARE.
SHE'S SO SELFISH I CAN'T STAND IT.
NO, SHE'S JUST LATE. SHE WOULDN'T ABANDON US IN THE FREAKING ENEMY CAMP.
RIGHT?
EVEN FOR P-PIZZ IT'S A BBBBIT M-MUCH.
I CALLED A CAB.
YOU CAN COME WITH ME IF YOU WANT.
I'M R-RINGING HER. THIS IS A WANKER M-MMMOVE.
BOLLOCKS. VOICEMAIL...
RING

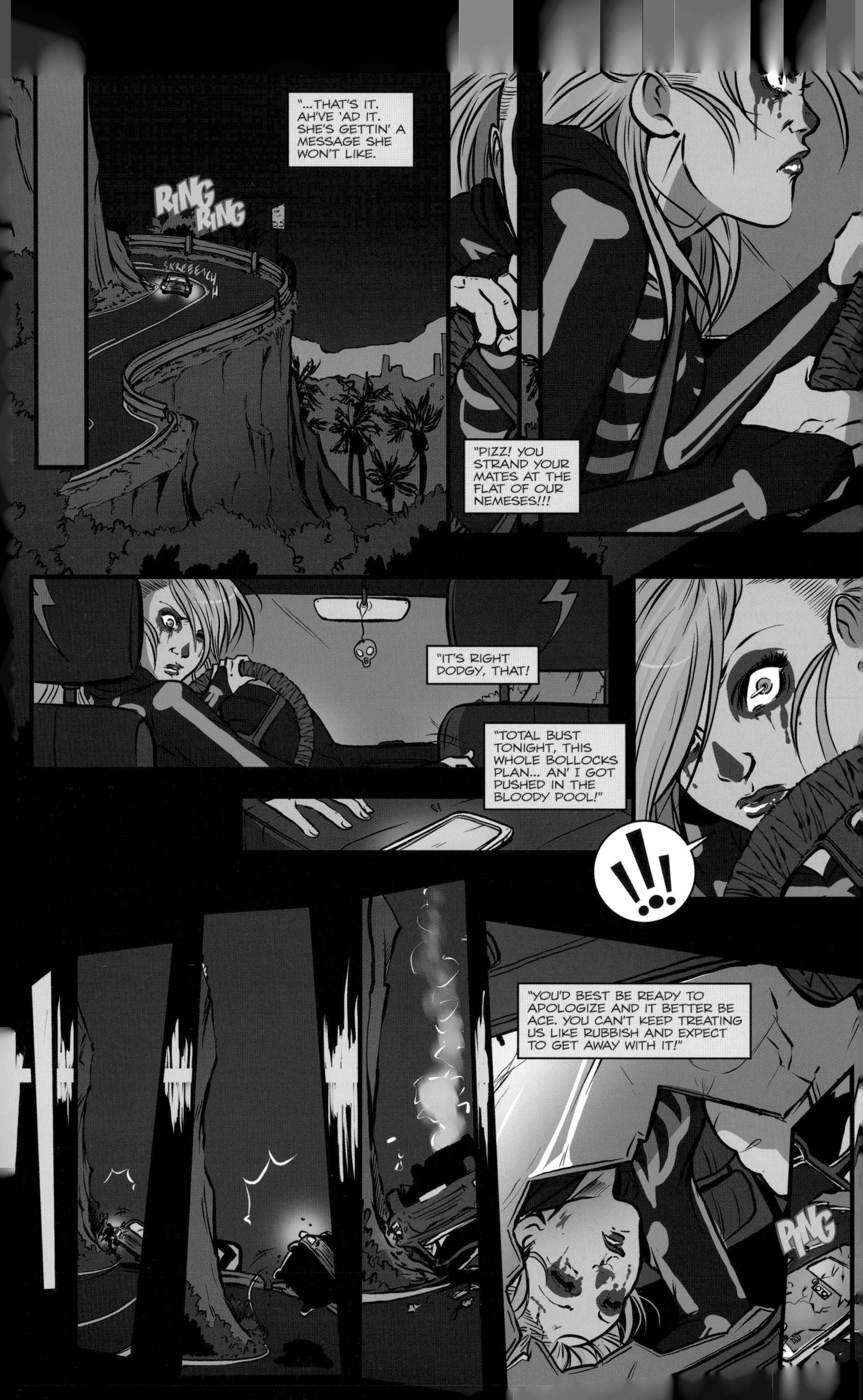
"...THAT'S IT. AH'VE 'AD IT. SHE'S GETTIN' A MESSAGE SHE WON'T LIKE.
RING RING
SKREEEEECH
"PIZZ! YOU STRAND YOUR MATES AT THE FLAT OF OUR NEMESES!!!
"IT'S RIGHT DODGY, THAT!
"TOTAL BUST TONIGHT, THIS WHOLE BOLLOCKS PLAN... AN' I GOT PUSHED IN THE BLOODY POOL!"
!!!
"YOU'D BEST BE READY TO APOLOGIZE AND IT BETTER BE ACE. YOU CAN'T KEEP TREATING US LIKE RUBBISH AND EXPECT TO GET AWAY WITH IT!"
PING

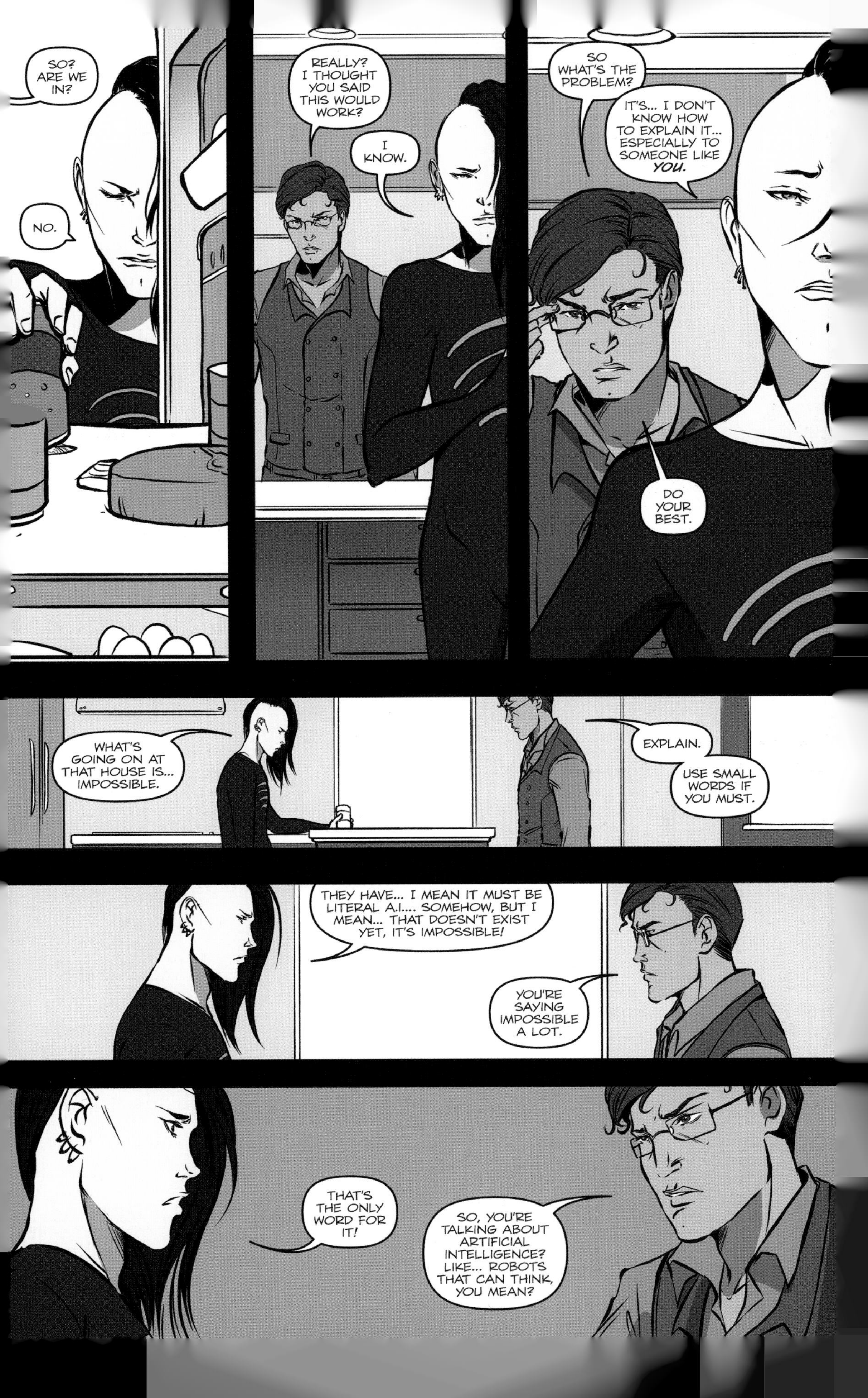
SO? ARE WE IN?
NO.
REALLY? I THOUGHT YOU SAID THIS WOULD WORK?
I KNOW.
SO WHAT'S THE PROBLEM?
IT'S... I DON'T KNOW HOW TO EXPLAIN IT... ESPECIALLY TO SOMEONE LIKE YOU.
DO YOUR BEST.
WHAT'S GOING ON AT THAT HOUSE IS... IMPOSSIBLE.
EXPLAIN.
USE SMALL WORDS IF YOU MUST.
THEY HAVE... I MEAN IT MUST BE LITERAL A.I.... SOMEHOW, BUT I MEAN... THAT DOESN'T EXIST YET, IT'S IMPOSSIBLE!
YOU'RE SAYING IMPOSSIBLE A LOT.
THAT'S THE ONLY WORD FOR IT!
SO, YOU'RE TALKING ABOUT ARTIFICIAL INTELLIGENCE? LIKE... ROBOTS THAT CAN THINK, YOU MEAN?

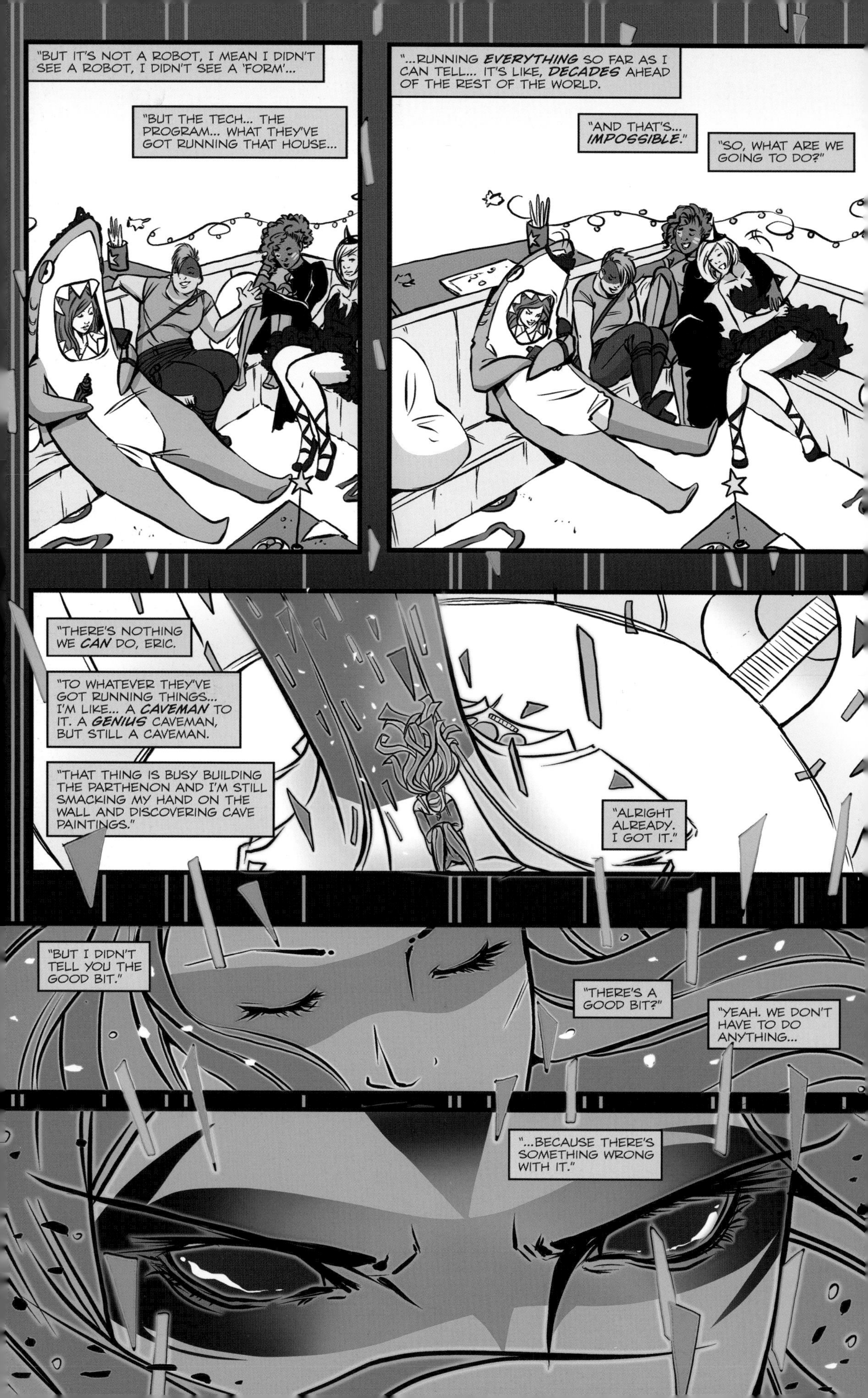
"BUT IT'S NOT A ROBOT, I MEAN I DIDN'T SEE A ROBOT, I DIDN'T SEE A 'FORM'...
"BUT THE TECH... THE PROGRAM... WHAT THEY'VE GOT RUNNING THAT HOUSE...
"...RUNNING EVERYTHING SO FAR AS I CAN TELL... IT'S LIKE, DECADES AHEAD OF THE REST OF THE WORLD.
"AND THAT'S... IMPOSSIBLE."
"SO, WHAT ARE WE GOING TO DO?"
"THERE'S NOTHING WE CAN DO, ERIC.
"TO WHATEVER THEY'VE GOT RUNNING THINGS... I'M LIKE... A CAVEMAN TO IT. A GENIUS CAVEMAN, BUT STILL A CAVEMAN.
"THAT THING IS BUSY BUILDING THE PARTHENON AND I'M STILL SMACKING MY HAND ON THE WALL AND DISCOVERING CAVE PAINTINGS."
"ALRIGHT ALREADY. I GOT IT."
"BUT I DIDN'T TELL YOU THE GOOD BIT."
"THERE'S A GOOD BIT?"
"YEAH. WE DON'T HAVE TO DO ANYTHING...
"...BECAUSE THERE'S SOMETHING WRONG WITH IT."

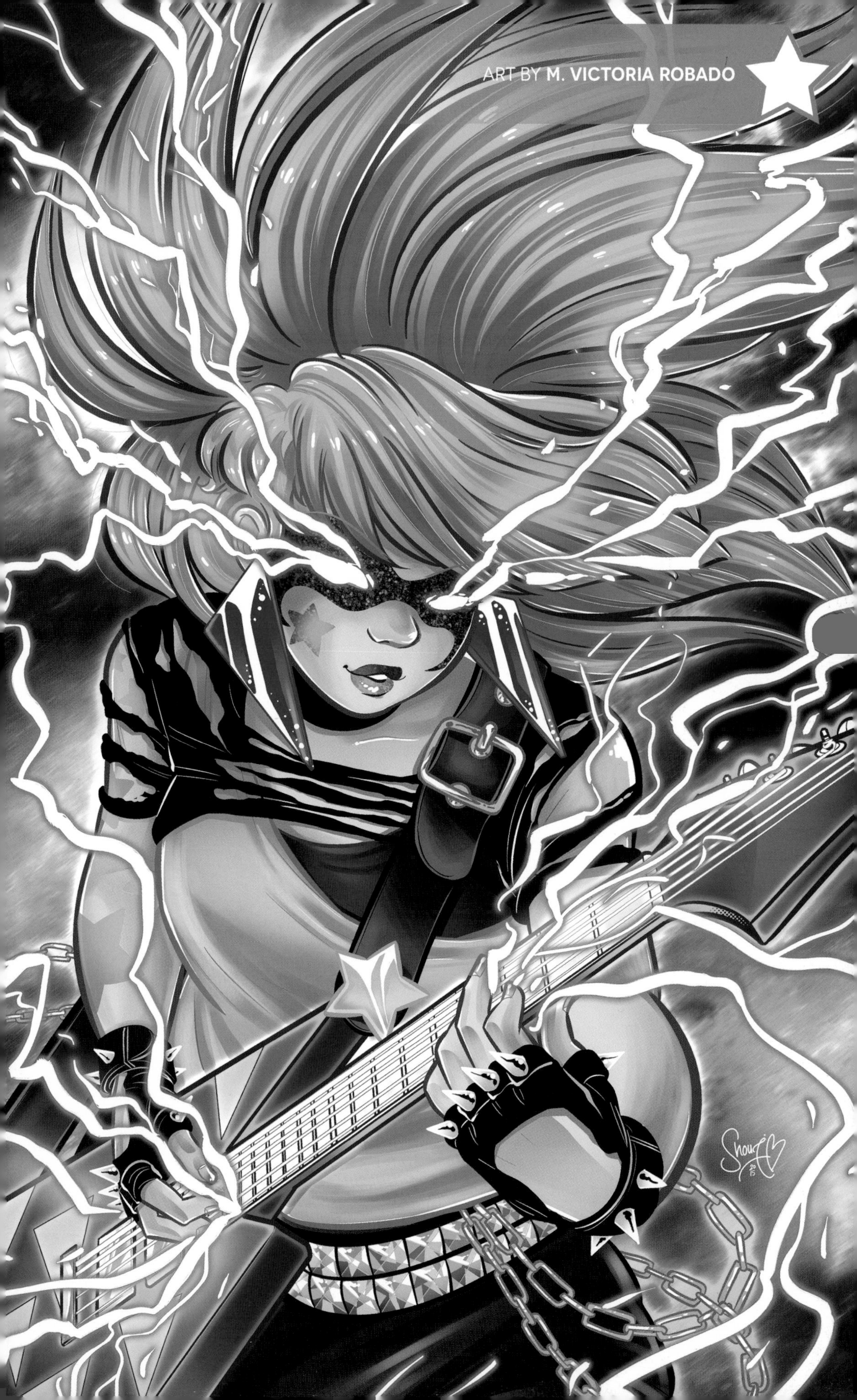

ART BY **M. VICTORIA ROBADO**

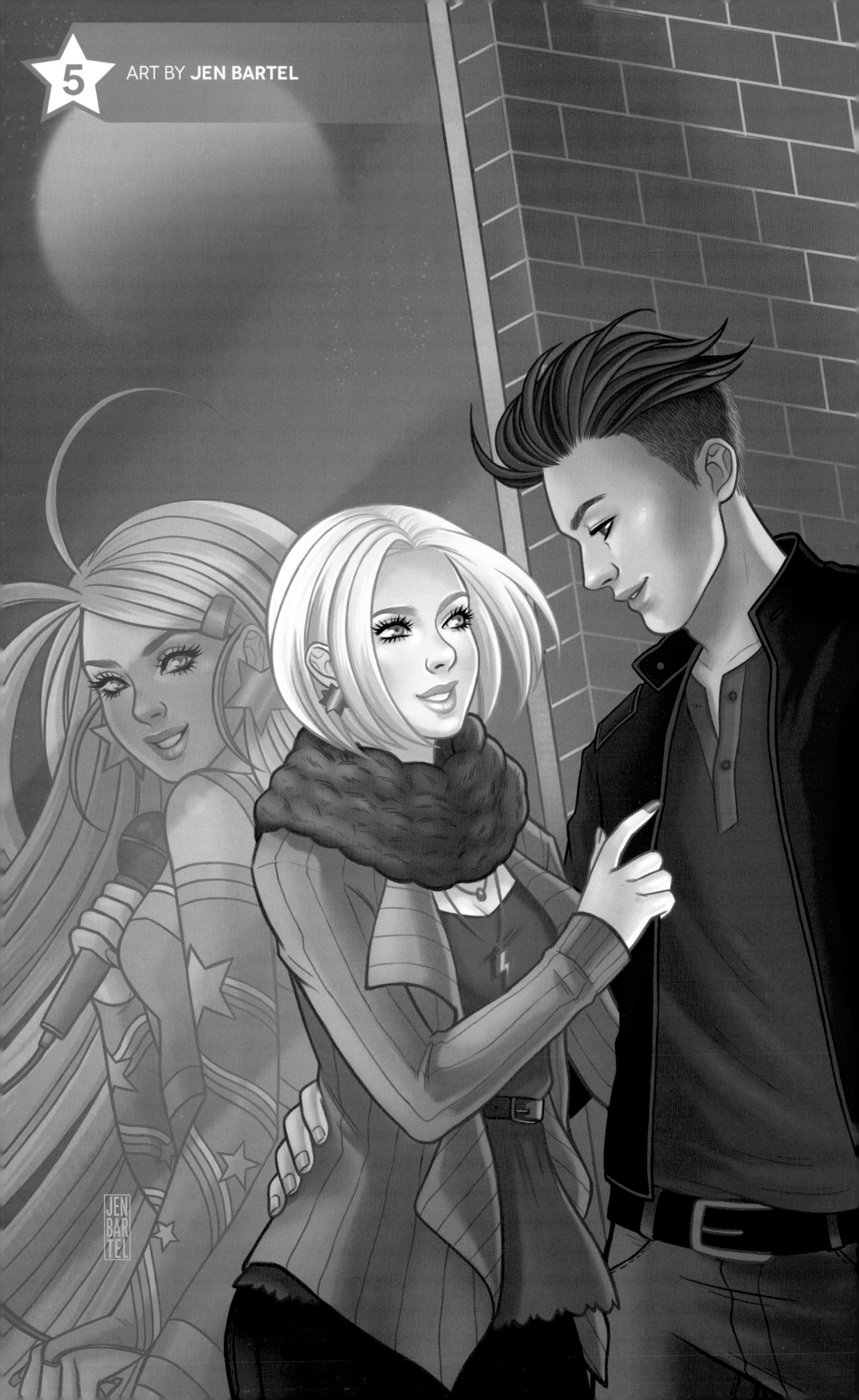
5
ART BY JEN BARTEL
JEN BAR TEL

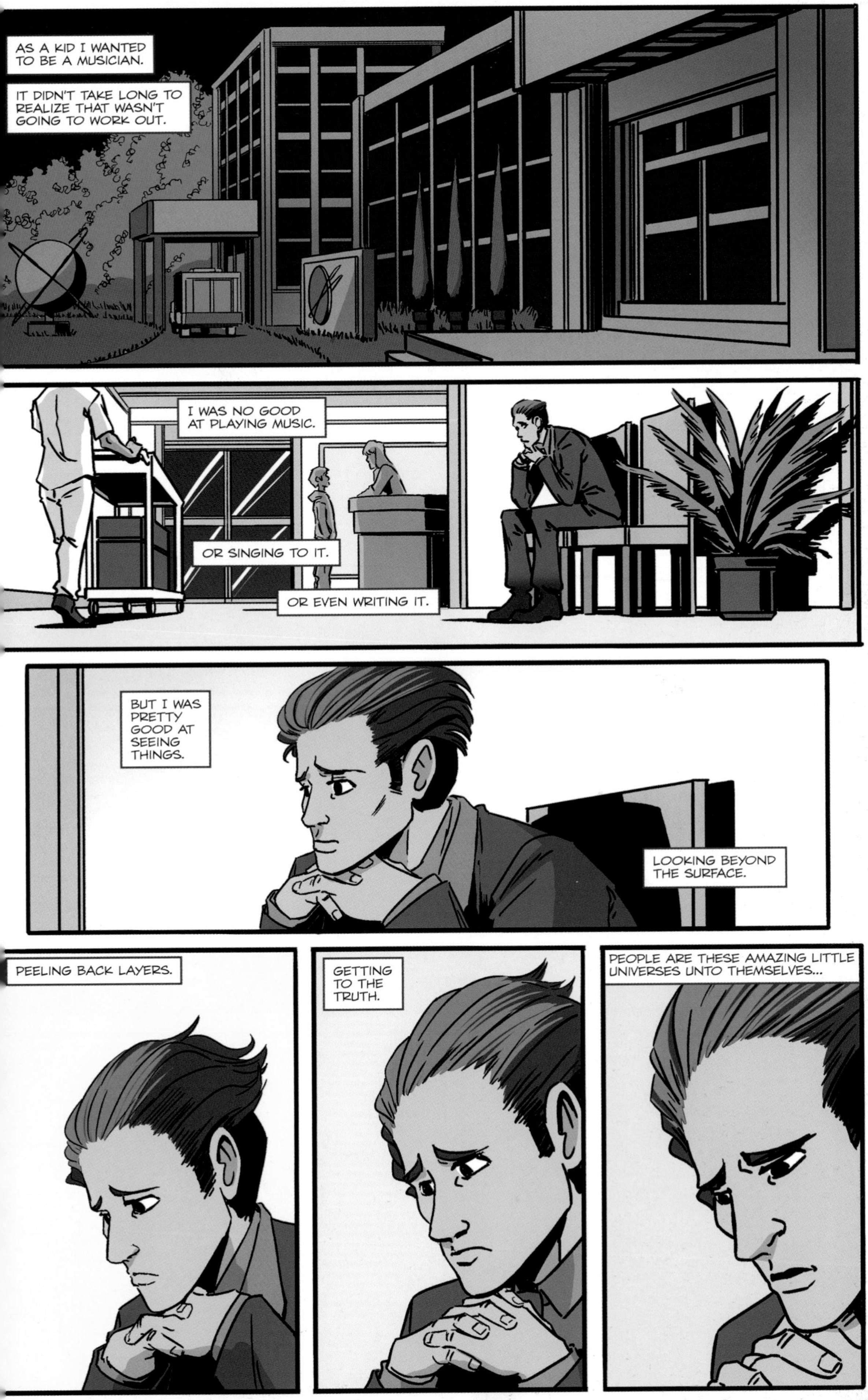
AS A KID I WANTED TO BE A MUSICIAN.
IT DIDN'T TAKE LONG TO REALIZE THAT WASN'T GOING TO WORK OUT.
I WAS NO GOOD AT PLAYING MUSIC.
OR SINGING TO IT.
OR EVEN WRITING IT.
BUT I WAS PRETTY GOOD AT SEEING THINGS.
LOOKING BEYOND THE SURFACE.
PEELING BACK LAYERS.
GETTING TO THE TRUTH.
PEOPLE ARE THESE AMAZING LITTLE UNIVERSES UNTO THEMSELVES...

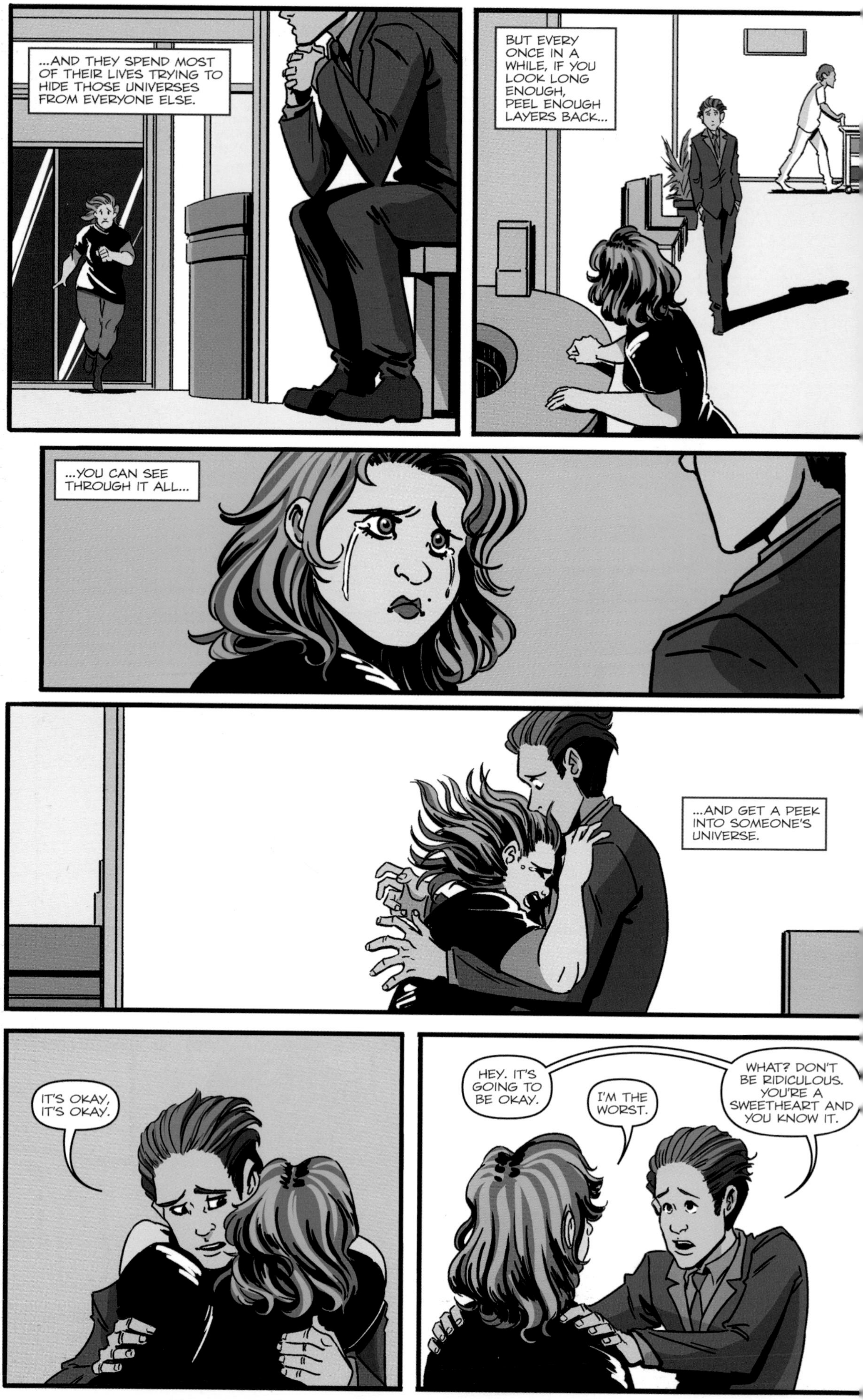
...AND THEY SPEND MOST OF THEIR LIVES TRYING TO HIDE THOSE UNIVERSES FROM EVERYONE ELSE.
BUT EVERY ONCE IN A WHILE, IF YOU LOOK LONG ENOUGH, PEEL ENOUGH LAYERS BACK...
...YOU CAN SEE THROUGH IT ALL...
...AND GET A PEEK INTO SOMEONE'S UNIVERSE.
IT'S OKAY, IT'S OKAY.
HEY. IT'S GOING TO BE OKAY.
I'M THE WORST.
WHAT? DON'T BE RIDICULOUS. YOU'RE A SWEETHEART AND YOU KNOW IT.

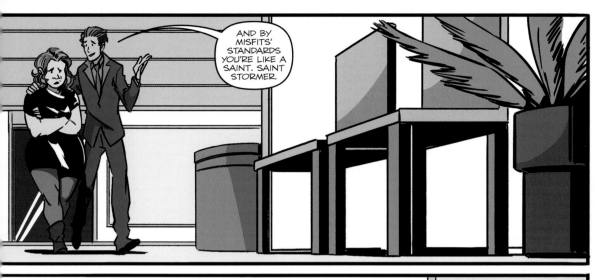

AND BY MISFITS' STANDARDS YOU'RE LIKE A SAINT. SAINT STORMER.

NO, I'VE BEEN AWFUL. SHE MAKES ME SO MAD.

SHE MAKES IT SO HARD TO BE NICE... AND THEN...

AND THEN WHAT?

AND THEN I FIND OUT THAT SHE HAS ME LISTED AS HER EMERGENCY CONTACT.

I MEAN, SHE MAKES IT SO HARD TO LOVE HER. IMPOSSIBLE. BUT THEN...

BUT THEN SHE SHOWS YOU SOMETHING VULNERABLE.

YEAH.

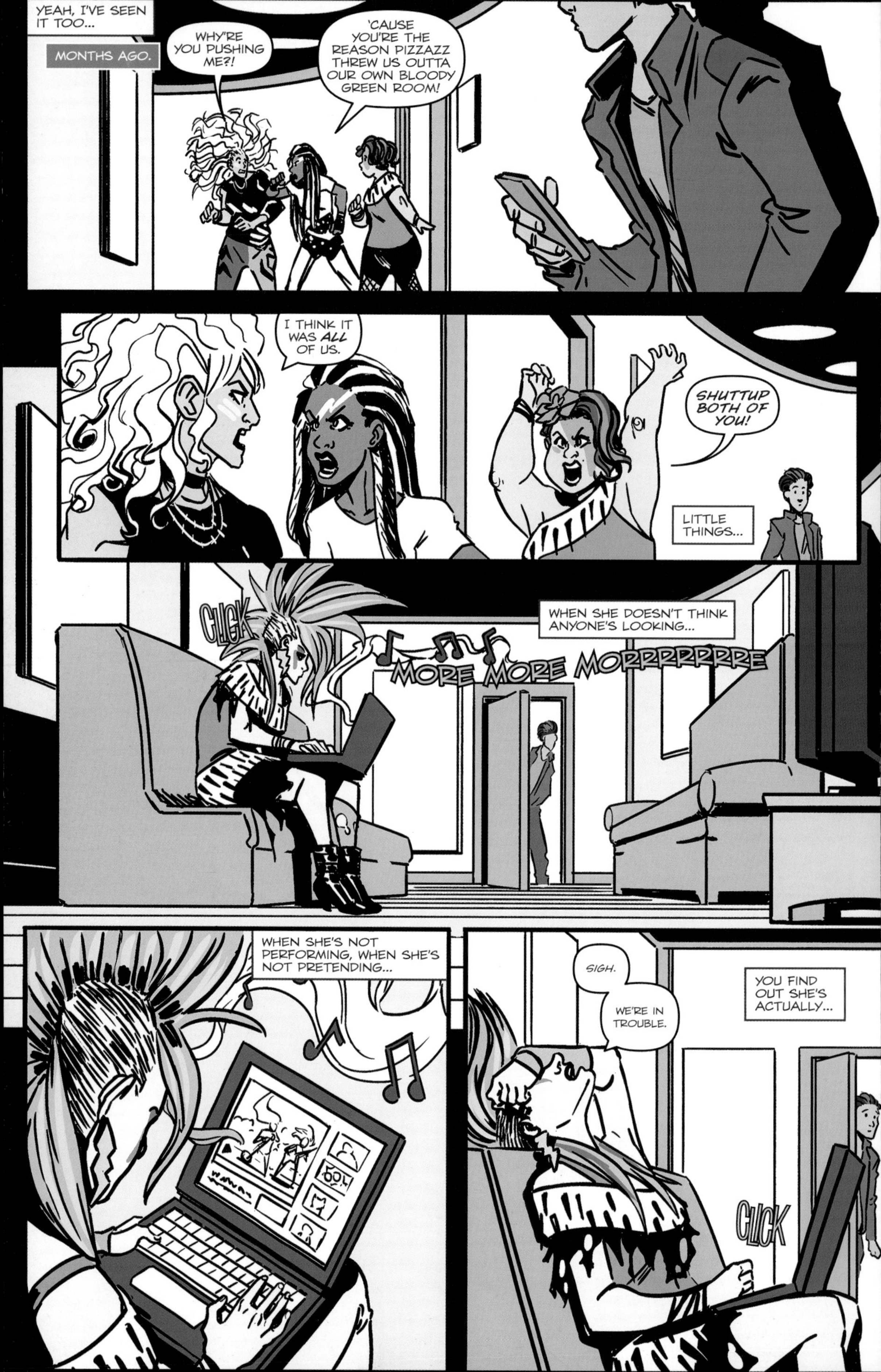
YEAH, I'VE SEEN IT TOO...
MONTHS AGO.
WHY'RE YOU PUSHING ME?!
'CAUSE YOU'RE THE REASON PIZZAZZ THREW US OUTTA OUR OWN BLOODY GREEN ROOM!
I THINK IT WAS ALL OF US.
SHUTTUP BOTH OF YOU!
LITTLE THINGS...
CLICK
WHEN SHE DOESN'T THINK ANYONE'S LOOKING...
MORE MORE MORRRRRRRE
WHEN SHE'S NOT PERFORMING, WHEN SHE'S NOT PRETENDING...
SIGH.
WE'RE IN TROUBLE.
YOU FIND OUT SHE'S ACTUALLY...
CLICK

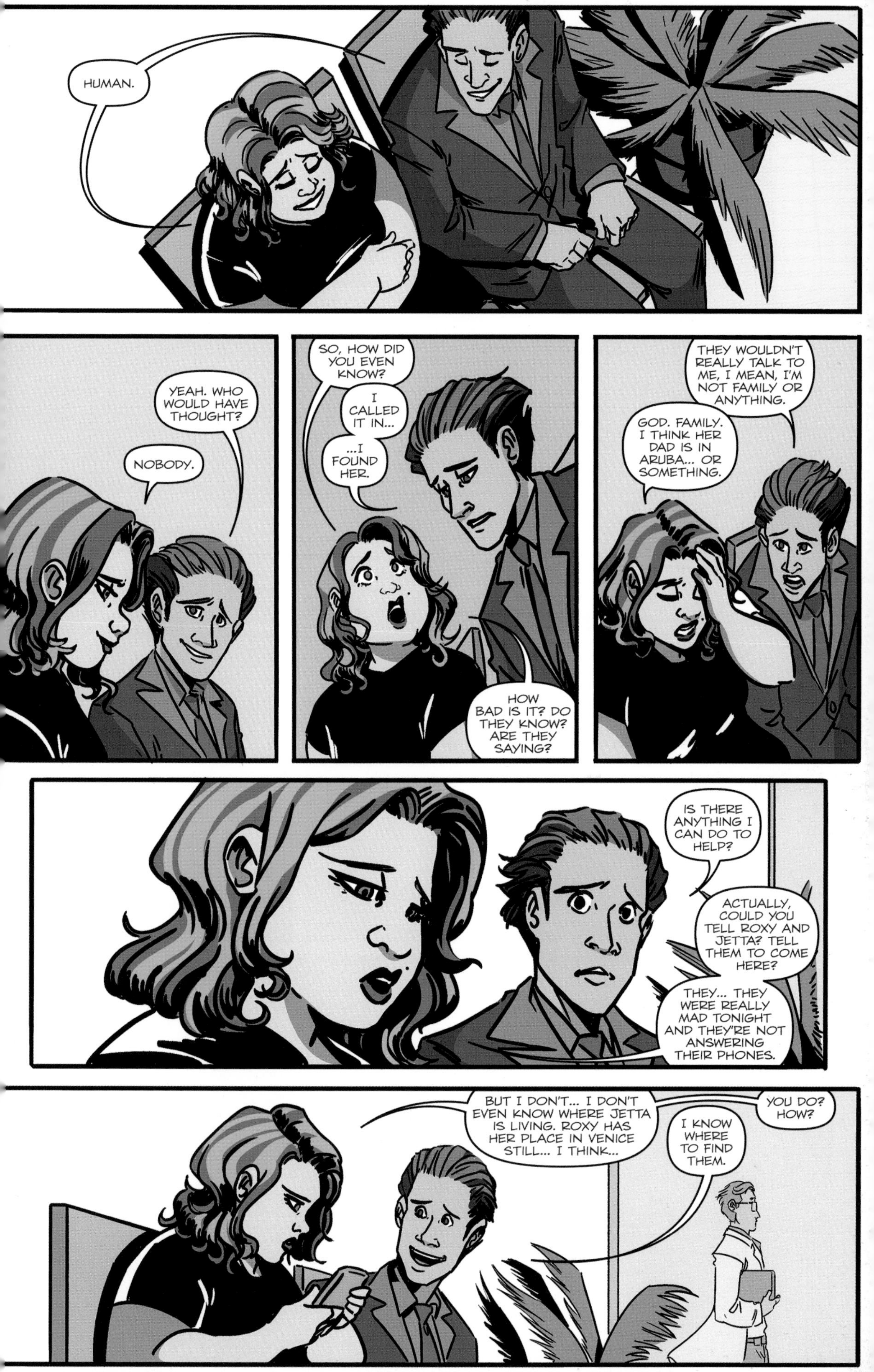
HUMAN.
YEAH. WHO WOULD HAVE THOUGHT?
NOBODY.
SO, HOW DID YOU EVEN KNOW?
I CALLED IT IN...
...I FOUND HER.
HOW BAD IS IT? DO THEY KNOW? ARE THEY SAYING?
THEY WOULDN'T REALLY TALK TO ME, I MEAN, I'M NOT FAMILY OR ANYTHING.
GOD. FAMILY. I THINK HER DAD IS IN ARUBA... OR SOMETHING.
IS THERE ANYTHING I CAN DO TO HELP?
ACTUALLY, COULD YOU TELL ROXY AND JETTA? TELL THEM TO COME HERE?
THEY... THEY WERE REALLY MAD TONIGHT AND THEY'RE NOT ANSWERING THEIR PHONES.
BUT I DON'T... I DON'T EVEN KNOW WHERE JETTA IS LIVING. ROXY HAS HER PLACE IN VENICE STILL... I THINK...
I KNOW WHERE TO FIND THEM.
YOU DO? HOW?

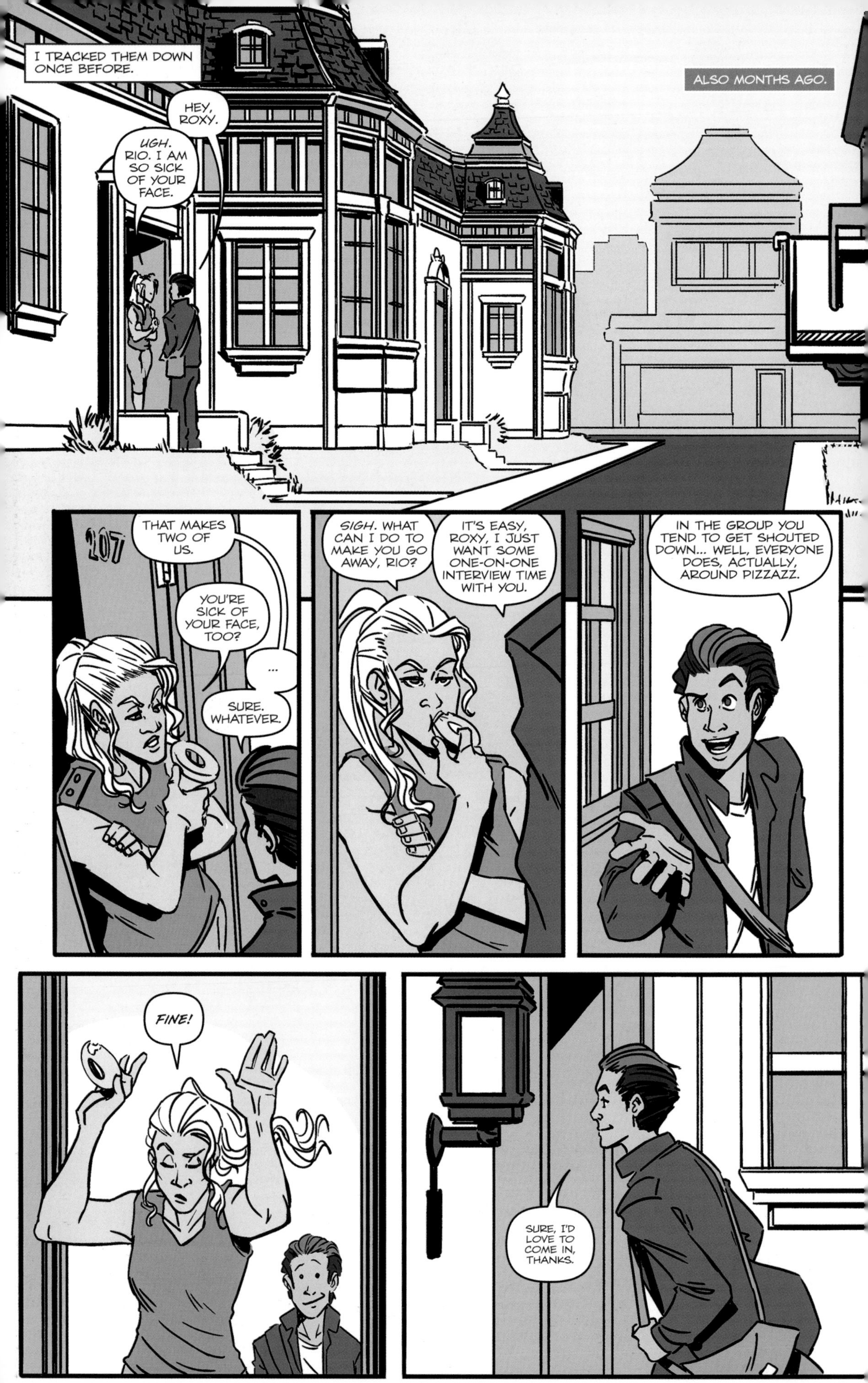
I TRACKED THEM DOWN ONCE BEFORE.
ALSO MONTHS AGO.
HEY, ROXY.
UGH. RIO. I AM SO SICK OF YOUR FACE.
207
THAT MAKES TWO OF US.
YOU'RE SICK OF YOUR FACE, TOO?
...
SURE. WHATEVER.
SIGH. WHAT CAN I DO TO MAKE YOU GO AWAY, RIO?
IT'S EASY, ROXY, I JUST WANT SOME ONE-ON-ONE INTERVIEW TIME WITH YOU.
IN THE GROUP YOU TEND TO GET SHOUTED DOWN... WELL, EVERYONE DOES, ACTUALLY, AROUND PIZZAZZ.
FINE!
SURE, I'D LOVE TO COME IN, THANKS.

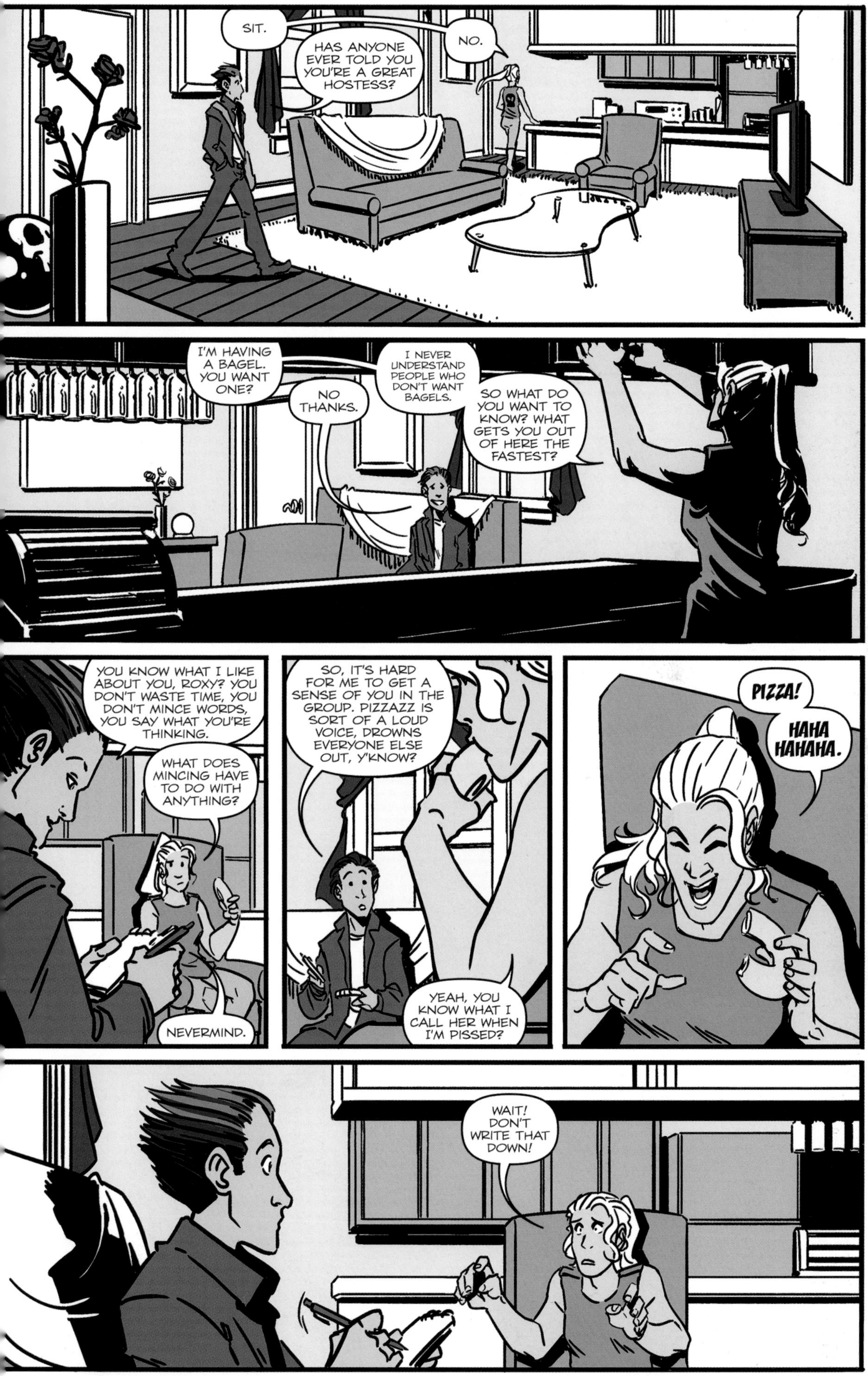
SIT.
HAS ANYONE EVER TOLD YOU YOU'RE A GREAT HOSTESS?
NO.
I'M HAVING A BAGEL. YOU WANT ONE?
NO THANKS.
I NEVER UNDERSTAND PEOPLE WHO DON'T WANT BAGELS.
SO WHAT DO YOU WANT TO KNOW? WHAT GETS YOU OUT OF HERE THE FASTEST?
YOU KNOW WHAT I LIKE ABOUT YOU, ROXY? YOU DON'T WASTE TIME, YOU DON'T MINCE WORDS, YOU SAY WHAT YOU'RE THINKING.
WHAT DOES MINCING HAVE TO DO WITH ANYTHING?
NEVERMIND.
SO, IT'S HARD FOR ME TO GET A SENSE OF YOU IN THE GROUP. PIZZAZZ IS SORT OF A LOUD VOICE, DROWNS EVERYONE ELSE OUT, Y'KNOW?
YEAH, YOU KNOW WHAT I CALL HER WHEN I'M PISSED?
PIZZA!
HAHA HAHAHA.
WAIT! DON'T WRITE THAT DOWN!

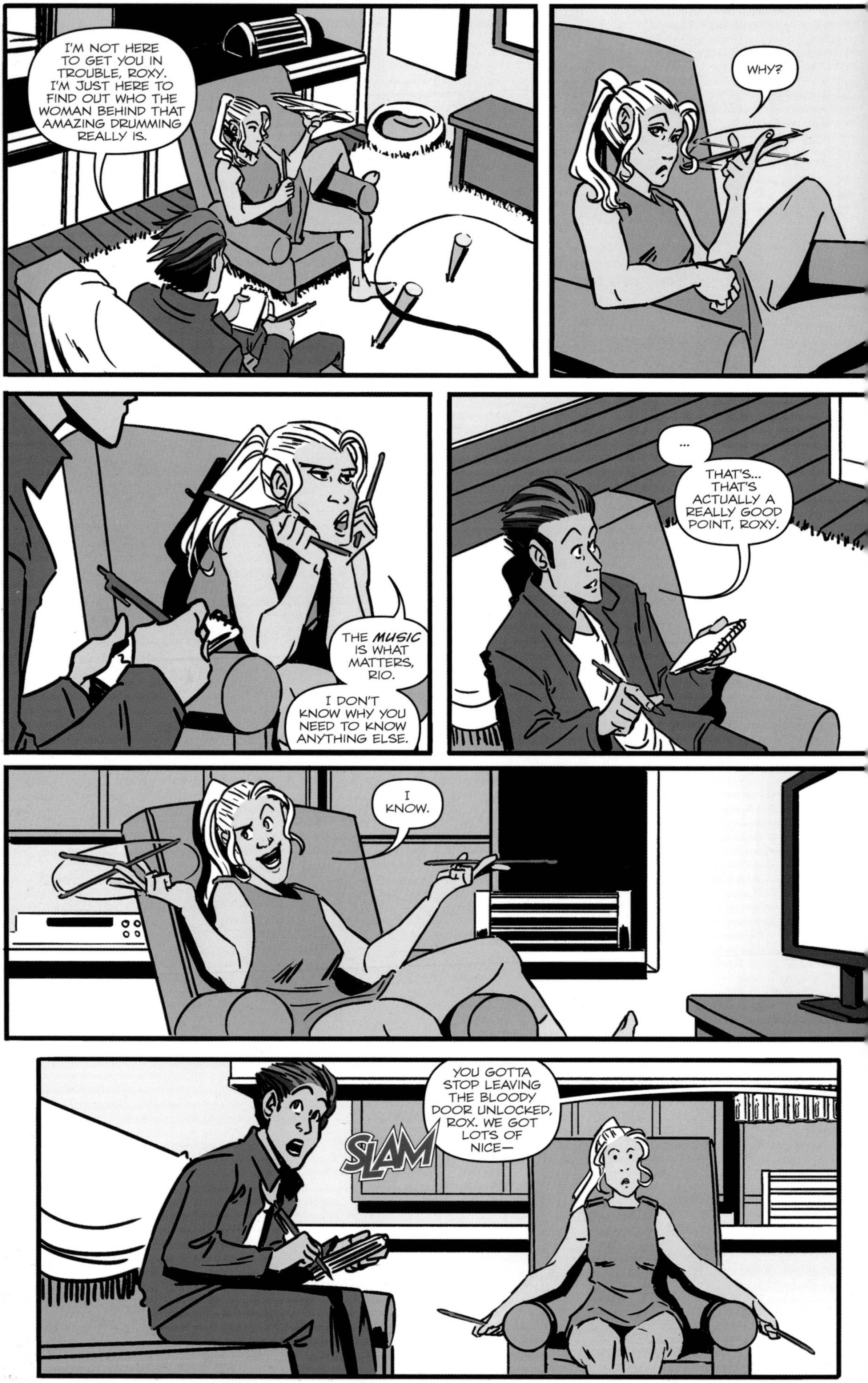
I'M NOT HERE TO GET YOU IN TROUBLE, ROXY. I'M JUST HERE TO FIND OUT WHO THE WOMAN BEHIND THAT AMAZING DRUMMING REALLY IS.
WHY?
THE MUSIC IS WHAT MATTERS, RIO.
I DON'T KNOW WHY YOU NEED TO KNOW ANYTHING ELSE.
...
THAT'S... THAT'S ACTUALLY A REALLY GOOD POINT, ROXY.
I KNOW.
SLAM
YOU GOTTA STOP LEAVING THE BLOODY DOOR UNLOCKED, ROX. WE GOT LOTS OF NICE—

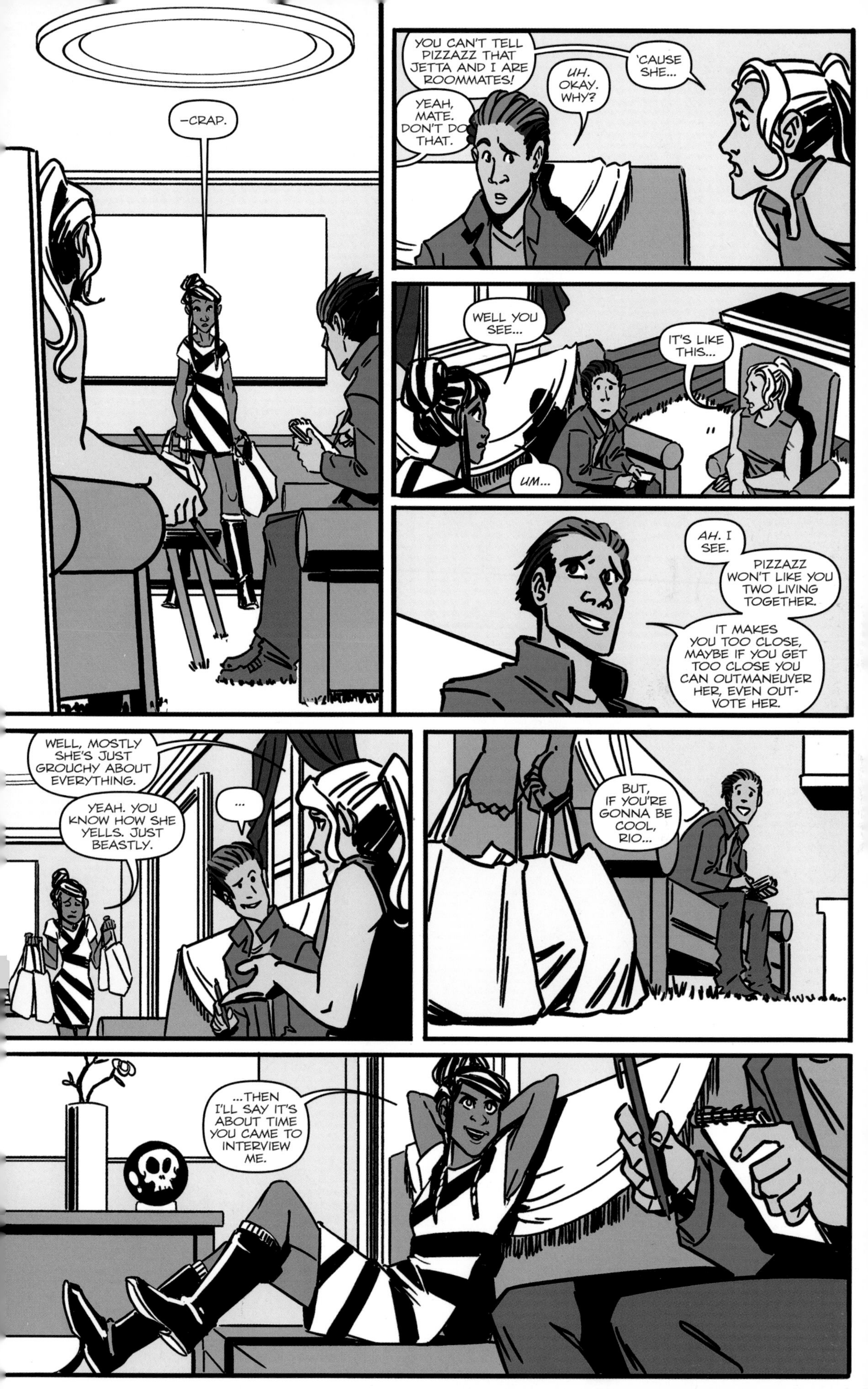
–CRAP.
YOU CAN'T TELL PIZZAZZ THAT JETTA AND I ARE ROOMMATES!
YEAH, MATE. DON'T DO THAT.
UH. OKAY. WHY?
'CAUSE SHE...
WELL YOU SEE...
IT'S LIKE THIS...
UM...
AH. I SEE.
PIZZAZZ WON'T LIKE YOU TWO LIVING TOGETHER.
IT MAKES YOU TOO CLOSE, MAYBE IF YOU GET TOO CLOSE YOU CAN OUTMANEUVER HER, EVEN OUT-VOTE HER.
WELL, MOSTLY SHE'S JUST GROUCHY ABOUT EVERYTHING.
YEAH. YOU KNOW HOW SHE YELLS. JUST BEASTLY.
...
BUT, IF YOU'RE GONNA BE COOL, RIO...
...THEN I'LL SAY IT'S ABOUT TIME YOU CAME TO INTERVIEW ME.

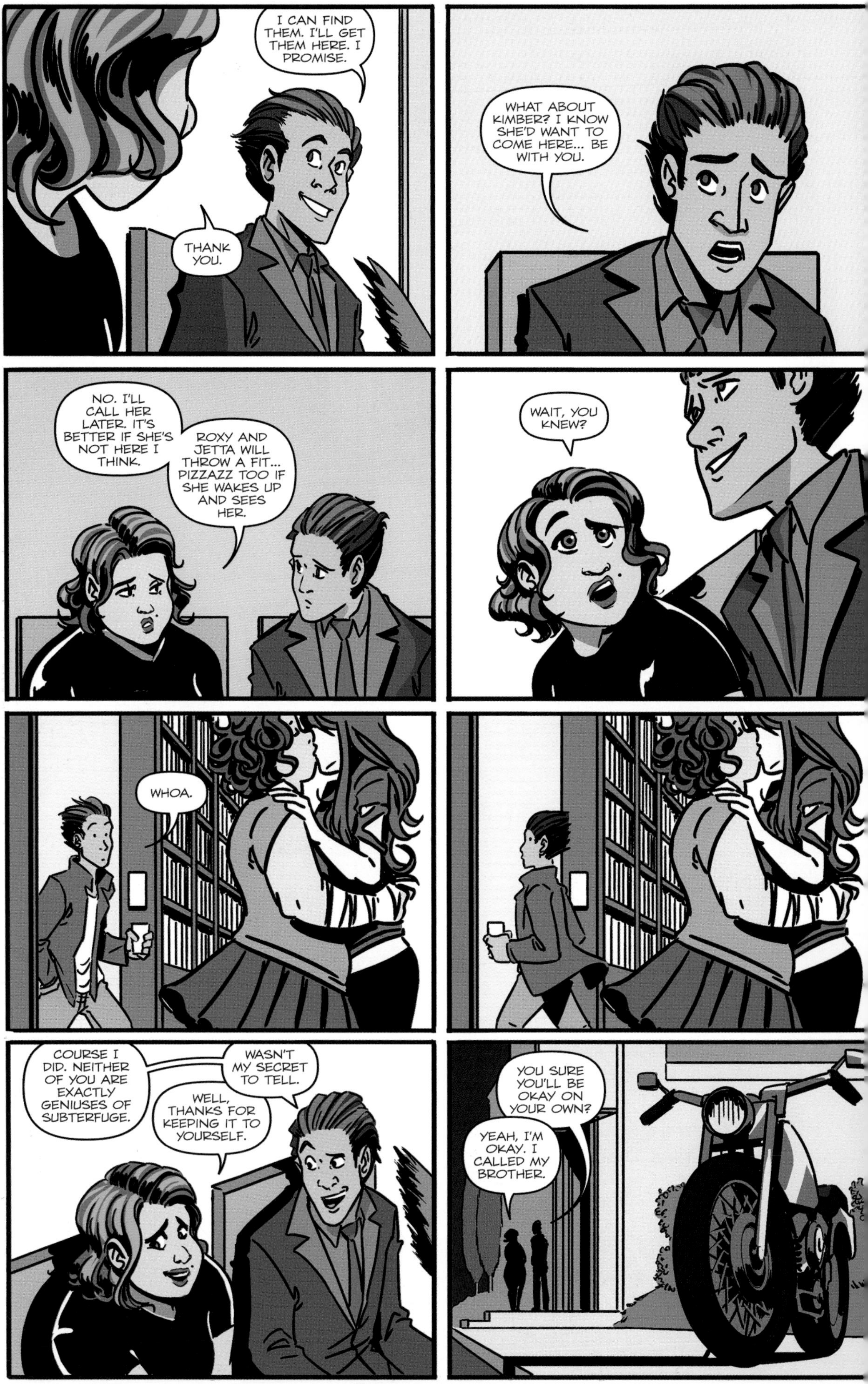
I CAN FIND THEM. I'LL GET THEM HERE. I PROMISE.
THANK YOU.
WHAT ABOUT KIMBER? I KNOW SHE'D WANT TO COME HERE... BE WITH YOU.
NO. I'LL CALL HER LATER. IT'S BETTER IF SHE'S NOT HERE I THINK.
ROXY AND JETTA WILL THROW A FIT... PIZZAZZ TOO IF SHE WAKES UP AND SEES HER.
WAIT, YOU KNEW?
WHOA.
COURSE I DID. NEITHER OF YOU ARE EXACTLY GENIUSES OF SUBTERFUGE.
WASN'T MY SECRET TO TELL.
WELL, THANKS FOR KEEPING IT TO YOURSELF.
YOU SURE YOU'LL BE OKAY ON YOUR OWN?
YEAH, I'M OKAY. I CALLED MY BROTHER.

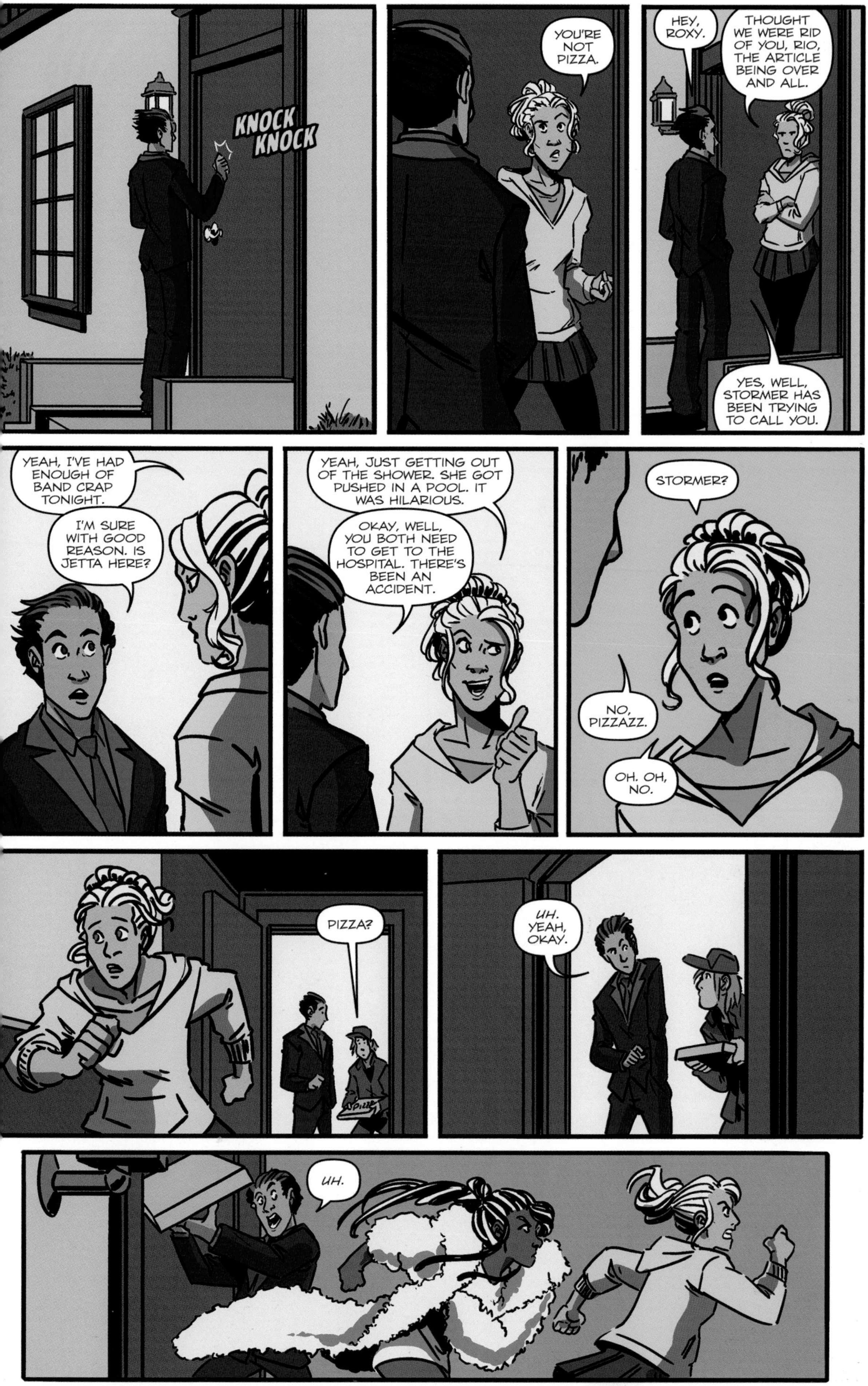
KNOCK KNOCK
YOU'RE NOT PIZZA.
HEY, ROXY.
THOUGHT WE WERE RID OF YOU, RIO, THE ARTICLE BEING OVER AND ALL.
YES, WELL, STORMER HAS BEEN TRYING TO CALL YOU.
YEAH, I'VE HAD ENOUGH OF BAND CRAP TONIGHT.
I'M SURE WITH GOOD REASON. IS JETTA HERE?
YEAH, JUST GETTING OUT OF THE SHOWER. SHE GOT PUSHED IN A POOL. IT WAS HILARIOUS.
OKAY, WELL, YOU BOTH NEED TO GET TO THE HOSPITAL. THERE'S BEEN AN ACCIDENT.
STORMER?
NO, PIZZAZZ.
OH. OH, NO.
PIZZA?
UH. YEAH, OKAY.
UH.

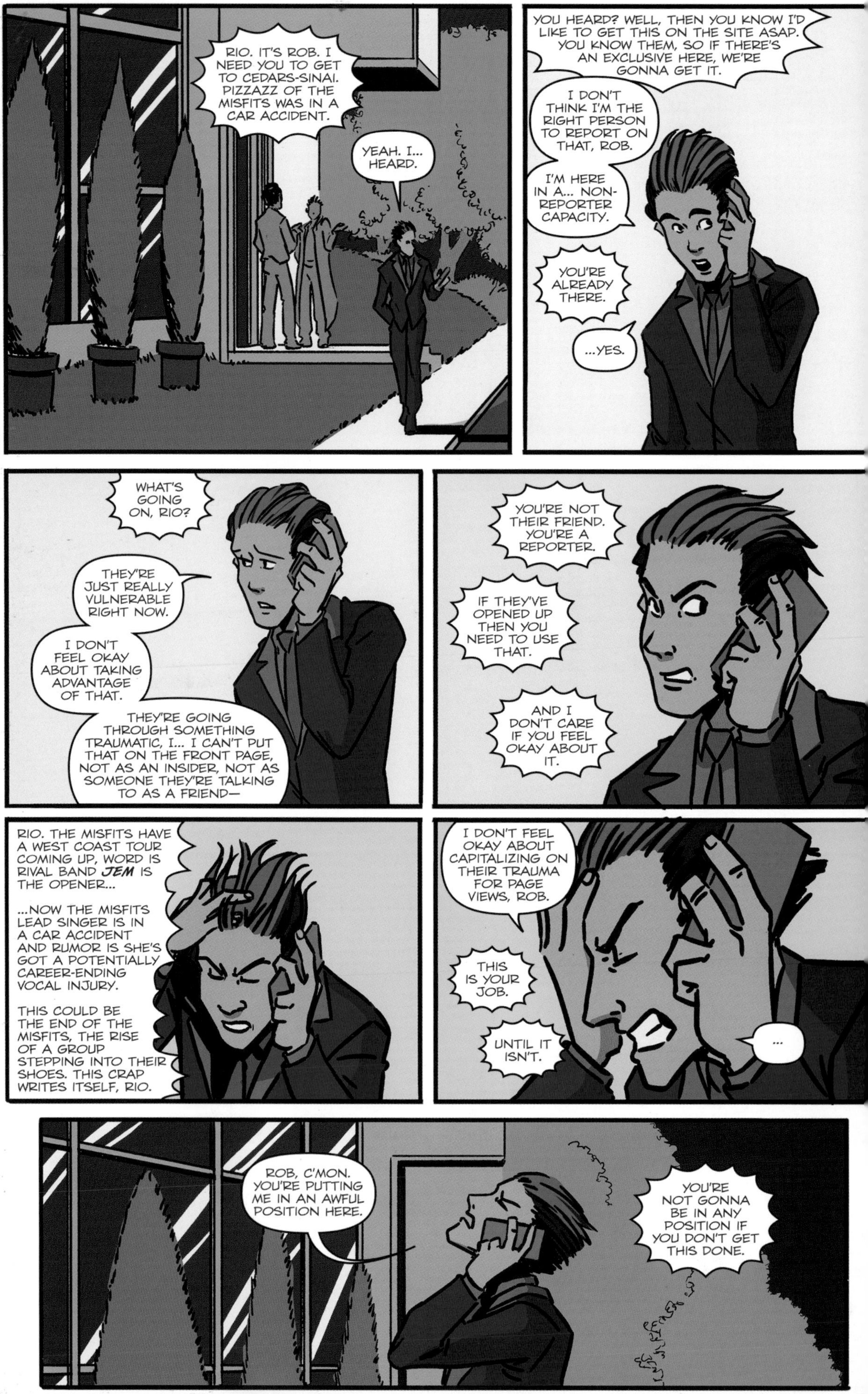
RIO. IT'S ROB. I NEED YOU TO GET TO CEDARS-SINAI. PIZZAZZ OF THE MISFITS WAS IN A CAR ACCIDENT.
YEAH. I... HEARD.
YOU HEARD? WELL, THEN YOU KNOW I'D LIKE TO GET THIS ON THE SITE ASAP. YOU KNOW THEM, SO IF THERE'S AN EXCLUSIVE HERE, WE'RE GONNA GET IT.
I DON'T THINK I'M THE RIGHT PERSON TO REPORT ON THAT, ROB.
I'M HERE IN A... NON-REPORTER CAPACITY.
YOU'RE ALREADY THERE.
...YES.
WHAT'S GOING ON, RIO?
THEY'RE JUST REALLY VULNERABLE RIGHT NOW.
I DON'T FEEL OKAY ABOUT TAKING ADVANTAGE OF THAT.
THEY'RE GOING THROUGH SOMETHING TRAUMATIC, I... I CAN'T PUT THAT ON THE FRONT PAGE, NOT AS AN INSIDER, NOT AS SOMEONE THEY'RE TALKING TO AS A FRIEND—
YOU'RE NOT THEIR FRIEND. YOU'RE A REPORTER.
IF THEY'VE OPENED UP THEN YOU NEED TO USE THAT.
AND I DON'T CARE IF YOU FEEL OKAY ABOUT IT.
RIO. THE MISFITS HAVE A WEST COAST TOUR COMING UP, WORD IS RIVAL BAND JEM IS THE OPENER...
...NOW THE MISFITS LEAD SINGER IS IN A CAR ACCIDENT AND RUMOR IS SHE'S GOT A POTENTIALLY CAREER-ENDING VOCAL INJURY.
THIS COULD BE THE END OF THE MISFITS, THE RISE OF A GROUP STEPPING INTO THEIR SHOES. THIS CRAP WRITES ITSELF, RIO.
I DON'T FEEL OKAY ABOUT CAPITALIZING ON THEIR TRAUMA FOR PAGE VIEWS, ROB.
THIS IS YOUR JOB.
UNTIL IT ISN'T.
...
ROB, C'MON. YOU'RE PUTTING ME IN AN AWFUL POSITION HERE.
YOU'RE NOT GONNA BE IN ANY POSITION IF YOU DON'T GET THIS DONE.

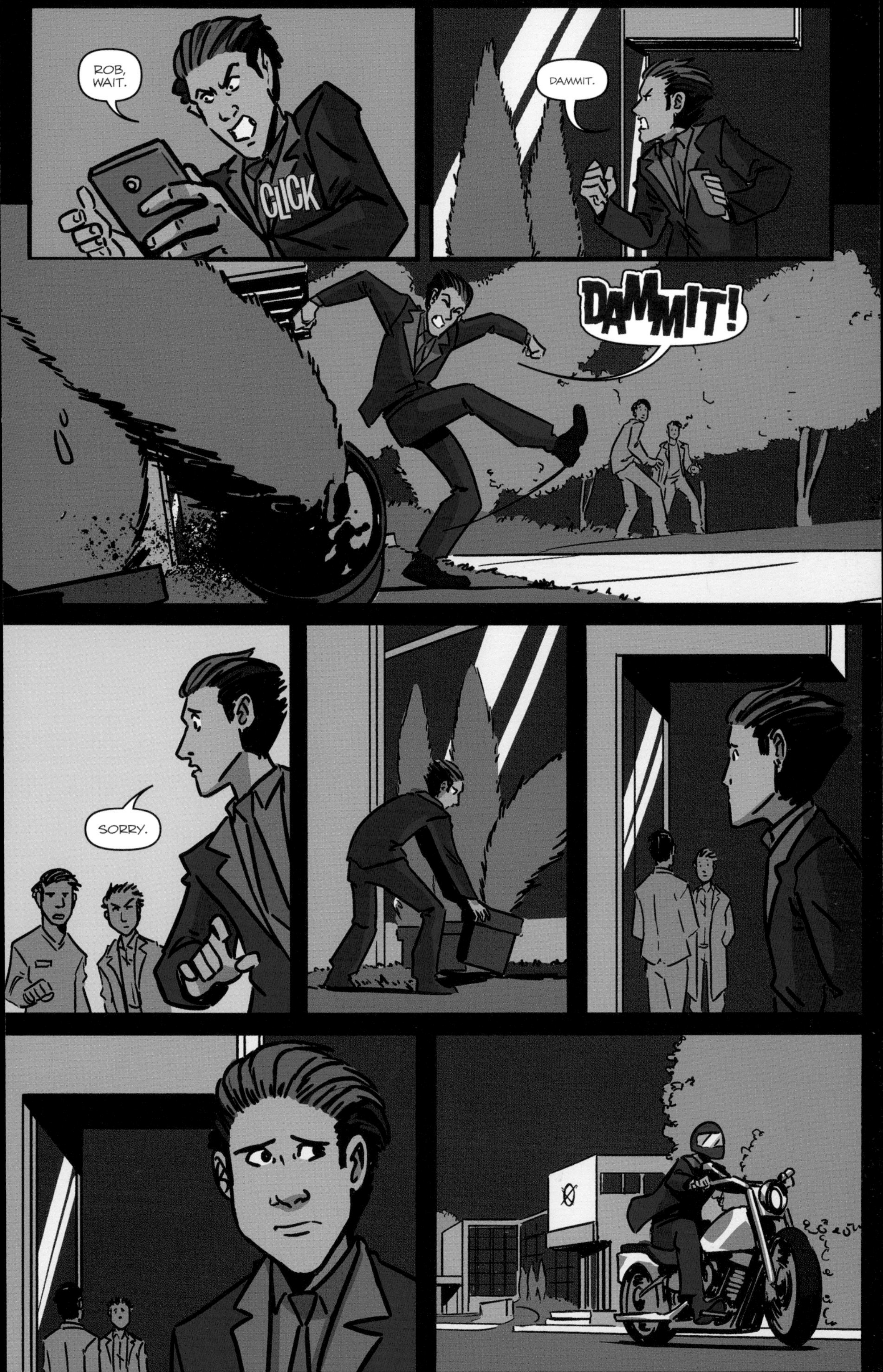
ROB, WAIT.
CLICK
DAMMIT.
DAMMIT!
SORRY.

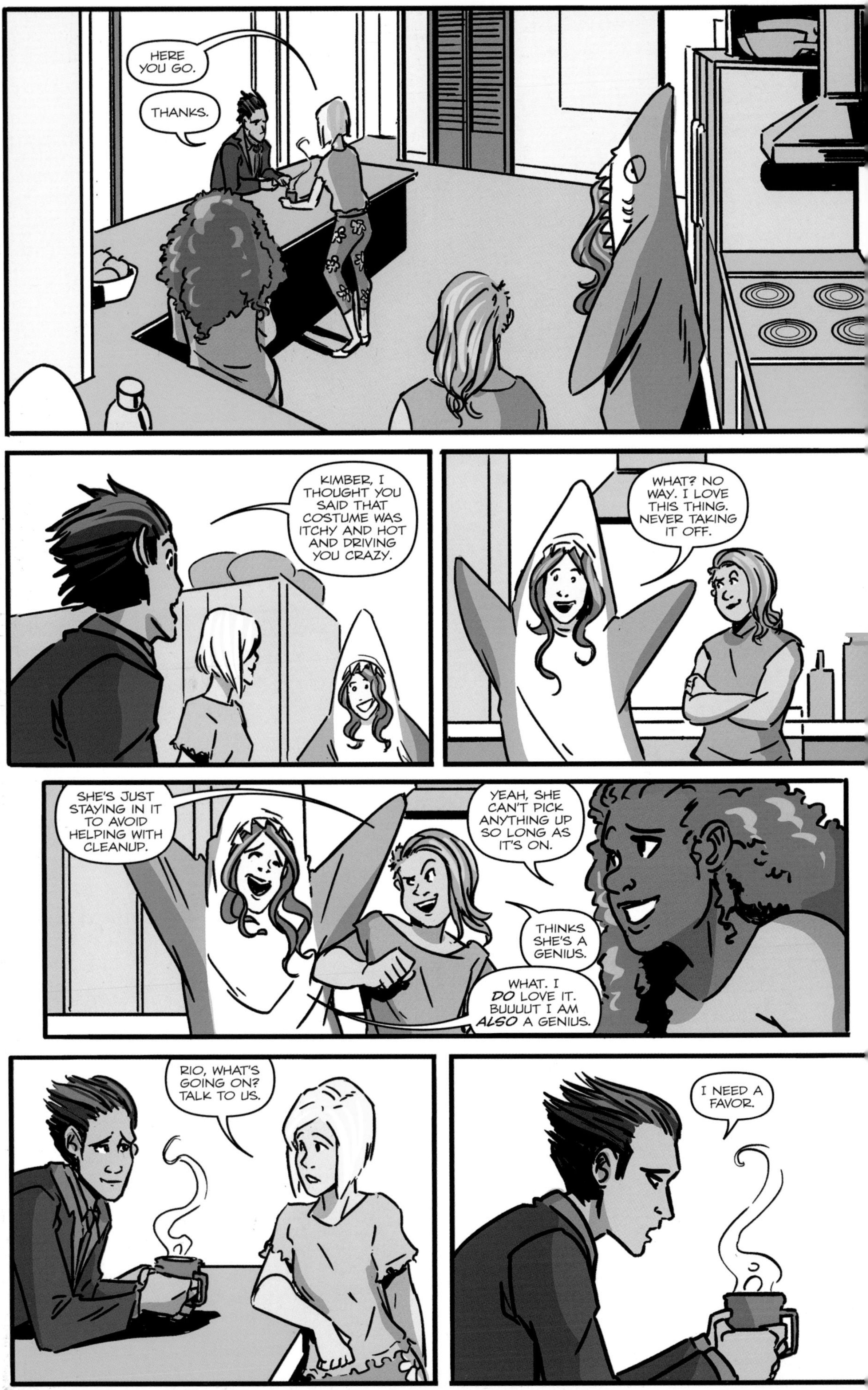
HERE YOU GO.
THANKS.
KIMBER, I THOUGHT YOU SAID THAT COSTUME WAS ITCHY AND HOT AND DRIVING YOU CRAZY.
WHAT? NO WAY. I LOVE THIS THING. NEVER TAKING IT OFF.
SHE'S JUST STAYING IN IT TO AVOID HELPING WITH CLEANUP.
YEAH, SHE CAN'T PICK ANYTHING UP SO LONG AS IT'S ON.
THINKS SHE'S A GENIUS.
WHAT. I DO LOVE IT. BUUUUT I AM ALSO A GENIUS.
RIO, WHAT'S GOING ON? TALK TO US.
I NEED A FAVOR.

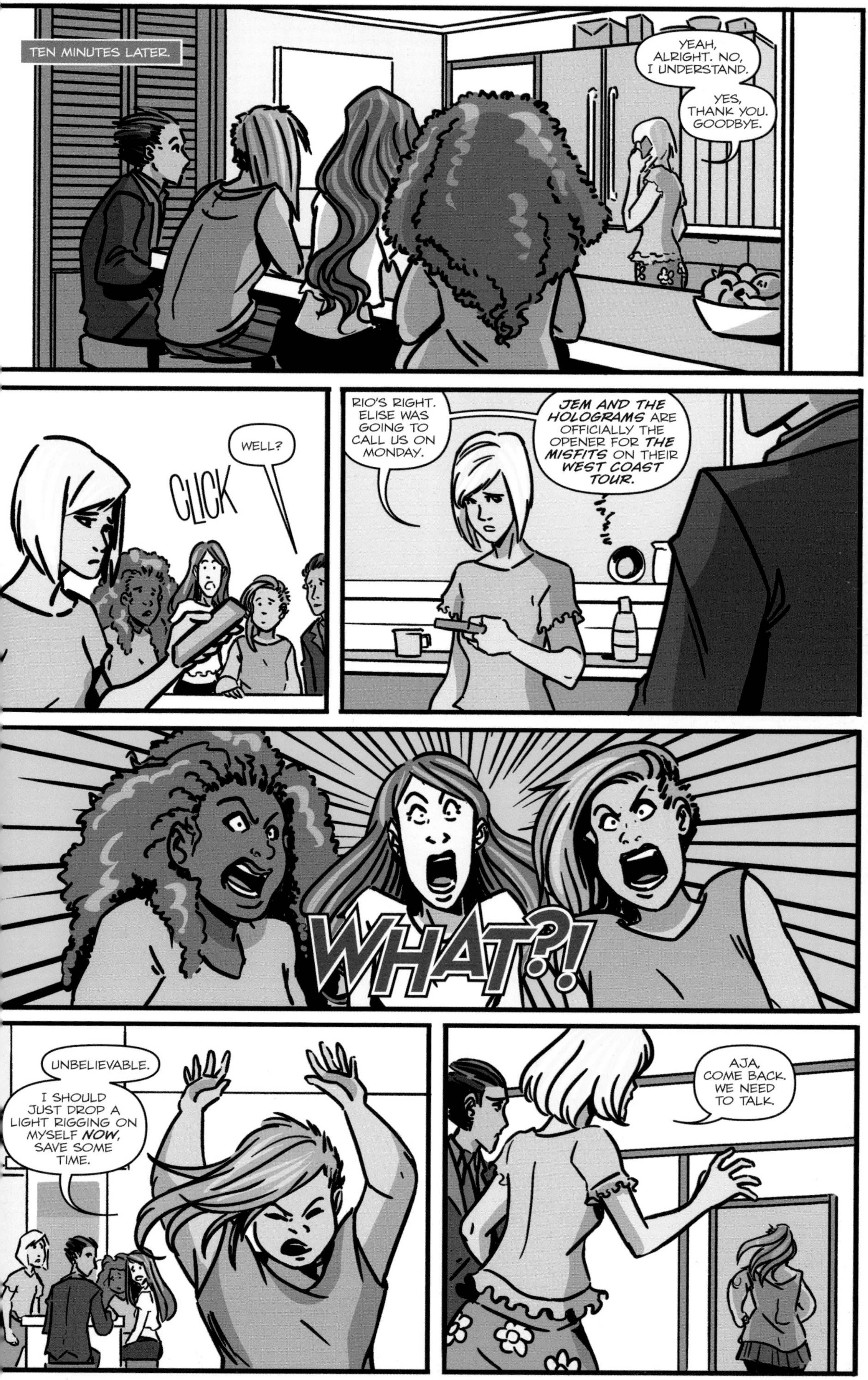
TEN MINUTES LATER.
YEAH, ALRIGHT. NO, I UNDERSTAND.
YES, THANK YOU. GOODBYE.
CLICK
WELL?
RIO'S RIGHT. ELISE WAS GOING TO CALL US ON MONDAY.
JEM AND THE HOLOGRAMS ARE OFFICIALLY THE OPENER FOR THE MISFITS ON THEIR WEST COAST TOUR.
WHAT?!
UNBELIEVABLE.
I SHOULD JUST DROP A LIGHT RIGGING ON MYSELF NOW, SAVE SOME TIME.
AJA, COME BACK. WE NEED TO TALK.

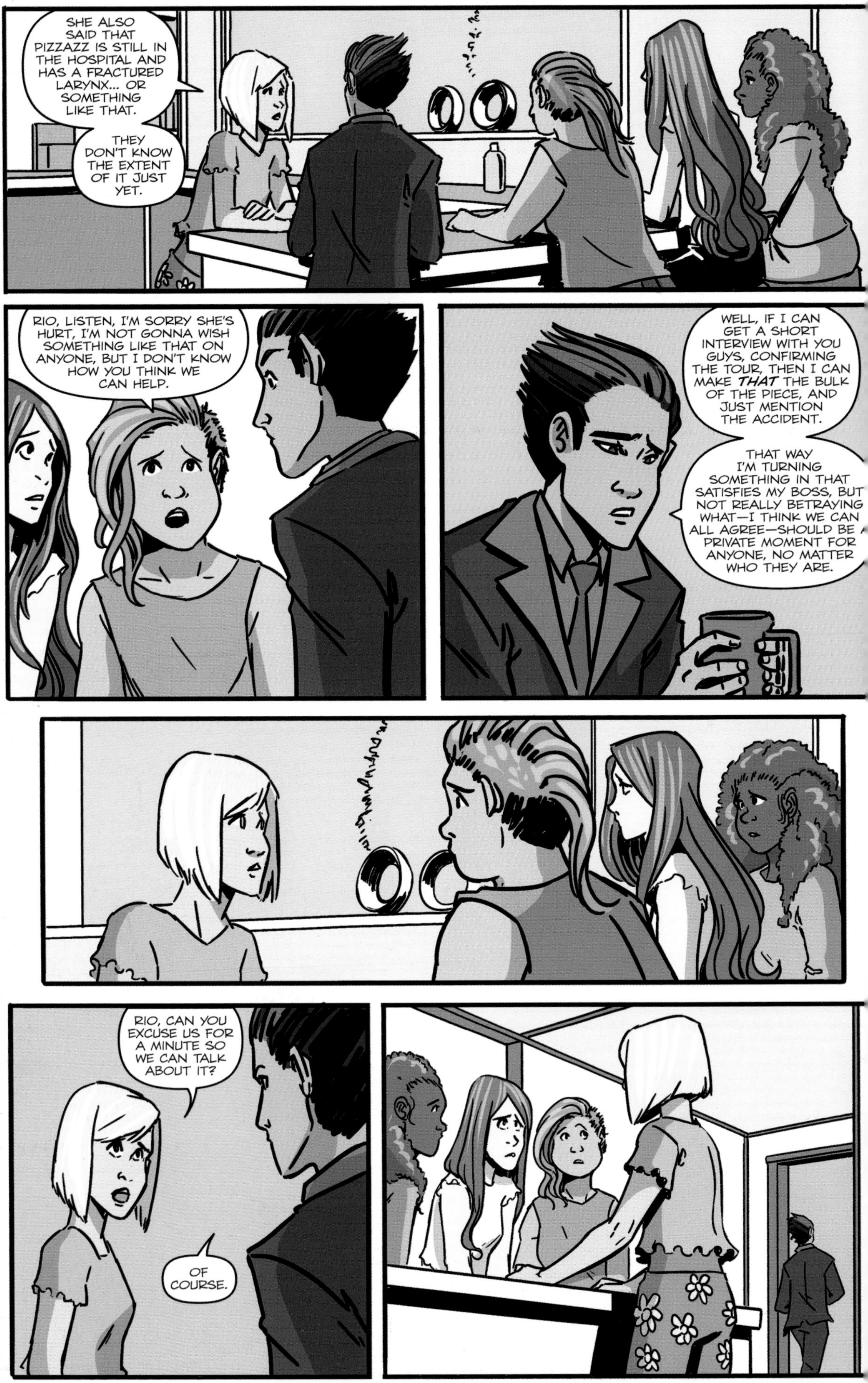
SHE ALSO SAID THAT PIZZAZZ IS STILL IN THE HOSPITAL AND HAS A FRACTURED LARYNX... OR SOMETHING LIKE THAT.
THEY DON'T KNOW THE EXTENT OF IT JUST YET.
RIO, LISTEN, I'M SORRY SHE'S HURT, I'M NOT GONNA WISH SOMETHING LIKE THAT ON ANYONE, BUT I DON'T KNOW HOW YOU THINK WE CAN HELP.
WELL, IF I CAN GET A SHORT INTERVIEW WITH YOU GUYS, CONFIRMING THE TOUR, THEN I CAN MAKE *THAT* THE BULK OF THE PIECE, AND JUST MENTION THE ACCIDENT.
THAT WAY I'M TURNING SOMETHING IN THAT SATISFIES MY BOSS, BUT NOT REALLY BETRAYING WHAT—I THINK WE CAN ALL AGREE—SHOULD BE A PRIVATE MOMENT FOR ANYONE, NO MATTER WHO THEY ARE.
RIO, CAN YOU EXCUSE US FOR A MINUTE SO WE CAN TALK ABOUT IT?
OF COURSE.

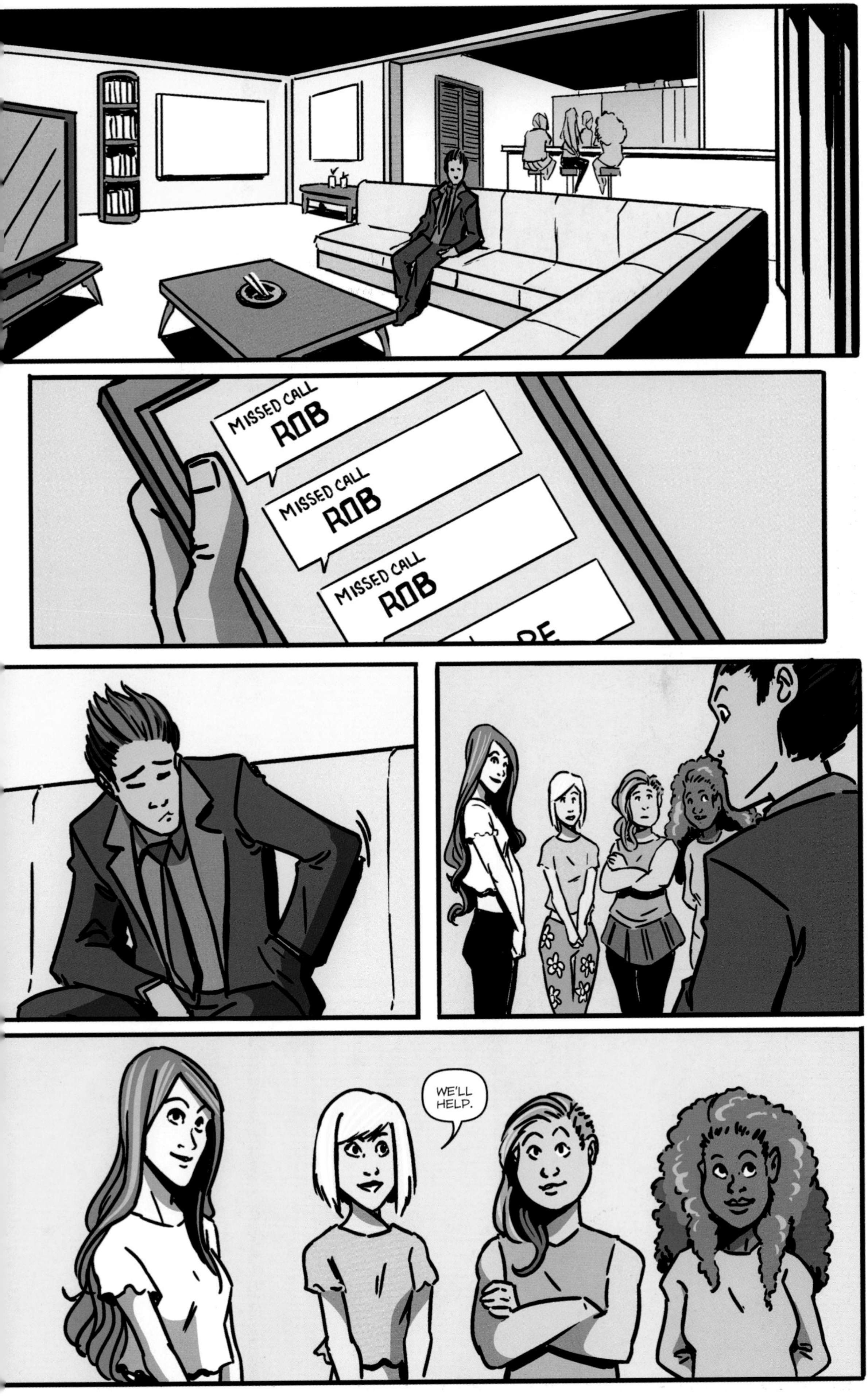
MISSED CALL
ROB
MISSED CALL
ROB
MISSED CALL
ROB
WE'LL HELP.

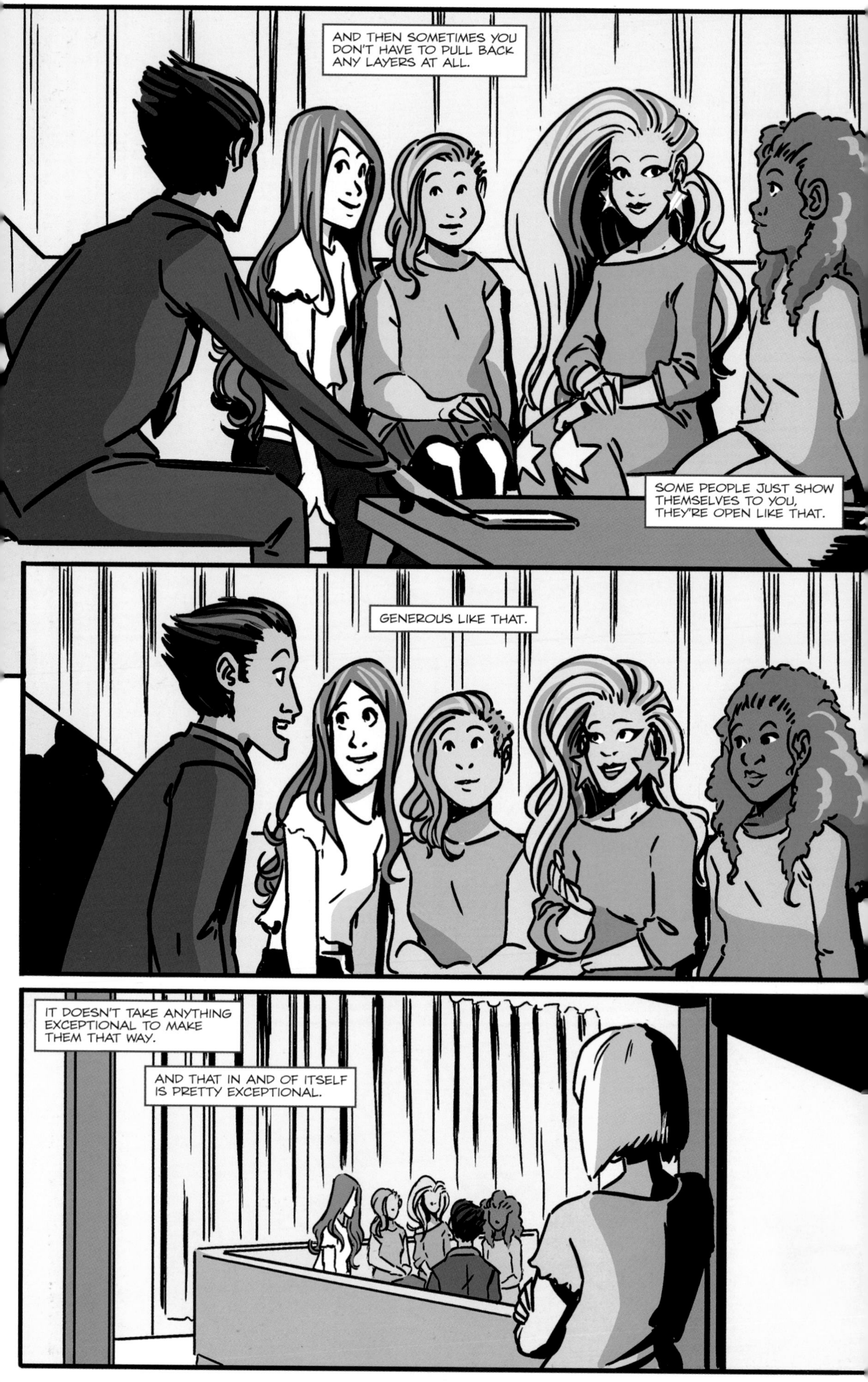
AND THEN SOMETIMES YOU DON'T HAVE TO PULL BACK ANY LAYERS AT ALL.
SOME PEOPLE JUST SHOW THEMSELVES TO YOU, THEY'RE OPEN LIKE THAT.
GENEROUS LIKE THAT.
IT DOESN'T TAKE ANYTHING EXCEPTIONAL TO MAKE THEM THAT WAY.
AND THAT IN AND OF ITSELF IS PRETTY EXCEPTIONAL.

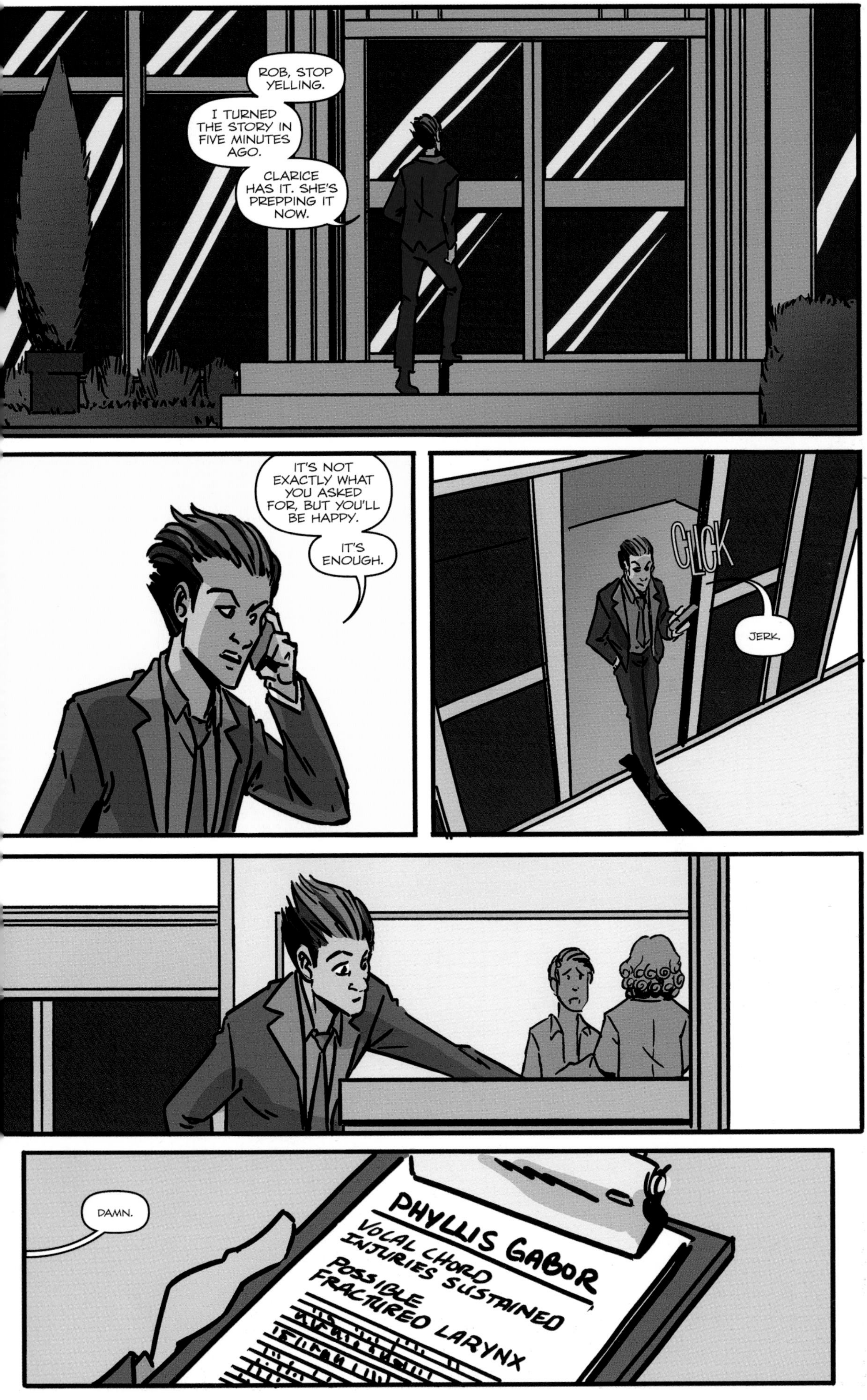
ROB, STOP YELLING.
I TURNED THE STORY IN FIVE MINUTES AGO.
CLARICE HAS IT. SHE'S PREPPING IT NOW.
IT'S NOT EXACTLY WHAT YOU ASKED FOR, BUT YOU'LL BE HAPPY.
IT'S ENOUGH.
CLICK
JERK.
DAMN.
PHYLLIS GABOR
VOCAL CHORD INJURIES SUSTAINED
POSSIBLE FRACTURED LARYNX

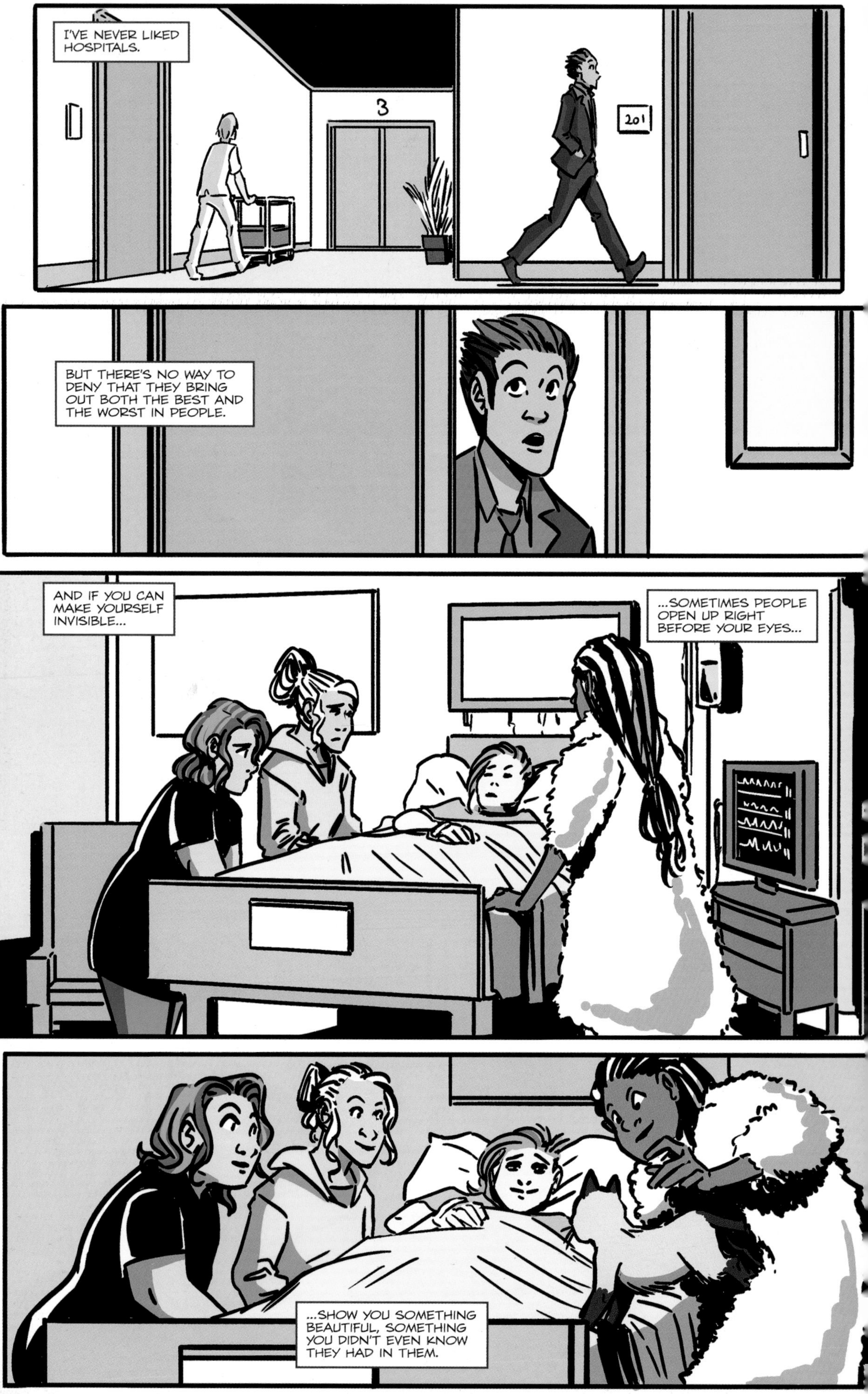

I'VE NEVER LIKED HOSPITALS.
3
201
BUT THERE'S NO WAY TO DENY THAT THEY BRING OUT BOTH THE BEST AND THE WORST IN PEOPLE.
AND IF YOU CAN MAKE YOURSELF INVISIBLE...
...SOMETIMES PEOPLE OPEN UP RIGHT BEFORE YOUR EYES...
...SHOW YOU SOMETHING BEAUTIFUL, SOMETHING YOU DIDN'T EVEN KNOW THEY HAD IN THEM.

ART BY **M. VICTORIA ROBADO**

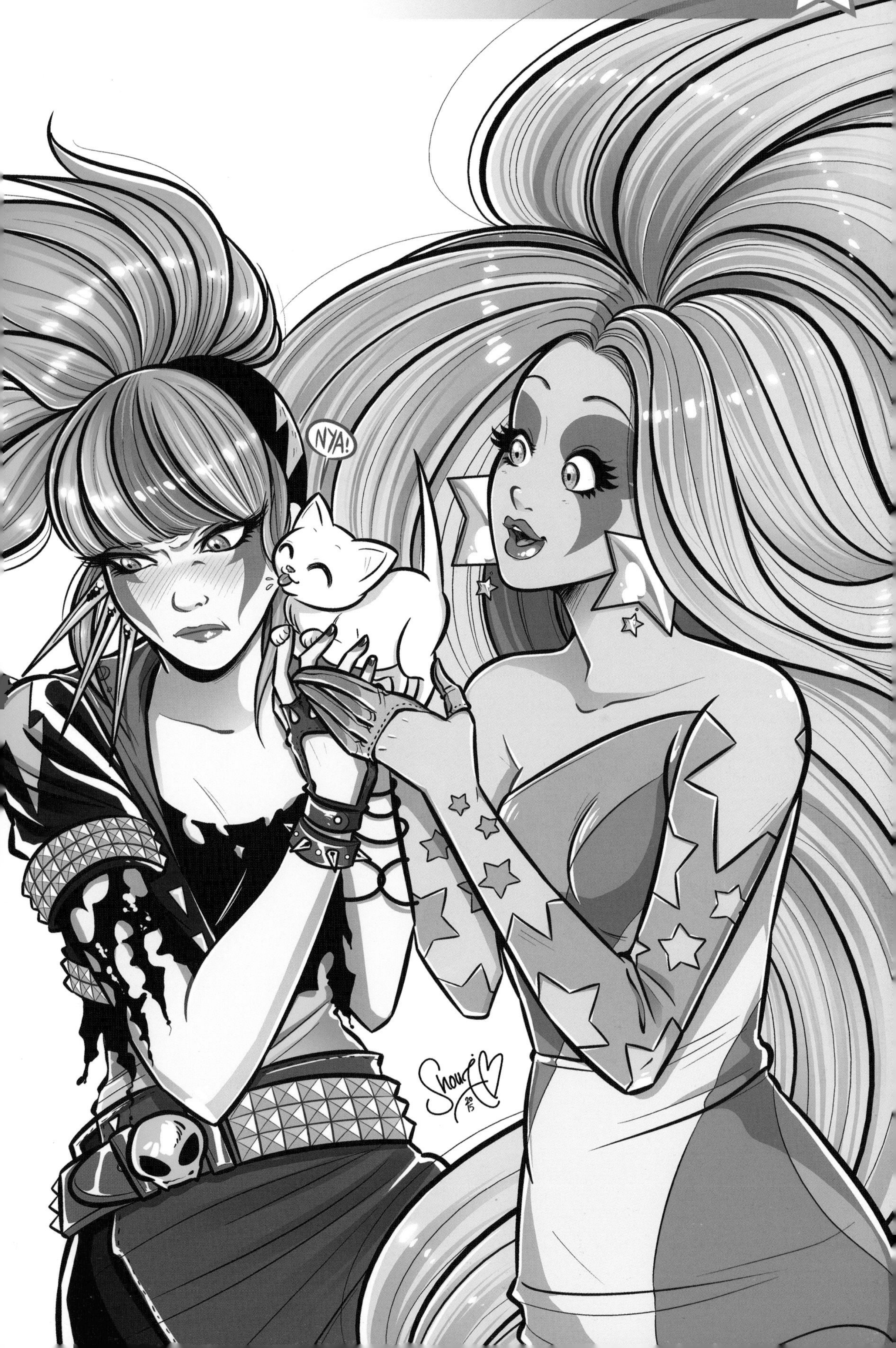
NYA!

6 ART BY **AMY MEBBERSON**

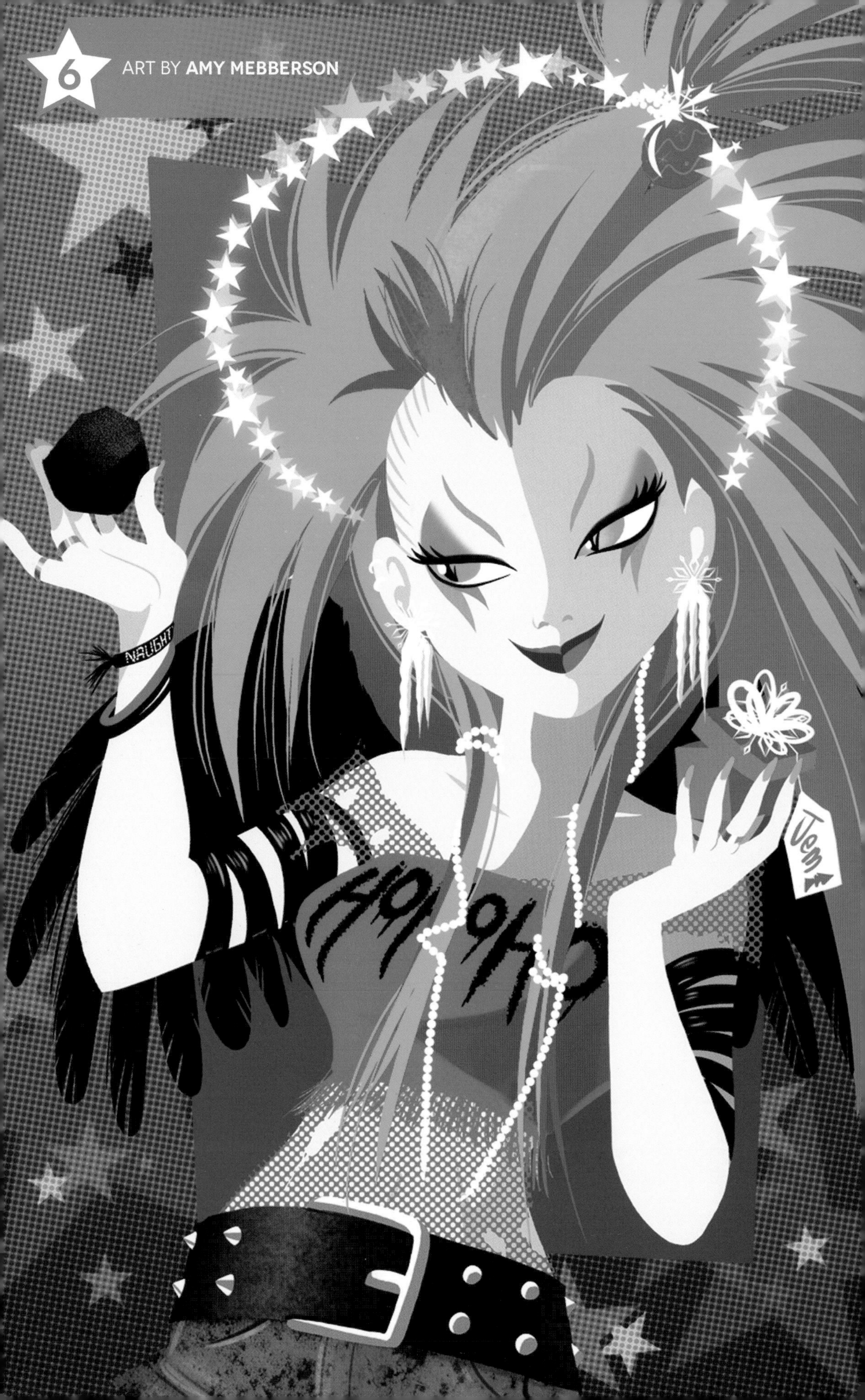
NAUGHT
Jem

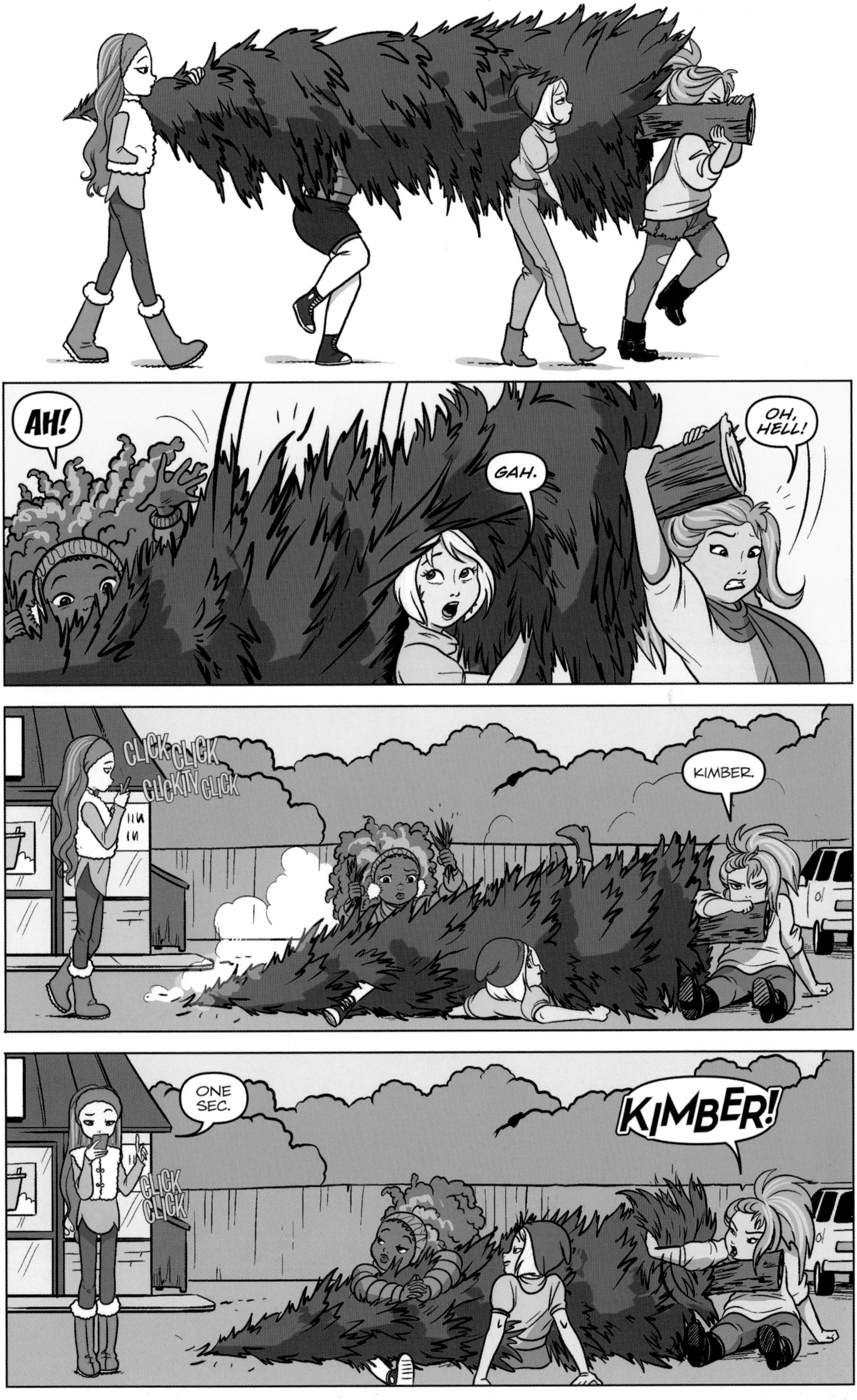
AH!
GAH.
OH, HELL!
CLICK CLICK
CLICKITY CLICK
KIMBER.
ONE SEC.
CLICK CLICK
KIMBER!

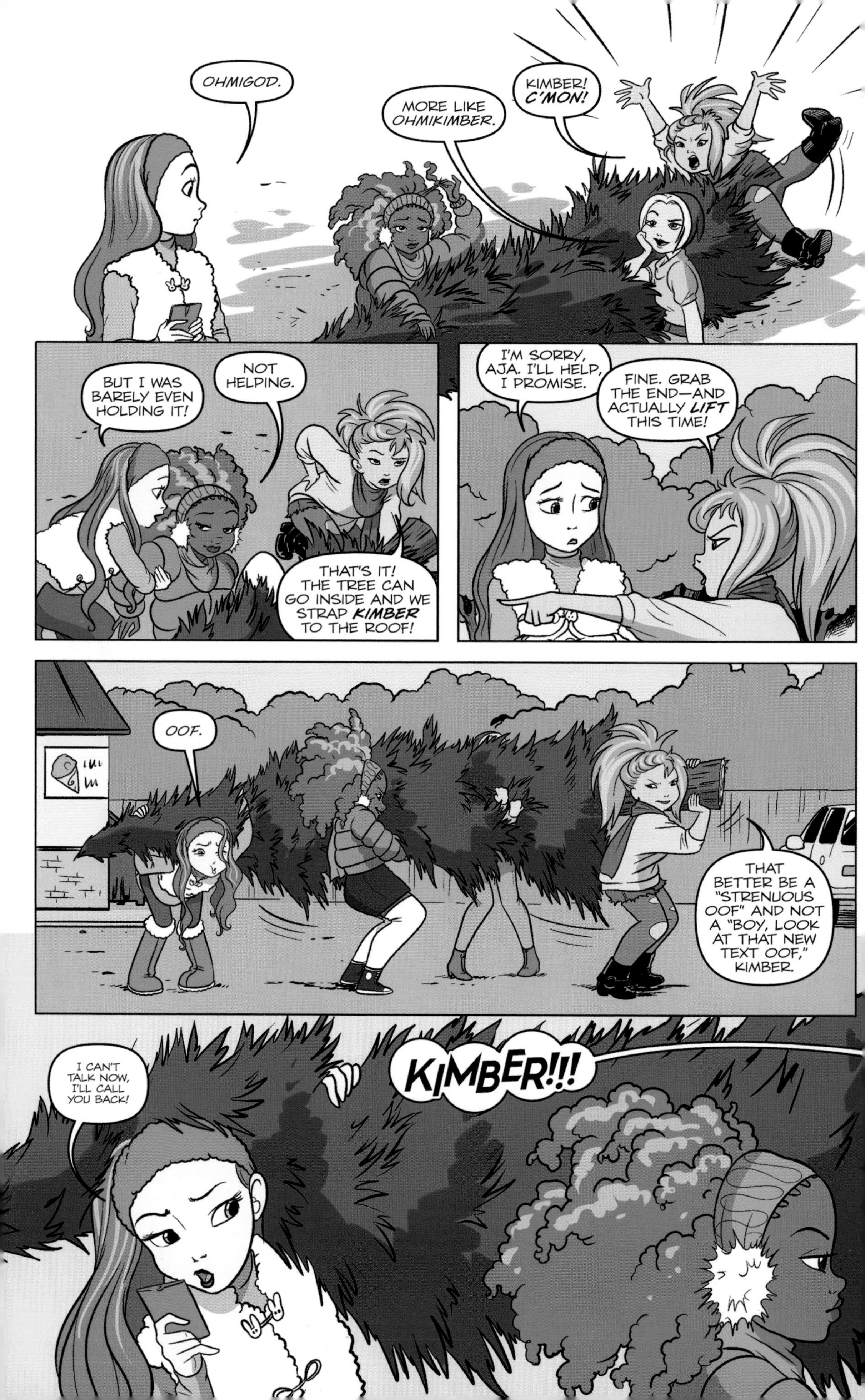
OHMIGOD.
MORE LIKE OHMIKIMBER.
KIMBER! C'MON!
BUT I WAS BARELY EVEN HOLDING IT!
NOT HELPING.
THAT'S IT! THE TREE CAN GO INSIDE AND WE STRAP KIMBER TO THE ROOF!
I'M SORRY, AJA. I'LL HELP, I PROMISE.
FINE. GRAB THE END—AND ACTUALLY LIFT THIS TIME!
OOF.
THAT BETTER BE A "STRENUOUS OOF" AND NOT A "BOY, LOOK AT THAT NEW TEXT OOF," KIMBER.
I CAN'T TALK NOW, I'LL CALL YOU BACK!
KIMBER!!!

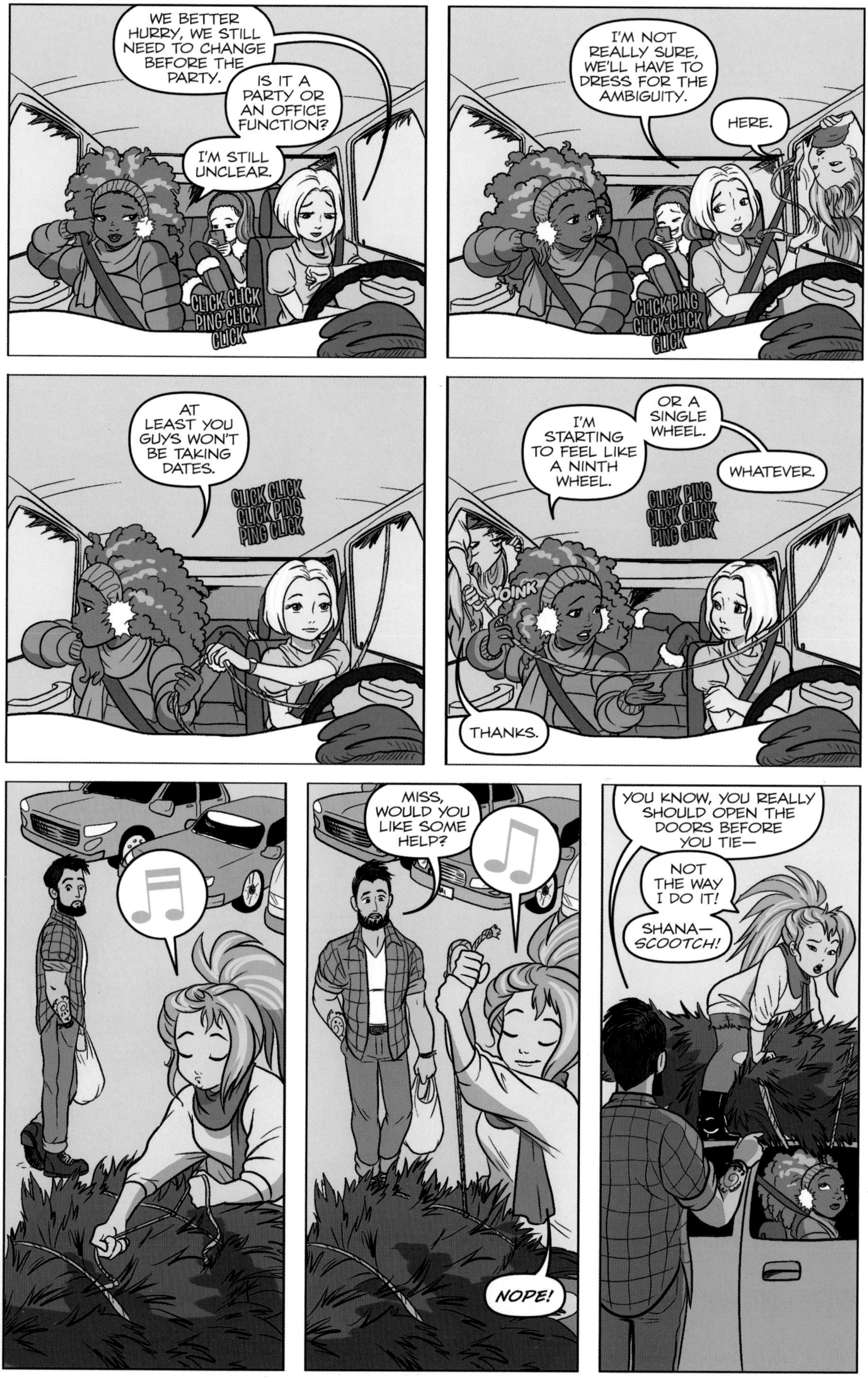
WE BETTER HURRY, WE STILL NEED TO CHANGE BEFORE THE PARTY.
IS IT A PARTY OR AN OFFICE FUNCTION?
I'M STILL UNCLEAR.
CLICK CLICK PING-CLICK CLICK
I'M NOT REALLY SURE, WE'LL HAVE TO DRESS FOR THE AMBIGUITY.
HERE.
CLICK PING CLICK-CLICK CLICK
AT LEAST YOU GUYS WON'T BE TAKING DATES.
CLICK CLICK CLICK PING PING CLICK
I'M STARTING TO FEEL LIKE A NINTH WHEEL.
OR A SINGLE WHEEL.
WHATEVER.
CLICK PING CLICK CLICK PING CLICK
YOINK
THANKS.
MISS, WOULD YOU LIKE SOME HELP?
NOPE!
YOU KNOW, YOU REALLY SHOULD OPEN THE DOORS BEFORE YOU TIE—
NOT THE WAY I DO IT!
SHANA—
SCOOTCH!

SCOOTCH
SCOOTCH

STEP BACK, PLEASE.

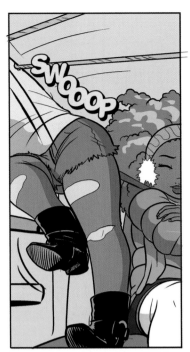

SWOOOP

WOW. YEAH... I MEAN, THAT'S... YEAH.

HEY, MY NAME IS FRITZ. YOU WANNA GO—

NOPE.

♥💔!

KINDA HARSH, AJA.

OH, PLEASE. HE'S EXTREMELY HANDSOME. HE'LL GET OVER IT.

YOU GET ASKED OUT EVERYWHERE YOU GO... I WANT THAT.

YOU WANT *THAT* SPECIFIC HANDSOME LUMBERJACK, SHANA?

NO, JUST, I MEAN, HOW DO YOU DO IT?

IT'S THE DISINTEREST.

DRAWS THEM LIKE FLIES TO HONEY.

I COULD BE DISINTERESTED!

YOU COULDN'T BE DISINTERESTED IF YOU TRIED.

IT'S WHAT MAKES YOU SO PERFECTLY SHANA.

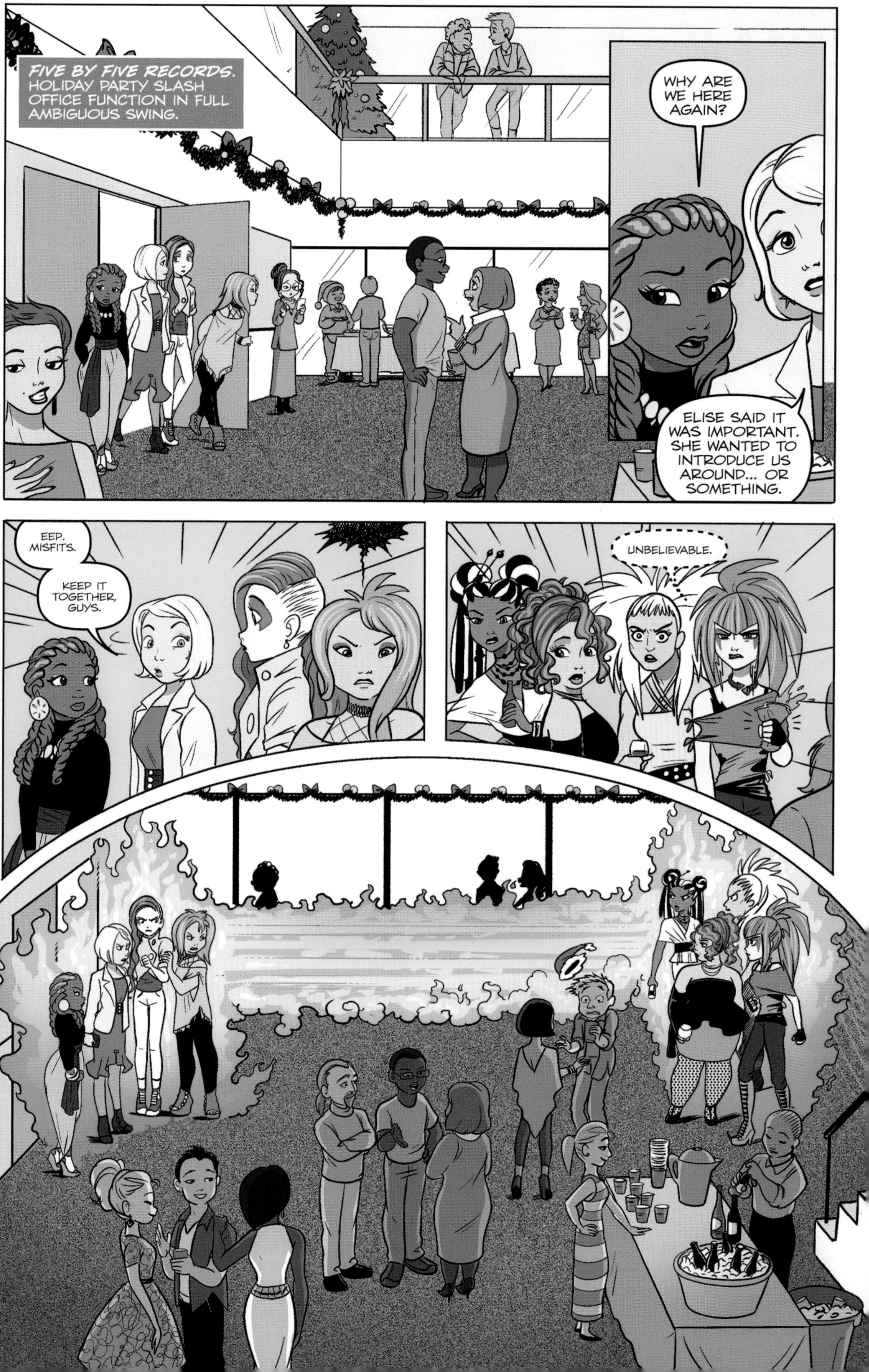
FIVE BY FIVE RECORDS.
HOLIDAY PARTY SLASH OFFICE FUNCTION IN FULL AMBIGUOUS SWING.
WHY ARE WE HERE AGAIN?
ELISE SAID IT WAS IMPORTANT. SHE WANTED TO INTRODUCE US AROUND... OR SOMETHING.
EEP. MISFITS.
KEEP IT TOGETHER, GUYS.
UNBELIEVABLE.

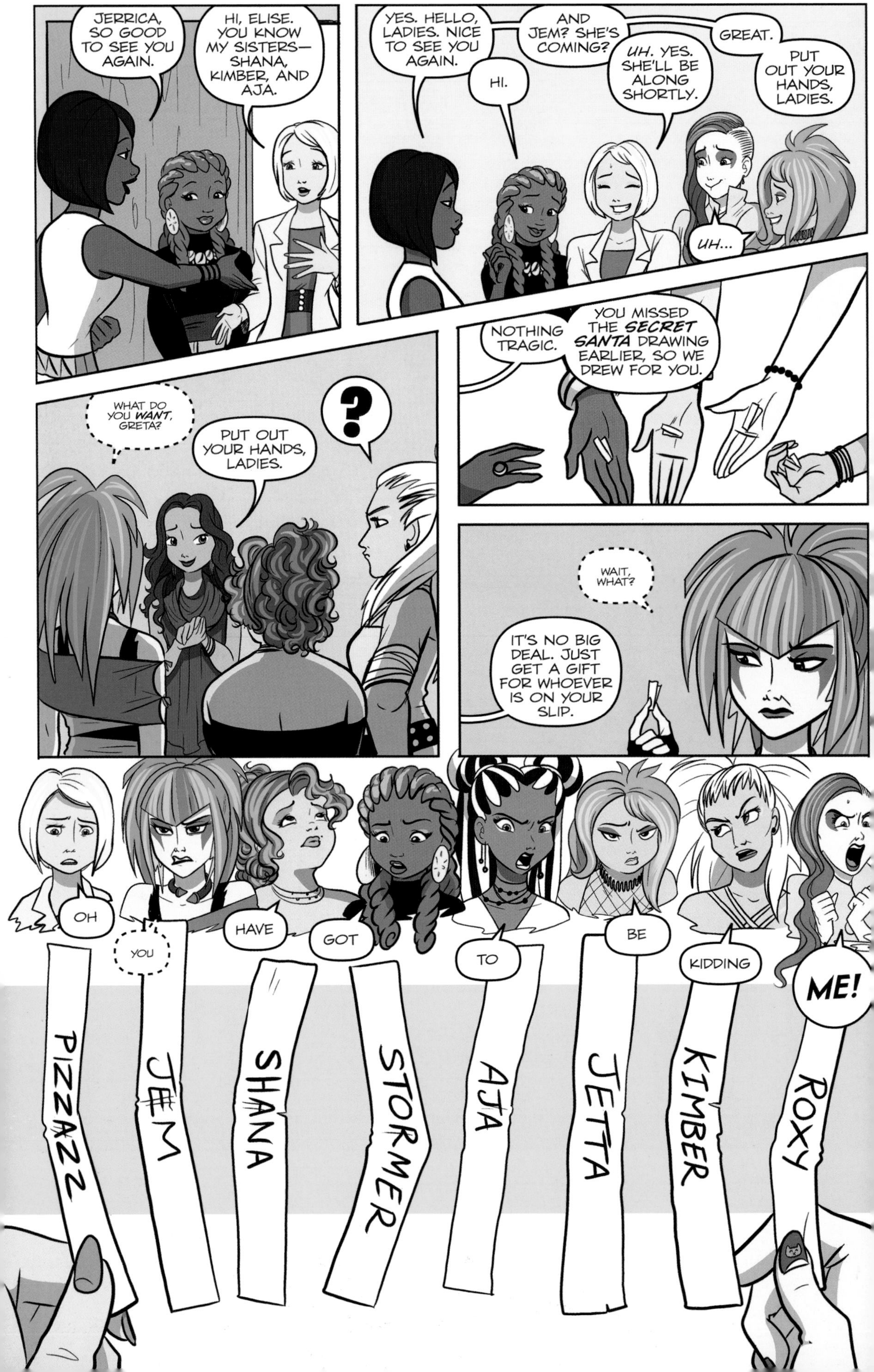
JERRICA, SO GOOD TO SEE YOU AGAIN.
HI, ELISE. YOU KNOW MY SISTERS— SHANA, KIMBER, AND AJA.
YES. HELLO, LADIES. NICE TO SEE YOU AGAIN.
HI.
AND JEM? SHE'S COMING?
UH. YES. SHE'LL BE ALONG SHORTLY.
GREAT.
PUT OUT YOUR HANDS, LADIES.
UH...
NOTHING TRAGIC.
YOU MISSED THE SECRET SANTA DRAWING EARLIER, SO WE DREW FOR YOU.
WHAT DO YOU WANT, GRETA?
PUT OUT YOUR HANDS, LADIES.
?
WAIT, WHAT?
IT'S NO BIG DEAL. JUST GET A GIFT FOR WHOEVER IS ON YOUR SLIP.
OH
YOU
HAVE
GOT
TO
BE
KIDDING
ME!
PIZZAZZ
JEM
SHANA
STORMER
AJA
JETTA
KIMBER
ROXY

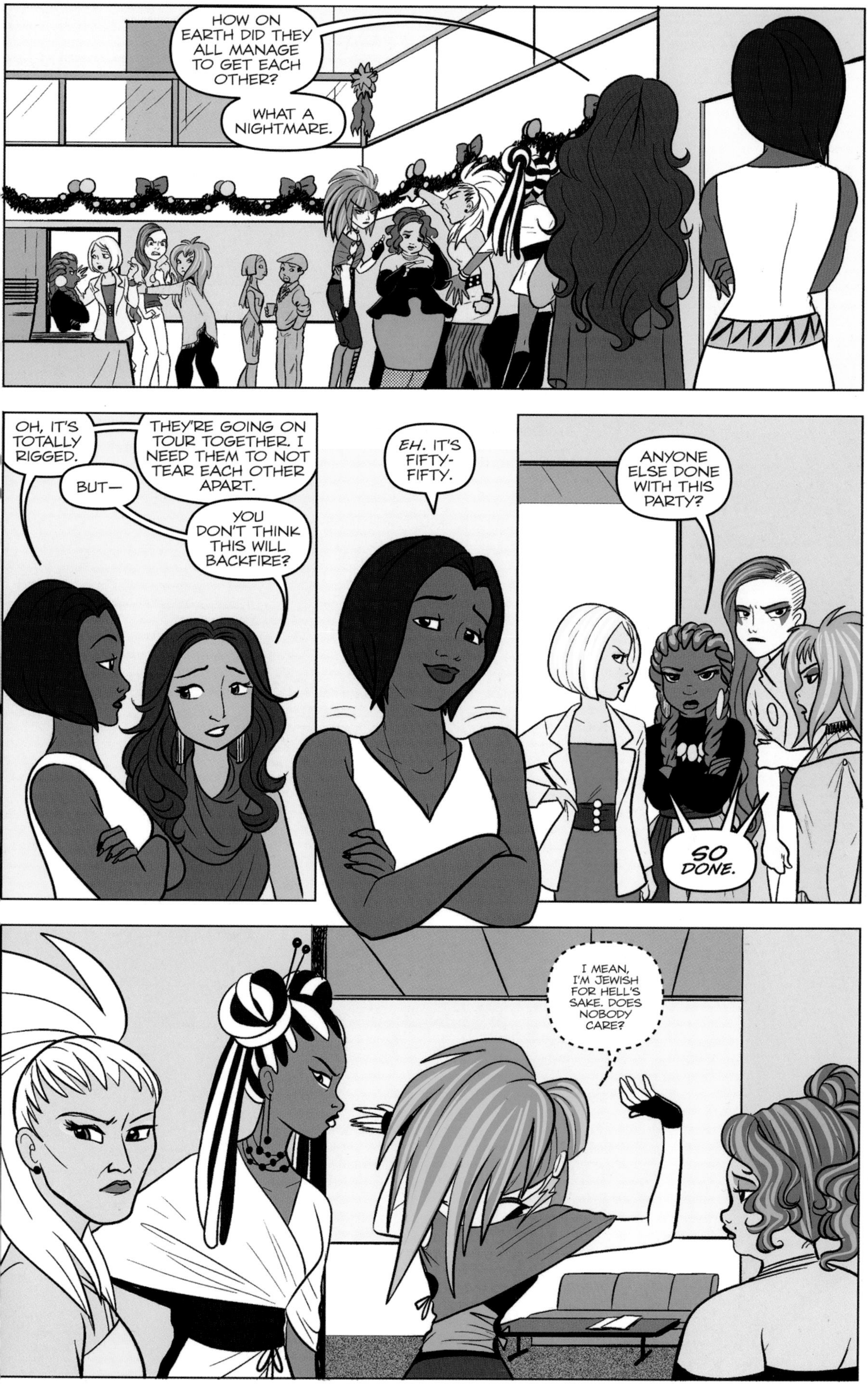

HOW ON EARTH DID THEY ALL MANAGE TO GET EACH OTHER?
WHAT A NIGHTMARE.
OH, IT'S TOTALLY RIGGED.
THEY'RE GOING ON TOUR TOGETHER. I NEED THEM TO NOT TEAR EACH OTHER APART.
BUT—
YOU DON'T THINK THIS WILL BACKFIRE?
EH. IT'S FIFTY-FIFTY.
ANYONE ELSE DONE WITH THIS PARTY?
SO DONE.
I MEAN, I'M JEWISH FOR HELL'S SAKE. DOES NOBODY CARE?

THIS BLOWS.

WE GOT RICKROLLED.

WHAT DOES THIS HAVE TO DO WITH RICK ASTLEY?

YOU KNOW, CLASSIC BAIT AND SWITCH.

LIKE FOR EXAMPLE TRICKING YOU INTO THINKING YOU'RE GETTING ONE THING... AN OFFICE PARTY...

...AND THEN GIVING YOU SOMETHING ELSE... LIKE FORCING YOU INTO A SECRET SANTA GIFT EXCHANGE WITH YOUR NEMESES.

THAT'S NOT WHAT RICK ROLLING IS.

GUYS. WHO CARES?

SURE IT IS, IT STARTED OUT BEING ABOUT THE VIDEO, BUT THE DEFINITION HAS CLEARLY EVOLVED, AJA.

C'MON.

GUYS.

C'MON WHAT? *THAT'S* YOUR ARGUMENT?

OHMIGOD SHUTTUP! I DON'T EVEN KNOW WHO RICK ASHLEY IS!!!

ASTLEY. HE'S—

I DON'T CARE!

I CARE THAT I HAVE TO BUY STUPID ROXY A PRESENT!

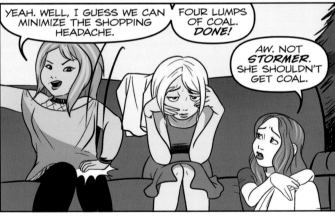

YEAH. WELL, I GUESS WE CAN MINIMIZE THE SHOPPING HEADACHE.

FOUR LUMPS OF COAL. *DONE!*

AW. NOT *STORMER*. SHE SHOULDN'T GET COAL.

AW. OKAY.

I GOT STORMER.

I'LL GET HER SOMETHING GOOD.

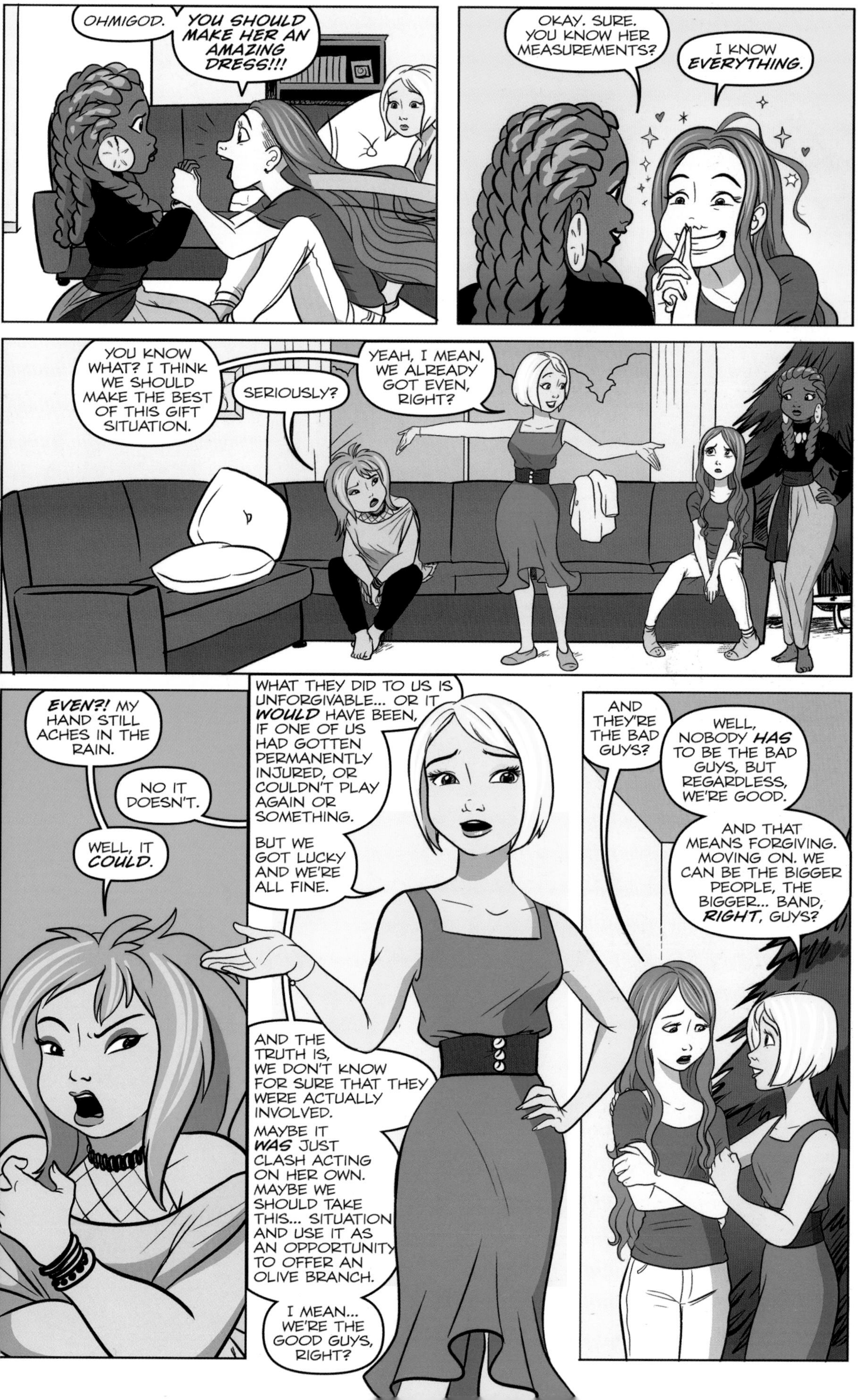
OHMIGOD.
YOU SHOULD MAKE HER AN AMAZING DRESS!!!
OKAY. SURE. YOU KNOW HER MEASUREMENTS?
I KNOW EVERYTHING.
YOU KNOW WHAT? I THINK WE SHOULD MAKE THE BEST OF THIS GIFT SITUATION.
SERIOUSLY?
YEAH, I MEAN, WE ALREADY GOT EVEN, RIGHT?
EVEN?! MY HAND STILL ACHES IN THE RAIN.
NO IT DOESN'T.
WELL, IT COULD.
WHAT THEY DID TO US IS UNFORGIVABLE... OR IT WOULD HAVE BEEN, IF ONE OF US HAD GOTTEN PERMANENTLY INJURED, OR COULDN'T PLAY AGAIN OR SOMETHING.
BUT WE GOT LUCKY AND WE'RE ALL FINE.
AND THE TRUTH IS, WE DON'T KNOW FOR SURE THAT THEY WERE ACTUALLY INVOLVED.
MAYBE IT WAS JUST CLASH ACTING ON HER OWN. MAYBE WE SHOULD TAKE THIS... SITUATION AND USE IT AS AN OPPORTUNITY TO OFFER AN OLIVE BRANCH.
I MEAN... WE'RE THE GOOD GUYS, RIGHT?
AND THEY'RE THE BAD GUYS?
WELL, NOBODY HAS TO BE THE BAD GUYS, BUT REGARDLESS, WE'RE GOOD.
AND THAT MEANS FORGIVING. MOVING ON. WE CAN BE THE BIGGER PEOPLE, THE BIGGER... BAND, RIGHT, GUYS?

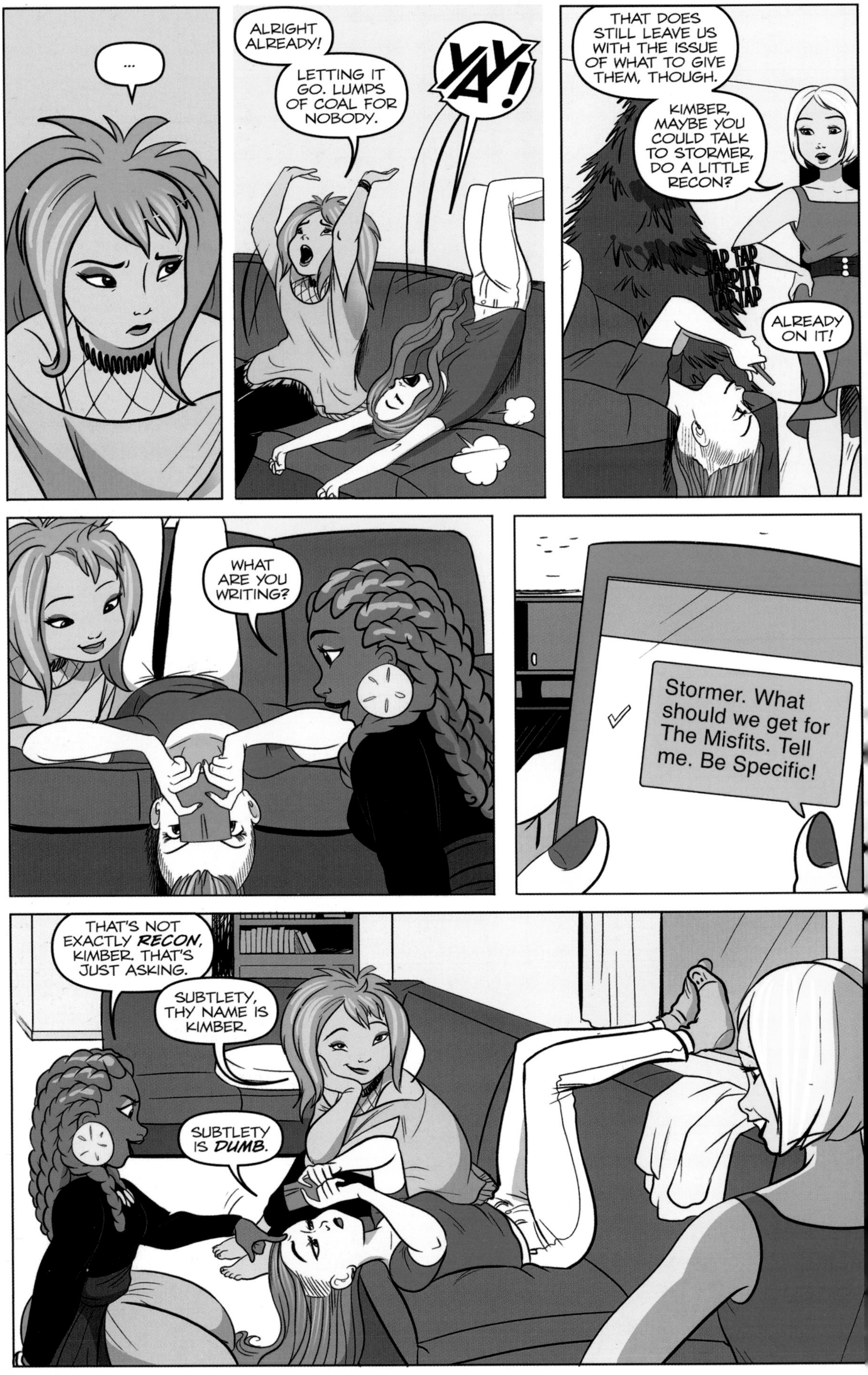
...
ALRIGHT ALREADY!
LETTING IT GO. LUMPS OF COAL FOR NOBODY.
YAY!
THAT DOES STILL LEAVE US WITH THE ISSUE OF WHAT TO GIVE THEM, THOUGH.
KIMBER, MAYBE YOU COULD TALK TO STORMER, DO A LITTLE RECON?
TAP TAP TAPPITY TAP TAP
ALREADY ON IT!
WHAT ARE YOU WRITING?
Stormer. What should we get for The Misfits. Tell me. Be Specific!
THAT'S NOT EXACTLY ***RECON***, KIMBER. THAT'S JUST ASKING.
SUBTLETY, THY NAME IS KIMBER.
SUBTLETY IS ***DUMB***.

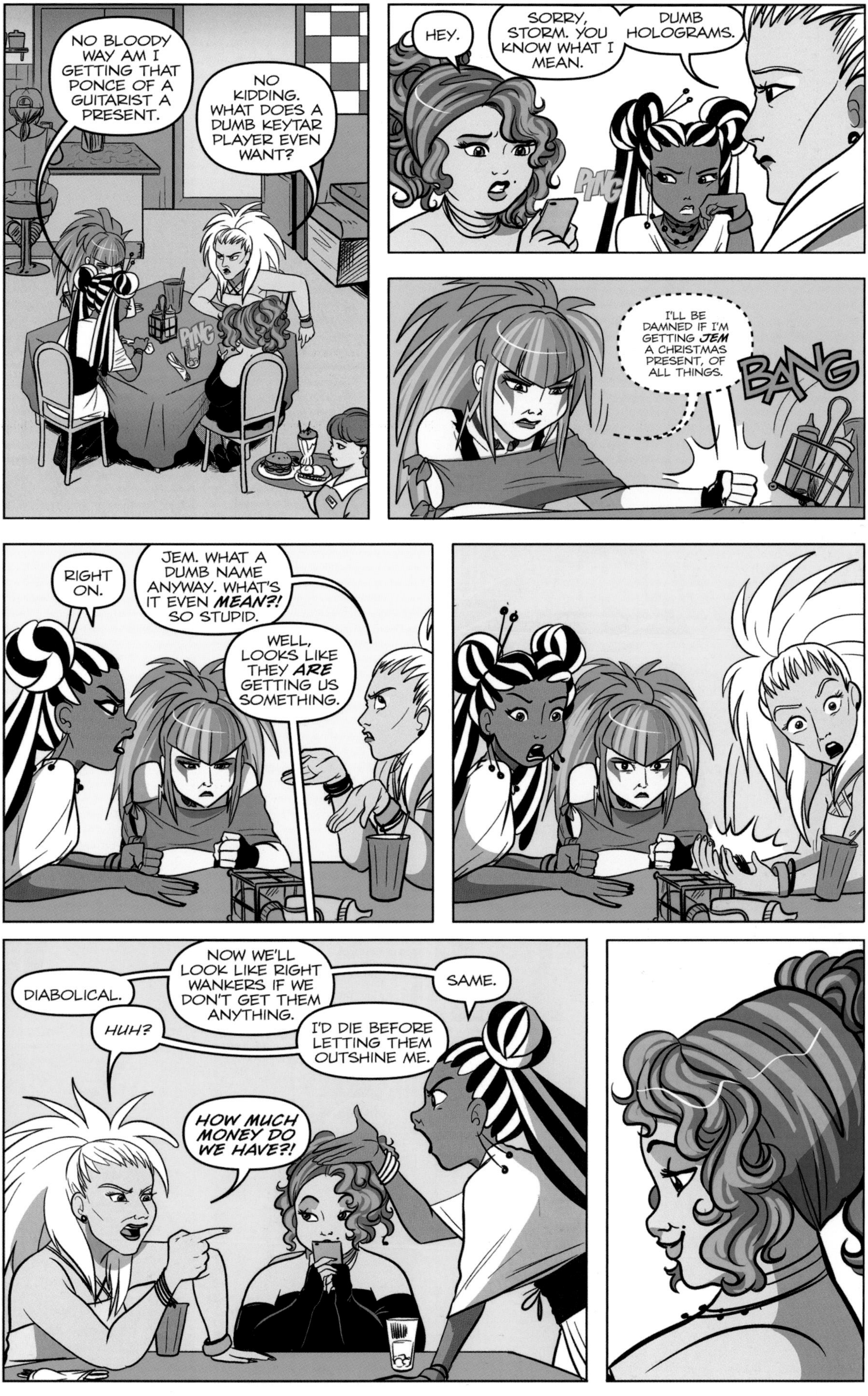
NO BLOODY WAY AM I GETTING THAT PONCE OF A GUITARIST A PRESENT.
NO KIDDING. WHAT DOES A DUMB KEYTAR PLAYER EVEN WANT?
PING
HEY.
SORRY, STORM. YOU KNOW WHAT I MEAN.
DUMB HOLOGRAMS.
PING
I'LL BE DAMNED IF I'M GETTING JEM A CHRISTMAS PRESENT, OF ALL THINGS.
BANG
RIGHT ON.
JEM. WHAT A DUMB NAME ANYWAY. WHAT'S IT EVEN MEAN?! SO STUPID.
WELL, LOOKS LIKE THEY ARE GETTING US SOMETHING.
DIABOLICAL.
NOW WE'LL LOOK LIKE RIGHT WANKERS IF WE DON'T GET THEM ANYTHING.
SAME.
HUH?
I'D DIE BEFORE LETTING THEM OUTSHINE ME.
HOW MUCH MONEY DO WE HAVE?!

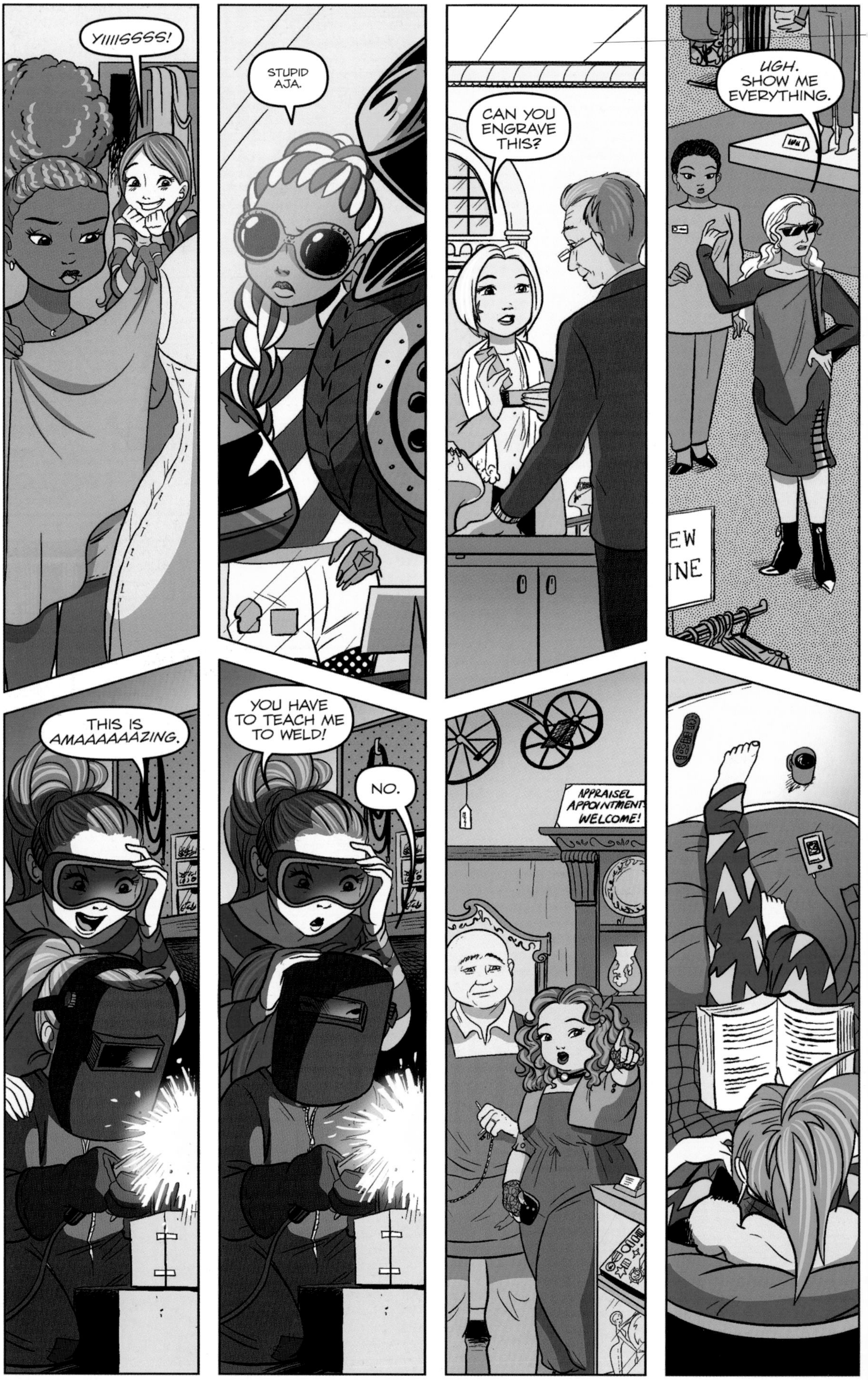
YIIIISSSS!
STUPID AJA.
CAN YOU ENGRAVE THIS?
UGH. SHOW ME EVERYTHING.
THIS IS AMAAAAAAAZING.
YOU HAVE TO TEACH ME TO WELD!
NO.
APPRAISEL APPOINTMENT
WELCOME!

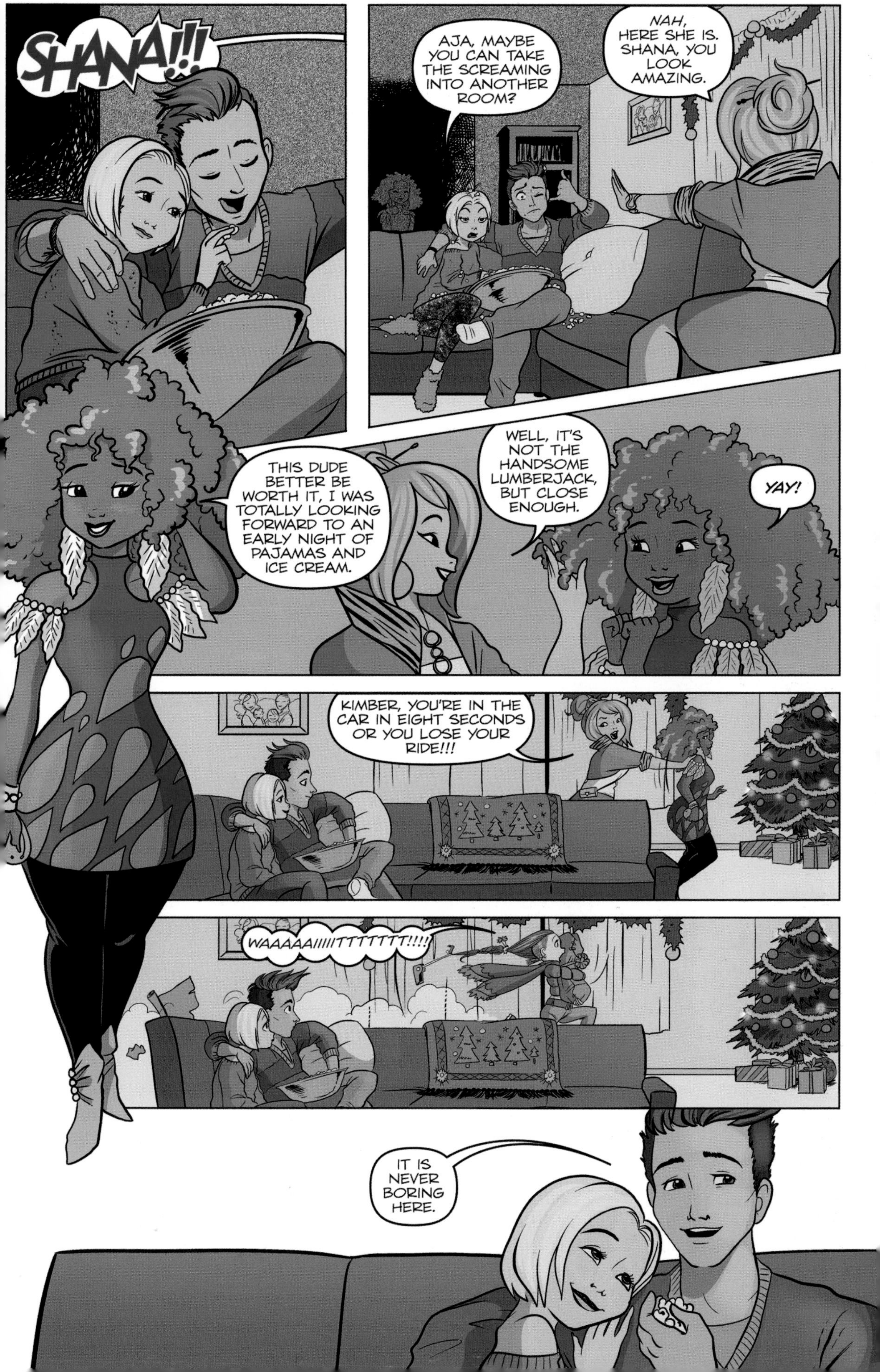
SHANA!!!
AJA, MAYBE YOU CAN TAKE THE SCREAMING INTO ANOTHER ROOM?
NAH, HERE SHE IS. SHANA, YOU LOOK AMAZING.
THIS DUDE BETTER BE WORTH IT, I WAS TOTALLY LOOKING FORWARD TO AN EARLY NIGHT OF PAJAMAS AND ICE CREAM.
WELL, IT'S NOT THE HANDSOME LUMBERJACK, BUT CLOSE ENOUGH.
YAY!
KIMBER, YOU'RE IN THE CAR IN EIGHT SECONDS OR YOU LOSE YOUR RIDE!!!
WAAAAAAIIIIIITTTTTTT!!!!
IT IS NEVER BORING HERE.

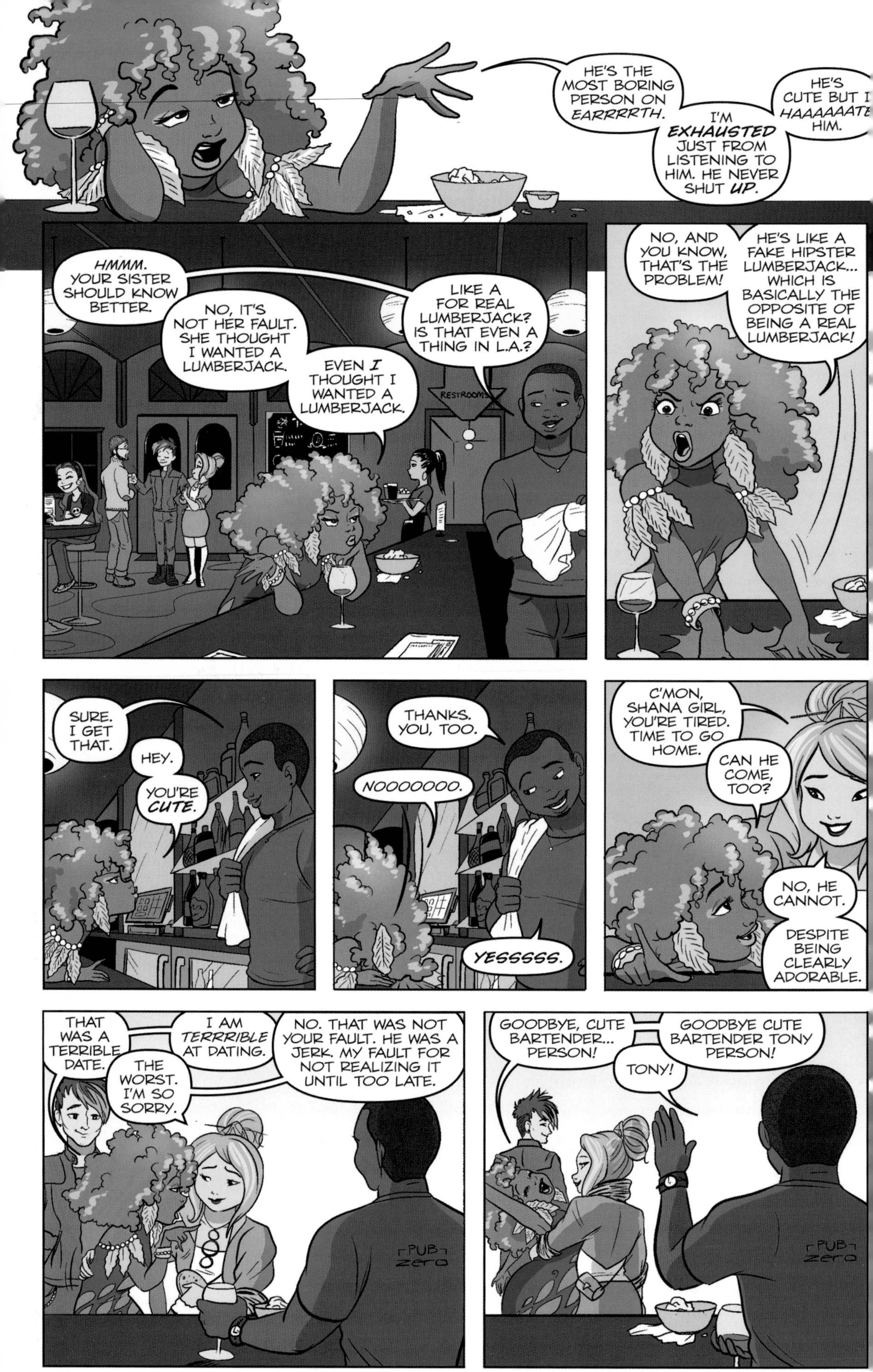
HE'S THE MOST BORING PERSON ON EARRRRTH.
I'M EXHAUSTED JUST FROM LISTENING TO HIM. HE NEVER SHUT UP.
HE'S CUTE BUT I HAAAAAATE HIM.
HMMM. YOUR SISTER SHOULD KNOW BETTER.
NO, IT'S NOT HER FAULT. SHE THOUGHT I WANTED A LUMBERJACK.
EVEN I THOUGHT I WANTED A LUMBERJACK.
LIKE A FOR REAL LUMBERJACK? IS THAT EVEN A THING IN L.A.?
RESTROOMS
NO, AND YOU KNOW, THAT'S THE PROBLEM!
HE'S LIKE A FAKE HIPSTER LUMBERJACK... WHICH IS BASICALLY THE OPPOSITE OF BEING A REAL LUMBERJACK!
SURE. I GET THAT.
HEY.
YOU'RE CUTE.
THANKS. YOU, TOO.
NOOOOOOO.
YESSSSS.
C'MON, SHANA GIRL, YOU'RE TIRED. TIME TO GO HOME.
CAN HE COME, TOO?
NO, HE CANNOT.
DESPITE BEING CLEARLY ADORABLE.
THAT WAS A TERRIBLE DATE.
I AM TERRIBLE AT DATING.
THE WORST. I'M SO SORRY.
NO. THAT WAS NOT YOUR FAULT. HE WAS A JERK. MY FAULT FOR NOT REALIZING IT UNTIL TOO LATE.
PUB zero
GOODBYE, CUTE BARTENDER... PERSON!
TONY!
GOODBYE CUTE BARTENDER TONY PERSON!
PUB zero

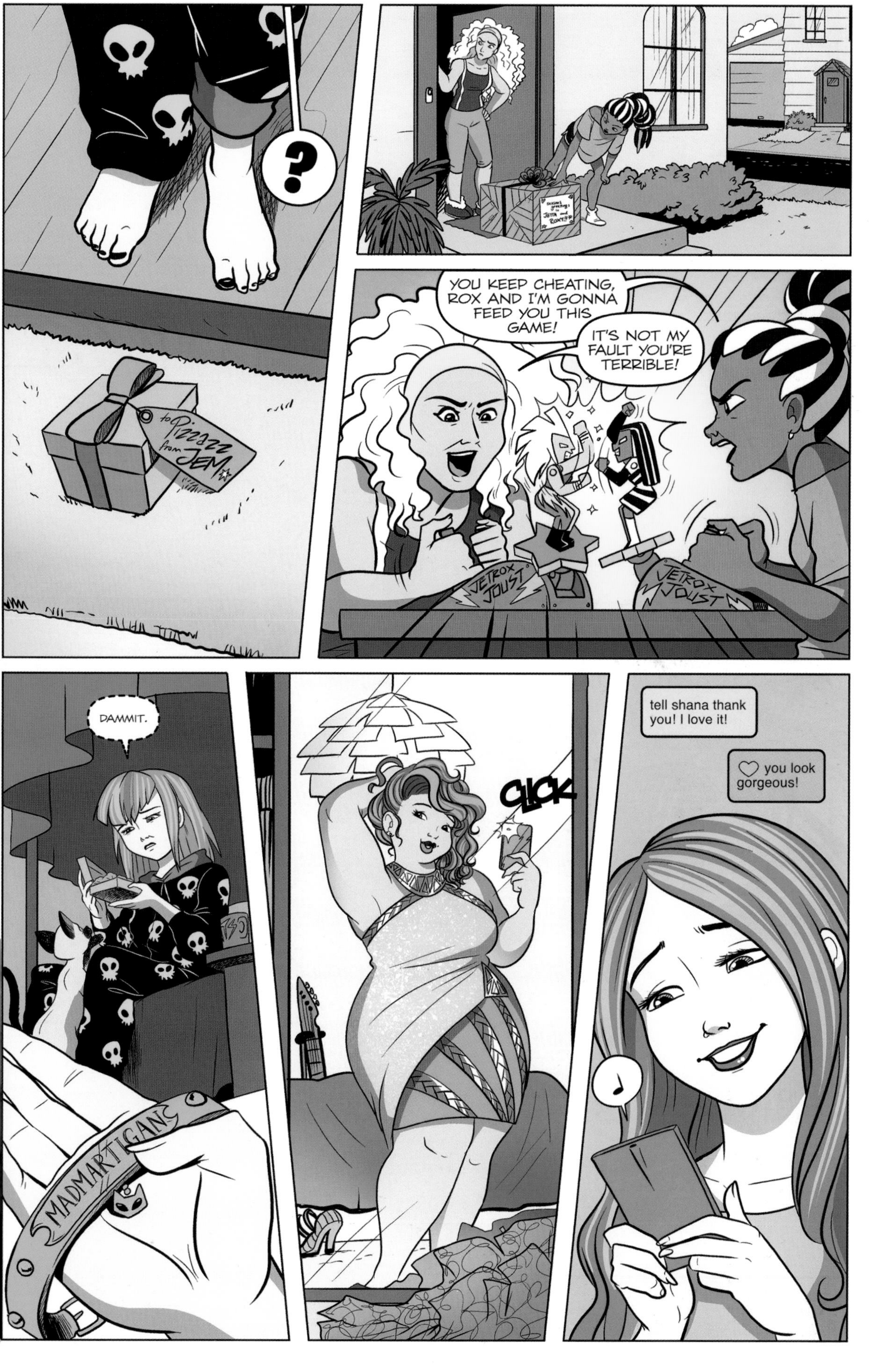
?
seasons greetings to JETTA and ROXY!!!
to Pizzazz from JEM
YOU KEEP CHEATING, ROX AND I'M GONNA FEED YOU THIS GAME!
IT'S NOT MY FAULT YOU'RE TERRIBLE!
JETROX JOUST
JETROX JOUST
DAMMIT.
MADMARTIGAN
CLICK
tell shana thank you! I love it!
you look gorgeous!

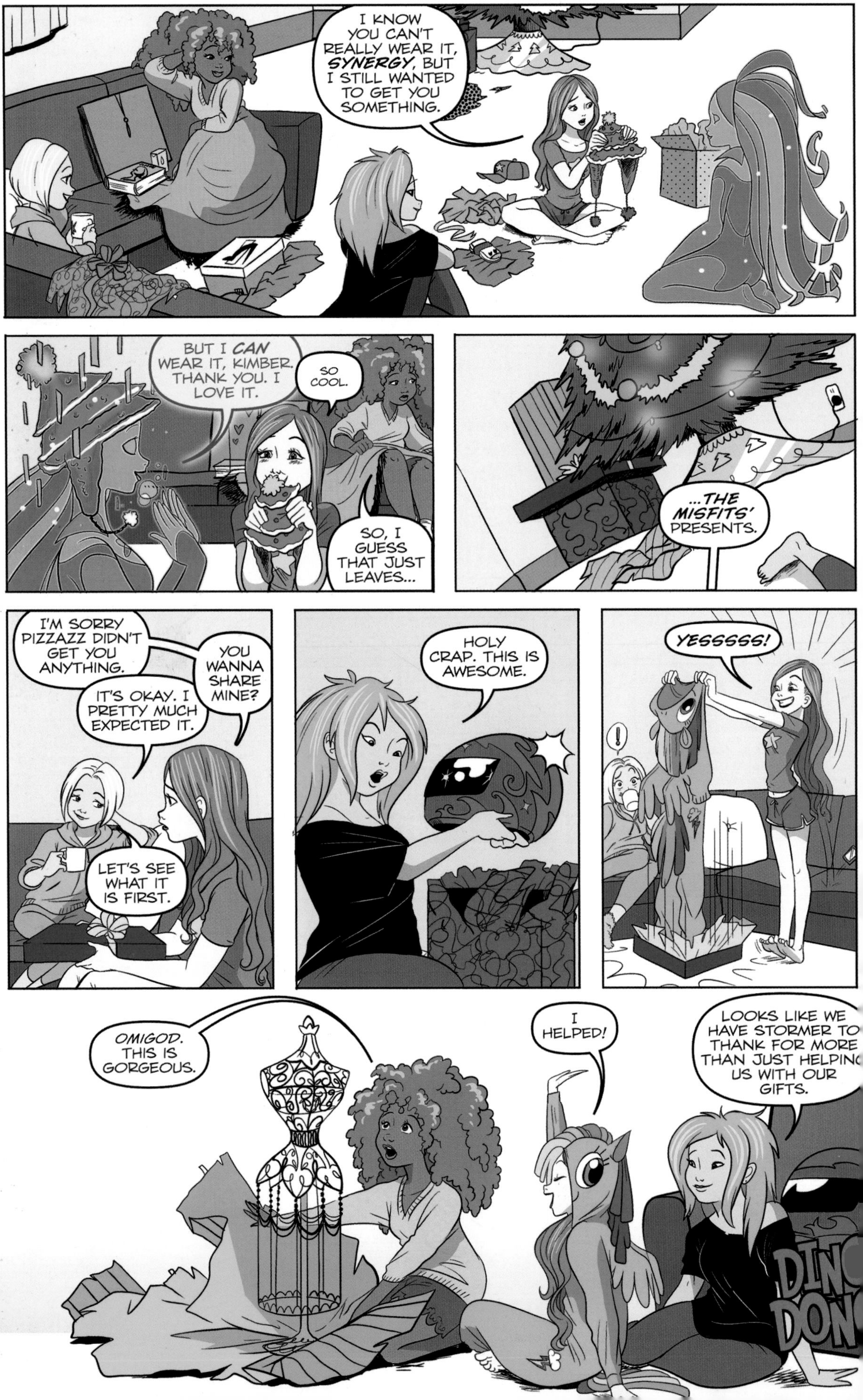
I KNOW YOU CAN'T REALLY WEAR IT, *SYNERGY*, BUT I STILL WANTED TO GET YOU SOMETHING.
BUT I *CAN* WEAR IT, KIMBER. THANK YOU. I LOVE IT.
SO COOL.
SO, I GUESS THAT JUST LEAVES...
...*THE MISFITS'* PRESENTS.
I'M SORRY PIZZAZZ DIDN'T GET YOU ANYTHING.
YOU WANNA SHARE MINE?
IT'S OKAY. I PRETTY MUCH EXPECTED IT.
LET'S SEE WHAT IT IS FIRST.
HOLY CRAP. THIS IS AWESOME.
YESSSSS!
!
OMIGOD. THIS IS GORGEOUS.
I HELPED!
LOOKS LIKE WE HAVE STORMER TO THANK FOR MORE THAN JUST HELPING US WITH OUR GIFTS.
DING DONG

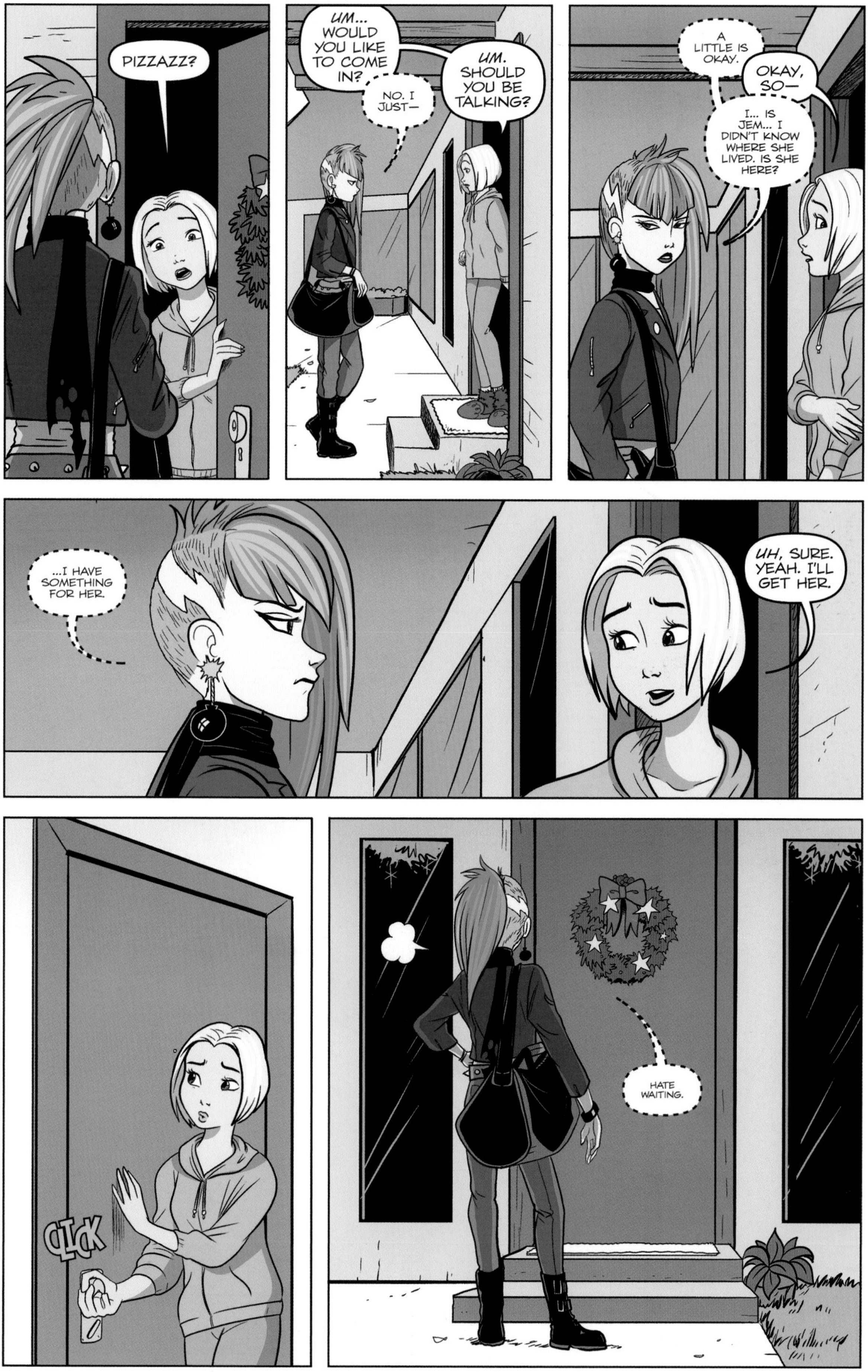
PIZZAZZ?
UM... WOULD YOU LIKE TO COME IN?
NO. I JUST—
UM. SHOULD YOU BE TALKING?
A LITTLE IS OKAY.
OKAY, SO—
I... IS JEM... I DIDN'T KNOW WHERE SHE LIVED. IS SHE HERE?
...I HAVE SOMETHING FOR HER.
UH, SURE. YEAH. I'LL GET HER.
CLICK
HATE WAITING.

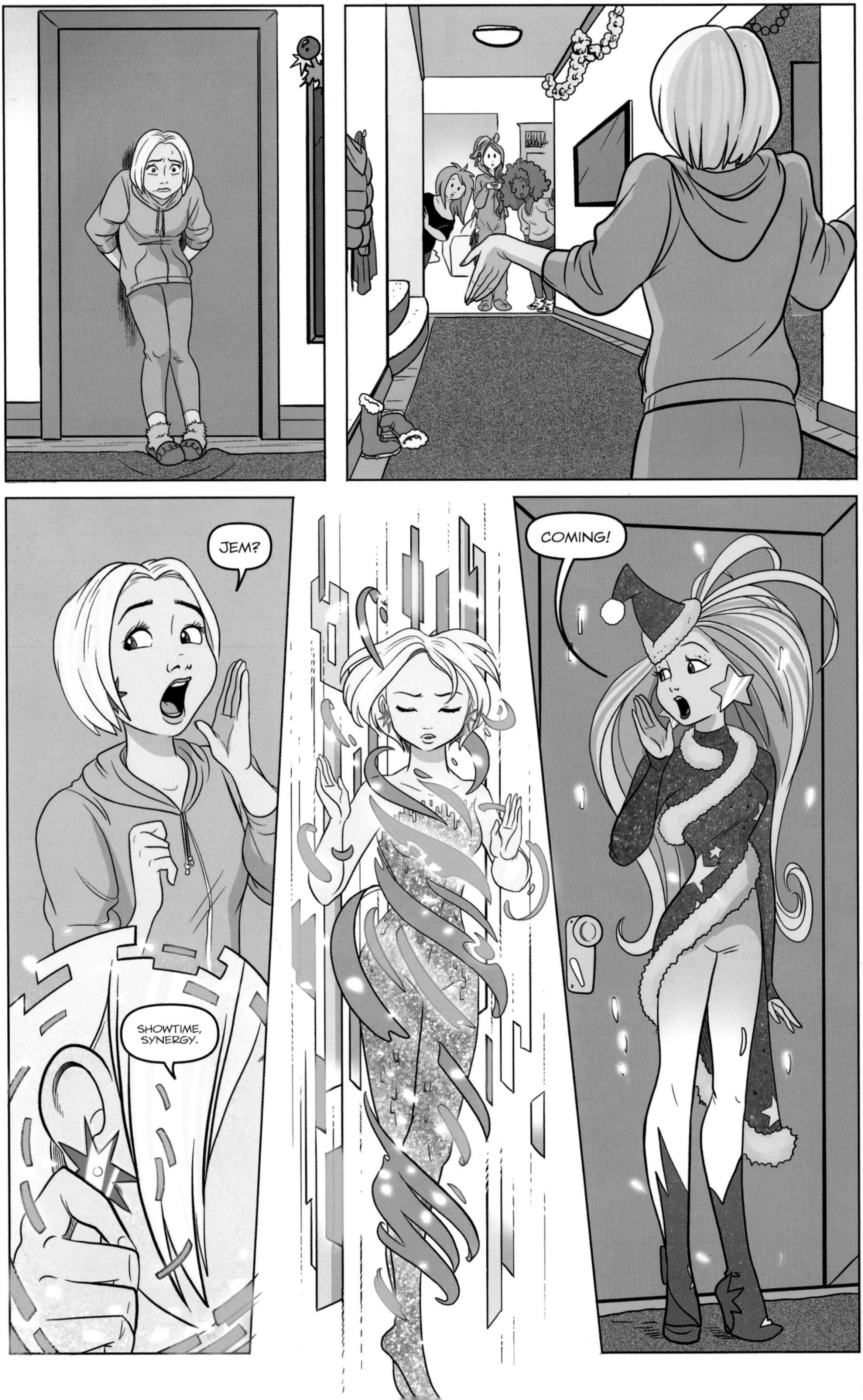
JEM?
SHOWTIME, SYNERGY.
COMING!

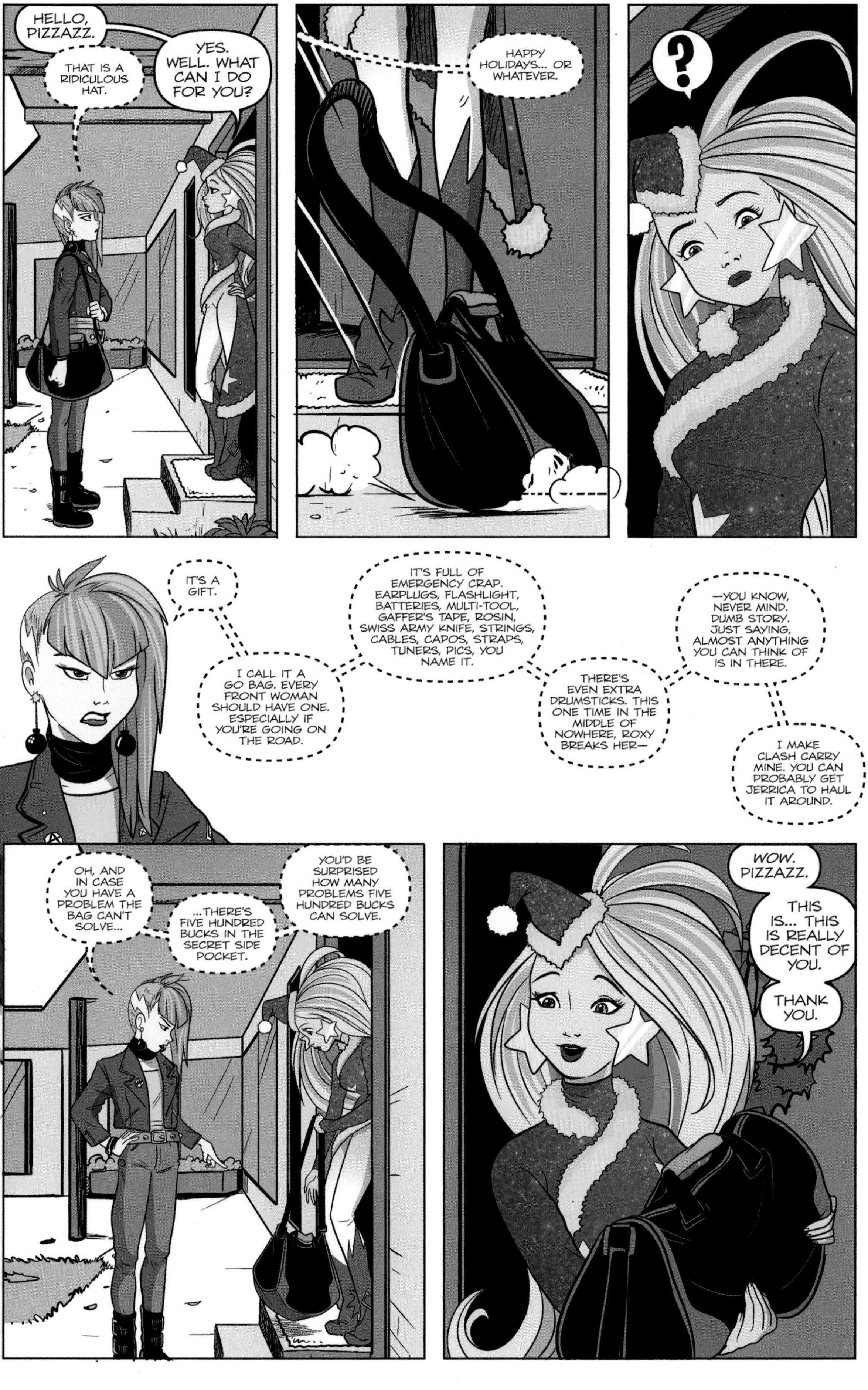
HELLO, PIZZAZZ.
THAT IS A RIDICULOUS HAT.
YES. WELL. WHAT CAN I DO FOR YOU?
HAPPY HOLIDAYS... OR WHATEVER.
?
IT'S A GIFT.
I CALL IT A GO BAG. EVERY FRONT WOMAN SHOULD HAVE ONE. ESPECIALLY IF YOU'RE GOING ON THE ROAD.
IT'S FULL OF EMERGENCY CRAP. EARPLUGS, FLASHLIGHT, BATTERIES, MULTI-TOOL, GAFFER'S TAPE, ROSIN, SWISS ARMY KNIFE, STRINGS, CABLES, CAPOS, STRAPS, TUNERS, PICS, YOU NAME IT.
THERE'S EVEN EXTRA DRUMSTICKS. THIS ONE TIME IN THE MIDDLE OF NOWHERE, ROXY BREAKS HER—
—YOU KNOW, NEVER MIND. DUMB STORY. JUST SAYING, ALMOST ANYTHING YOU CAN THINK OF IS IN THERE.
I MAKE CLASH CARRY MINE. YOU CAN PROBABLY GET JERRICA TO HAUL IT AROUND.
OH, AND IN CASE YOU HAVE A PROBLEM THE BAG CAN'T SOLVE...
...THERE'S FIVE HUNDRED BUCKS IN THE SECRET SIDE POCKET.
YOU'D BE SURPRISED HOW MANY PROBLEMS FIVE HUNDRED BUCKS CAN SOLVE.
WOW. PIZZAZZ.
THIS IS... THIS IS REALLY DECENT OF YOU.
THANK YOU.

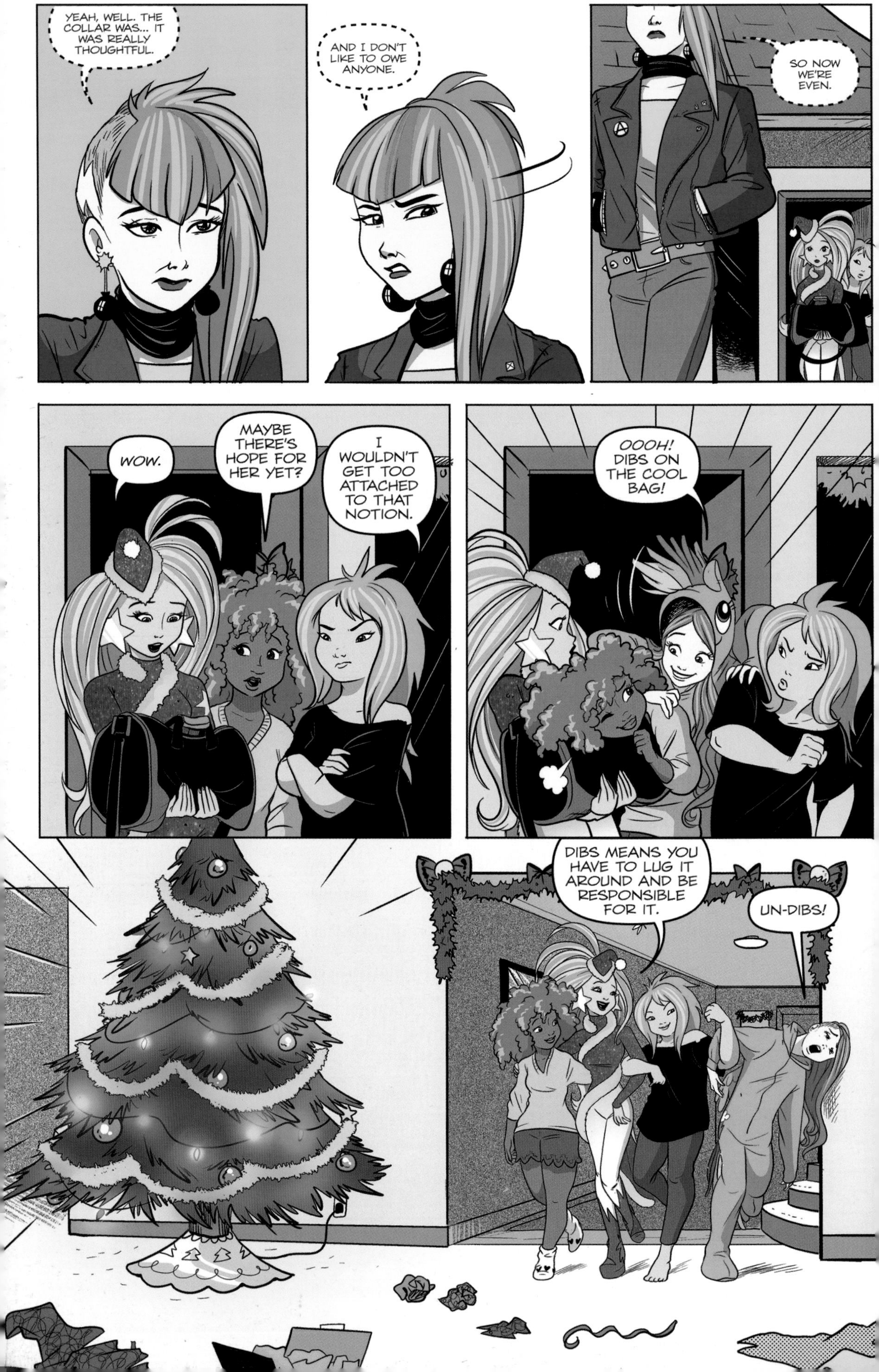
YEAH, WELL. THE COLLAR WAS... IT WAS REALLY THOUGHTFUL.
AND I DON'T LIKE TO OWE ANYONE.
SO NOW WE'RE EVEN.
WOW.
MAYBE THERE'S HOPE FOR HER YET?
I WOULDN'T GET TOO ATTACHED TO THAT NOTION.
OOOH! DIBS ON THE COOL BAG!
DIBS MEANS YOU HAVE TO LUG IT AROUND AND BE RESPONSIBLE FOR IT.
UN-DIBS!

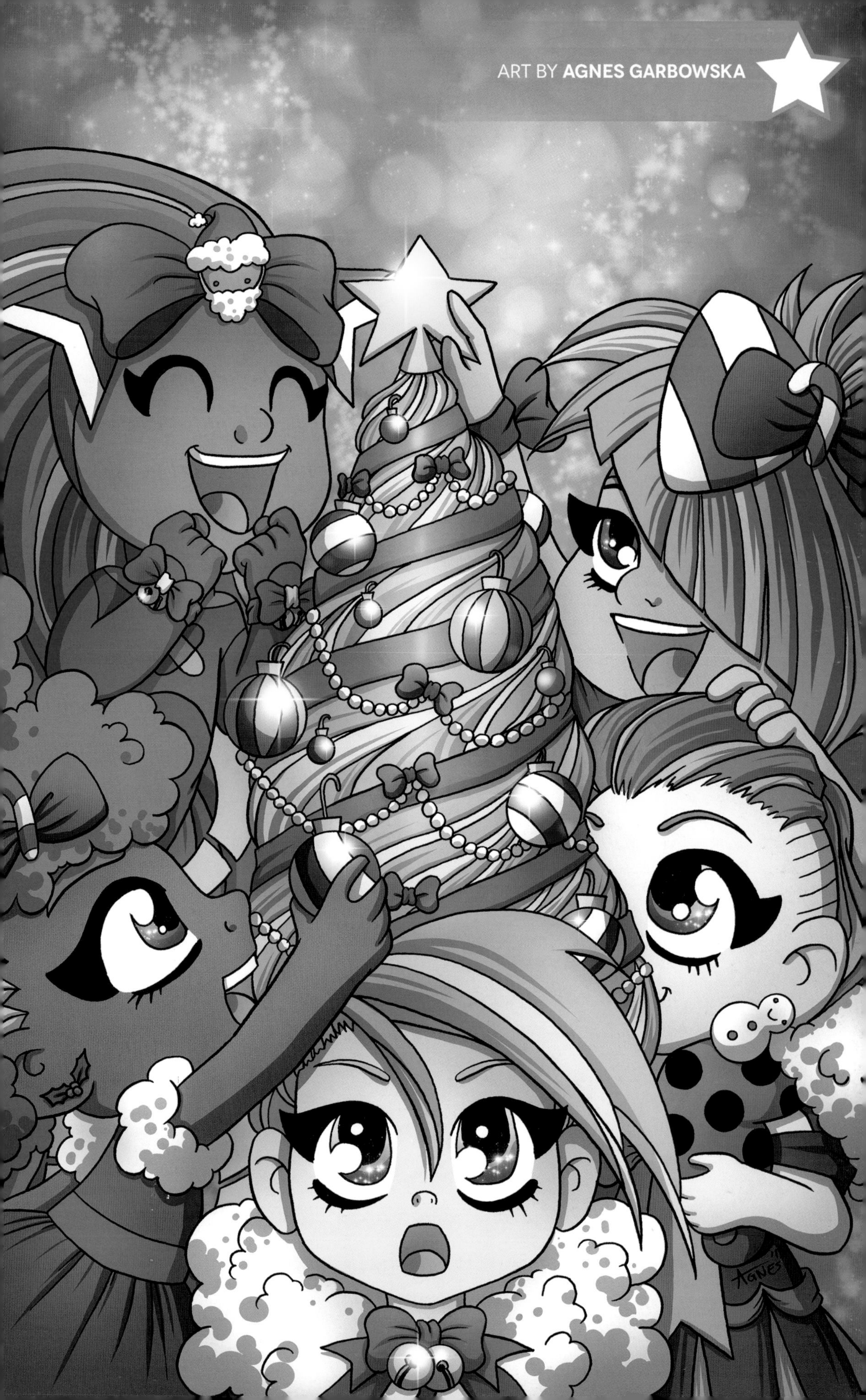
ART BY **AGNES GARBOWSKA**

ART BY **SOPHIE CAMPBELL**

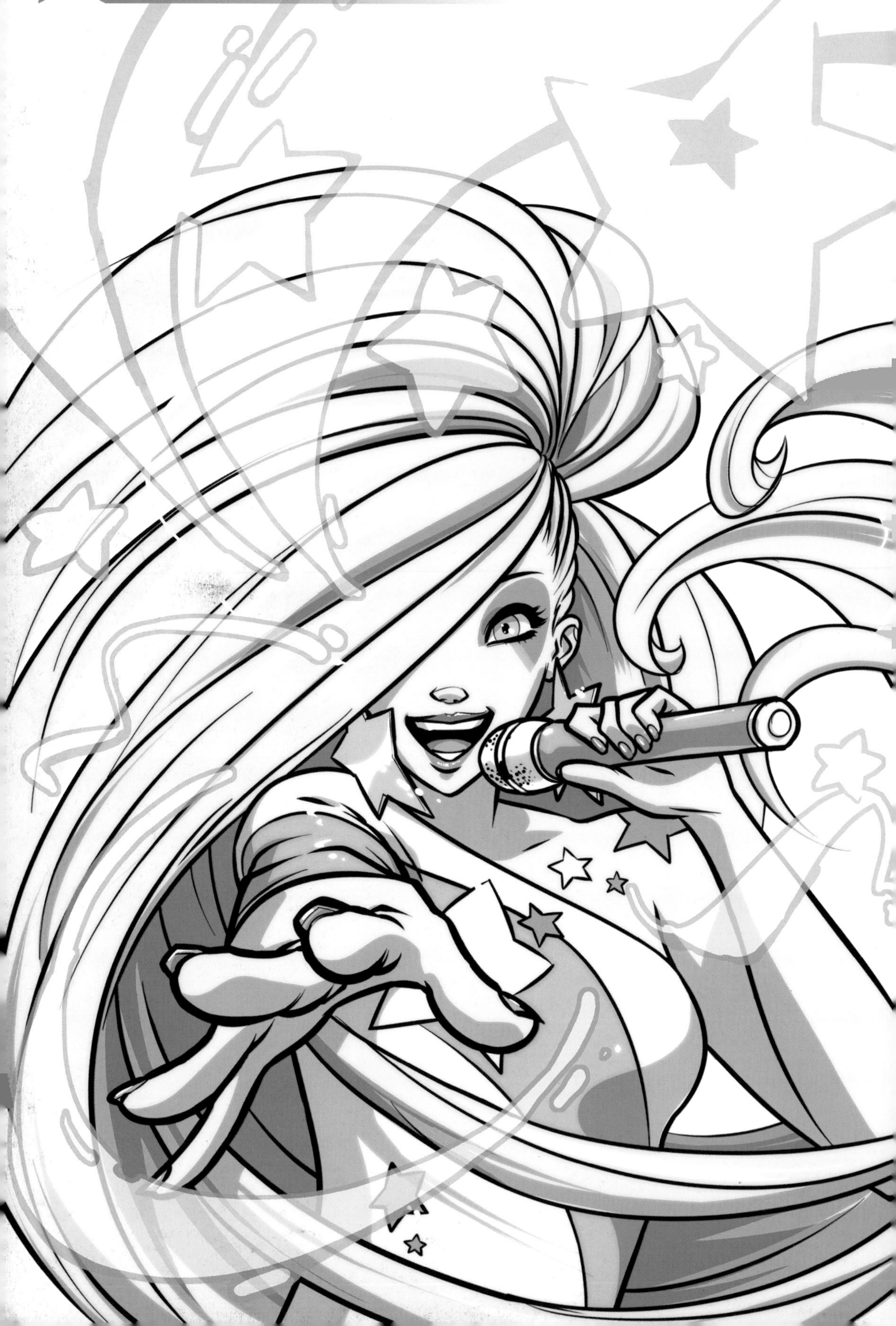

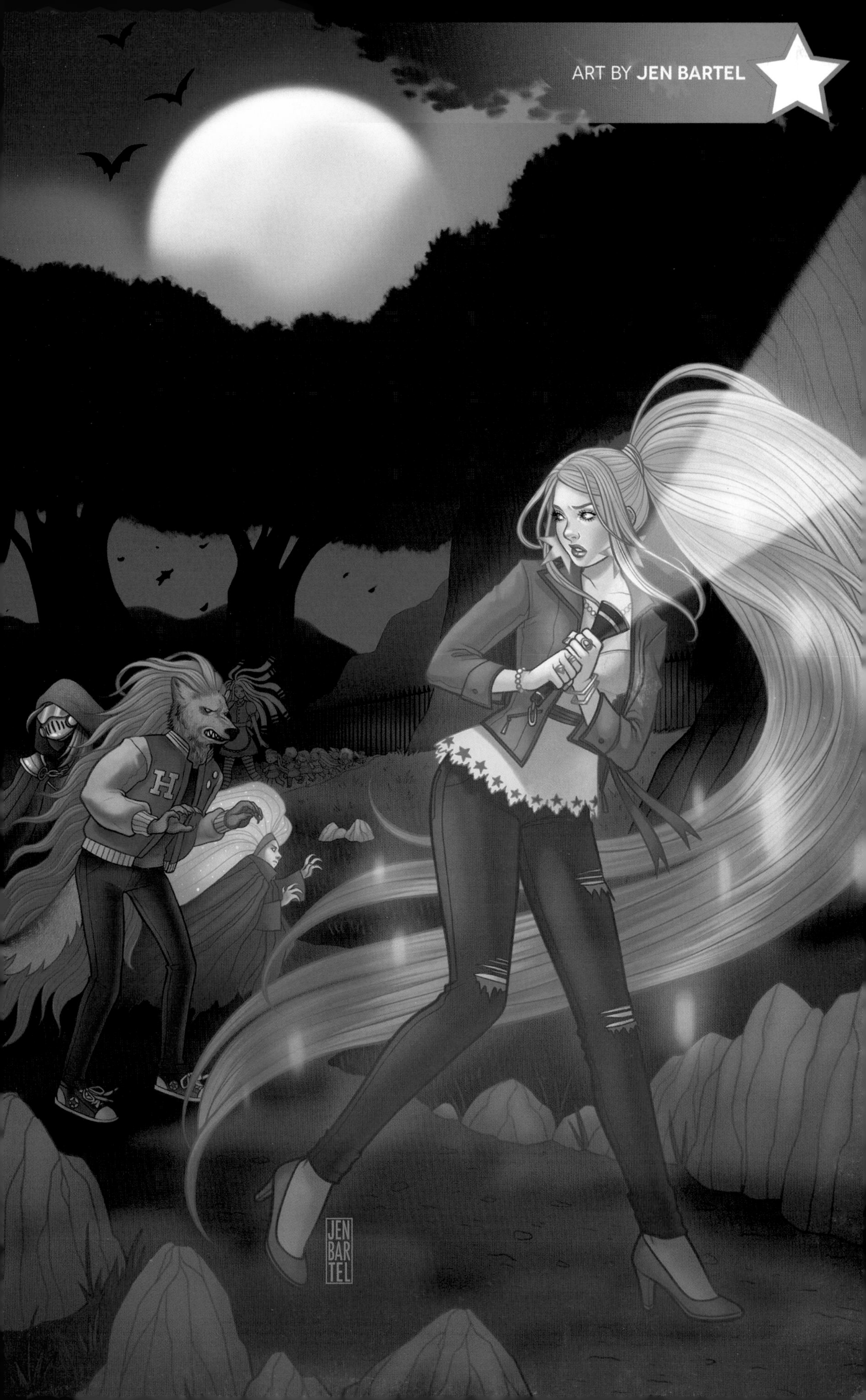
ART BY JEN BARTEL
H
JEN BAR TEL

ART BY **AMY MEBBERSON**

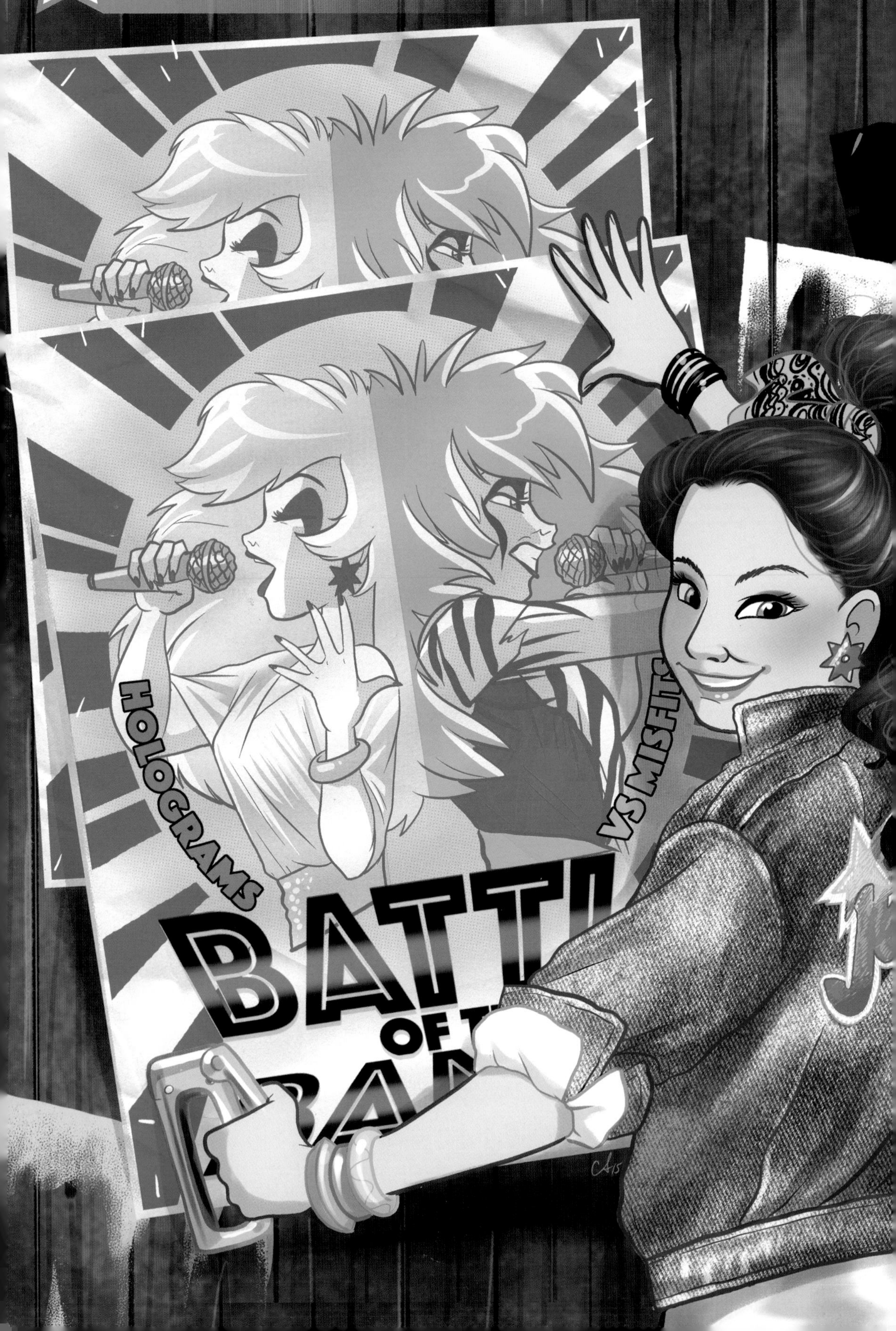
HOLOGRAMS
VS MISFITS

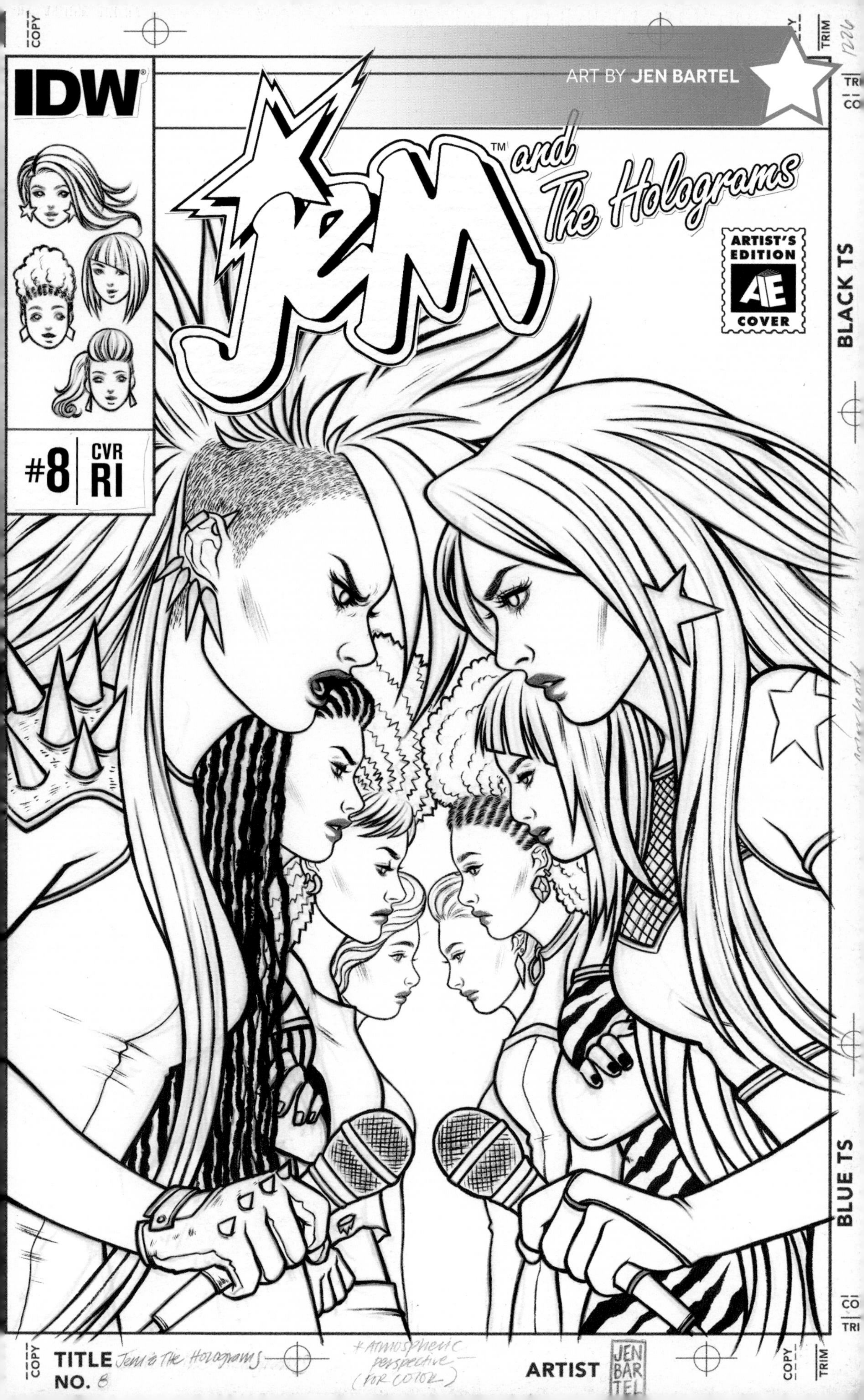

IDW
ART BY JEN BARTEL
JEM
and The Holograms
ARTIST'S EDITION
AE
COVER
#8
CVR RI
BLACK TS
BLUE TS
TITLE Jem & The Holograms
NO. 8
+ atmospheric perspective (for color)
ARTIST
JEN BARTEL

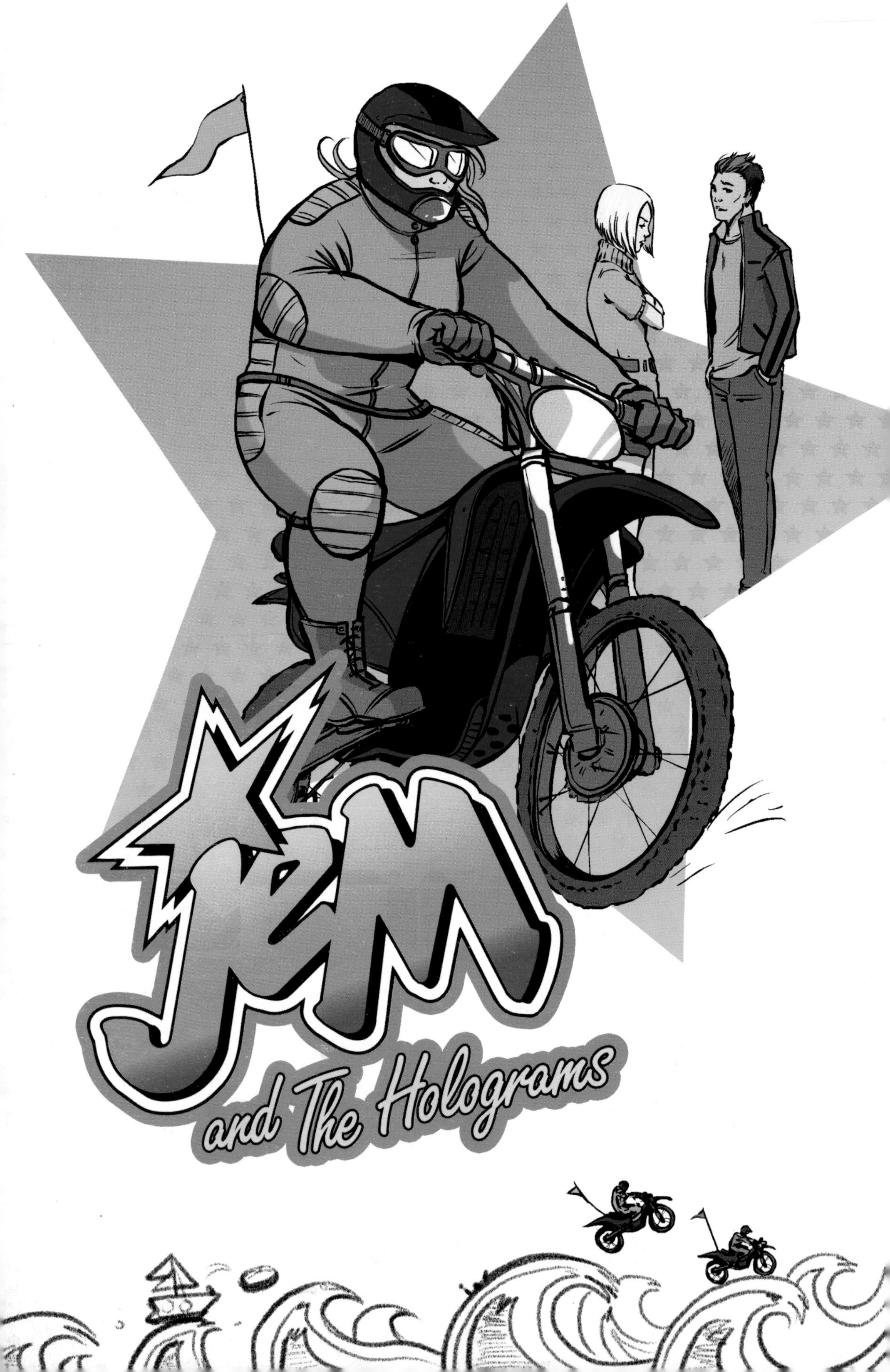

JEM
and The Holograms